Critical praise for this book

This is not only the most accurate biographical account of Robert Tressell, the Irishman who wrote the classic novel of English working-class life. It is also a life history of his book, and of its extraordinary impact on twentieth-century British socialism. Harker draws on a deep knowledge of the political and cultural history of the left in order to place Tressell and his work in their contexts. He rejects the reverential tone in which *The Ragged Trousered Philanthropists* is often discussed, subjecting its politics to a toughly critical appraisal. Tressell admirers may not agree with Harker's analysis, but they should be grateful to him for the way in which his meticulous research and challenging arguments will stimulate new discussion of *The Ragged Trousered Philanthropists*.

Jonathan Hyslop, *Professor of Sociology,*
University of Witwatersrand

The Ragged Trousered Philanthropists has been described as 'the bible' of the English left, and by Arnold Kettle as the 'real foundation of socialist realist literature in Britain'. Yet the novel and its author, writing under the name Robert Tressell, have suffered scholarly neglect out of all proportion to their influence. With the benefit of previously unpublished source materials, this 'biography' of a book weaves it into the history of British socialism, from its first publication in 1914, three years after the death of its author, through the reconstruction of the original text after over forty years of abridged versions, to the burgeoning of the 'Tressell heritage industry' from the 1980s. Concluding with a passionate reaffirmation of its spirit, Dave Harker has produced what will undoubtedly become the unignorable benchmark study of the one book by 'the greatest socialist writer Britain has produced'.

Bruce Johnson, *School of English, University of New South Wales*

Without doubt *Tressell* is the most researched and comprehensive study of *The Ragged Trousered Philanthropists*, tracing its influence on social, political and literary thinking from when it was first published through to the present day. Able to quote from previously unpublished material Dr Dave Harker has produced a most interesting and informative book, invaluable to the ordinary reader and student alike. It is essential reading for all those who seek a fuller understanding of the ll Family Papers

As the anti-capitalist movement grows and disgruntled Labour Party members and trade-union and other activists across the world look to it for a way forward, so there is a renewal of ideas. This book makes a most valuable contribution to this process, showing in rich detail how one of the key socialist works of the last century has never stopped stimulating debate and argument on the all important question: What is to be done?

Geoff Brown, trade-union tutor, Manchester

Dave Harker uses the history of Robert Tressell and his book to illuminate the failures of the left in Britain. This is a sharp and uncomfortable read for everyone who claims to be a socialist.

John Edmonds, outgoing General Secretary, GMB

By following the extraordinary history of The Ragged Trousered Philanthropists and the inspired (if varied) effect it has on generations of workers, artists and intellectuals, Harker manages to give us a fresh and compelling insight into the shifts and changes within the British radical (and not so radical) left in the twentieth century. It operates as multi-layered detective story — first, into the enigma of the elusive Tressell himself; second, the extraordinary tale of the re-emergence of the full text after almost fifty years; and, finally, the vicissitudes, visions, compromises and downright betrayals of socialism. I only wish I had had this book to guide (and challenge) me when I was first adapting the book for the stage.

Stephen Lowe, playwright

Dave Harker's Tressell traces the career of a remarkable novel that has had an extraordinary influence since its publication in 1914. It has had over a million copies sold all over the world, and in the UK it has circulated among millions of workers and converted innumerable persons to socialism. Harker sets the history of The Ragged Trousered Philanthropists against a changing political background and shows its significance for today. His book is the product of painstaking and devoted scholarship that attests to his love for his subject.

Paul Siegel, professor emeritus at Long Island University and
author of REVOLUTION AND THE TWENTIETH-CENTURY NOVEL

Dave Harker's absorbing and instructive work of political, literary and human history recaptures the astonishing vitality of Tressell's classic working-class novel across nearly a century. Combining meticulous research and an appropriately combative tone, Harker reveals how this tale of exploited workers has survived the exploitation of publishers and the invocations of dubious fellow travellers to retain its inspirational message for the left. Tressell lives!

Peter Bailey, Professor of History,
University of Manitoba

About this book

Not many novels about working-class life have been reprinted over a hundred times in the UK, the USA, Canada, Australia, Germany, Russia, the Netherlands, Czechoslovakia, Bulgaria and Japan. Even fewer have sold over a million copies. Hardly any have been so often adapted for the stage, or featured on television and radio. Above all, none has been passed from hand to hand so often by workers, and gets taken to their hearts.

The Ragged Trousered Philanthropists is straightforward and highly readable, but it is also a very odd book. After all, novels don't usually explain key points of Marxist theory. True, it has humour, parody, pathos, irony, rage, little victories, defeats, arguments and ideas, and it is brim full of contempt for the ruling class. But isn't capitalism irreversibly triumphant in the twenty first century? And isn't the book too hard on workers? Anyway, what practical political appeal can a tale of isolated socialists, fighting for a Co-operative Commonwealth, possibly have today?

Tressell: The Real Story of 'The Ragged Trousered Philanthropists' describes the author's life, puts the book in its historical context and traces its success over the past ninety-odd years. It shows that The Ragged Trousered Philanthropists is about socialist values and their continued relevance at a time when we are being told that capitalism is here for ever; that greed is good; that war, famine, poverty, racism and oppression are natural, normal and permanent features of life on Planet Earth. Crucially, Tressell's passionate, compassionate denunciation of the capitalist 'system' is about hope, so little wonder The Ragged Trousered Philanthropists is selling very well indeed in these anti-capitalist days.

About the author

Dave Harker has been a trade union and socialist activist for over thirty years. He co-edited *The Big Red Song Book* (Pluto Press, 1977 and 1981), which sold fifteen thousand copies, and wrote *One for the Money: Politics and Popular Song* (Hutchinson, 1980). His *Fakesong: The Manufacture of British 'Folksong', 1700 to the Present Day* (Open University Press, 1985) was one of eleven volumes in the Popular Music in Britain series, which he co-edited. He also edited two books of workers' songs and verse, *Songs from the Manuscript Collection of John Bell* (1985) and *Songs and Verse of the North East Pitmen, c. 1780–1844* (1999) for the Surtees Society at Durham University. Dave was a university teacher until 2000, when he retired in order to become more involved with education. He a member of the Socialist Alliance.

TRESSELL

The real story of

The Ragged Trousered Philanthropists

DAVE HARKER

ZED BOOKS
London & New York

Tressell was first published in 2003 by
Zed Books Ltd, 7 Cynthia Street, London N1 9JF, UK,
and Room 400, 175 Fifth Avenue, New York, NY 10010, USA

www.zedbooks.demon.co.uk

Designed and typeset in Monotype Joanna by Illuminati, Grosmont
Cover designed by Andrew Corbett
Printed and bound in the EU by Gutenberg Printers Ltd, Malta

Distributed in the USA exclusively by Palgrave, a division of
St Martin's Press, LLC, 175 Fifth Avenue, New York, NY 10010

A catalogue record for this book is available from the British Library
Library of Congress Cataloging-in-Publication Data available

ISBN 1 84277 384 4 (Hb)
ISBN 1 84277 385 2 (Pb)

Contents

For Reg,

and all those struggling against the capitalist 'system'

to build the Co-operative Commonwealth

Thanks to:

David Alfred
Ann Bates
Neil Bates
Chris Bessant
Ian Birchall
Emma Bircham
Eric Bolton
Gila Breitenbach
Alex Bromley
Paul Brook
Geoff Brown
Alan Burgess
Ron Clarke
Christine Coates
Janet Cole
Andy Coles
Brigit Collins
Dave Cope
Tina Corry
David Craig
Andy Croft
Julian Davies

Gary Day
Graham Draisey
John Edmonds
Russell Edwards
Keith Flett
Sheila Gammon
Clive Griggs
Charley Hall
Michael Harker
Jim Herlihy
Trevor Hopper
David Horsfield
Jonathan Hyslop
Fred Inglis
Alain Kahan
Matt Kelly
John Lovell
Stephen Lowe
Annie Makepeace
Mike Matthews
Donal McCracken
Arthur Mendelsohn

Renate Mitchell
John Monks
Donald Muir
Dennis Nolan
Derek Norcross
Sean O'Donoghue
Gerda Ott
Barbara Phillips
Mary Phillips
Kenneth Price
Dave Renton
Jacqueline Slocombe
Harold Smith
Judith Smith
Mike Smith-Rawnsley
Andy Strouthous
Else Tonke
Ray Walker
Patrick Ward
Sam Webb
Peter Wicke

Illustrations

The following pictures are from the Robert Tressell Family Papers, reprinted here with the kind permission of Reg Johnson: Kathleen Noonan's Birthday Book (p. xx); Robert and Kathleen Noonan, c. 1895 (p. 5); Noonan's '98 Association Membership card (p. 7); Robert Noonan with model airship, c. 1905 (p. 16); Kathleen Noonan, c. 1910 (p. 46); Reg Johnson, c. 1967 (p. 192).

The picture of Elizabeth Noonan, c. 1895 (p. 4), is reprinted courtesy of NASA Cape Town Archives Repository CSC 2/1/1/336, no. 30.

The picture of George Hicks, 1927 (p. 110) is reprinted with kind permission of the Trades Union Congress.

At time of going to press all efforts have been made to locate the copyright-holder of the picture of Grant Richards (p. 125).

The picture of Fred Ball, c. 1940 (p. 153), is reprinted with kind permission of Mrs Jacqueline Slocombe, the widow of Fred Ball.

The picture of Jack Beeching, 1979 (p. 181), is reprinted from the original dust-jacket of *An Open Path* with the kind permission of his widow, Charlotte Mensforth.

The picture of Joan Johnson (p. 211) is reprinted with the kind permission of the *Morning Star*.

Abbreviations

A publication history of

The Ragged Trousered Philanthropists

23 April 1914	London: Grant Richards (from 1927, The Richards Press). Reprinted thirteen times.
May 1914	New York: Frederick Stokes.
May 1914	Toronto: Macmillan (using British copies).
May 1918	London: Grant Richards (from 1927, The Richards Press). Reprinted seven times.
Early 1920s	Russia: All Union Council of Trade Unions.
1925	Berlin: Neuer Deutscher Verlag.
1927	Berlin. Universum Bücherei für Alle. Reprinted once.
1933	Amsterdam: De Arbeider Pers.
April 1940	Harmondsworth: Penguin. Reprinted four times.
October 1942	Melbourne: Lothian (Penguin). Reprinted once.
October 1955	London: Lawrence & Wishart. Reprinted twelve times to 2002.
1955	Moscow: Foreign Languages Publishing House. Reprinted once.
1958	Berlin: Aufbau-Verlag.
1961	Prague: Státni Nakladatelstvi Krásné Literatury, Hudby a Uměni.
1962	New York: Monthly Review Press.
1964	Bulgaria.
February 1965	London: Panther. Reprinted twenty-four times.

1971   Japan: Tama Shobo.

1978   New York: Monthly Review Press (undated).

1981   Toronto: HarperCollins Canada.

1987   Moscow: Khudozhestvennaia literatura.

1991   London: Paladin.
        Reprinted six times.

1993   London: Flamingo.
        Reprinted ten times to 2003.

April 2002   Kuckenshagen, Germany: Scheunen-verlag.

Those who have been set on golden chairs to write
Will be questioned about those who
Wove their coats.
Not for their elevated thoughts
Will their books be scrutinised, but
Any casual phrase that suggests
Something about those who wove coats
Will be read with interest, for it may involve characteristics
Of famous ancestors.

Whole literatures
Couched in the choicest expressions
Will be examined for signs
That revolutionaries too lived where there was oppression.
Pleading appeals to immortal beings
Will prove that at that time mortals sat over other mortals.
That delicious music of words will only relate
That for many there was no food.

But at that time will be praised
Those who sat on the bare ground to write
Those who sat among the lowly
Those who sat with the fighters.
Those who reported the deeds of the fighters
With art.

from Bertolt Brecht, 'Literature will be Scrutinised'

Preface

A very odd book

Not many novels deserve to have their biography written. But then, not many have been published in three different versions and given over eighty printings by seven UK publishers. Fewer have been adapted for the stage so many times, taken on tour, featured in television and radio documentaries, and, after nearly ninety years in print, can inspire people to try to raise the money to make them into a film. Hardly any have had at least three printings in the USA, two in Canada and two in Australia, plus four in Russian, five in German, and one in Dutch, Czech, Bulgarian and Japanese, or sold well over a million copies worldwide. Above all, no other novel about working-class life is passed from hand to hand by millions of workers and gets taken to their hearts.

The Ragged Trousered Philanthropists (RTP) is clear, straightforward and eminently readable; but in many ways it is a very odd book. After all, novels do not usually explain key points of Marxist theory. True, it has humour, parody, pathos, irony, rage, little victories, defeats, arguments and ideas, and it is brimfull of hatred and contempt for the capitalist 'System', the ruling class and their hangers-on. But surely capitalism is irreversibly triumphant in the twenty-first century? And anyway, the book is very hard on workers, above all on the socialist Frank Owen. Are all its readers sentimental masochists?

For some jaded readers The Ragged Trousered Philanthropists supports the idea that the working-class is – apparently, always has been – too selfish, short-

xviii   Tressell

sighted or downright stupid to act in its own interests. Its socialist ideas, we are told, were put into practice by serious organisations, but sadly they failed to catch on. The explanations vary. Usually, this sort of world-weary despair comes from former members of the Communist Party; but we can also hear it nowadays from the increasingly homeless Labour left, and even from a few people who once thought they were revolutionaries. After all, the story goes, we were the best, and if we failed nobody else could possibly do any better. Some of them have forgotten that Lenin called that sort of thing 'communist arrogance'.

On the other hand, there are those who believe that Tressell's book has near-magical powers. Not long ago in North London a paper-seller was asked if she had read the book, since it would do more good than selling *Socialist Worker*.[1] It's a thought, of course; and it speaks volumes about those who believe ideas alone can change the world. But is it *true*? *Tressell* will argue that while socialist ideas must be available all the time, only when people's experience changes will they fully explain oppression and its causes, and offer a way forward.

The Ragged Trousered Philanthropists is about *hope*. It is about socialist values and their continued relevance when we are being told that capitalism is here for ever; that greed is good; that war, famine, poverty, racism and every form of oppression are natural, normal and permanent features of life on Planet Earth. More that that, it is a passionate denunciation of the capitalist 'system' worldwide. *Tressell* will not indulge in post-Communist cynicism, sectarianism, woolly idealism, or uncritical ancestor-worship – the seductive but self-defeating idea that all that socialists have to look forward to is the past – or in any other form of sophisticated despair. Nor will it support those insidious forms of British nationalism and anti-intellectualism so often found in backward parts of the reformist left. Instead it will show how *The Ragged Trousered Philanthropists* was produced, reprinted, distributed and put to work throughout the labour movement, and after almost a century is still used as a weapon in the struggle. It has remained relevant because it is not only manifestly against the capitalist 'System', internationally, but leaves the future open for those of us who want to change it.

Memory and forgettary

The most important sources for *Tressell* are the Robert Tressell Family Papers. Thanks to Reg Johnson, the author's grandson-in-law, I have enjoyed privileged access to this material. However, RTFP is such a large and growing collection that full references would make the Notes completely unwieldy. So quotations from original Noonan documents, correspondence and taped interviews involving Kathleen Noonan Lynne, Joan Johnson, Reg Johnson and Len Green, and from reviews, newspaper cuttings and periodical articles, flyers, programmes and ephemera relating to RTP, can be taken to come from originals or copies in RTFP, unless specifically referenced elsewhere. The memories of Tressell's daughter, Kathleen Noonan Lynne, were systematically interrogated only from 1967, when she was in her mid-seventies. The consistency of her responses is impressive. Of course, as she acknowledged, a distinction has to be made between what she was quite sure about, what she was fairly sure about, and what she believed was probably the case. So on the few occasions when her memory conflicts with reliable documentary evidence, 'forgettary' may have taken place.

My second major source was John Charles Stuart Beeching, who was born in St Leonards in 1922. His grandfather had worked with men who had known Robert Tressell. In the late 1930s Jack joined the Communist Party, then went to London to work as a Party full-timer. In the early 1940s he served in the Royal Navy Fleet Air Arm, was torpedoed, and took part in the Anzio landings. After the war he became involved in London radical culture as a poet, and was appointed Secretary of the CP's Writers' Group. In the early 1950s he was made a director of Lawrence & Wishart, the CP publishing house, and was central to the publication of the 'complete' edition of RTP in 1955. Otherwise unsourced quotations from Jack are from the letter and two tapes he sent me a few months before his death in December 2001. Copies are in RTFP.

My third major source ought to have been the archive of Frederick Cyril Ball, who researched Tressell of Mugsborough in the years 1942–50. His main sources for the period up to 1911 were the memories of the author's elderly niece, Alice, plus those of Bill Gower, Len Green, William Ward, Edward and Phoebe Cruttenden and Alf Sellens. These accounts were supplemented by material from George Gallop, John Whitelock, J.H. Poynton, and Messrs Boreham, Noakes, Philcox, Cradduck and Burr. But from 1967 Ball had privileged access to Kathleen Noonan Lynne, and by 1973 the material for his second biography, One of the Damned, amounted to seventy-six trays of notes.[2] Apparently, he never kept his own correspondence with publishers, the BBC and other institutions and individuals.[3]

Sadly, with the exception of William Ward's important letter, Ball's other unique material, including his copies of the correspondence between Jessie Pope and Grant Richards, have gone missing. Consequently, wherever that material is cited here from Ball's books, readers need to be aware of its uncertain status. It is, to say the least, a sad end to a lifetime's work on 'Robert Tressell'.

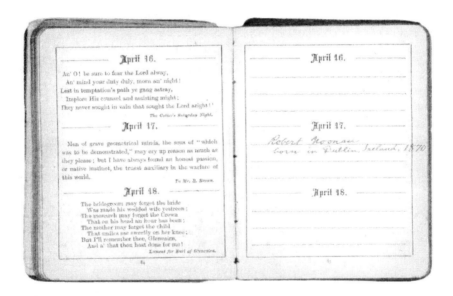

Kathleen Noonan's Birthday Book

I

Who was Robert Tressell?

Dublin

The author of *The Ragged Trousered Philanthropists*, the classic English working-class novel, was not born in England, or into the working class, but he often tried to put people off the scent. Apparently, he told Stuart Ogilvy that he hailed from Liverpool, and that his father had been an Inspector in the Royal Irish Constabulary.[1] Yet William Ward understood he was born in Cleveland Street, off Tottenham Court Road, London.[2] However, he wrote in his daughter Kathleen's Birthday Book, under 17 April, that he was 'born in Dublin, Ireland, 1870'. Kathleen was led to believe this took place in Merrion Square, and that her paternal grandfather was Sir Samuel Croker, 'an officer in the army' who 'had his head bashed in during the Phoenix Park riots', and 'a silver plate put in under the skull'.

Some of this turns out to be true. Samuel Croker was born in 1790 or 1791, and joined the Royal Irish Constabulary around 1820. By 1825 he was Sub-Inspector (Chief Constable) in Dungarvan, County Waterford, and later in Carrickbeg, County Tipperary. He retired from the RIC in 1840 on a large pension of £400 a year; but he was Resident Magistrate in Ennis, County Clare, until 1 April 1843.[3] In 1862 Inverine Castle was mortgaged to him, but by then he lived in Dublin. A birth certificate from No. 3 South City District shows that a son, Robert, was born on 18 April 1870 to Samuel Croker, 'Pensioner', and Mary Croker (formerly Noonan), of 37 Wexford Street. A register at St Kevin's Church, Harrington Street, Dublin, records that Robert Croker was christened on 26 April. The priest noted the father was not a Catholic. One sponsor was Maria Hannah

Croker; the other was the mother, 'Maria Noon', of 37 Wexford Street. Yet
that house was tenanted by a Dr Daly.

Samuel Croker lived at 1 Winslow Terrace, Rathgar,[4] with his wife, Jane
Usher Croker. They married in 1827, and three sons and two daughters
survived. Yet Mary Anne Noonan had at least three daughters, plus Robert
and another son, all of whom claimed Samuel Croker as a father. Fortunately, Samuel was well-off. In August 1873 he conveyed 145 Great Britain
Street, Dublin, a commercial property yielding over £27 rent a year, to
Mary Anne Noonan, 'spinster', of 38 Bes[s]borough Avenue, North Strand.
In June 1874 Samuel Croker, 'retired Resident Magistrate, of London',
signed a settlement (registered in August), giving Mary a £100 annuity
from his pension, though Mrs Croker still tenanted 1 Winslow Terrace,
Dublin.[5]

Reportedly, Robert's niece, Alice Meiklejon, understood he was a 'very
sensitive and impressionable child', and 'very fond of his father'.[6] Kathleen
believed he was brought up as a Catholic, and had a 'well fed, well
clothed and happy childhood and a good education'. He spent some time
in Forest Gate, London. Once, after he stayed out too long, his father
'whipped' him so hard that he got tired, and the older brother 'got off
scot free'. On another occasion, dressed in a 'Jack Tar' suit of 'long white
pants and sailor blouse', Robert 'ran away from home, and was brought
back by a policeman, who had found him sleeping under a tree, with a
loaf of bread and a carving knife'. Evidently, Samuel Croker died, 'raving',
at some point between late 1874 and December 1875, when 16-year-old
Mary Jane Noonan married, giving her father's name as 'Samuel Noonan',
'Deceased'. (Confusingly, she was called 'Mary Ann Noonan' by the clerk.)

In 1875 'Mrs Numan' continued to live at 38 Bessborough Avenue; yet
by 1876 that address was home to John O'Reilly.[7] Apparently, Alice understood that she remarried, 'sooner than was then thought proper', and the
stepfather 'never took kindly to the children'. The older ones soon left,
and some of them went to England. Robert, the youngest, was 'extremely
self willed', and left before completing his education, though he later
complained about his stinted schooling.[8] Kathleen believed her paternal
grandfather was a landowner who 'left the collecting of rents and estate
management to his agents, and lived in comfort himself without bother-
ing about the conditions of his tenants'; and since Robert grew up during
the Irish Land War, she assumed he left home because 'he could not live
on the income from absentee rentals'. In any event, probably from 1886,

aged sixteen, Robert earned his own living. He never saw his mother again; but at some point he took her surname and became Robert Noonan.

Cape Town, Johannesburg and back

Diamonds were 'discovered' – that is, recognised by white people – in South Africa in 1867, near Kimberley, on the border between the British-controlled Cape Colony and the Boer republic of the Orange Free State. By 1872 the region had the largest diamond mine in the world. Its capital, Cape Town, was a major port and the British Navy's 'Gibraltar of the South', and between 1865 and 1891 its population more than doubled to 67,000. Kathleen understood her father worked his passage there, perhaps from Liverpool, in 1888, aged 18, or 'possibly a little younger or older'. She and Alice believed he had never been apprenticed; and Ward thought he probably learned his trade in South Africa. In any event, on 15 October 1891, Robert Phillipe Noonan, 'Decorator' of 78 Strand Street, Cape Town, giving his age as 23 (not 21), married 18-year-old Elizabeth Hartel of Cape Town, with one parent's consent, at the Protestant Holy Trinity Church.

The Noonans lived in Rosebank, Mowbray, a middle-class suburb, and Kathleen was born on 17 September 1892. They were 'happy' until 1894 (possibly the year Robert's mother died); but then he suspected Elizabeth was having an affair. She 'denied it, & I had no proof, so forgave her'. 'Business was bad & I left for Johannesburg partly for that'. On 7 April 1895 Kathleen was baptised at the Protestant St Peter's Church, Mowbray; but at some point after September she was 'put in a convent'. From 15 September Elizabeth was in Johannesburg; but by December she was back in Cape Town, and definitely had an affair. She went to Johannesburg again, but returned in March 1896. When Robert got to Cape Town in April she was 'in the family way', and the child was born in August. Eventually, she admitted that Thomas Lindenbaum was the father.[9]

On 21 November 1896 Robert Philip Noonan filed for divorce in the Supreme Court, Cape Town, on the grounds of the adultery of Elizabeth Noonan ('born Hartle'). She ignored five summonses, and did not appear in court on 26 or 27 February 1897. Noonan insisted he had 'supplied her with sufficient funds'; but Thomas R. Lindenbaum, a 30-year-old 'head cart driver' of German origin from Mowbray, testified that he 'had intercourse with her' and 'used to pay her when I was with her'. 'She told me

Elizabeth Noonan
c. 1895

her husband had c[augh]t her with a man named Saunders & that is why he went to Johannesburg'. Robert got his divorce, and Elizabeth was 'declared to have forfeited all benefits arising from the marriage in community of property', though she had nothing when they married. Robert got custody of 'the minor child'.[10] Kathleen, then aged 4, dismissed 'any question of my mother being "impossible"'. Her father told her she was 'very much' like her mother, who she was led to believe was a French Catholic, called Madeleine, who died of typhoid fever. 'I used to think I was Kathleen Elizabeth until R[obert] wanted to know where I got the Elizabeth from'. By now, if not before, she was in a Johannesburg convent.

Gold had been 'discovered' in Boer-controlled Transvaal in 1886. During 1894–95 the number of new buildings in Johannesburg almost doubled; and by 1897 its population of nearly one hundred thousand consisted mainly of single men. Most whites were British immigrants, and about a

Robert and Kathleen
Noonan, c. 1895

thousand of them were from Ireland. That January, Noonan gave his birthday as 17 April 1871 (not 1870), his last place of residence as Ireland, and
his date of settlement in Johannesburg as 15 August 1896.[11] He got work
at Herbert Evans & Co., founded in 1889, the largest decorating business
in town. For 'nearly three years', he 'worked under' Stewart Ogilvy. The
foreman found him 'a very good signwriter – indeed, the best I have ever
known', with 'the makings of a brilliant artist'. Ordinary tradesmen got
£5 a week for working 9 a.m. to 5 p.m. on weekdays, with an hour for
lunch, and 9 a.m. to 1 p.m. on Saturdays. But Noonan got £7 or more,
so perhaps he was made a junior 'foreman' in 1898, when Evans & Co.
opened a separate signwriting department.[12]

Ogilvy recalled that Johannesburg 'offered little, outside of hard
drinking, by way of amusement', and Noonan was 'an interesting and
entertaining companion' with 'a brilliant and versatile mind'. He was 'an

extremely pleasant fellow, and the best of company, and we became very
friendly'. Ogilvy understood that his friend's domestic life was 'not happy',
and that he 'was separated from his wife'. Noonan 'lived in a little world
of his own and was very fond of writing, especially articles dealing with
everyday life', and his 'All meals a shilling' appeared in a 'little paper
dealing with local topics'. He 'had an eye for queer characters, and would
follow them about, endlessly listening to their conversation, and taking
voluminous notes of how they looked and what they said' for a 'book of
his impressions of the people of Johannesburg', which had to be 'shelved
owing to the troubled times'.[13]

In January 1897 Noonan had had dealings with the Commissioner for
Mines. He later told Ward of 'mining swindles that he put money in
while in South Africa', and was accused of being 'quite willing to make
a Profit out of the miners, but no gold being there you lost your money'.
On 12 June 1898 Robert Phillip Noonan leased Lot No. 16, Block No. 2 of
'the farm Turffontein No. 198 Witwatersrand Goldfields, in the District of
Heidelberg', known as Forest Hill. The 99-year lease was registered with
the Registrar of Mining Rights at Johannesburg, but it gave him no mineral
rights. Noonan was committed 'forthwith' to 'neatly and substantially'
fence the property, to accept that 'no dwelling or place of business of less
value than £200 shall be erected thereon', and to agree not to sell, sub-
lease or hire the land 'to any Arab, Malay, Chinese, Coolie, Indian or other
coloured person'. Moreover, any such persons could not live there 'unless
he or she is in the bona fide employ of the Lessee'. He had to pay £3 a year,
quarterly in advance, and did so up to 31 December 1899. But no building work was carried out.[14]

Kathleen recalled that her father was 'quite fond' of his servant, 'Sixpence'. He 'may have christened him or he may already have had that
name – they had all kinds of, to us, funny names'. All 'Sixpence' ever
stole was a 'green and gold sash'. Robert 'used to imagine him strutting
in front of his wives, wearing nothing but his loin-cloth' and the sash,
but 'never begrudged it'. Kathleen didn't 'think the colour question ever
arose in those days', though a man was 'attacked by Kaffirs at a farm near
the Convent' during 1897. She had been 'put in' the Convent of the Holy
Family in Regent Street, Johannesburg, which was run by the Holy Sisters
of Bordeaux. It was 'far from being cheap', and day girls 'used to be
brought to school in carriages'. Kathleen was given a necklace with a
diamond, a ruby and a pearl; and her nurse, Mary Eulalie ('not a Negro'),

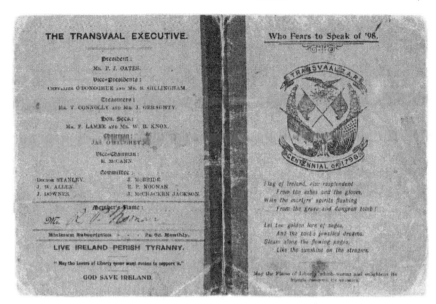

Noonan's '98 Association card

accompanied her to school. Robert visited on Sundays, and 'all the girls got excited' since he gave prizes. So it 'all seems to point to good financial circumstances'.

Noonan may not have belonged to a trade union in Cape Town, but, probably before the end of 1897, he became Secretary of the Transvaal Federated Building Trades Council. In fact the *Transvaal Leader* noted it was 'called together by Mr Noonan' in Johannesburg, and its first public act was to 'protest against the employment of black skilled labour'. Subsequently, architects insisted that only white skilled workmen should be employed. So Noonan 'at least acquiesced' in white supremacist views. On the other hand, the English socialist paper the *Clarion* was given away to subscribers of South Africa's first socialist newspaper, the *Johannesburg Witness*; and in May 1899, as Trades Council Secretary, Noonan went to the launch of the International Independent Labour Party, formed by British trade unionists and German socialists. The IILP saw the Boers as victims of British imperialism, and Noonan, who vigorously denied disparaging President Kruger, was elected onto the committee.[15]

R.P. Noonan was also on the Transvaal Executive Committee of the Centennial of 1798 Association, which commemorated the United Irishmen. The Vice-President, Sol Gillingham, was a well-to-do Pretoria baker, and probably linked the Boers with the revolutionary Irish Republican Brotherhood. A Committee member, John MacBride, was subsequently shot by the British after the Irish Republican Easter Rising of 1916. An ordinary member, Arthur Griffith, was anti-imperialist, pro-capitalist and a racist, but later became President of Sinn Fein.

Ogilvy was sure that Noonan was 'active in the formation of the Irish Brigade'. His rooms were on Pritchard Street, between Smal Street and Van Wielligh Street, and he and 'a lot of other wild Irishmen used regularly to meet, and concert their plans'[16] at John Joseph Mitchell's small cleaners' and dyers' shop at 106 Pritchard Street, between Smal Street and Delvers Street. From early August 1899, for six weeks, 'small clandestine meetings' took place on Sundays, the miners' day off. On 3 September, at a meeting of the '98 Centenary Committee, it was suggested that an Irish Brigade be formed to fight alongside the Boers, should Britain declare war, and a week later a larger meeting approved the proposal. Three days after that the First Irish Transvaal Brigade was authorised by the Boer leaders. MacBride emerged as second-in-command; Mitchell was elected Captain. On 2 October the officers went to Pretoria to receive their commissions. For the next three days recruits enlisted at the Brigade's offices at the corner of Pritchard Street and von Wielligh Street; and on 5 October they marched to the railway station, bound for the Transvaal and the Natal Border.[17] War broke out six days later.

Herbert Evans had closed his business at the end of August;[18] so Noonan was out of a job, with a child to support, and the Irish Brigaders were to be unpaid. Did he join? He usually kept his affairs to himself. When Kathleen asked him where he was going, he very often said 'I'm going to see a man about a dog.' But he was particularly reticent about his ill-health. Once he is said to have blamed it on the age of his parents;[19] yet Kathleen was told 'again and again' that 'he attributed his chest condition to drinking whisky to keep warm, when riding across the veldt at nights, and getting chilled'. We know that MacBride worked at Langlaate goldmine. So, for a time, did Griffith; and '98 Association Meetings took place there.[20] No full muster rolls have survived for the 1st or the 2nd Irish Brigades, yet all but forty members have been tracked down, and Noonan's name is not among them.[21] Moreover, he left no trace in the Republic's Detective Branch papers.[22]

Reportedly Ogilvy believed Noonan was 'very much opposed to the war', and that he 'disappeared into the blue very shortly before the Boer war broke out'. Alice understood her uncle had 'been in trouble with the authorities', and that he had a terrible journey in an open truck on the last train going south from Johannesburg.[23] So did Len Green and others. The last train heading south before war broke out left on 9 October 1899, carrying the remnant of sixty thousand recent, mainly British, immigrants who could not afford passenger fares. They were 'packed – seventy, even a hundred at a time – into "Kaffir-trucks" (or coal trucks or cattle trucks, it was all the same)', and arrived in Cape Town after three days and nights of being 'exposed to the spring rains, and covered in mud and coal dust'.[24] Any weak chests probably got weaker.

Fred Ball once speculated that it was 'extremely likely' that Noonan 'left Johannesburg as a prisoner and spent the rest of the war behind bars' in Cape Town, before being deported, while Kathleen travelled to England in the care of the British Consul's wife.[25] Kathleen rejected all of this. Her father once thought of remarrying, but the woman didn't want responsibility for the child; so in 1897 he had written to his widowed sister, Adelaide Rolleston, whose husband had worked in the British Consulate in Santiago, Chile. He asked her to 'keep house for him' and 'be a mother' to Kathleen, while 'he could take the place of Arthur's father'. In fact he sent money for the fare, but Adelaide spent it going to see Mary Jane in England, so he had to send more. Kathleen understood that 'just about or before the time when I was 7', which was on 17 September 1899, her father left Johannesburg 'on business' to meet Adelaide and her son Arthur, and 'to arrange a home for us all in Rondebosch, near Cape Town'. Her aunt was used to maids, and there 'were never any plans for her to go to Johannesburg'; so her father's journey 'had nothing to do with the Irish Brigade' and he left 'on his own, and not under duress'.

Kathleen left 'much later' in 1899. But she was told by her father that 'the real reason for the Boer War was the diamond mines', and she was 'very anti-British'. At school prayers 'everyone would be praying for the British to win, and I used to be praying for the Boers'. Once, English officers came and 'gave us all little Union Jack buttons', but she 'threw that button down and put my foot on it and twisted it around a few times', then sat down in the middle of the chorus of 'God Save the Queen'.[26] She left Johannesburg with 'a Frenchwoman', Mme Vaillant, who was 'probably a friend of the Sisters'. They travelled to Durban by train 'in ordinary carriages' and 'perfect comfort', then on to Cape Town by boat, where Kathleen mistook her aunt for a maid. Adelaide was 'very vain', and 'never really forgave me'.

The Noonan–Rolleston foursome lived in Rondebosch, a well-to-do residential area. They had a maid – 'probably a dark girl' – but Kathleen could not recall a school, or remember her father's work. In October 1900 Kitchener stationed troops at Cape ports. During 1901 the horrors of the British concentration camps became known, and Kitchener ordered the Boers to surrender before 15 September. Early that month, after a few days in the Hotel La France in Cape Town, Robert, Kathleen, Adelaide and Arthur sailed from Durban on the Union Castle Line's SS *Galician*. Kathleen thought they left so she could be 'educated properly'. Noonan may have been particularly stressed, since he hit her for the one and only time for being 'impudent' to someone on the boat. Yet he also played practical jokes, and (as 'George Washington') wrote several flimsy sheets of a hand-written 'bulletin' of news and gossip. *The Evening Ananias* was named after the character in Acts, Chapter 5, who 'fell down and gave up the ghost' after being found out a liar.[27]

Hastings

Kathleen thought she spent her ninth birthday, 17 September 1901, near Las Palmas, so the foursome probably arrived in London soon after. A fellow-worker understood that Noonan 'remained for some time in London', but that 'his physique being against him, he had a bitter struggle for an existence'.[28] Kathleen believed they stayed only a week or two, 'possibly until luggage, transport, etc., was arranged', and then accepted an invitation from Mary Jane Meiklejon (née Noonan) to 'dear, sunny Hastings', or, rather, to 38 Western Road, St Leonards.[29] Ward recalled they arrived there before the Boer War ended on 31 May 1902. Robert and Mary Jane's sister Ellen visited from Liverpool, but that was the last Kathleen saw of her.

Noonan was a 'compact' five foot three inches, and weighed about nine stone; while his hair was 'quite thin on top', and he had 'a kind of sandy moustache'.[30] But locals noticed 'the pink spots which appeared on his cheeks in moments of excitement';[31] and Ward thought his eyes 'seemed to have a light behind them', which 'might be due to ill health'. He 'certainly was on the frail side'. One workmate found he was 'a great sufferer from lung and chest troubles'.[32] Kathleen recalled he had 'recurrent attacks of bronchitis and would cough and cough'. Hastings might seem an odd choice for an anti-imperialist, but it was, after all, a health resort.

In 1851 the town had 17,000 inhabitants, but in the 1860s cheap railway fares led to a speculative building boom. Thomas Carlyle experienced 'Nothing but dust, noise, squalor, and the universal tearing and digging as if of gigantic human swine, not finding any worms or roots that would be useful to them!' He leased a furnished house in St Leonards, 'bearing marks of thrifty, wise, and modestly-elegant habits in the old-lady owners just gone from it', but it turned out to be 'decidedly the worst-built house I have ever been within'.[33]

When Noonan arrived Hastings had a population of over 60,000, and was generally prosperous, yet it was particularly vulnerable to international economic fluctuations. British 'idlers' had long sent huge amounts of capital abroad, but the seriously rich had now begun to follow their money and to spend it overseas. Nationally, the building trade was already in severe depression, and as sharpened competition led to speed-ups, unemployment began to rise. In Hastings the slump was deeper still, because the boom had brought many workers from the countryside and the North of England. Many, like Jack Beeching's grandfather, were craftsmen who now had to work 'very much below their level of skill'. In 1902, 143 painters applied to the local Charity Organisation Society.[34]

Eventually, Noonan got a start with Bruce & Co. The basic rate was sevenpence (less than 3p) an hour, for from 56 to 70 hours a week; though he could gild, grain and write signs and coffin plates, so he may have got an extra halfpenny.[35] Ward first met him when he used to 'look after the shop in Queens Rd selling Paperhangings, Glass &c & to do the sign writing & Graining'. Noonan said he was 'very sorry to be doing me out of work, I said you have got to work for a living the same as I have so do the best you can'. Yet Noonan was more of a 'Decorative Artist than a common sign writer', and he told Ward he 'had not been used to trade work'; so he was 'often in bed between 10 & 11', though he 'could not get to sleep before 4 am and then had to get up at 6 o'clock'. He 'used to say he could not carry on & would like to Pass out'.

Noonan was known as a 'brilliant scenic painter', but was often given 'washing off' and distempering to do.[36] Indeed, he may have taken notes for 'Misery' from Bruce & Co.'s foreman, before leaving 'under a cloud'.[37] Ward knew 'he was fed up according to his talk', and that he 'worked there for a few months, then was missing for a few weeks', but 'did not know he was going away'. He understood Noonan 'spent most of the time in hospital' in London. But about five or six weeks later Ward saw him in Hastings, writing the name of a house, working for Burton & Co., Builders, Decorators and Funeral Directors.

At first Kathleen attended the private Aylsham House School, run by Mrs Glenister in Milward Crescent, and may then have moved to the Roman Catholic convent. She remembered a 'little boy spit at me and call[ed] me pro-Boer', and from some time in 1902 she boarded at the fee-paying St Ethelburga's Girls High School, a Roman Catholic convent at Deal in Kent. She didn't recall coming home for holidays, but 'probably did'. Yet there were good boarding schools in Hastings, so it was 'quite possible' she had become 'a bone of contention' between her father and Adelaide, who showed 'continual resentment at the mode of living' he had chosen, and wanted him to set up on his own. Kathleen felt there was 'no puzzle in his not attempting to "better" himself', since 'he was there to find out the TRUE facts of working conditions and to find out how they could be improved'.

However, Mary Jane's welcome soon 'wore out', once it became clear that Robert was not well-off, so they moved to 1 Plynlimmon Road, nearer the breadwinner's work. In 1903 Noonan rented attic Flat 5 in Grosvenor Mansions, a newish building in Milward Road. Late that year he painted the east wall in Christchurch, Ore, and did stencilling at Christ Church, St Thomas of Canterbury Catholic Church and the Convent Chapel, St Leonards.[38] During 1904 Kathleen moved to St Andrew's Church of England Elementary School, Hastings, presumably because money was tight.

Raymond Postgate thought that 'the deadness of the union so depressed' Noonan 'that he did not re-enrol' in Hastings;[39] though George Hicks claimed he had joined in London, then transferred his membership to the South Coast.[40] There had been seventy members in the Hastings branch of the painters' union in the 1870s, but in October 1904 there were seven, and Noonan's name was not among them.[41] That same month the Turf-fontein Estate Limited, whose head office was at Old Jewry in London, began proceedings against Noonan in the Witwatersrand High Court for failing to keep up payments on his plot of land. They did not know where to find him. Notices were placed in Johannesburg papers, but he was not represented on 10 November when the court gave leave to sue for £15. On 14 February 1905 The Honourable Sir James Rose-Innes KCMG cancelled

Noonan's lease, and awarded costs (with interest) against him, in his absence.[42]

At that time Noonan was painting St Andrew's Church chancel in Hastings, reportedly for eightpence an hour, plus overtime. Kathleen recalled that he 'used to keep on until the early hours of the morning working alone in the darkened church with just the light he needed to see what he was doing', sometimes until 4 a.m. At Easter 1905 he got a photograph and £5 from the vicar, Henry W. Jeanes, 'as a Souvenir of his most artistic renovation', which was later misattributed to 'a member of the congregation'.[43] He also painted St John's and some nonconformist churches. Workmates began calling him 'Raphael'.[44]

Noonan kept his head down politically, but the local *Observer* noted he was 'summoned for obstructing PC Curtis in the execution of his duty' on 6 November 1905, as he 'cautioned a lad who was lighting a squib in Havelock-road'.

> Defendant interfered, and called witness, who was in plain clothes, a coward. Defendant took his coat off, and put himself in a fighting attitude. He refused to give his name, but subsequently did at the station. – Defendant, who referred to notes, cross-examined the witness, who said that Noonan was very excited, and it was owing to that that he declined to show his authority as a constable. He admitted that the boy complained that witness hurt his shoulder. – P.C. Hoadley said defendant was making a great disturbance, and there was a big crowd round. – Mr Noonan, a decorator of 115, Milward-road, gave his version of the affair on oath. He had bought his children some Chinese crackers. One of them tried to light one, and he saw a man, apparently a civilian, come up to his boy, seize him violently by the shoulder, and begin stamping on the squib. He interfered to protect the boy, and took off his overcoat with the intention of defending himself ... he did not give his name and address because Curtis did not treat him properly.

The case was found to be 'fully proved', and Noonan was 'fined 10s and costs (£1 9s), or seven days' hard labour'.

Presumably Noonan paid up, but money was still a problem. So while he painted a scenic wall in the Buchanan Hospital for free, on Christmas Day he was writing a coffin plate for cash.[45] He worked a few months at Burtons, then for a St Leonards firm; but he told Ward he 'was treated very bad by them' and was 'off again' because he 'could not put up with it', and 'asked me if I would write the Coffin Plates for him'. Burtons 'had a contract at the Municipal Hospital 6d each allowed for plates in case he came back'. Come back he did, and with his politics sharpened.

Extreme socialist opinions

Ward thought Noonan was 'Roman Catholic and Proud of it', yet his future publisher understood that was only before his reading on religious matters 'convinced him that neither Roman Catholicism in particular nor Christianity in general had any sound basis'. Reportedly, Noonan told a friend that 'there's only one religion as ridiculous as the Roman Catholic and that is the Protestant', and that 'God is a devil who lets little children suffer'.[46] Yet a frequent visitor at Milward Road was Father George O'Callaghan, the Roman Catholic Pallotine priest from Star of the Sea parish. Kathleen remembered them 'talking half-way into the night', until O'Callaghan was sent to New York in 1905.

Kathleen, who later became a Christian, liked to think of her father as an 'agnostic' who did not lose faith but 'had never been intellectually able to accept it' in the first place. He believed in 'the historical Jesus and His teachings, but not in His divinity', yet 'followed His teachings more than the most truly christian people I have ever met'. On the other hand he 'had nothing but the uttermost contempt for those who professed christianity and yet failed so lamentably to show it in their lives'. He could not abide 'clergy who pandered to their wealthier parishioners and ignored the underfed and shabby ones', and he had 'no use' for the religion taught at her convent schools. She knew he performed the 'strychnine' trick on a preacher called Hubbard, though he regretted it when he got home. So he was no bigot, but he was pulled by militant atheism.

Noonan was also a very cultured man. Kathleen understood he learned Latin and Greek at school, or from his father, and he spoke French fluently, making her practice at meal-times. He could 'keep up a conversation in German and Spanish', had some Boer Dutch, Italian and Gaelic, and owned French and German books. Besides 'the usual classics', she recalled, there were works by Zola, Dickens, Voltaire, Paine, Plato, Scott, Pliny, Macaulay, Josephus, Gibbon, Spencer, Huxley, Ruskin and Morris, plus Blatchford's *Merrie England*, Aristotle's *Poetics*, Plutarch's *Lives*, a set of *University Magazines*, and 'books on religion'.

Kathleen owned works by Meredith and other writers. She recalled being taken by her father to see a film about Raffles, and to His Majesty's Theatre to see 'The Bohemian Girl', *Les Cloches de Corneville* and *Madame Butterfly*. But he stopped her singing commercial songs of the day because they were 'common' and 'rubbish', and he 'wouldn't read "trash"'. Reportedly, he enjoyed Eugène Sue's *Mysteries of Paris*, Bram Stoker's *Dracula* and Conan Doyle's Sherlock Holmes stories. His close friend Bill Gower recalled that he owned works by Fielding, Shakespeare, Shelley, Byron, Whittier and Oliver Wendell Holmes, many of which he found on second-hand book-stalls or at Reeves's shop in Hastings Old Town. Gower loaned him Edwin Arnold's *Light of Asia* and Ernst Haeckel's *Evolution of Man*, and knew he read Darwin with great interest. Ruskin was 'a favourite'; Morris influenced him 'a great deal'; but for Swift he had 'the greatest admiration'.[47]

Noonan used his books as a lending library. Len Green, then a young paperhanger, recalled: 'We paid a penny a week' and 'every Friday he'd come over to see my dad and he'd bring one book over and then take the other away'. Len was 'made up' with Zola's *Lourdes*. Evidently, Noonan used the Free Library for technical books;[48] and Ward found he was 'very keen on all transport & railways to come under one management (all over the world[)]'. Yet in the typed introduction to his series of drawings illustrating 'The Evolution of the Airship', Noonan noted:

> The most powerful navy that could be built, the strongest fortifications that the wit of man could devise, or the most numerous and efficient army in the world, would all be comparatively helpless and at the mercy of the nation possessing a fleet of airships so designed as to be capable of carrying quantities of high explosives.

Probably in 1905 Noonan was photographed beside the large model air-ship he had made. Kathleen remembered he sent the design to the War Office, who refused to consider it unless he provided a full-scale working model, which was an economic impossibility. Someone suggested he offer it to Germany, but 'in spite of being a wicked Irishman, he didn't'. He smashed the model out of frustration.

But why would an Irish anti-imperialist want to help the British state? According to Ball, some people noticed Noonan's 'slight Irish accent,[49] though Kathleen recalled no such thing. He sang 'various Irish songs', such as 'Come Back to Erin', 'The Harp that Once' and 'Dark Rosaleen', which they all joined in. He also had 'an Italian harp with ram's heads round the top of the fluted front column' but 'only 5 strings', and he played Irish jigs. He remained fond of Wolfe Tone and Robert Emmet; but he thought 'it wasn't any use giving the Irish Home Rule' unless 'she got rid of the whiskey' and 'the priests'. Perhaps his Irish nationalism mellowed as socialist convictions grew.

Robert Noonan and model
airship, c. 1905

One workmate apparently saw Noonan as an 'idealist' who was 'convinced that the only hope of the workers was in the establishment of a co-operative commonwealth, in which the means of life were owned by the community, and goods produced for use'.[50] Kathleen believed his socialist ideas came from 'an innate sense of justice combined with compassion', backed up by reading. Yet he would sing:

> There was a man lived down our street,
> Who was full of aches and pains,
> He fell out of the window one day
> And dashed out all his brains.
> And when he found he had no brains,
> What do you think he did?
> He became a member of parliament
> Where brains he did not need!

For a time, this scepticism may have led to abstentionism. Kathleen re-called leaning out of the window with Arthur at Milward Road during the January 1906 general election, singing:

> Don't vote for either of the bounders
> Throw old Thomas in the sea
> Du Cros he is no good
> He wants to tax your food
> Socialism is the thing for you and me.

The next they knew Adelaide was 'dragging us back in, saying, just because my father wanted to live that kind of a life, there's no reason why people shouldn't behave like civilised beings'. 'Dad wasn't in favour at all' with his 'very proper' sisters, because 'he was going to try to make things better for the working man'. Alice told Fred Ball that her uncle had 'always been extremely vehement and very very bitter', and held 'extreme socialist opinions'.[51]

2

The two souls of Mugsborough socialism

From radicalism to socialism

Robert Noonan was not the first Hastings radical. According to an obituary in a September 1899 issue of the *Hastings and St Leonards Standard*, Alfred ('Toby') King was born around 1837, and brought up in the Church of England. But after digging trenches in the Crimean War he became a follower of the rationalist and atheist Charles Bradlaugh, and attended the London Reform Bill demonstration of 1885. King was 'a deep thinker and greater reader', 'one of his favourite occupations being to instruct the young men in the district' in history and politics in the evenings and on Sunday afternoons. His *Ireland's Woes and Ireland's Foes* 'had a great circulation among the local Radical party'. He ridiculed the House of Lords and the Church, and stopped his children showing deference to the gentry.

King combined theory with practice. When Tory boatmen caused 'some disturbance' at a Liberal meeting, this 'veritable Goliath' 'picked them up, one by one, by the scruff of the neck, and dropped them over the balustrade'. One broke a leg, so King incurred 'the utmost'

BITTERNESS OF THE WATERMEN who meant straightaway to be revenged. Therefore, after the next meeting, he was to be waited upon, and things made warm for him. His labourers at the Market Garden at Tivoli got wind of the affair, and to a man at once decided to stand by their master, to whom they all owed so much in many ways, and form a bodyguard. After the meeting there was a great crowd, but after that had thinned down a bit, Mr King started to walk up Bohemia-road to his home, with his bodyguard of labourers, each armed with a stout oak stave, which he had up his sleeve ready for the attack. The boatmen followed filling the air with threats, and as they began to close in, the Radicals in front brandished their staves to the dismay of the followers.

Liberal radicalism evidently had a cross-class appeal. Socialism followed.

By 1880 the mid-Victorian capitalist boom had begun to collapse. Britain's economy had declined relative to those of Germany and the USA, but orthodox economics failed to explain the situation. Marx's ideas were not generally known. Only 'a few ill-printed copies' of the English translation of Marx and Engels's *Communist Manifesto* were to be found, and even then only 'in the most advanced revolutionary circles'. But in 1880 Henry Mayers Hyndman, a Cambridge-educated non-practising barrister, read *Capital* (in French) on a Cunard liner bound for the USA. He concluded that 'the only way out of the existing social difficulties was the inevitable development from capitalism to socialism', though 'this could never be peacefully brought about except by a thoroughly educated industrial democracy'.[1] Yet his grasp of Marx's thought was partial. For example, it is true that Marx thought that 'at least in Europe, England is the only country where the inevitable social revolution might be effected entirely by peaceful and legal means'; but he 'never forgot to add that he hardly expected the English ruling classes to submit, without a "pro-slavery rebellion"'.[2]

In June 1881 Hyndman founded the Democratic Federation, which advocated adult suffrage, land nationalisation, Irish independence and the abolition of the House of Lords. In August 1884, as the 'Great Depression' deepened, it became the Social-Democratic Federation, also demanding triennial parliaments, equal electoral divisions, payment of MPs, criminalisation of electoral corruption and self-government for colonies and dependencies. But the SDF was tiny, largely London-based and middle class. Engels noted that they 'haven't got 400 paid-up members', while readers of Hyndman's *Justice* were 'sentimental bourgeois'.[3] Soon after, the Federation left wing, including William Morris, walked out, criticising Hyndman's 'arbitrary rule'. They founded the Socialist League, advocated 'Revolutionary International Socialism', and wanted theoretically trained working-class cadres who would lead others from 'Education towards Revolution'.[4]

During 1885, SDFer George Smart, an unemployed painter, was elected to the Salford School Board; but Hyndman accepted Tory money to stand Federation candidates against Liberals, and most working-class members left. The theoretical level of those who remained was not high. Marx's *Wage Labour and Capital* appeared in *Justice*, but one of the few working-class

members, Harry Quelch, had to teach himself French in order to read
Capital. The first English edition of Volume 1 appeared in 1887, in the USA.
In the UK events were moving on. That November, two hundred people
were treated in hospital, and three died of their injuries, after police
attacked a Trafalgar Square demonstration. The SDF leaders blamed the
victims, while Engels noted that the Federation was not only sectarian,
seeing itself as 'the one true church', but also an 'army of officers sans
soldiers'.[5] Then Quelch, a Hyndman loyalist, was made editor of Justice.
He published articles favouring workplace organisation, while other SDFers
agitated at Bryant & May's match factory, and led the gas workers' and
dockers' struggles of 1889.[6]

Meanwhile, reformist socialists had begun to organize. The Fabian
Society was founded by London-based middle-class intellectuals in January
1884. In 1890 Fabian Essays in Socialism, edited by the playwright George
Bernard Shaw, hailed the 'inevitable' progress of democracy, but denounced
'Insurrectionism'. It sold 25,000 copies in one year, while Fabian Tracts
went on to sell over a third of a million. For years there was only one
working-class Fabian, the painter W.L. Phillips; but their reformist ideas
were influential. Will Thorne, a hero of 1889, felt 'Something could be
done by Parliament', though not 'with every interest except labour represented'. He believed unions were more effective than 'vague indefinite
appeals to revolution', since they offered workers 'a definite, clearly-lighted
road out of their misery'.[7]

The left was polarising. William Morris left the Socialist League, accepted
the Marxist theory of the state and the need for revolution, and called
himself a Communist. He found the bureaucratic state socialism of Edward
Bellamy's Looking Backward unconvincing, so he wrote News from Nowhere. In
1890 it was serialised in his paper, Commonweal, then published as a book
in 1891. Morris knew that revolutions involved bloodshed, though the
ruling class would use violence first; so he did not duck the likely general
strike or civil war before a 'Co-operative Commonwealth' might come
into being. By 1892–3 he understood that revolutionaries should use
parliamentary elections tactically. Then came Blatchford.

Robert Peel Glanville Blatchford was an anti-socialist who was converted after visiting Manchester's slums and reading Morris and Hyndman's
What is Socialism?, sent to him by a Liverpool workman. He became convenor
of Manchester Fabian Society and, in December 1891 (having accepted a
£1,000-a-year job on the new Workman's Times), began publishing the Clarion,

a socialist penny weekly unattached to any party, whose circulation settled down at 30,000 copies. In 1892 he helped found the Manchester and Salford Independent Labour Party, which soon had seven hundred members. In January 1893 delegates from the Fabian Society, various socialist societies and the SDF founded the Independent Labour Party. The ILP argued for the eight-hour day and the collective ownership of the land, mines and minerals, and all other means of production, distribution and exchange. Yet unity negotiations failed, because of anxieties about the bourgeois Hyndman, while the SDF distrusted union-sponsored MPs with Liberal support and insisted on a socialist programme.

Blatchford declined a leading position in the ILP. He accepted a mediated version of Marx's labour theory of value; but while he had read and 'worshipped' Morris, he 'had not read Marx, and was inclined to scorn those who claimed that they had'. He acknowledged that unions were necessary, but believed them to be insufficient, since the 'British workman' was 'his own worst enemy, and he will never be materially better in mind or in condition until he is learned enough, wise enough, honest enough, and generous enough to become his own best friend'.[8] He saw himself not as a general but a 'recruiting-sergeant' for socialist ideas.

In November 1893 Blatchford published *Merrie England*, which was against the anarchy of the market, the factory system, usury, economic imperialism and individualism, and for land nationalisation, the division of labour on a social basis and a universal right to useful work. He did not understand the role of the state in maintaining capitalist social relations, and he had 'no "system" ready cut and dried'. 'Let us once get the people to understand and desire Socialism, and I am sure we may very safely leave them to secure it.' Socialists should 'join a Socialist Society and help to get others to join', and 'send Socialist workers to sit upon all representative bodies', including parliament, 'with definite and imperative instructions' to act on the working class's behalf.[9] However, he also advocated joining both the SDF and the ILP, as he had done himself.

By 1894 'a million people had passed through' the SDF, yet only 4,500 remained.[10] Privately, Engels felt 'driven to despair by these English workers, with their sense of imaginary national superiority, with their essentially bourgeois ideas and viewpoints, with their "practical" narrow-mindedness'.[11] The ILP now had the support of Keir Hardie's *Labour Leader*, but it was fixated on elections. However, Blatchford's *Merrie England* was extremely influential. It retailed at one shilling (5p), and sold 30,000 copies. Reissued in a smaller format in 1894 it sold 25,000 more, and there were 200,000 advance orders for the penny edition, of which George Lansbury's SDF branch sold 'thousands', after members had 'wearily struggled' with *Capital* and Engels's *Socialism Utopian and Scientific*.[12] At least a million copies were sold in Britain alone. Following Blatchford's lead, working-class *Clarion* readers canvassed, recruited and sold the literature of both the ILP and the SDF, while Julia Dawson organised Clarion Vans to take 'the New Religion into remote places'.[13]

Socialism on the Sussex coast

Eastbourne was fairly remote when George Meek was born there in 1868. His father was a plasterer who had moved from Hastings in search of work. In the early 1870s, during a slump in the building trade, George's parents emigrated to the USA, leaving the boy with his grandparents. Soon after this, his father was killed, and his mother returned. In 1880 a shoe-maker who was 'a strong Radical and an atheist' lent the boy books, and argued that the Liberals 'were the friends of the poor working people'. George became 'an ardent liberal'. But in the mid-1880s he heard William Morris speak at socialist meetings in London, and back in Eastbourne he met a man who 'spent many hours preaching the gospel of advanced Radical-Republicanism'. After a period in the USA he joined Eastbourne Liberal Club in 1887, and registered working-class voters.

At this point Meek knew of only one Eastbourne socialist. But in 1891 his religious faith was undermined by reading Bellamy's *Looking Backward*, and by a militantly atheistic house-painter from Nottingham. In 1892 Meek stopped working for the Liberals and subscribed to *Justice*, the *Workman's Times* and the *Clarion*. The following year he advised his audience at an open-air meeting to join the ILP, and was promptly expelled by the Liberal Association. He got in touch with the SDF and the Fabians, sold pamphlets on the Eight-Hour Day Demonstration in London, and heard speakers like John Burns (made famous by the 1889 Dock Strike) and the Fabian Shaw. Meek returned to Eastbourne, began working as a Bath-chair man, tried to form a union, and was blacklisted. Along with some reporters and compositors, he organised a Fabian Society branch, which held several open-air meetings, but soon collapsed because most members left town.

Meek spent time in prison for debt; then in 1895 he began distributing the *Clarion*, and sold or gave away over five hundred copies of *Merrie England*.

He formed the Eastbourne Clarion Scouts, but they were accused of being 'anarchists and engaged in the manufacture of bombs', so this 'small, but select' band of compositors and carpenters withered away. In London, once again, Meek collected his letters at the *Clarion* office, heard Hyndman speak at the SDF Hall in the Strand, and visited the Anarchists' Club Autonomie in Windmill Street. He also got in touch with the Communist Club in Charlotte Street, off Tottenham Court Road.[14] (Curiously, both places were close to where Noonan once claimed he was born.)

Around this time Edward Cruttenden, a shop man in a Hastings fancy goods store, wrote to the local *Observer* asking to 'hear from any friends of labour who will assist to set the progressive movement on its legs in the town'.[15] Meek recalled that for 'some years, being the greater part of the time the only Socialists in our respective towns, we maintained a regular correspondence, and he biked over to see me now and then'.[16] There had been unionisation. A Beehive Coffee-House, probably named after the London trade-union paper run by George Potter, a carpenter, had existed in Hastings since the 1860s; and in 1894 Hastings Trades Council was founded, apparently at Cruttenden's suggestion. It took root. In the later 1890s Cruttenden and his wife Phoebe advertised for socialist contacts in the *Clarion*. The first response came from a bakery worker, F J Pay, who lived two doors away, and there was a short-lived attempt to set up an SDF branch.[17]

Yet socialist unity was hard to build on the ground when the issue of reform or revolution remained unresolved. Tom Mann had tried to bring the leaderships of the ILP and SDF together in 1897, but failed. Nationalism was a key issue. In 1898 ex-Sergeant Blatchford announced:

> I am a sincere advocate of peace, and an unwavering opponent of war. And, being what I am, I am in favour of keeping a large and efficient fleet, of strengthening the defences of our empire, and of making our army as fit as science and discipline can make it. While doing this, let us try hard to secure concord amongst the nations.

Evidently, 'our empire' transcended class lines. In October 1899, when war broke out in the Transvaal, Blatchford wobbled closer to the Tory defenders of empire: 'I cannot go with those Socialists whose sympathies are with the enemy.' In Labour clubs and Labour churches his portrait was taken from the wall, while so many working-class readers gave up the *Clarion* that it 'almost died'.[18]

As for unions, Blatchford believed the 'average trade unionist' was 'not a hopeful person', but was 'narrow, and shallow, and selfish', and 'objects strongly to the trouble of thinking'. During 1900 he founded the Clarion Fellowship, 'to promote social intercourse, and to work for whatever is thought desirable'. Each local Fellowship coordinated the Cinderella Clubs, Scouts, Cycling Clubs and Glee Clubs: 'They needed no rules, scorned committees, and their only official was a single devoted Secretary.' But since 'the great mass of the workers are too apathetic and selfish to be moved', 'it is to the younger and better educated working men and women that the champions of Socialism most profitably appeal'.[19]

Meanwhile, trade unionists organised. In February 1900 the Trades Union Congress formed the Labour Representation Committee. Its 375,000 affiliated members vastly outnumbered the ILP's 13,000 and the Fabians' 861; while the SDF claimed 9,000, but probably had a thousand in fifty branches. SDfers forced their leaders to enter the LRC, but they failed to get their 'class war' perspective adopted. Then the LRC ran candidates in the September general election. They published no socialist principles, but two were unopposed by the Liberals, and got elected. Other reformists organised, too. The National Democratic League, a radical body with Labour sympathies, which supported the Liberal Party in elections, was founded that same month. Its secretary was Tom Mann. Hastings socialists followed his lead. Their secretary was Frank Willard, a Christian Socialist, and they held Sunday evening meetings at the Fish Market; but Hastings NDL was probably moribund before Robert Noonan arrived.[20]

The bastards aren't worth saving

By 1902 Britain's economic crisis had deepened, and Blatchford was arguing for municipal socialism on a moral basis: 'I do not hate the rich: I pity the poor.' Unlike the SDF, he was 'dead against the idea of revolution':

> I do not think revolution is *possible* in Britain. Firstly, because the people have too much sense; secondly, because the people are by nature patient and kindly; thirdly because the people are too *free* to make force needful.

Instead he wanted 'a revolution of *thought*. Let us once get the people, or a big majority of the people, to understand *Socialism*, to believe in *Socialism*, and to work for *Socialism*, and the *real* revolution is accomplished.' He sensed that France, Germany, Holland, Belgium and America were 'eager to take our coveted place as general factory, and China and Japan are changing swiftly from customers into rival dealers'. But 'even if we have a perfect fleet, and keep entire control of the seas, we shall still be exposed to the risk of almost certain starvation during a European war'. Evidently, socialism could be built only when 'our empire' was safe.

Who would achieve that? Blatchford did not want 'to ask too much of the mass of working folks, who have been taught little, and mostly taught wrong, and whose opportunities of getting knowledge have been but poor'; but

> I should like to see the Trade Unions federated, and formed into a political as well as an Industrial Labour Party on lines similar to those of the Independent Labour Party.
> Or I should like to see the whole of your 2,000,000 of Trade Unionists join the Independent Labour Party.
> Or, best of all, I should like to see the Unions, the Independent Labour Party, and the great and growing body of unorganised and unattached socialists formed into one grand Socialist Party.

Britain for the British aimed at 'Socialism' on a cross-class basis.[21]

Hyndman's attitude to the Boer War helped to crystallise the SDF's internal opposition. In September 1899 he supported an anti-war rally in Trafalgar Square, but soon began writing of the 'abominable war on behalf of German-Jew mine owners and other international interlopers' in the 'Jewish international'.[22] Meanwhile, about 1,700 SDFers in ninety branches collaborated with ILPers, and tried to improve their socialist understanding. The London printer Tommy Jackson went to Jack Fitzgerald's classes in Marxist theory, and ordered Engels's *The Origin of the Family* from the USA. Yet Hyndman denounced the dead Engels in *Justice*, and abused Quelch 'like a pickpocket' for printing his translation of Marx's *The Poverty of Philosophy* at the Twentieth Century Press.[23]

Disagreements among European Marxists helped polarise the SDF further. Two socialists had joined a French government that included General Gallifet, the butcher of the Paris Commune;[24] and at an international congress in September 1900 Karl Kautsky argued in favour of socialist participation in bourgeois governments under specific circumstances. The SDF delegation supported what V.I. Lenin called the 'india rubber' resolution, but their decision was strongly attacked at the subsequent annual conference; and by March 1901 James Connolly and his allies had captured the Scottish district committee. That July Hyndman convinced a majority of the executive that anti-war agitation was 'a waste

of time and money',[25] and that the best outcome would be a British
victory. In August he led the SDF out of the LRC and into the wilderness,
then walked out of the executive.

Russian events had an impact, too. From April 1902 the Social Democrat Lenin shared Quelch's office, though Hyndman favoured the Social
Revolutionaries. By August Connolly's Scottish SDF group had a monthly
paper, The Socialist, and convinced Marxists entered the fray. Schoolteacher
John Maclean noted: 'Merrie England is the primary school of Socialism, but
Das Kapital is the university.'[26] But in 1903 Quelch forced Connolly and his
eighty co-thinkers out of the SDF. They were mainly engineers from cen-
tral Scotland, though another small group of what became the Socialist
Labour Party was based at the Communist Club, Der Kommunistischen
Arbeiter Bildungs Verein, behind a restaurant in Charlotte Street, London.

For SLPers, Marxist training was almost compulsory; and, fortunately,
Charles Kerr & Co. of Chicago and the Labor Publishing Company in New
York were printing the first English versions of basic texts by Marx, Engels,
Kautsky, Labriola and Plekhanov. SLP members barred themselves from
holding official union positions, even though they looked forward to
revolutionary action through industrial unions. Yet Marxist terminology
was discouraged in street-speaking: 'Any word ending in —ation (unless
it's fornication) makes 'em look glassy-eyed and very sad.' So Marxism
was 'soft-pedalled to the point of silence'; and the key point that Marx
and Engels learned from the Paris Commune, the need for a dictatorship
of the proletariat to defend a revolutionary victory, was routinely fudged.[27]

Further splits developed. In 1904 another 140 dissidents were squeezed
out of the SDF, but, sadly, rather than join the SLP they formed the even
more sectarian Socialist Party of Great Britain. In what remained of the
SDF an 'air of gloomy antagonism to the bone-headed working man was
extremely prevalent'.[28] Jim Connell, the author of 'The Red Flag', lamented that 'For over 20 years, we have been trying to convert people to
Socialism, and we found that to keep them we must re-convert them 365
times each year'. Hyndman, too, was 'utterly disgusted' with 'workers
here in general and with our party in particular. Neither deserve to have
men of ability from the educated classes to serve them. It is a waste of
life. They are not worth the personal sacrifice and continual worry.'[29]

Tommy Jackson recalled that for years afterwards former SDFers

> thought their duty done when they had told the workers with reiterated
> emphasis that they had been and were being robbed systematically, and

given them an exposition of how the trick had been worked. From this the workers were to draw a moral conclusion that the robbers ought to be stopped, and to reach a practical decision to wage a class war upon the robbers. When their audience didn't reach this decision ... members were wont to conclude that 'the bastards aren't worth saving'.[30]

Yet the situation was contradictory. Quelch argued: 'We cannot have Socialist unity under the LRC, which contains anti-Socialists'[31] But Hyndman sympathised with the 1905 Russian Revolution, and at least one SDFer ran guns. Moreover, the Federation now accepted the affiliation of socialist societies, including Clarion supporters, and SDF trade-union delegates on the LRC won a resolution in favour of the public ownership of all means of production, distribution and exchange. Hyndman, under rank-and-file pressure, had to argue for unity with the ILP; but he was saved by James Ramsay MacDonald, an ex-SDFer, who saw the ILP as the 'legitimate heir of Liberalism', and favoured 'biological evolution'.[32] In 1903, as LRC Secretary, MacDonald had negotiated a secret electoral deal with the Liberals.

In the January 1906 general election the SLP and the SPGB urged working-class voters to abstain. Yet Hyndman came within 400 votes of winning Burnley, and Tom Kennedy, a friend of John Maclean, won almost 2,000 votes in North Aberdeen. Every other SDF candidate came bottom of their poll. The Liberals gave twenty-two LRC candidates a clear run, and twenty-nine, half of them ILPers, were elected. Within days they constituted themselves as the Labour Party, elected Keir Hardie as Chairman, and claimed all but a million affiliated members. They had made no manifesto commitments of a socialist character, and their favourite reading was Ruskin and Dickens, followed by the Bible. The only living authors they read were the Webbs; and while two had opened one of Marx's works, one of them admitted that the pages were mostly uncut.[33]

The main source of socialist ideas for most British workers remained the Clarion and Blatchford's books. Yet his Not Guilty: A Defence of the Bottom Dog of 1906 relied on Darwin, Haeckel, Spencer and Kropotkin. It argued that 'The cause of most of our social and moral troubles is ignorance', and that 'Humanism is a better religion than Christianity'.[34] As for the SDF, when J.R. Campbell, organiser of 'Marxist circles' for Glasgow workers, asked 'What is a Capitalist?', a ship-welder responded: 'A capitalist is a bastard of the first water!'[35] That may well have been true, but such a level of theoretical understanding did not produce socialist cadres capable of analysing a situation politically and then acting appropriately.

While there was 'a sharp division of opinion about the leadership of Hyndman', in the SDF, members largely confined themselves to propaganda:

> The normal SDF branch numbered something between a score and fifty – the regular attenders at a branch meeting being somewhat better than a dozen. The customary routine was, after the 'minutes' and correspondence, to fix arrangements for the Sunday propaganda meetings, and for any week-day meetings there might be. The life-activity of the Branch centred around these propaganda meetings. If the Branch possessed a Hall or meeting-room one meeting would take place there as a matter of course, usually on the Sunday evening. A morning meeting, or meetings – perhaps an afternoon one – might be held in the open air at some customary 'spouting-place', to advertise the indoor meeting, and to gather a collection and sell 'literature'.
>
> Usually the Branch had a speaker or speakers who was (or were) the main-stay. But other speakers would be obtained if possible, from other branches, particularly for the indoor meeting. A small branch or a big one without an indoor meeting place would have to rely exclusively upon its outdoor pitch or pitches – save for special occasions when a crack-speaker could be obtained.
>
> There was seldom much discussion about appointing a speaker or speakers from among the Branch members. Some comrade would establish himself as a local favourite and he would take the 'stump' as a matter of course. The appointment of a 'chairman', and a platform-carrier left more room for argument, though this too was settled often by local conditions – when, for example, it was often necessary for the 'chairman' to silence rowdy inter-rupters by laying-out one or two per meeting. A comrade who could 'use 'em' was, in these circumstances, much in demand.

Speeches 'usually took the form of a general statement of Socialist aspira-tions, a general criticism of capitalism and its evils, and a special appli-cation to current happenings, particularly the doings of the local Borough or Town Council'. Some orators preferred 'concentrating exclusively upon local issues, and "immediate demands" or "palliatives"', and others on 'accentuating and emphasising the revolutionary objective, the conquest of power by an insurgent proletariat'. Socialists everywhere had to relate to these 'sharply contrasting trends'.[36]

Hastings SDF

By 1900 Hastings Trades Council was supported by bakers, postmen, plumbers, teachers, bricklayers and painters. Delegates sat on the Housing of the Working Classes Committee, and several were socialists. The secre-tary, the painter John Lamb, formed branches of the Municipal Employees Association, which soon had 250 members, and also the National Union of Shop Assistants, Warehousemen and Clerks. In 1901 he and Toby King Junior stood as Labour candidates for the School Board. They lost, but attracted a thousand votes apiece.

In 1902–3, when Robert Noonan settled in the town, there seems to have been a political lull. But in 1905 there was talk of standing an LRC candidate at the municipal election. More people were coming out as socialists. A. Munday, the Shop Assistants' local leader, lived at Mr and Mrs Crump's Gordon Temperance Hotel, which was advertised in the ILP's *Labour Leader*. By 1906 Hastings Trades Council represented eight hundred workers, including carpenters, railwaymen, shop workers, clerks and municipal employees. In that January's general election the Tory courted trade unionists, and the Liberal got Trades Council support, but there was no socialist candidate.[37]

However, in April 1906 Hastings socialists were instrumental in forming a branch of the Democratic Association, which contained Liberal councillors as well as Labour supporters. Its programme included adult suffrage, one person one vote, automatic registration, election expenses to be defrayed from state funds, secret ballots, payment of MPs and the extinction of the House of Lords. Within a fortnight they had a hundred members. The Trades Council agreed to help them to form a Municipal LRC, and donated £5. League activities included leafleting, postering, issuing addresses, holding meetings on the beach on Sunday mornings and at the Fish Market on Sunday evenings, and sending delegations to the Municipal Council.[38] The branch chairman, Frederick Owen, addressed over a hundred people on 3 June.

Hastings was experiencing a sharp version of the economic crisis. In July the *Mail and Times* lamented that 'ridiculously cheap' railway fares meant that 'the day tripper in multitude deteriorates' this 'watering place'.[39] Nationally, the *Clarion* argued for 'fusion' on the left, so the socialist majority on the Hastings Democratic League committee invited H. Pay to speak. He was a blacklisted bakery worker, a member of Tunbridge Wells SDF, and a friend of Noonan's. By August the League was repelling Radical Liberals;[40] but it attracted working-class men like Alf Sellens, Noonan's pal and fellow painter.[41]

Brighton SDF had been revived in March, and Eastbourne ILPer George Meek had put a notice in the *Clarion*. An 'assembly' of the Clarion Fellowship was formed, Meek was elected secretary, and he began to use the *Clarion* network.[42] In June 200 Clarionettes heard SDFers E.J. Pay of

Tunbridge Wells and Joe Young of Brighton on Eastbourne beach. There
was a 'ripping' collection, and 'every scrap' of literature was sold. A Hastings contingent was present.[43] In July Meek found 'a few societies scat-
tered about', but 'mostly disconnected and they left ample room for more'.
So he invited socialists in Kent, Sussex, Surrey and Hampshire to Eastbourne. In August over fifty delegates formed the South-Eastern Federation of Socialist Societies,[44] and agreed to 'swap and obtain speakers and
open up new spheres of activity'.[45] Hastings Clarionettes were represented.[46] Meek acknowledged that the ILP's strength was 'due more to the
efforts of the *Clarion* and its writers than any other one agency', and he
wanted 'Socialists of all names and grades to work together for organisation and propaganda'. He 'had occasion to quarrel with the *official* attitude
of the ILP', but the SEFSS was 'open alike' to SDF and ILP branches, *Clarion*
readers, Fabians and other socialists.[47] By August, seven socialist societies
had 'actually or practically affiliated', including one from Hastings.[48]

Hastings working-class politics were polarising fast, and Alf Cobb was
central to the process. He was born in Hackney in 1874. His father, a
socialist baker, encouraged him to read Marx, and they both joined the
ILP in 1893. In 1900 Alf and his wife agreed to separate, and he took their
daughter to Hastings. In quick succession he was secretary for a drapery
firm, ran a florist's shop, and worked for a large wholesale greengrocer.
In 1904 he got credit to open his own greengrocer's shop, but was bank-
rupted in 1906. By then he was running a Marx study group. Later that
year Councillor March suggested forming a Hastings branch of the SDF.
Frank Willard resigned as Democratic League secretary and wrote to *Justice*
asking local socialists to get in touch.[49]

In September 1906 Robert Noonan, his friends Bill Gower and Edward
Cruttenden, and other socialists met at the Cricketers pub in South Terrace,
Hastings. A second meeting followed. On 12 October Hastings SDF held
its first public meeting at Mrs Lewcock's Ye Olde Beehive Dining Rooms
at 32 Pelham Street. Frederick Owen was in the chair, and there was a
'good attendance'.[50] The branch was well above the minimum require-
ment of six members, and larger than the Sheffield branch had been four
years previously.[51] Reportedly, Cobb looked on his friend Noonan as a
'visionary'.[52] But Noonan, Cruttenden, Gower, Cobb and his Marx study
group all signed up,[53] not for the reformist ILP, but for the largest 'Marxist'
organisation they could find.

3

Ragged trousered philanthropists

The reds of the southeast

Hastings SDF was challenged immediately. The Railway Clerks' Association demanded that the Trades Council withdraw its delegates from the local Labour Representation Committee, and sever its connection with what it called the 'Social Democratic League'. Only thirty-five delegates voted against.[1] Yet the SDF refused to be sectarian, and their winter propaganda campaign's first speaker was ILPer George Meek.[2] In November the branch's first report to *Justice* claimed over eighty members. Clarion Vanner and SDFer Tom Kennedy was invited, and received 'wild enthusiasm' for 'advocating a revolutionary policy'. Hastings socialists reported that Kennedy had 'braced them up to continue the fight', and argued that the SEFSS should have its own Clarion Van.[3] Len Green recalled: 'Wild horses wouldn't stop him'; and Kathleen Noonan remembered having a meal with Kennedy at the Cruttendens. At the November municipal elections the Trades Council president nearly won the working-class Hollington and Silverhill ward, but there was no LRC candidate.[4]

Late in 1906 *Justice* was enlarged from eight pages to twelve, and SDF national membership was said to be six thousand. But there were problems in keeping the educational programme going, since 'most of the able men deserted the ranks' for the Socialist Labour Party. Many SDFers had, at best, only 'a certain knowledge of Marxism'. In Glasgow, John Maclean took classes in economics and industrial history, and grasped the 'whole original scope of Marx's thought', so he was 'an absolute godsend'.[5] But not every branch had a John Maclean.

In December 1906 Hastings Education Committee refused to adopt the Provision of Meals Act for schoolchildren, and the local SDF intervened. But the economic crisis deepened, and by January 1907 over six hundred unemployed people were applying to the Distress Committee. Even the fishing industry was in decline; and up to five hundred artisans and labourers marched

> in organised processions through the town to raise funds and solicit public sympathy. Fronted by a brass band repeatedly playing the same mournful tune, the men tramped daily often for five hours at funeral pace behind a large banner which read 'In aid of the Genuine Unemployed'.

The SDF officially disapproved of 'begging', yet workers wanted answers and solidarity. At this point, reportedly, the local *Observer* and the *Mail and Times* stepped up their anti-socialist campaign. Alf Cobb lost his job, failed to emigrate to Canada, ran a shop, became a buyer for hawkers, and then took to a barrow himself.[6]

Green believed Cobb was one of Noonan's 'greatest friends', but Kathleen felt they were not 'kindred spirits'. She bought Cobb's fruit, but wasn't sure she got full measure, and she never saw him at their home. Reportedly, Hastings SDF split over Cobb's sexual politics. In any event Willard and Owen left, and others followed. Willard claimed the Democratic League had three times the Federation's membership, but Cobb noted:

> Mr Willard refers to Karl Marx and twits the SDF members with either not having read his works or with having forgotten them. Mr Willard is extremely fortunate to have been able to purchase them and afterwards to spare the time to read, and moreover, understand them, but here allow me to say that membership of the SDF is not denied to those who have not been able to tackle Marx or even to those who have failed to agree with him, but it is open to anyone, male or female, Christian or otherwise, who believes in the 'complete emancipation of labour from the domination of capital and landlordism, to be replaced by the Socialisation of the means of production, distribution and exchange'.

Any sectarianism, in other words, was not to be laid at the SDF's door.[7]

On 6 April 1907 Hastings SDF told *Justice* they were holding regular Thursday meetings at the Pelham Dining Rooms: 'With the help of our Tunbridge Wells comrades we have planted a healthy little branch of the SDF in this old Cinque Port which we hope will grow.'[8] SDFers argued at the Trades Council, and at the Debating Society, whose committee shifted its meetings to Thursday, so as to clash.[9] Reportedly, SDFers had their names posted in the police station. Meetings were held in secret in the Central Hall or at the Cruttendens' home at 16 Wellington Square, and members walked there separately, while visiting speakers had a body-guard. Comrades Thompson and E.J. Pay had to leave the town in order to eat; yet Cobb turned down well-paid jobs offered by those anxious to see an end to his political activities.[10]

On 16 April a meeting chaired by the secretary of the Trades Council discussed forming a branch of the Independent Labour Party. Cobb and Edward Cruttenden attended. Cobb noted that the SDF did not form branches where the ILP already existed, and argued that 'by joining the ILP people can escape being called Socialists'. Hastings ILP was officially formed in May, and had strong union links. It met on the seafront in summer and indoors in winter. Belatedly, the SDF applied to join the Trades Council, but the chair argued that if they 'had any sympathy with the true cause of labour they would be trade unionists', and the application was withdrawn.[11]

The 1907 SDF conference voted for a united socialist party, but the leaders ignored the resolution. As for the ILP, Meek noted that during the first months of his unity campaign he had the help of the *Labour Leader* (as well as the *Clarion* and *Justice*); but then its support was withdrawn. The ILP's national secretary informed him that they were

> forming exclusively ILP Federations throughout the country, and that they 'did not approve of hybrid Federations'; this in spite of the fact that they had been instructed to 'co-operate with other socialist organisations wherever possible' by their own National Conference! Similarly J.R. MacDonald wrote a letter to me telling me we should advise the ILP not to co-operate with the SDP [sic] whenever asked.

Meek was sacked from his day job on 13 May. Since 'the work of disruption was already beginning' at the top he 'determined to make a tour round the three counties to try to stop it' at the grassroots by linking 'socialists who lived in unorganised towns and districts'. He began with Hastings SDF, where he was 'very kindly received both by my old friends Mr and Mrs Cruttenden and the local society'. He explained his plan, and they 'approved of it, giving me, the former hospitality for the night, and the latter three shillings towards my expenses'.[12] He told *Justice* that their Hastings branch was 'in fine fighting trim with a well-organised summer campaign ahead of them', and that they were a leading light among 'The Reds of the South-East'.[13]

Socialist MPs were now being elected. In July Pete Curran stood as an openly socialist candidate for the Labour Party in Jarrow and won; and Victor Grayson, arguing for 'pure revolutionary socialism', won a by-election in the formerly safe Liberal seat of Colne Valley, 'notwithstanding the underneath efforts' of the ILP leaders, and the refusal of the Labour Party leadership to endorse his candidature.[14] Yet Ramsay MacDonald demonstrated his 'fixed determination to widen the breach between the ILP and the SDF as much as possible'. So while Meek won support from ILP branches, the National Administrative Council 'strongly deprecated' joint action with the SDF.[15]

Hastings SDF prospered. In July sixty copies of _Justice_ were sold at Harry Quelch's meeting, and Edward Cruttenden rejoiced: 'ten months ago a copy of _Justice_ was not to be had in the town'. Robert and Kathleen Noonan were there. The SDF had arguments that cut. When Cobb debated a Liberal the ILP meeting had to be cancelled. SDFers were bold. They had a woman speaker, Miss Kathleen Kough from London.[16] They were exciting. At one meeting Kathleen gripped a pamphlet so hard while singing 'The Red Flag' and 'The Internationale' that it was 'all screwed up and nobody could read it'. Thanks to Noonan and Gower they had imagination. These two had given slide shows as The South Coast Amusement Co.; and soon Hastings SDF had its own socialist van. Acting on Noonan's idea, it carried lantern slides and Cobb's 'caustic commentaries' round the streets of the town.[17] Nationally only seven Clarion Vans were on the road.

Meek doggedly argued for socialist unity. In July he told H.G. Wells:

We must work together loyally as comrades: all disintegrating intrigues must be discouraged. The sectionalism both of the trade union and Socialist movements is a hindrance to the progress of the workers towards emancipation. In all probability the Liberal Party will go to pieces in the near future. A strong _united_ Socialist party must be ready to take its place.[18]

On 4 August the SEFSS's annual conference at Tunbridge Wells was attended by forty-eight delegates. Ten ILP branches, six SDF branches, four Clarion Fellowships, three socialist societies and one Fabian society were represented. ILP loyalists came down to put the leadership's line, but 'a vote of censure upon J.R. MacDonald was carried by a large majority'.[19] Meek resigned his secretaryship, and, as planned, his place was taken by a Tunbridge Wells comrade who was in both the ILP and the SDF, and a broad-based committee was elected. Yet soon after, Meek's relations with Eastbourne Clarion Fellowship deteriorated, and he was 'kicked out',

allegedly for being 'not respectable'. He blamed MacDonald. He was offered an ILP organizer's job at a 'decent salary', but that would have put
him at the leadership's mercy, so he declined.[20]

On paper, the Labour Party looked impressive. Almost a million people
were affiliated. Yet as troops shot strikers in Belfast that August, 'Beyond
asking a couple of questions', Labour MPs 'did nothing';[21] and they accepted the protectionast Imperial Preference ('Tariff Reform') policy. The SDF's
paid-up membership was still six thousand, but its leaders were sectarian,
abstract propagandists, and poor Marxists. Quelch continued to believe,
against Marx, that an 'Iron Law of Wages' made union activity at best a
'stepping-stone' to political action.[22] The SLP was good at Marxist propaganda, publishing up to eleven penny pamphlets a month, some of them
in editions of ten thousand; and sales of The Socialist rose from three to
four thousand. But it was sectarian and tiny, and the nearest of its fifteen
branches to Hastings were in London and Southampton. The sectarian
SPGB published Marxist literature also; but its offices were raided, its
printing machinery damaged and its type destroyed. From Hastings, it
was probably invisible.

Getting jeered at for his pains

During 1907 the national economic crisis forced the political pace. Unemployment reached its highest level for over twenty years. In Hastings
the outlook was particularly grim. In September James Loveday had been
unable to find work, but the police refused to allow him to play his
whistle-pipe in the streets. Loveday, near starvation, had walked into the
sea and drowned.[23] Socialist ideas drew audiences. In October a Mr Potter
gave a lecture at an ILP meeting, and used a diagram 'showing the annual
proportionate distribution of national wealth' very like 'The Oblong'.[24]
But in November, 151 skilled workers registered with the Distress Committee, and 73 of them were painters.[25] The ILP organised a packed meeting
at the Market Hall, but all they could suggest was to urging the Corporation
to help. Their three unemployed parades were 'more disciplined and tightly
controlled', but mustered 'on average barely a hundred men', since only
those registered with the Distress Committee were allowed to march.[26]

Hastings SDF continued to thrive. In August Cobb told the Observer that
for years 'Mr Chubb's shop has been a kind of depot for Socialist Literature'

A socialist who wanted *Justice, Labour Leader,* or *Clarion,* 'was always sure of getting them' there. Mr Chubb prevaricated:

> although I knew 'The Clarion' to be Mr Blatchford's mouthpiece and he was an agnostic, I thought it was a Labour paper. 'The Labour Leader' I fancied was to tell labourers where work was to be had and 'Justice' I imagined was a paper devoted to police reports etc.

In October Kennedy's Clarion Van returned to Hastings, got a good reception, and stayed for a second week. In December the Brighton socialist William Evans urged the unemployed to make themselves an unmitigated nuisance to the authorities by visiting councillors' homes, especially those 'in the more fashionable quarters', until they acted.[27]

At some point during 1907 Robert Noonan had a row with his boss, Burton, about taking too much time over a job. Reportedly, he threatened to 'knock his bloody head off', and 'finished up by storming out and turning the key in the lock on the outside'. Fortunately, Noonan's skills remained in demand. Working for Adams & Jarrett of St Leonards allowed him to add to his notes for 'Misery'. Robert, Kathleen, Adelaide and Arthur may have moved to an 'area flat' in Warrior Square at this time.[28] Kathleen insisted they 'mostly lived on his workman's wages', and 'received no financial aid from his family', so any 'riotous living' depended on 'spasmodic sources of income', possibly from articles. In July she helped the family economy by winning a two-year local education committee bursary worth £18. But while she and Arthur were 'always well dressed, probably because my aunt made most of our clothes', Kathleen remembered 'brown paper being put in as an inter-lining in dad's coat'.

In public Robert Noonan was always taken to be an ordinary member of the working class; though he was clearly 'a skilled artisan':

> In the week he was dressed like his mates, except that he always wore his trilby hat to work, never the cap common to most working-men. He always wore a painter's apron, and made little effort to keep it clean, but he didn't sport the painter's white jacket. On Sundays, he dressed smartly, almost dapperly, usually in a grey 'fashionable' suit, soft hat or 'stetson' set at a tilt, and he liked to carry a walking-stick.[29]

Kathleen recalled his kindness to workmates. He gave up drinking the hot toddy that a doctor had prescribed in order to encourage a man with an alcohol problem, only to find he was drinking 'just about as much as usual'. He also liked cricket, but his spare time was mainly devoted to politics.

Reportedly, Noonan wrote leaflets, manifestoes and election addresses. He distributed handbills and sold literature at SDF 'open-airs', and if people couldn't afford to buy it he gave it away. He took part in deputations to the council, made bannerettes, posters and banners for unemployed marchers, and collected money for them in a tin.[30] He was 'a lovable man to those who knew him well', but 'very quick in temper when any affront to Socialism was offered. To him the class war was not an empty phrase, but something that really existed, daily, hourly. The notion of an armistice he would have scorned.'[31] Once, when someone insulted the red flag flying over the rostrum, Noonan chased him across the beach until comrades restrained him.[32] Yet he had few gifts as an orator, and Kathleen thought he was 'not physically fit enough' anyway. Green used to hear Cobb and others on Sunday afternoons – 'very interesting. Sometimes they were cheered.' But he recalled Noonan 'lecturing on socialism on the sea front and getting jeered at for his pains'.

Noonan's propaganda skills were those of close-quarter argument. Gower 'never met any man, however well-educated and high up, who didn't appear intellectually inferior to Bob, even in ordinary conversation'.[33] He would often be seen on the outskirts of the crowd, asking in a very low, quiet voice:

> 'You agree then that your children are not good enough for a better standard of living?'; 'Do you agree that your children are not fit to be properly educated?'; 'Can you tell me why your children should have shoes on their feet?' 'What makes you think that you are entitled to food and clothing?'

Gower recalled him 'at twelve o'clock at night surrounded by a little group, still going strong'.[34]

He also argued at work. Green worked with him at West Dean, Hollington Park. There was 'this old-fashioned chimney-corner, where we used to cook all our bloaters'. At dinner time, as they drank out of jam-jars or condensed milk tins, they 'used to lay about all round this big room, the kitchen', and 'have meetings'. 'I've heard say that he was bad-tempered, but he never was', though 'he used to lose his temper when people were so ignorant, and they wouldn't take any notice of what he was saying'. They 'used to delight in hearing him talk, you know, to pass the time away'. He got jeered: 'Yeh, "you silly bugger" and all that.' But the 'well-educated' were 'greatly interested', and Green's dad 'used to uphold him'.

Kathleen assumed her father performed the 'Great Money Trick' with workmates, but hoped he 'didn't rant at them'. A Mr Harmer recalled 'a

kindly man' who was 'strong willed and at times a firebrand in argument'. J.H. Poynton had 'many discussions about the different aspects of
the socialist movement' with the man he knew as 'Bob Newland', who
won respect as 'an exceptionally good man at his trade'. He was 'sometimes pessimistic, but always held firm to his belief that some day the
workers would rise to power'.[35] Some working-class men were frequent
visitors to Noonan's flat, and he made 'numerous converts' who later
built up the Labour movement in the town.[36]

Noonan's problem was how to persuade the maximum number of
workers in the little spare time he had. Kathleen knew he got 'exasperated
beyond words'. He 'would come home furious and sometimes even contemptuous of fellow workers', and begin 'ranting about the stupidity of
the men', scandalised about their willingness to live in houses which
were not as good as their employers' stables'. 'He couldn't make them
understand that there was something wrong with the *system*', or 'make
any real impression on those he wanted to reach by just telling them at
meal times'. So she believed he 'gave up talking to the workers and set
about his book. Maybe that would wake them up and others like them.'

The Ragged Trousered Philanthropists was probably under way by 1907, yet
even Noonan's apprentice, Cradduck, was kept in the dark.[37] Ward did
not know, either, but 'could understand our talks' better when he read
the book. Poynton understood that it 'was written over a period of many
months'. 'Few of his comrades or friends knew he was writing; indeed I
know he was very shy about it.' But it 'was made up from a collection of
real incidents and talks that had taken place in the various jobs'. The
Moorish drawing room decoration 'was carried out by Bob almost alone'
in 'a large house in Hollington Park'.[38] Green had no idea about the
book, though the original of 'Old Philpot' told him later that Noonan
'used to come to his house and do a lot of writing down there'.

Neither meek nor mild

By 1908 it was clear that Labour MPs were not going to get Liberals to
enact socialist measures. Even the 'Right to Work' bill was stopped in its
tracks, and Labour MPs failed to vote against the army estimates and
conscription. Moreover, a motion to amend the Labour Party constitution
so as to make socialism one of its aims was successfully opposed by ILP
leaders. The SDF now claimed a membership of over ten thousand, but

the sectarian leaders voted against reaffiliation to the Labour Party. Blatchford was losing it completely. His perspective was restricted to 'the Cau-
casian race', excluding what he called 'inferior races';[39] and he wrote of
'The Coming German War against Great Britain', in which 'the success of
the German pan-Teutonic, anti-English, anti-French scheme of aggression
would throw back Socialism in Europe for fully two generations.'[40] Like
Hyndman, Blatchford's 'socialist' policy was to boost the armed forces,
and to put nation before class, as international capitalist competition led
to an arms race in these 'Dreadnought days'.

In January 1908 Hastings charitable funds were at their lowest ebb for
two years, and the numbers registered with the Distress Committee rose
sharply. The council was pressurised into spending £100 on free school
meals, but dropped the halfpenny rate as soon as winter was over. An SDF
speaker from London found it strange that Hastings was advertised as a
health resort when several hundred children were underfed.[41] Noonan
still did his bit. In a parliamentary by election that March he made mince-
meat of the carpetbagger Irish Tory, Arthur Du Cros;[42] but there was no
Labour candidate. In April the ILP postman Leonard Watson was elected to
the local Board of Guardians,[43] and Hastings SDF switched meeting nights
so members could to go to the Debating Society. Alf Sellens replaced
Edward Cruttenden as branch secretary; and Alf Cobb took over in July.
Police watched SDF activities, and harassed socialist speakers. Cobb responded with nightly meetings.[44] But sometimes he got stones through
his windows.[45]

Economic agitation tended to come from outside Hastings. In August,
a group of Midlands Hunger Marchers reached Bulverhythe, only to be

met by a detachment of police and prohibited from going along the seafront. They unsuccessfully remonstrated against this decision for over three
hours, loudly cursing the Hastings police as blacklegs and blackguards before being directed to a rear route via Boscobel Road. They had tramped
from town to town along the South Coast dragging a horseless four wheel
van piled full of progressive literature.[46]

Someone very like Noonan was photographed in Wellington Square, next
to a placard proclaiming 'We demand the Right to Live'.[47] In September
the National Union of Teachers started a trust fund to buy boots for
Hastings children. In October Tom Kennedy drew well over a thousand
people to a Sunday meeting. Soon after there was a national shift. Dissident ILP branches joined the SDF and became the Social-Democratic Party.

In December Hastings SDP was rewarded with a visit by Hyndman. Apparently, Noonan wanted to put a streamer across a street, or trail one behind a large box kite, though he settled for a four-sided sandwich board on condition that the man was paid union rates. Yet the socialists who sang 'The Red Flag' in the Royal Concert Hall were drowned out by rowdy youths singing 'God Save the King'.[48]

By early 1909 Noonan's nephew Arthur was in the choir at St John's, complete with 'Eton suit and mortar board', and Adelaide's conformism seems to have hardened at their 'social descent'. She and the boy moved out. Robert may have been a bit of a snob, too. Kathleen recalled that he was 'always raving' about a woman he saw on a tram, though 'when he heard her talk that finished him'. He was used to a self-contained flat, but had to settle for rooms at 241 London Road, St Leonards, on the line between the working-class and middle-class communities. Kathleen saw herself as a 'working-man's child', yet they 'were never as hard up as the characters in the book', and she 'never learned to cook, or to do the washing'. When they could afford it they took their evening meal – they both liked steak-and-kidney pudding – at a 'little restaurant' nearby; but when money was tight she cooked, though not very successfully. Once, she dirtied a plate so her father would think she had eaten half the soup, though that was the only occasion she recalled being short of food. She had three months away from school because she was 'very anaemic', yet her name was one of the first on St Andrew's School honours board, and both she and her father hoped she would become a teacher. Robert's chest was not getting any better, but he spent more time in the evenings and at weekends, writing.

Kathleen believed RTP was 'started and finished' at 241 London Road. She recalled 'books – books up to the ceiling'. Noonan's political armoury probably contained Bellamy's Looking Backward, Morris's Useless Work versus Useful Toil and News from Nowhere, H.G. Wells's New Worlds for Old, some Froude, Fabian publications, and Blatchford's Clarion, Merrie England, Britain for the British, Not Guilty and God and My Neighbour.[49] Kathleen recalled no Marx, but supposed he 'must have' had some.[50] Yet Noonan not did quote Marx in RTP; and, like almost all British working-class socialists of his day, he may have read none at all. An apprentice painter knew him as a 'keen Socialist of the William Morris type'.[51] Ward, who 'did not agree altogether about the socialist ideas', recalled that Noonan 'used to say Parliament could alter it any time they liked if they had men there who honestly wanted to better the worker'. But he had a clear political agenda to argue against. An Anti-Socialist Union campaign had begun in Hastings; and the London Municipal Society's The Case Against Socialism threw down the gauntlet to 'evolutionary' reformists.

Hastings SDP fought back. In March 1909 they produced a local edition of Justice, criticising the council for buying the loss-making Electric Light Company, and noting that the profitable Gas Company (which had many councillors as shareholders and directors) was left well alone. At the council by-election the SDP got eighty-six votes; and in June Chubb the newsagent complained that socialist propaganda was 'doing its deadly work upon the minds and feelings of people, who, a short time back, would not hold in with any one of their tenets'. Socialist meetings lasted till half-past nine. Chubb demanded to know: 'What are the Anti-Socialist League doing to stem the tide?'[52] In July Cobb and two other SDPers were fined for spreading the word to Bexhill, yet the Clarion Van's literature sales were 'comparatively low', since demand was 'well met by local branches'.[53]

In January 1910 Hastings SDP's one hundred and fifty members decided against contesting the parliamentary seat only for lack of funds; but by summer the branch was under Cobb's vigorous leadership, and the council was rattled. A new by-law banned religious and political meetings at the usual beach venues, so Justice organised speakers who refused to pay fines and were prepared to go to jail.[54] Noonan attended meetings less often now, though he produced posters, leaflets, and election addresses.[55] He also painted a banner. Poynton put the idea to him: 'He at once consented, and we worked on it hanging up in a bedroom wall at 139, Marina, on Saturday and Sunday afternoons'.[56] It depicted, 'inset in a shield, the writhing serpent "Capitalism" being strangled by a shirt-sleeved worker in a desperate struggle, with, on each side a torch wreathed with a scroll'; and it was 'unfurled at a large meeting on the beach by Tom Kennedy'.[57]

Yet Noonan's health was worsening. Kathleen recalled rubbing his chest with Elliman's Embrocation, though he suggested she should 'get the kind for horses'. As for medicine, he 'would not measure the prescribed dose but just drink it out of the bottle'. He often didn't feel well enough to go to work until after breakfast, and often did so only for a few days at a time. Yet Kathleen stayed on at school. She remembered a blue-printed letterhead – 'R.P. Noonan, Signwriter & Decorator, 241 London Road' – and that her father wrote show cards for shopkeepers and coffin plates for Poor Law funerals. Gower recalled him saying: 'I've got to make some money or I'll die in the work-house!' Reportedly, he asked for his SDP membership to be cancelled since he could not be sufficiently active.[58]

Noonan's writing had now become his main political activity, and he had a local stimulus. In May 1908 George Meek had taken H.G. Wells's advice and 'returned to literature'. His 70,000-word draft book was ready by March 1909.[59] Edward Cruttenden was friendly with Meek, and he often saw Noonan writing on Sunday mornings. He recalled that he 'lent George Meek's book' to 'Bob', who said

> he could do something better and stronger and after that he did not attend our meetings very regularly, said he had something important on hand and we should know later on what it was. His daughter said her father was always writing so we let him get on with it.[60]

George Meek: Bath Chair-Man was published by Constable in May 1910. Blatchford's *Clarion* pronounced his struggle for socialist unity 'hard, if hopeless';[61] but Robert Noonan found the book 'too Meek and Mild'.[62]

Robert Tressell

Kathleen recalled a large writing table near her father's bedroom fireplace, with 'papers all over it':

> sometimes he'd be writing and he wouldn't like what he'd written, and he'd just screw it up and ... throw it aside. But you daren't go and clear it up again, because it was quite possible, if you cleared up these papers and threw them out, he'd want them back.

So 'you had to leave him to ... clear up his mess'. He was reading Dickens and Fielding; but theirs were novels *about* working-class life, by outsiders, and, in any case, according to RTP's future publisher, 'when the work was started the author had no intention of writing a book but had in mind the writing of a series of pamphlets. It was only when it was begun that he found it turning into a novel under his hand.'

Noonan wrote 1,674 quarto pages, plus a title page, a five-page list of forty-five chapter numbers and headings, a five-page Preface, a five-page unfinished draft of Chapter III, 'Mugsborough. Sweater, Rushton, Didlum and Grinder', and produced several unpaginated drawings. He wrote on one side of 'New Rolled Linen' paper, using different pens and inks. No surviving pages show signs of being screwed up, but several have deletions of up to half a sheet, scribbled over so as to be illegible, or completely obliterated with ink. (A passage on the labour process met this fate.) He made few spelling mistakes, and corrected many which slipped through. Ampersands appear frequently; his use of apostrophes and hyphens was inconsistent; and while did not always capitalise words like 'monday', he was fond of capital letters for ironic or sardonic stress.

Many pages look like fair copies, but minor alterations are frequent. Bert White had been a year older; Sawkins's wages went up a penny an hour, and Barrington's a halfpenny. Most children's names were altered, and Robert Starr became John. Abbreviations for 'bloody' were sometimes restored, or altered (for example, to 'damn'), though 'b——er' was usually left. The term 'government' was replaced with 'State' in the 'Great Oration', and the 'mob' at Rushton's nomination became a 'crowd'. The 'Great Money Trick' was originally performed by Barrington, and a verse from Edward Carpenter's 'England Arise' was pasted over the chorus of the 'The Internationale'. Kathleen recalled that his pen name 'was to have been Robert Croker', but 'he was afraid people might say "Croker by name and Croaker by nature"'. Poynton believed that 'he was so often seen at some shop front, working on trestles' that 'Tressell' was more appropriate. The title was characteristic: 'Bob used to say that the workers were the real philanthropists, but didn't know it.'[63]

The *Ragged Trousered Philanthropists* was probably completed by April 1910 Kathleen understood that any proceeds would help them 'travel around the world together in a little tramp ship, visiting all the unusual ports'. Reportedly, Noonan wanted a Hyndman preface, though nothing came of that.[64] The book was offered to three publishers:

> The first seems to have returned it without reading it, frightened, it would seem, by its length and by the fact that it was not typed. The second did not have the actual manuscript but on being written to replied that his list was too full. The third had the manuscript and returned it.

Constable's found it 'too unwieldy', and Blatchford may have seen it, too. Then Noonan gave up. Kathleen believed the 'apparently unread' manuscript 'would probably have had the fate of the model of the airship if I hadn't rescued it': 'You can't destroy that – I want it.' But she was lectured about how, if the book brought any royaties, before she 'could take any interest from that money you'd have to be sure that the people who were providing that interest ... were being properly paid'.

In the summer of 1910 Kathleen took five honours in Oxford local examinations, and won a place at Whitelands College, though acceptance was 'not financially possible'. However, she also won a bursary to St Helen's Pupil Teacher Centre, Orr, and their landlord made her a bicycle to save tram fares. She thought money difficulties 'started the Canada project', and that her father intended starting a business,

> this time forgetting his ragged trousered philanthropists, who would not listen to sense, and for whom he had written the book – and make some money to leave me in more comfortable circumstances. He said at times that he wished he had not been such a dreamer, and then I would have been better off – financially, that is.

So she believed that when he left for Liverpool it was in order 'to make arrangements for us both to go to Canada'. One workmate understood he went 'with a view to working his passage'.[65] Poynton thought he suffered from 'chronic asthma', saw he was 'getting worse', and was 'advised to go to Canada, as the climate was more likely to suit him'.[66] Emigration was common enough. Between 1901 and 1911 Hastings' population declined by five thousand, and hundreds emigrated to Canada.[67]

Yet Noonan's departure was sudden. Allegedly, he told Gower that a South African doctor had diagnosed tuberculosis;[68] so his friend believed the novel was 'almost an autobiography'. The part 'in which Owen is stricken with haemorrhage, is literally true; he told me of the occurrence and his fears for the future of the children'.[69] Green recalled that, after 'a bit of a laugh', 'Bob' would 'always place his left hand over his side, as though it was a great exertion'. 'I said to him, one day, "Bob, what's the matter with you?" He says, "I've only one lung".' Green 'was convinced that it was ... TB', because his friend 'used to say Wun Lung, you know, in Chinese – used to write it on the wall'. Noonan smoked, and worked with lead-based paints, but Kathleen believed he had 'broncho-pneumonia', since he 'never had any chest haemorrhages' and was 'always treated for bronchitis'. 'If he had thought he had T.B. I do not think he would have kissed Arthur and me and he was always affectionate.' He 'definitely was not ill when he left. He was very well for him.' So if he had been coughing blood it was probably a recent occurrence, though he may have left so as to avoid contact with loved ones, especially if it had to be in Hastings Workhouse.

Noonan left St Leonards in August 1910. He probably gave away his books and other possessions, and took his original pounces and designs by William Morris, plus some tools and drawings. Kathleen began working as a teacher at her aunt Mary Jane's school at St Leonards (for her keep, but no salary); but she understood this was only 'until he sent for me after he had made all the arrangements' in 'a few weeks'. He may have stopped off in London. Frank Jackson recalled being present at a send-off in a pub, where a collection was taken to help Noonan on his way;[70] and a Mr McLoughlan had 'various reminiscences' of him at the Communist Club and the Club Autonomie, though he may have been mistaken, since he thought the year was 1913.[71] Kathleen speculated that he may have 'stayed with Maurice Reckitt – I don't know how well he knew him – or with Tom Kennedy' in London; but 'it could not have been for very long as his letter came from Liverpool in August'.

Kathleen assumed her father stayed with his sister Ellen in Liverpool, but apparently he took lodgings with James and Mary Anne Johnson at Erskine Street.[72] Robert Quigley, Michael Collins's personal envoy, is said to have heard Noonan speak at the Pier Head; and Bower later claimed he was pointed out to him[73] by S.H. Musten, a Sussex syndicalist.[74] In any event Noonan was admitted to the General Ward of the Royal Liverpool Infirmary on 26 November. Gower thought it was the 'Royal Free Hospital', and recalled that his friend 'expressed his gratitude for the kindness shown to him by the staff there', but 'his health had all gone to pieces, and he would not mind much when the end came'.[75] According to Ward, Noonan believed that if a worker had 'not much to keep him in old age' then 'it was not worth him living'; so when he 'slipped out of it all' it seemed something he 'had been waiting years to do'. Yet Robert told Kathleen, 'cheerfully', that he was 'in hospital, quite happy and decorating the ward for Christmas and friendly with the patients'. He never gave her 'any idea of finality', so she was 'not unduly worried', since he 'was always getting sick', then getting better again.

About six weeks later she received a terse telegram: 'Your father died at 10.15 last night', Friday 3 February 1911. The Death Certificate gave his trade as 'Sign Writer (Journeyman)', and his address as Erskine Street. The cause of death was 'phthisis pulmonalis', a wasting of the lungs associated with tuberculosis, and 'cardiac failure'. The Sister sent Kathleen a 'very nice letter' telling her 'how much he was liked', and that 'he'd died of "broncho-pneumonia"'. These were 'probably dad's instructions ... preventing them from telling me how terminal his illness was in order to delay my heartache.' 'No mention was made of T.B.' One acquaintance

Kathleen Noonan
c. 1910

believed he died of 'consumption';[76] but bronchial pneumonia could have developed into TB in Liverpool, and the possibility of a hospital cross-infection cannot be excluded. Eventually, Kathleen acknowledged it 'may have been T.B.' at the end. 'One of the symptoms of T.B. is optimism and after all his other times of illness he probably expected to recover as he had then.' His last letter, which 'fell to pieces after being treasured and constantly read and re-read', told Kathleen that 'if it were true that circumstances compelled us to live apart from each other permanently – then I would much prefer not to continue at all'. Fear of TB? The hospital records were destroyed, so we will never know for sure.

It took a week to bury him. The Sister asked about funeral arrangements, and Kathleen thought the delay was 'probably caused by them writing to St Leonards for instructions'. The 18-year-old had 'never had anything to do with death or funerals and anyway was in a state of shock for weeks afterwards': 'the bottom fell out of my world, and I do not remember the days immediately following'. Financially, she was 'completely dependent on my aunt'. 'The hospital staff must have thought me heartless, for my aunt would not make it possible for me to go to Liverpool, or make any arrangements'. Instead, Mary Jane 'told' her 'just write', 'tell them "to proceed in the usual way"' and 'make the usual arrangements'. Kathleen 'didn't ever know what that meant': 'what an awful thing that was for her to do'. Her aunt Ellen 'did nothing about the funeral', and the landlady presumably claimed his effects in lieu of rent. Apparently he had no trade-union insurance.

Robert Noonan was buried on 10 February 1911, a few yards from Walton Gaol and near Walton Hospital, the former workhouse. Walton Park Cemetery was formerly the burial ground of Liverpool's Overseers of the Poor. Alan O'Toole discovered that the burial took place under a Relieving Officer's order, in a 'public grave', which contained people interred wholly at the public charge, and some whose relatives could afford a coffin and service but not a burial plot. Such graves were up to twenty five feet deep and could take several weeks to fill. Noonan's body was interred with twelve others. Ball found no record of his death in the Hastings papers, and believed none of his effects reached there.[77] In 1926 Gower still did not know where his friend was buried;[78] and ten years after that Bower had no idea 'however and wherever he lived and died'.[79] Even the name of the cemetery was not known until 1968; and the burial site was not located until 1970. The grave remained unmarked until 1977. Today, rough grass grows around it, and the gilding has almost weathered away.

4

A faithful picture of working-class life?

Where was Mugsborough?

The Ragged Trousered Philanthropists is a slightly pretentious title, but the subtitle, 'Being the Story of Twelve Months in Hell, Told by One of the Damned', is not.
Neither is the unfinished draft Preface:

> In writing this book my intention was to present, in the form of an inter-
> esting story, a faithful picture of working-class life – more especially of
> those engaged in the Building trades ...
> I wished to describe the relations existing between the workmen and
> their employers, the attitude and feelings of these two classes towards each
> other; the condition of the workers during the different seasons of the year,
> their circumstances when at work and out of employment; their pleasures,
> their intellectual outlook, their religious and political opinions and ideals.
> (11)[1]

Whatever its shortcomings, 'Robert Tressell' insisted, 'the work possesses
at least one merit – that of being true. I have invented nothing' (12).

So where was Mugsborough? The draft Preface calls it 'a small town in
the south of England' (11). Yet in the unfinished draft Chapter III it was
a 'resort' of 'about eighty thousand inhabitants', 'built in a verdant valley',
'about two hundred miles from London', with the south coast 'one
hundred miles away' (631) – that is, somewhere off the Welsh coast, near
Llanelli.[2] And if Mugsborough was meant to represent Hastings, where
are the holidaymakers and the beach? Where is the equivalent of Eastbourne, Brighton, or any nearby town? Even the Beano is a 'weary journey'
along a main road (472), and the countryside is rarely mentioned.

Mugsborough is like Hastings in some ways. Employment comes from tourism, public utilities, shops, domestic service, building and home-working, and the town experiences a similar economic crisis. Crass notes that 'more than 'arf of the damn stuff' in the shops 'comes from abroad' (20); and Easton complains: 'There don't seem to be 'arf the work about that there used to be' (278). As Jack Mitchell noted, the overall movement of the book is 'everyday capitalism: slump–boom–slump', with the second slump deeper than the first.[3] Yet the world economy appears to bear down on Mugsborough mainly because 'well-to-do', upper-class 'patriots' had 'adopted the practice of going on the Continent to spend the money they obtain from the working people of England' (631).

Mugsborough time is different. The narrative begins in November and takes just over a year; but winter takes three-quarters of the book. Yet RTP can be dated internally. The year 1906 saw the Tariff Reform, the debate over the Education (Provision of School Meals Act), and the election of 'them there Labour members of parliament' – 'a lot of b——rs what's too bloody lazy to work for their livin'!' (281). In Hastings that February 'several very respectable painters' were unable to get relief from the Distress Committee: 1,515 people got out-relief, and 425 were in the work-house.[4] In August an article in the local *Weekly Mail and Times* was headed 'Hands and Brains', as is Chapter 11.[5] The *Daily Mail Year Book* for 1907 is quoted (107). That January the Hastings unemployed marched all week;[6] and in Mugsborough Slyme and Crass worry they might 'drive all the gentry out of the place' (310). There is a Mugsborough by-election, just as there was in Hastings in 1908; and 'miserable Old Age Pensions' (511) came in on 1 January 1909. A 1909 newspaper headline, 'It's Not My Crime', is almost exactly the title of Chapter 6.[7]

International history and politics get very short shrift in the book, though we learn that Jack Linden's son died in the Boer War of 1899–1902, five years before the narrative present (77). Moreover, Mugsborough has no history of working-class struggle, even though in 1830–31 there were thirteen 'Captain Swing' incidents near Battle, three miles from Hastings, and 'riots' even closer at Bexhill.[8] There is no reference to Chartism,[9] to the nationally important London match girls' strike of May 1888, or to the gas workers' and dockers' struggles of 1889.[10] Yet Len Green saw Noonan, Cobb and Ben Tillett, the dockers' leader, walking together on Hastings sea-front after a meeting at the Market Hall. However, we hear about working-class defeats, like the miners' strike at Featherstone

in 1893, where the shooting of 'rioters' was sanctioned by the Liberal
Home Secretary, H.H. ('Featherstone') Asquith. But while we learn nothing
of the Russian 'dress rehearsal' for revolution of 1905, RTP highlights the
three civilians shot in Belfast in 1907. Of course, this is a novel, not a
history book; but Mugsborough does seem like a Dickensian prison-hulk,
moored off the coast, safely under the control of armed warders.

Any Hastings worker-writer who used his own name, or those of real
and influential figures, would have risked economic, legal and possibly
physical reprisals. Yet Noonan's satirical pseudonyms appear unnecessarily
unrealistic. The monopolistic ownership of Mugsborough's *Daily Obscurer*,
Weekly Chloroform and *Weekly Ananias* is realistic enough. Adam – a damn –
Sweater controls two of them, and he is also the leading draper, with 'a
large wholesale business in London and shops all over the bloody country'
(19). Amos Grinder, the leading greengrocer, owns another. Cobb's biog-
rapher, Mike Matthews, believes Charles Eaton, a Hastings draper and
Mayor in 1904, and Stanley Weston of the grocers, Paine Rogers & Co.,
who was Mayor in 1906, were likely models.[11] The Mugsborough bourgeoisie is presented with 'a kind of allegorical rigour', though we rarely
seen them at home.[12] The petty-bourgeois Mr Wireman, the electrical
engineer; Mr Toonarf, the architect; and Mr Lettum, the estate agent, are
even less rounded. Mr Snatchum, the predatory undertaker, might seem
implausible, yet Kathleen heard from her father about 'One lift out and
one lift in' (561). A. Smallman, a small grocer risking bankruptcy by
giving credit to customers who spend their cash at the Monopole Provision Stores, is realistic enough, and so are Mr Latham, the venetian-blind-
maker, and his son, those 'men who did piece-work at home' (254). After
all, so did Mr Noonan. Yet only the Old Dear seems completely alive.

As for the female majority, Mrs Starvem and A. Harpy (a pub landlady)
have a kind of vitality; but Mrs Grosare, Mrs Bilder, Mrs Daree, Mrs
Butcher, Mrs Taylor, Mrs Baker and Mrs Slodging are characters as thin as
cards in a game of Unhappy Families. Generally, Mugsborough women
are 'more or less exposed, languishing, collapsed or ill'.[13] But the
domestic lives of working-class women are represented realistically; and
the interiors of their homes are 'probably a fair picture'.[14] Mary's sweated
homeworking, machining blouses for Sweater, is entirely believable; yet
few Mugsborough working-class women have outside jobs, and even
fewer are seen doing them. Ruth's domestic service for Mrs Starvem had
been

a series of recollections of petty tyrannies, insults and indignities. Six years of cruelly excessive work, beginning every morning two or three hours before the rest of the household were awake and ceasing only when she went to bed exhausted, late at night. (51)

Noonan apparently told a workmate about just such a case.[15] Yet that skivvying took place before Ruth married, and is not directly represented in RTP.

The ideology of the heterosexual nuclear family is hegemonic in Mugsborough. Even the socialist Owen attacks the single man, Slyme, for not being one of those 'who live natural lives' (296). Interestingly, Noonan described Kathleen's 'lack of interest in the male' as 'un-natural'; and she felt 'sheltered', even 'sequestered' at home, having spent years in boarding schools, partly in consequence of her parents' divorce (which she had no idea about) and her aunt's antipathy (which she did). Yet unlike the Noonans, the Eastons are reconciled. However, except for middle-class 'charity' work, most Mugsborough women are not shown as being socially active, let alone politically engaged. Where, for example, are the Mugsborough suffragettes? We know they were active in Hastings.[16]

Noonan stresses that 'no attack is made upon sincere religion' (12). Indeed, Frankie's atheist parents allow him to go to Sunday school, and give him twopence for the Easter Offering. Yet distinctions are made between the Church of the Whited Sepulchre and its vicar, Mr Habbakuk Bosher, and the Shining Light Chapel, where the Reverend John Starr is contrasted to the regular preacher, Mr Jonydab Belcher. (Tom Mann knew a Reverend Belcher in Hackney.[17]) But while RTP ignores some Protestants' records in fighting oppression, the Catholic Church is let off the hook completely.[18] Secular alternatives are ignored, yet Socialist Sunday Schools visited Hastings in 1906 and 1907.[19] Instead, Noonan focuses on the bosses' involvement in religious and charitable institutions. Mrs White's exploitation is supervised by Mrs Didlum. 'Another specious fraud was the "Distress Committee"' (376). The Organised Benevolent Society depends on mindless widows like Mrs M.T. Head, Mrs M.B. Sile and Mrs Knobrane. Mr Sawney Grinder, Amos's nephew, is its secretary. (Hastings and St Leonards Society for the Organising of Charitable Relief and Repression of Mendicity was formed in 1891, and Noonan's description was 'probably accurate', according to a later secretary.) For all that, RTP assumes its readers possess biblical knowledge about Ananias, and Pontius Pilate, *aka* Nimrod, that 'Mighty Hunter before the Lord' (31).

The balance of Mugsborough class forces

Mugsborough employers understand their class interests, and they mono-
polise political power as 'Brigands' and 'Bandits' on the Municipal Council. Adam Sweater is mayor and all-time 'Chief' of the dominant Liberal
'Band', and has been mayor several times before. Nepotism and corruption are normal. Sweater angles for the council to take over his drains,
and Grinder plans to open the Kiosk after ratepayers subsidise its re-
furbishment. The chief electrician is bribed. Mr Oyley Sweater (some
relation) is Borough Surveyor. True, Councillor Weakling, a retired sur-
geon with a belief in Darwinism, argues for adopting trade-union rates of
pay; but he gets the 'dirty kick out' by working-class voters at the election
(612). Thanks to their 'semi-imbecile constituents' (212), Rushton, Didlum
and Grinder, those 'wise, practical, philanthropic, fat persons whom the
people of Mugsborough had elected to manage their affairs, or whom
they permitted to manage them without being elected', increase their
majorities (371). Yet even as Noonan was writing, Hastings municipal
employees acted as 'informers' for the SDP. In 1908 Cobb denounced the
pilfering of garden-plants from public parks, and in 1910 he damned the
'Forty Thieves'.[20]

Mugsborough councillors dispense class justice as magistrates. Ruth
Easton fears her husband will be 'taken off to jail for a month, the same
as Mrs Newman's husband was last winter' (62). Newman is imprisoned
for not paying poor rates, and his wife gets three shillings a week for
herself and three children. Five or six men a week were 'captured by the
police and sent to jail' for the same reason in summer (458). This class-
based power is so ingrained that Mr Didlum JP suggests that the Council
Engineer's pay rise 'be extended from a fortnight to one calendar month
with hard la—— he begged pardon – with full pay' (388–9). All this is
believable.

In Hastings 'scarcely a week passed without a large batch of respectable
people being hauled before the Borough Magistrate for non-payment of
rates'.[21] A painter's 'terrible fall' was recorded in May 1905. (The dead
man was 55, and the policeman who attended was Frederick Philpot.[22])
One contemporary of Noonan's reportedly

> kept his family alive for a whole winter on bread and parsnips, and told
> how the unemployed went out at night stealing fences from public grounds
> in order to get firewood. Some families even burnt the inside doors of their
> houses.[23]

In July 1906, a child's body was taken to the Borough Cemetery in a sack and buried without religious ceremony: 'The anguished mother was heard to cry out that her child was buried like a dog.' Yet the acting chaplain 'was harshly maligned by fellow passengers as he travelled to the Cemetery by tram', and an anonymous correspondent exposed his callousness in a local paper.[24]

Queen Victoria and King Edward VII are ignored by RTP's republican author. Hastings returned Tory MPs in 1886, 1892 and 1895. A Liberal won in 1900; but then, against the national trend, the Tories got the seat back in 1906, held on to it in a snap by-election in 1908, and again in the general election of January 1910. In Mugsborough, Sir Graball D'Encloseland is the Tory candidate; but after visits by Lord Ammonegg and Sir Featherstone Blood, the Liberal wins the election. So Philpot's initial resignation – 'They're hall the same; working the horicle for their own benefit' (27) – *seems* realistic. The Mugsborough class war looks to be over, and the workers lost.

In Hastings Len Green testified that Adams & Jarrett's really was known as 'Makehaste and Sloggem', and he knew 'Misery' well. 'Everything – get it done cheap.' 'If they was going to do it with three coats put on, they put two.' Poynton agreed: 'Old Misery was known to nearly all builders' workers in the district and the description of him is a perfect pen picture of the man.'[25] Yet in Mugsborough this character has several names. Hunter was 'on the point of starting on his own account when Rushton offered him a constant job as foreman, two pounds a week, and two and half per cent of the profits'. But while he 'was entitled to a week's notice instead of an hour's notice', he was 'little better off financially than when he started for the firm'. So *Misery* 'realised now that Rushton had had considerably the best of the bargain', and his 'heart failed him at the thought of having to meet on an equal footing those workmen whom he had tyrannised over and oppressed', should he ever be sacked (32–3). *Nimrod* and *Pontius Pilate* had crossed both a class and a moral boundary.

Noonan represents class struggle at work, realistically, as a *contradictory* phenomenon. Yet only towards the end of the book does the narrative voice come off the fence to celebrate Bill Bates' and the Semi-drunk's attempted drenching of Hunter: 'Unfortunately, they were too drunk and excited to aim straight' (444). Only near the end are we offered the psychic satisfaction of the rate-cutting estimator using a razor to cut his own throat. More realistically, the site foreman, Crass, is marginally better

off than most tradesmen, but largely because Mrs Crass's boarders
pay twelve shillings and their daughter is in service. His position at work
is not secure. He thins Misery's paint, and whispers to Sawkins: 'Is the
b——r gorn?' (44). But when Misery threatens an 'alteration' Crass's 'fat
face had turned a ghastly green with fright' (171).

Gradually, sides are marked out. Harlow defends Bert against Misery.
Easton 'had it in his mind to say that Nimrod seemed to hate the sight of
all of them', but 'made no remark' to Crass (103–4). Easton tells Owen
privately: 'The bloody rotter's no friend of mine either' (109). Harlow
and Philpot are openly angry when Owen looked set to be sacked on a
Monday, and everyone except Crass and Slyme sympathises. Yet Crass and
Harlow laugh quietly at Misery's envy of Owen's skills, then let Philpot in
on their merriment. Generally, RTP suggests it is not so much a person's
character as their relative power at the point of production which is
fundamental to class society. 'They all cursed Crass', but 'if any one of
them had been in his place they would have been compelled to act in the
same way – or lose the job' (217). Noonan had probably lived this contradiction in South Africa.

These contradictions extend outside working hours. Crass gets six and
a half pints of beer and two selections on the polyphone for a penny; yet
he, Slyme and Sawkins cough up for the subscription for Newman's family.
After all, Crass's position is largely based on his patronage power over the
lumpenproletarian Semi-drunk, Besotted Wretch and Dick Wantley, so he
needs Slyme, who toadies and survives 'The Slaughter'. Yet Slyme remains
vulnerable. Harlow promises not to tell about the wallpaper scam, and
occasionally solidarity is returned: when Owen challenges craft elitism,
Slyme does not come to Crass's assistance. But while the class in itself is
shown in the early stages of formation, and on the road to becoming a
class for itself, Noonan's technique of naming does tend to reinforce the
idea that the 'System' is fixed. An Iron Law of Capitalist Social Relations
often seems to flatten out contradictions through which, if Marx was
correct, change might come.

According to Green, RTP represented Mugsborough workers realistically. The story about the missing beer 'was a thing that I actually wrote
for Bob Tressell on the job up at Hollington Park. I did it on a bit of
lining paper'. The real Philpot drank the beer money: 'next morning he
shows up' and 'he'd borrowed the money off his sisters or somebody,
that's why they called him the Absconding Secretary of the Light Refresh-

ment Fund'. Of course, a 'lot' of RTP 'took place on other jobs'; and there may have been 'inventions', but 'mostly it was authentic'. Some Mugsborough workers, like Mr Budd, Miss Wade, Mr Partaker and Jim Smith, have names, but most are one-dimensional. In Hastings the 'Man in the Moat' was 'well known to everybody for his dirty habit of spitting all round him while he was smoking',[26] and the 'man with a red tie' may have been Noonan's self-portrait, though that neckwear was usually the badge of an ILPer.[27] But 'the man with the patches on the seat of his trousers', the 'man on the pail', a 'new man', a 'very tall, thin man', 'the man with the metallic voice', the 'stranger' from London, the 'tall man with a very loud voice', the 'little man', 'another paper-hanger', the 'man with the copper wire stitches in his boot' and the 'man with the scarred face', are nameless. And while RTP stresses the potentially creative role of labour, in Mugsborough it is dominated by its opposite: the 'dozens of men out of employment already' (217).

RTP calls itself 'this history' (207), but Noonan reportedly called the book his 'Diary'.[28] Like many diary entries, work in Mugsborough is repetitive, but under capitalist social relations that is realistic enough. As in Hastings, building workers have a 9½-hour day in winter, during the week, from 7 a.m. to 5.30 p.m., with an unpaid half-hour for breakfast and dinner, plus a half-day of 6.30 a.m. to 1 p.m. on Saturdays. In summer they work from 6 a.m. to 5.30 p.m. on weekdays, less breakfast and dinner, making ten paid hours a day, plus Saturday mornings. But Noonan shows how the working day is much longer. For a six o'clock start Bert leaves home just after five, because he has a forty-five-minute walk, making a thirteen-hour day, assuming he gets up on time. Green and his father 'were so hard up in that time that we hadn't got a real clock', and 'on several occasions' they went out in the dark only to find out from a suspicious policeman that 'it's only been damned four o'clock'. Green told the story, and Noonan 'added to it' (64–6). As we have seen, he was used to a 9-to-5 day and a 44-hour week in Johannesburg.[29]

Realistically, working poverty is endemic in Mubsborough. Easton's wages, 'taking good times with bad ... did not average a pound a week', so he struggled; whereas when he was single 'he always had enough to live on and pocket money besides' (49). Equally realistically, Noonan shows how workers were split by craft hierarchies. Sawkins's fivepence an hour is twopence less than the rate, while labourers get fourpence. Harlow complains: 'We've got to teach a b——r like 'im so as 'e can do us out

of a job presently by working under price' (98). Yet most men accept the
lowered rate of sixpence halfpenny, while Crass is exempted, and Owen
gets eightpence for the Moorish Room, making 200 per cent profit for
his employer. In Johannesburg the cost of living was high, but Noonan
got at least three shillings and twopence an hour, and ordinary tradesmen
got two shillings and threepence.[30]

Noonan's draft Preface claims that, so far as he dared, he 'let the characters express themselves in their own sort of language and consequently
some passages may be considered objectionable' (12). Yet workers' grammar, syntax and vocabulary usually coarsen when they are being servile,
and when the narrative voice (or Owen) is about to damn their opinions.
Jack Beeching confirmed that 'the tone, the dialogue, the attitudes' of RTP
were 'absolutely as I remember them from my boyhood' in St Leonards
in the 1920s. Yet, strangely, there are no Irish building workers, and Ireland is mentioned only in passing. Beeching believed Noonan was not
'one of these chaps', and looked down on them, but Ball found otherwise: 'Not from a single person I interviewed nor in any reminiscing
about Robert did I ever hear of any hostility to English people because
they were English'. Moreover, Ogilvy 'had no difficulty whatever in iden-
tifying some of the characters portrayed as being derived from the oddi-
ties Noonan had subjected to such close examination and study during
the years he lived on the Rand'.[31] Mugsborough was *everywhere*.

The only real remedy

RTP's draft Preface stresses that the book was 'designed to show the conditions resulting from poverty and unemployment',

> to expose the futility of the measures taken to deal with them and to
> indicate what I believe to be the only real remedy, namely – Socialism. I
> intended to explain what Socialists understand by the word 'Poverty': to
> define the Socialist theory of the causes of poverty, and to explain how
> Socialists propose to abolish poverty.

This was necessary since 'not only are the majority of people opposed to
Socialism, but a very brief conversation with an average anti-socialist is
sufficient to show that he does not know what Socialism means' (11). Yet
RTP was a novel, not a tract, so the 'main object was to write a readable
story full of human interest and based on the happenings of real life', 'the
subject of Socialism being treated incidentally' (12).

The key to RTP's politics is the role of narrative voice. It tells us 'Every-one was afraid' (41); and when Crass intimidates Bert he does not answer. It reads workers' minds: 'Hunter's silence seemed more menacing than his speech' (118). It speaks on behalf of the oppressed: 'The men work with their hands, and the masters work with their brains. What a dreadful calamity it would be for the world and for mankind if all these brain workers were to go on strike (147). It mimics 'common-sense'.

> People always take great care of their horses ... But ... If they work a man to death they can get another for nothing at the corner of the next street ... If he does not like the hirer's conditions he need not accept them. He can refuse to work, and he can go and starve. There are no ropes on him. He is a Free man. He is the Heir of all the Ages. He enjoys perfect Liberty. He has the right to choose freely which he will do – Submit or Starve, Eat dirt, or eat nothing. (275–6)

Crucially, this is not part of a dialogue between characters, but a dis-embodied monologue:

> Extraordinary as it may appear, none of them took any pride in their work ... On the contrary, when the workers arrived in the morning they wished it was breakfast-time. When they resumed work after breakfast they wished it was dinner-time. After dinner they wished it was one o'clock on Saturday.
> So they went on, day after day, year after year, wishing their time was over and, without realising it, really wishing that they were dead. (97)

Time is 'the enemy' (47). Deaths are 'boxin' up jobs', a source of work: 'we can't grumble: we've 'ad one nearly every week since the beginning of October' (136). There is little labour mobility: Owen goes to London, but he comes back penniless and in worse health. The only escape routes for Mugsborough workers are suicide or death. To some extent, this was realistic: in 1901–11 suicides were a weekly phenomenon in Hastings.[32] Yet if the capitalist 'System' was ever to be changed, Mugsborough seems the most unpromising place to start.

According to the narrative voice, workers are plant pots for capitalist propaganda. Newspapers contain 'seeds which, cunningly sown in their minds, caused to grow up within them a bitter undiscriminating hatred of foreigners' (21). They are mad. 'If these people were not mentally deficient they would of their own accord have swept this silly system away long ago' (69). They are infantile. The 'grown-up children were gathered round outside the entrance, worshipping' D'Encloseland's car (376). They are thick. The 'argument was generally too obscure to be grasped by men whose minds were addled by the stories told them by their Liberal and Tory masters' (395). They are atomised, with 'very little sympathy for each other at any time' (445). They have no self-respect. 'Our children is only like so much dirt compared with Gentry's children', and their pleasures are not for 'the likes of us' (485). They can be depraved. The 'drunken savages' make the four brakes look like 'so many travelling lunatic asylums' (489, 494). So they are to be pitied. 'Truly the wolves have an easy prey'(591).

We are simply told that, 'in the face of such colossal imbecility it was absurd to hope for any immediate improvement'. Bates' calling Crass 'a good nigger-driver', and the frequent references to the 'savage' and 'savagery' add to the pervasive fatalism.[33] Yet while most Mugsborough workers are given few directly attributed thoughts, they often challenge capitalist social relations by small deeds. Philpot boozes surreptitiously, steals turpentine and counsels Owen: 'Charge up to six o'clock on yer time sheet and get some of your own back' (124). Even Slyme breaks unused rolls of wallpaper so as to be able to claim for hanging them, and insists: 'We must get our own back somehow, you know' (221). Nimrod's paint is oiled down. Rushton gets one of his own cards covered in excrement, and it spoils his breakfast. Nothing fundamentally changes, yet seeds of resistance keep popping up. Was Mugsborough exceptional?

It is true that the economic position of British workers deteriorated during Noonan's first years in Hastings. The Taff Vale Judgment of 1901 made union funds liable for damages, and the period up to 1904 was a low point for strike days. Few strikers won. The Taff Vale decision was reversed in 1906, but as RTP was being written the economic crisis deepened. By 1908 unemployment among trade unionists had trebled to almost 8 per cent since 1900, and real wages were 9 per cent lower; yet strike days quadrupled to over ten million. In 1909 almost a million people claimed out-relief, and strike days fell to 2.75 million; but in September a strike over the minimum wage in a South Wales pit spread rapidly to the whole Cambrian Combine. It was led not by the official South Wales Miners' Federation, but by the South Wales Unofficial Reform Committee, which struggled against the employers, union officers and Board of Trade officials to impose a compromise settlement, even before massive detachments of police and troops were dispatched by Winston Churchill. From November 1909 to July 1910 there was a series of spontaneous strikes in shipyards in Northeast England. In January 1910 the

Durham miners struck for three months over wages, against their union leaders' advice, and overall strike days shot up once again. So as Noonan wrote the economic situation was massively contradictory, and we might reasonably expect a realist novel to take some account of that.

Of course, Hastings was an industrial backwater. Alf Sellens reportedly remembered 'nothing I can recall as direct struggle', 'no fights for better conditions' in the local building trade, until after 1918.[34] Len Green knew it was hard to stay in the union: 'In the winter-time they come along and they got plenty of work but they only paid us halfpenny below the figure, because they had to take it cheap, and you had to work under rate, see.' But he refused to be a victim. His boss knew he liked a smoke:

> 'The next time I catch you smoking I'll fine you. I'll fine you sixpence every time'. Well, he caught me three times in a week. He knocked off eighteen pence. But ... perhaps one firm hadn't got a job of papering, another had ... I chucked him off altogether.

Employers were socially vulnerable, too: 'Old Jarrett, his wife divorced him.'

Jack Beeching's grandfather, like Noonan, worked for Eldridge & Cruttenden, one of two large builders in St Leonards – 'a lot of crooks, both of them'. He was a gilder 'obliged to work as a painter', but he was

> a militant sort of chap, and when he got too heavy to go up a ladder they sacked him. He earned a living – or managed to survive, thanks to his wife's dressmaking – as a sick-visitor for a Friendly Society, and running the Mechanics' Institute, which had a library. It was this sort of world of mutual self-help – Friendly Societies, the union, and camaraderie, solidarity, in defence of their means of livelihood.

So RTP was right about 'this sense of despair' and 'futility', but it did not show the 'basic, radical militancy and human solidarity'. Such contradictions offered the possibility of development, and therefore of hope.

By 1910 British socialism was polarising. At that January's general election the Liberal majority was wiped out, and there was dissatisfaction among socialists at the forty Labour MPs' class-collaborationism. Curran lost Jarrow, and Grayson lost in the Colne Valley, but his supporters seceded from the ILP, and a reform movement began inside the organisation. As for the SDP, Hyndman conceded that the failure to address working-class concerns had cost the organisation dearly. Tom Kennedy argued that sectarianism was the root cause, and pressed for reunification with the Labour Party. Blatchford, however, ignored the election, being unable to 'enthuse about cabbages'. Instead he focused on 'the menace of the pan-German "world policy", and supported the Navy League's demand for £50 million for destroyers and the extension of the Rosyth naval base.[35] By 1911 he had lost faith in the working class completely.[36] There was a crisis of socialist leadership and, realistically, this also appears in RTP.

The monologic militant

Frank Owen is the nearest RTP comes to having a working-class hero. His name may have derived from Frank Willard and Frederick Owen, both of whom left the SDF to join the ILP in 1907; and it may also have been a reference to the utopian socialist Robert Owen. But Noonan's Owen is defined as being very *different* from the start. Like Noonan, he is an incomer, with 'a suggestion of refinement' about him (16). In fact he is worryingly exotic. Mrs Linden 'looked curiously at the Atheist as he entered the room', and 'was surprised to find that he was not repulsive to look at, rather the contrary. But then she remembered that Satan often appears as the angel of light' (74). Owen is also a very special worker. He can afford to produce designs for the Moorish Room in his own time, and his unusual skills mean that 'The Slaughter' doesn't touch him. He is a trade unionist, a socialist and a teetotaller before the story starts, so he does not have to be shown being convinced. Yet the narrative voice stacks the odds against him from the beginning. His complexion is 'ominously clear, and an unnatural colour flushed the thin cheeks' (16). Soon after, he is 'seized with a violent fit of coughing' (25). Then 'Symptoms of the disease that had killed his father began to manifest themselves' – 'consumption', or TB – and he begins 'gradually abandoning himself to hopelessness' (67, 68).

The narrative voice stresses Owen's isolation at work. He was 'generally regarded as a bit of a crank' (16); and he soon gets labelled 'as mad as a March hare' (28). He is a utopian. There 'was no reason to believe or hope that the existing state of things would be altered for a long time to come' (68). Besides, he was 'a bit orf is onion about Socialism' (190); and at the end of the book Sawkins 'thought of the talk there had often been about Owen being mad, and felt half afraid of him' (606). The narrative voice comments that people arguing for socialism 'were undoubtedly mad' if 'they hoped to do so by reasoning with the others!' (496). He even *talks* differently, in the same 'standard English' as the narrative voice. As Eric Bolton noted, Owen 'never drops his aitches, nor mispronounces long words and he is always grammatically correct'.[37] So, unsurprisingly, his speeches 'sounded almost like something out of a book' (29). One worker wonders out loud 'wot the bloody 'ell 'e thinks 'e is? A sort of schoolmaster?' (160). Crass tells him to his face: 'You can't never get very far without supposing some bloody ridiclus thing or other' (28). So he gets the mock-heroic title of 'Professor' (223).

Very occasionally, the narrative voice comes to Owen's support, as in the case of the Tory *Obscurer*'s 'carefully cooked statistics' (17). Harlow, a Liberal, ridicules a Tory workmate on the question of media bias: 'If you're goin' to believe all that's in that bloody rag you'll want some salt' (20). So the position is by no means hopeless. Of course, Owen is asked big questions, yet too often he gives abstract responses. Easton wants to know: 'wot do you reckon is the cause of poverty, then?' Owen replies:

> The present system – competition – capitalism … it's no good tinkering at it. Everything about it is wrong and there's nothing about it that's right. There's only one thing to be done with it and that is to smash it up and have a different system altogether. (157)

However, he suggests no political strategy for smashing the 'Money System'. Instead, he stays at the level of socialist *ideas*, though they make some headway. Philpot acknowledges: 'I agree with a lot that 'e ses. I've often thought the same things myself' (190); and Easton confides: 'a great deal of what Owen says is true. But for my part I can't see 'ow it's ever goin' to be altered, can you?' Harlow responds: 'there's one thing very certain; it won't be done in our time' (232). Yet the narrative voice lets slip that even Tory workers were 'disgusted and angry with Grinder' (479).

So what *was* the 'Nemesis which was overtaking the Capitalist System' (630)? Owen downplays trade unionism. It is a quarter of the way into the book before he hints that 'we could help ourselves to a certain extent if we would stand by each other. If, for instance, we all belonged to the Society'. But first he is barracked, and then he accepts being silenced: 'after all, that's another matter' (165–6). Over half-way through RTP we learn that Mugsborough Trades Council was 'formed of delegates from all the different trade unions in the town', though the narrative voice insists that a worker had told the Grinder that 'there was scarcely one of the local branches of the trade unions which had more than a dozen members' (371–2). So 'Ninety-nine out of every hundred of them did not believe in such things'; and 'Trades Union rules were a dead letter' (422). In reality,

Harry Quelch of the SDF/SDP argued that workers had to use their trade-union organisations to

> get control of the political machinery of the country, and use it for the advancement of their class. By this means they could, if they chose, achieve as much in a year or two as would be gained in a century by the old methods of trade agitation and strikes.[38]

Moreover, the Hastings Branch of the Painters' Society had more members than that of Brighton, a town over four times its size.[39]

There is individual defiance in Noonan's Mugsborough, but it is rarely *generalised*. Owen gradually wins the argument, but he tends to lose the vote, largely because he separates theory and practice. His ideas are never tested in practice. He is not around when Newman, who 'had never worked under price' and 'had sometimes gone hungry rather than do so', 'went off feeling like a criminal' after Nimrod beat him down (36). He is ignorant of the fact that Harlow 'had at one time belonged to the Union' and was 'rather ashamed of having fallen away from it' (165–6). He misses an opportunity for agitation when most men's wages are cut to sixpence halfpenny an hour while he decorates the Moorish Room on eightpence. The death of one of his few socialist converts, Philpot, gives him a chance to agitate, but he abstains. Yet it isn't all hopeless. The Painters' Society, of which Owen is secretary, have a whip-round for Mrs Newman; and the secretary of the Trades Council, of which Owen is a member, writes to the *Obscurer*.

Owen tries to unpick bourgeois ideology one nonsense at a time, and he can be gratuitously rude. So Crass sets him up as a snob: '"you think your opinion's right and everybody else's is wrong". "Yes", replied Owen' (156). The majority are told that 'the majority are mostly fools' (161). The narrative voice agrees. 'Of course! It wasn't necessary to think about these things at all! Nothing could ever be altered.' Then Owen bursts out: 'It seems to me that you all *hope* it is impossible to alter it' (300). So he 'continued to make himself objectionable and to incur the ridicule of his fellow workmen' (458), and gets beaten up at the election.

˙Crucially, the monologic militant avoids *dialogue*. When Harlow complains that he was 'always sayin' that everything's all wrong ... but why the 'ell don't you tell us 'ow they're goin' to be put right?' Owen replies: 'It doesn't seem to me as if any of you really wish to know' (108). When the man on the pail asks that same question, Owen retorts: 'Well, that's not what we're talking about now, is it?' (290) When Harlow asks again, Owen begins to answer: 'The way to alter it is, first to enlighten the people as to the real cause of their sufferings, and then ——' (300) – but then Crass interrupts. At home, Nora tells Frankie: 'they won't listen, they don't want to hear' (86).

> Don't you think it will be any use, then, for me to tell them what to do to the Idlers?' asked Frankie, dejectedly.
> 'Hark!' said his mother, holding up her finger.

Then Owen reinforces her doubts: 'all their lives they have supported and defended the system that robbed them, and have resisted and ridiculed every proposal to alter it. It's wrong to feel sorry for such people; they deserve to suffer' (88–9).

This Blatchford-like pessimism about the working class gets amplified back at work. Owen talks to workers about the 'working class' as 'they' (160–61).[40] The narrative voice reports that he 'listened with contempt and anger' to a man 'who grumbled at the present state of things, yet took no trouble to think for himself and try to alter them, and who at the first chance would vote for the perpetuation of the System which produced his misery' (354). He considers individual terrorism, and what stops him is not the politically self-defeating character of such activity but the economic realities. Listening to Hunter, he 'felt that he would like to take him by the throat with one hand and smash his face in with the other'. 'And then?'

> Why then he would be sent to goal, or at the best he would lose his employment: his food and that of his family would be taken away. That was why he only ground his teeth and cursed and beat the wall with his clenched fist. So! And so! and so! (42)

Frustration reinforces the pull of elitist abstentionism.

Hyndman always argued that 'a slave class cannot be freed by the slaves themselves',[41] and Owen tells workers to their faces, 'You should not be allowed to vote' (22). (Many could not until 1918.) Soon, we are told,

> there sprang up within him a feeling of hatred and fury against the majority of his fellow workmen. *They were the enemy* ... *They were the real oppressors* ... *They* were the people who were really responsible for the continuation of the present system ... No wonder the rich despised them and looked upon them as dirt. *They were despicable. They were dirt.* They admitted it and gloried in it. (46)

Yet the narrative voice tells us, if not Owen, that some workers had begun to see how socialist ideas fitted their experience. 'Some of them began to wonder whether Owen was not sane after all', and Philpot 'had suddenly grown very serious' (29). Owen is fly enough to cast the most likely converts, Philpot, Harlow and Easton, as 'the working classes' in 'The Great Money Trick', so they could experience the swindle at close range; and those made 'unemployed' by the 'kind-hearted Capitalist' 'even threatened to take some of the things by force' (227, 229). Thereafter, Philpot becomes supportive; and Owen can get away with the comment that the Liberal Party 'consists for the most part of exploiters of labour' (311–12). But what is the practical political alternative?

Police constable socialism

To some extent, Noonan was moving beyond Blatchford and Hyndman, and towards a Marxist theory of ideology. Owen does not have to start from scratch, since Mugsborough workers are already lukewarm about religion. Everyone but Slyme concurs when Philpot refers to "eaven – if there is sich a place', and nobody disagrees when Cross suggests 'this world is 'ell' (155). Even the narrative voice acknowledges that at Easter, 'not more than one working man in fifty went to any religious service' (404). And militant atheism appears when Hunter is challenged to take 'strychnine' by 'two unbelievers' at the 'Open Air'; though these 'well-dressed young men' were 'evidently strangers and visitors' (248).

But while Owen understands something of the power of bourgeois ideology on others, it also attacks him:

> Usually, whenever Owen reflected upon the gross injustices and inhumanity of the existing social disorder, he became convinced that it could not possibly last; it was bound to fall to pieces because of its own rottenness ... But always, after one of these arguments – or, rather, disputes – with his fellow workmen, he almost relapsed into hopelessness and despondency, for then he realised how vast and how strong are the fortifications that surround the present system; the great barriers and ramparts of invincible ignorance, apathy and self-contempt, which will have to be broken down before the system of society of which they are the defences, can be swept away. (396)

The narrative voice sometimes colludes with this hopelessness by letting workers off the hook. It 'was not so much to be wondered at that none of them had the courage to openly resent the conditions under which they had to work, for although it was summer, there were many men out of employment, and it was much easier to get the sack than it was to get another job' (458).

Owen has socialist ideas, and a general analysis, but, like Blatchford, assumes people must change before they can tackle the 'System', and not, as Marx believed, during the process of struggle itself. So theory is privileged over practice. With the help of his lending-library Owen converted the 'small number of Socialists – not more than half a dozen altogether – who did not join in the applause' for Grinder at the Beano (479). But rather than arguing for activity and winning little victories, he indulges in rhetoric: 'The time will come, and it's not very far distant, when the necessaries of life will be produced for use and not for profit' (505). All he can suggest are 'palliative' reforms, like public works for the unemployed; and he defends the pay of Labour MPs. To sort out Bert's freezing working conditions he resorts to the Society for the Prevention of Cruelty to Children, not working-class organisation. (Kathleen recalled that her father nearly got the sack for doing something similar.) Yet in Mugsborough, as in Hastings, raising workers' confidence was the key. We are shown a leaflet, *What is Socialism?*, and a Brotherhood card; but where are the union and Trades Council minutes, membership cards for socialist groups, cuttings from socialist papers and socialist speakers' notes? Where are the collective socialist solutions to collective working-class problems?

The working-class socialist Owen is all but written off by Noonan half-way through the book, when his mouth 'suddenly filled with blood' (358). After that he is reduced to anarchist fantasies about capitalism making 'these miserable wretches' sufficiently enraged to 'turn upon their oppressors and drown both them and their System in a sea of blood' (398), while the narrative voice stresses the forces ranged against socialism, especially in the reception for the Socialist Van:

> Crass, Dick Wantley, the Semi-Drunk, Sawkins, Bates and several other frequenters of the Cricketers were amongst the crowd, and there were also a sprinkling of tradespeople, including the Old Dear and Mr Smallman, the grocer, and a few ladies and gentlemen – wealthy visitors – but the bulk of the crowd were working men, labourers, mechanics and boys.
> ...many of them had their pockets filled with stones and were armed with sticks – several of the Socialists were in favour of going to meet the van to persuade those in charge from coming. (463)

The van kept coming and 'made several converts' (467); but, unlike Hastings, the locals were too scared to form a socialist party branch. So hope had to come from outside.

Barrington, the only other convinced socialist in the book, is reminiscent of SDPer Tom Kennedy, though Green presumed he was an invention. He appears briefly, early on, and is conspicuous for being 'a good deal taller than the majority of the others', and 'well and strongly built' (17). 'Nobody knowed exactly who 'e was or where 'e come from, but anyone could tell 'e'd been a toff' (257). For a long time he remains a silent and mysterious figure, until it 'began to be rumoured that he shared Owen's views' (461). But like Owen he lets the bosses off the hook: 'It is the bad employer' who 'sets the pace and the others have to adopt the same methods – very often against their inclinations' (482). He also dodges the problem of class-consciousness. The new 'Professor' is just as monologic, reducing Crass and Slyme to barracking and then to silence.

Barrington *sounds* revolutionary: 'you must fill the House of Commons with Revolutionary Socialists' (538); yet he has no understanding of the class character of the state. So he ignores the ruling-class backlash which Marx was sure would occur if a revolutionary programme was enacted by a parliamentary majority. Harlow accepts that 'Socialism was a beautiful ideal', even if 'it was altogether too good to be practical, because human nature is too mean and selfish' (505), but he is understandably confused by how the expropriators could be expropriated without force. So while his conversion is 'greeted with loud cheers from the Socialists', and Philpot declares the vote for socialism carried 'unanimously', the narrative voice lets slip that 'the majority were against it' (541–2).

For most of the time in RTP the 'System' seems to be a peculiarly British problem. Owen is heavily ironic about the 'Tariff Reform paradise' with 'Plenty of Work' (13), potential 'foreign' aggression and 'foreign competition' (229, 230). But for all the references to 'Imperialists in broken boots' (421), the issue of Empire is fudged. True, Barrington refers to capitalism's problems in Germany and the USA; and makes a case for a British Citizen Army and Navy to defend 'our homes and our native land' (539–40). For the rest, he wants capitalists replaced with state capitalism by 'Police Constable Socialism'.

According to Barrington, 'Public Ownership' would intervene in the commercial world, and then lead automatically and inevitably to the defeat of private capitalists, without running the risk of imperialist war. So his politics owe most to Bellamy's *Looking Backward*, where capital concentrated itself, as Marx generally predicted that it would, and 'All that society had to do was to recognise and co-operate with that evolution.' The 'whole

mass of the people was behind it', and socialist parties 'had nothing to do
… except hinder' the 'most bloodless of revolutions'.[42] Barrington also
seems close to Victor Grayson; yet the latter's short experience as an MP
had convinced him that the 'Parliamentary game is played out' in the
'chloroform chamber', and that the Labour Party had 'done all it could
constitutionally': 'it needs more'.[43]

For the most part both Owen and Barrington follow Blatchford's advice
that socialists should convince people individually of the merits of socialism, then let them get on with it. Yet while they argue most opponents
to a standstill during a by-election, Barrington's confidence is clearly shaken
by the renegade: 'There's something in what you say … but it's not all.
Circumstances make us what we are; and anyhow, the children are worth
fighting for' (586). Of course, such renegades existed. In March 1908
Cobb reported to *Justice* that a one-time SDFer from Canning Town, a gas-
worker called J. Allen, had spoken for Tariff Reform, since he 'was tired of
playing the martyr' and 'his new occupation paid him better'.[44] But to
publicise such acrid cynicism, then fail to contradict it, is self-defeating. In
any case, Grayson knew a socialist lecturer who was offered £4 10s a
week to push Tariff Reform, but who replied: 'Soul not for sale'.[45]

Barrington was even more different than Owen. The narrative voice
eventually acknowledges that he 'did not care a brass button whether he
got the sack or not' (545). His 'manner of life was the subject of specu-
lation on the part of his former workmates, who were a little puzzled by
the fact that he was much better dressed than they had ever known him
to be before, and that he was never without money'. And there was
something odd about all the 'Socialist pamphlets and leaflets he gave away
broadcast' (568). Almost at the end of the book Barrington privately
explains to the Owens: 'I did not work for Rushton because I needed to
do so in order to live. I just wanted to see things for myself; to see life
as it is lived by the majority. My father is a wealthy man' (621). So he
leaves Mugsborough workers much as he found them, without strategy
or tactics, but he intends fitting out another Socialist Van and coming
back with more socialist ideas.

Why bother? As Raymond Williams noted, there is 'hardly a line'
between the book's savage criticism of workers and 'a certain kind of
reactionary rendering of the working class and working people as ir-
redeemably incapable of improving their conditions'.[46] At one point, Owen
even justifies individualism: 'No one can be blamed for doing the best he

can for himself under existing circumstances' (274); and he writes off white-collar workers – the very ones who were organising in Hastings – as doing work 'for the most part of no utility whatever' (289).

Bill Gower was sure that Owen 'was Noonan';[47] but Kathleen believed that Barrington and Owen were 'a composite picture' of her father, who

> would get exasperated when he could make no impression on the workmen when trying to get them to better their conditions. He would say they deserved to suffer but that it was their children who would have to suffer, which was so terribly frustrating to him.

He had 'a well-fed childhood; he knew another life', while his workmates did not. So 'he couldn't see why they'd be so stupid and put up with anything, when there wasn't any real need if they only had some gumption'.[48] He 'could quite plainly see what was wrong', but he 'didn't see the method by which it could change'.

The Ragged Trousered Philanthropists is characterised by a highly contradictory and selective realism, and its socialism is deeply contradictory and problematical. It occasionally chimes in with elements of the insidious 'socialist' nationalism being preached by Hyndman and Blatchford. After all, even Grayson was 'willing to defend even this rotten country – willing to prefer the English plunderer to the German plunderer'; though he also hoped that the socialist movement's 'international cord' would bind it together, and 'believed the day was coming when they would have to look to their guns'.[49] Noonan's narrative voice exhorts workers to 'Blame the system', and to fight the 'Battle of Life' (217, 218); but it doesn't say how, or who the officer corps might be. Of course, he wasn't Lenin. But Marx's idea that the emancipation of the working class would be the act of the Mugsborough working class seems very remote indeed.

5

The damnably subversive book

The study of Marxism had been negligible

The Ragged Trousered Philanthropists was close to the cutting edge of British socialist thought in 1910, and well to the left of most reformists and trade unionists. That year the miners' union instructed its MPs to leave the Liberals and join Labour's parliamentary group, thereby making the Liberal government dependent on Labour (and Irish) votes. The Liberals restricted the power of the Lords, but recognised the importance of separating working-class politics from economics, so they retained the 1909 judicial ban on unions financing political parties. One per cent of the population still owned two-thirds of the wealth, and the capitalist 'System' remained firmly in place. As one working-class militant put it: 'We have spent thousands of pounds on the Labour Party, with absolutely no return.'[1] Maybe the parliamentary road to socialism was a dead-end?

In July 1910 Tom Mann began publishing the Industrial Syndicalist, and in May 1911 he resigned from the SDP, convinced that 'industrial organisation' was 'THE means whereby the workers can ultimately overthrow the capitalist system'.[2] That June 500 Liverpool seamen refused to sign on, and within days 70,000 workers had struck work. Mann led the strike committee. On 4 August they won. Then a railway strike flared up, and the state sent two gunboats and 2,000 troops to Merseyside. Soon 150,000 railway workers were on strike, plus 220,000 in other industries, and practically every UK regiment was mobilised. Two men were shot dead by troops escorting prisoners to Walton Gaol, just across the road from where Robert Noonan had been buried six months before.

Some organised socialists rethought their position. In Glasgow, Harry
McShane failed to get his ILP branch to join the SDP, so he and two
others left 'to get in between the two' and 'preach class struggle, revolution, and extra-parliamentary activity without being anti-parliamentarian'.[3]
In September a Socialist Unity conference at Salford brought delegates
from 70 SDP, 36 ILP, and 30 Clarion branches, plus forty other socialist
societies. Some 40,000 ILPers (including Victor Grayson) joined with the
SDP to form the British Socialist Party. Tom Kennedy was on the Executive.
    The BSP aimed for the 'transformation of capitalist competitive society
into Socialist or communist society'. Like Noonan, it wanted 'the establishment of the Co-operative Commonwealth'. Its 'Methods', like Barrington's,
were 'The Education of the People in the principles of Socialism', and the
establishment of 'a militant Socialist Party in Parliament and on Local
Bodies, completely independent of all parties which support the capitalist
system'. Like Tom Mann, the BSP wanted the 'closest possible co-operation
with trade union organisations, and the advocacy of industrial unity of all
workers as essential to bring about the socialisation of the means of
production'.[4] Subs were a shilling a year, so the level of economic commitment was not high, and neither was the level of theoretical understanding.
One leading BSPer argued that 'it was not necessary to understand Marxism
in order to understand Socialism'.[5] McShane found the BSP became 'pretty
much like the old SDP'. Many left, and serious socialists who remained
were 'in struggle against the leaders' policy'.[6]
    Socialists in the ILP felt frustrated. In Eastbourne, George Meek

    did hope the Labour Party would have done something before now, but
    most of its leaders appear to be more concerned in taming the Party which
    sent them to Parliament to their own hands than in endeavouring to for-
    ward the interests of their supporters. The latest news is that Independent
    Labour Party branches are not allowed to communicate with each other
    respecting the resolutions they wish to submit to its Annual Conference:
    they must move only to the strings it suits J.R. MacDonald to pull ... What
    is the use of all our devotion and sacrifice when any specious trickster can
    undo half what we have done?

The SEFSS was 'flourishing', but it too was in 'ferment':

    On the one hand is the conservative element pulling towards mere Labourism
    – perhaps Liberalism; on the other the uncompromising Socialists who see
    no sense in being led out of the swamps of the old political parties with the
    idea of forming a definite independent Socialist party of their own only to
    be led back again.

> Although I have ceased to take a very active part in politics for some time, I am entirely in sympathy with the latter. Some day the workers will tire of mere politicians of every shade and will organise themselves for the definitive struggle with Capitalism. Then, thoroughly grounded in the economics and ethics of Socialism, they will know what to do.[7]

However, what Meek did was to emigrate to Canada.

Hastings SDP was still thriving. In October 1911 they published *The Hastings & St Leonards Citizen, A Monthly Journal of the People*, which retailed at one penny. It noted the failure of the electricity company, ridiculed the local Tory MP, savaged the Liberals for using troops against workers, criticised Lib–Lab MPs and published extracts from *Justice* and the *Clarion*, stressing the need for socialists to 'teach the workers to be "class-conscious"'. It plugged *The Great Strike Movement of 1911 and Its Lessons*, and argued against low pay and for trade unions. It was against employing a German band, but acknowledged that it was 'Capitalism which sweats the worker in Germany every bit as much as it sweats the worker in England'. Readers were urged to vote for Alf Cobb in the municipal elections.

The November *Citizen* advertised speakers, including Quelch, at the Electric Picture Palace, noted that the police ban on Ben Tillett had been thwarted by an 'immense and sympathetic' crowd, and proclaimed that 'over fifty percent of those present were associated with the local branch of the SDP'. It welcomed the new BSP and supported the SEFSS. Those who wanted municipal investment to tackle unemployment should vote for Cobb. The anxious Tories and Liberals put up a single candidate, yet Cobb lost by only thirty-three votes. In December, when he lost a by-election by thirty-two votes, a 'vast crowd of several thousand had gathered in Queen's Road to hear the result'. 'Groans and shouts of dismay greeted the declaration'; and his supporters carried him shoulder high. Sadly, he prosecuted a Tramway Company worker for overcrowding his vehicle, not the bosses whose policy it was, and he also attacked railway workers' strike leaders.[8]

Nationally, the 'Great Unrest' was well under way. In February 1912 a million miners went on strike and won. Their unofficial manifesto, *The Miners' Next Step*, argued that 'Political action must go on side by side with industrial action'. Labour MPs must be accountable, but the 'old policy of identity of interest between employers and ourselves' had to 'be abolished, and a policy of open hostility installed'.[9] Thirty-eight million strike days were recorded in 1912, and in 1913 real wages were almost back to 1900 levels. That June Meek was back in Eastbourne, but in January 1914 he argued that votes for women was 'not a working class' measure. He was also against Labour policy on the sale of the local park, since the 'town' needed 'all the wealthy residents we can possibly get', though it felt strange to be working alongside Liberals and Tories.[10]

The high point of the Great Unrest came during the winter of 1913–14. Dublin was paralysed for six months by a lock-out of 20,000 workers, and over 9 million strike days were recorded in the first seven months of 1914. That March there had been another attempt by the International Socialist Bureau to forge unity on the British left, yet most socialists did not understand the class nature of the state, or the need for a revolutionary party, and many were pulled by Hyndman and Blatchford's idea of a 'national' socialism. In August Meek urged Eastbourne hoteliers to employ Englishmen who were unfit for active service instead of 'aliens'. He also tried to enlist; but, predictably, he was rejected because of his poor eyesight.[11] Late that year even Alf Cobb was pulled into the bosses' 'Great War'.[12] So was one of the possible models for Harlow.[13] The overwhelming majority of European reformist socialists got behind 'their' states. On that issue, Mugsborough was everywhere, too. A few 'advanced' workers were open to Bolshevik ideas in Glasgow, Manchester, South Wales and London; but the BSP had declined from 376 to 85 branches with 1,100 members, and 'the study of Marxism had been negligible'.[14]

A remarkable human document

In August 1910 Kathleen Noonan had begun teaching what she called 'subnormal children' at her aunt Mary Jane's Registered School for the Blind at 48 Kenilworth Road, St Leonards. Jennie's husband, J.B. Meiklejon, may have come down in the world, but she was also Principal of a 'Special Affiliated School for the Feeble Minded' at 37 Carrisbrooke Road. Kathleen fell in love with their son, but recalled that her aunt 'did not approve of cousins marrying'. So Paul and his sister Ruby convinced her 'that it was better to work for strangers and be properly paid rather than remain at home for practically nothing', then 'got busy and found me a job' as a 'nursery governess for a little girl'. By spring 1913 she was working in North Finchley. Paul worked in London as an actor, and they met on her day off. But in June his family paid his fare to Canada and gave him a small allowance, 'just enough to prevent him from making any real effort'. By August Kathleen had moved across North Finchley to be nurse to the Mackinlays' five children, but 'Mrs M. knew I would only be with them until Paul sent for me'.

Kathleen kept her father's manuscript at the bottom of her trunk in the Japanned tin box he had made for it – one 'like cash boxes', with a handle on the top. It was 'just my treasured possession'. One day Mrs Mackinlay saw the box, 'asked if it was full of treasure' and was allowed to take a look. Kathleen was always referred to as 'Miss Noonan', and ate with the family. One day, Jessie Pope took afternoon tea. Miss Pope was a professional journalist and writer of children's books, and had rooms or a flat next door. Kathleen remembered her as a 'small, neat person'. Young Alison Mackinlay recalled

> a very vivid character who managed to produce humorous verse for *Punch* while living in rather drab surroundings looking after an ailing and aged mother. She was unable to pronounce her 'R's' but would repeat 'Round the ragged rocks the ragged rascal ran' to amuse the children.

Miss Pope was told about the manuscript, asked to see it, became enthusiastic, and took it away to read. She later claimed she 'consented without enthusiasm' to read this 'work of a socialistic house-painter', 'expecting to be neither interested nor amused', but found she 'had chanced upon a remarkable human document'.[15] Her cousin, Pauline Hemmerde, the 'innocently adoring and too often unpaid secretary' of an 'under-capitalised' publisher, suggested Pope should offer him the book.[16]

Thomas Franklin Grant Richards was born in Glasgow in 1872. He was the son of a university lecturer, and was educated at the City of London School. In 1888 he started work in wholesale publishing, and later moved to the *Review of Reviews*; but in 1896 he set up as a publisher with £1,400 borrowed from relations. He wanted George Bernard Shaw on his list, but the Fabian dramatist insisted that *Plays Pleasant and Unpleasant* be printed by unionised labour. Richards 'had few notions of what made a Union house', yet his sympathies were 'all left-wing'. He bought the radical Liberal *Star*, and even the socialist *Justice*, though that felt like 'committing a crime against the State'. So he agreed. However, he was in the habit of giving large commissions, and inviting people to expensive restaurants, and by April 1905 he was bankrupt. The firm was put in his wife's name and he 'reached what seemed to be the end' of his 'Socialist interests'. In fact he praised Edward Clark, who 'ran some good cargoes of printed matter' for him during a strike, though 'many strikers had bloody knuckles as the result of attempting to stop him'.[17]

melancholy maudlin manner'.[28] She also standardised ironic capitals, tinkered with vocabulary and punctuation, and made workers' speech more 'illiterate'. 'He's' became 'E's' and 'The Pandorama' became 'The Pandoramer'. She bowdlerised inconsistently. 'Bloody' was often retained, but 'b——r' was either left out, or became 'swine', 'bleeder', 'damn' or 'blighter'. 'Gord' went; but 'Christ', 'Damn' and ''ell', often stayed. The Semi-drunk's 'dreadful expression' became 'something', and 'orf 'is bleedin' perch' is rendered, banally, as 'into the roadway'.

The bourgeoisie is let off lightly. Didlum's repossessed furniture, and his purchases from Sheriff's sales are screened, as is his exploitation of women homeworkers. Grinder has no monopoly of greengrocery whole-saling, or the power to smash uncooperative retailers. The leading capital-ists' control of the press is censored, and their ignorance of astronomy vanishes into thin air. References to stolen venetian blinds and a table go missing. Rushton's attempt to seduce Miss Wade is veiled. Frankie receives no information about 'Idlers' and 'bejewelled loafers' with signs of 'drunk-enness', or the fact that some women 'tried to conceal the ravages of vice and dissipation by coating their faces with powder and paint'. The Semi-Drunk's support of the brewery industry is halved: the 'Old Dear' no longer gives tick; and the narrative voice's anger at those who 'have the insolence' to say that drink was the cause of poverty evaporates.

Bodily functions are eliminated. The 'Art of Flatulence' and Belcher's 'chronic flatulence' are blown away. Cross does not go to the toilet, farting is not allowed, and the excrement-smeared card which put Rushton off his breakfast is wiped, as is Charley's blood, 'oozing from the broken heel of his boot'. Easton's moustache, 'stuck together with saliva and stained with beer', is shaved. Details of poisons and prostitution are censored, as is the court judgment that a worker's suicide was caused by 'Temporary Insanity'. References to a 'corfin plate' and wages for lifting corpses, and details of the pauper funeral, are buried.

Religious hypocrisy is whitewashed. Frankie's education about the vicar, and the subversive behaviour of Jesus, are spirited away. Owen's disbelief in an 'individual god' is left in, but his spirituality, looking at the stars, is left out. The exploitation of the chapel cleaner is brushed under the carpet. The clergyman's thirty shillings for four burials a day, and his unclean linen, are laundered. Rev. Starr's 'bolstering up the characters of the despicable crew of sweaters and grinders' who paid him four guineas a day, and the description of them as 'a pack of wolves', are muzzled.

Hunter and Slyme are protected from scorn when at chapel. Slyme's seduction of Mrs Easton fails, so their child has to go, too. Hospital collection boxes, which workers fill for fear of being 'marked', disappear. The sarcastic chapters on the church-run jumble sale, the Organised Benevolent Society and the Distress Committee interrogation, are all removed. So Noonan's crucial demonstration of the systematic links between the Church of England, charity and the capitalist clique are broken.

Local politics are made less corrupt. Sir Graball D'Encloseland's 'Great Speech' goes unreported, as does his huge salary and Lord Ammonegg's rewards for 'consideration of other considerations'. The 'Forty Thieves' nickname vanishes. So does the 'Band', and its monopoly over the mayoral role thanks to a 'community composed for the most part of ignorant semi-imbeciles, slaves, slave-drivers and psalm-singing hypocrites'. The plants taken for councillors' gardens, the fattened-up ducks and geese for their tables, and the fact that such 'Daylight robberies were of frequent occurrence', are unaccountably mislaid. Out go the Kiosk scam, 'Vive la System', and the 'secret council of war' over the Electric Light Co. and Gas Company. Dr Weakling's opposition becomes febrile.

Street politics are policed. 'The March of the Imperialists' chapter heading is halted, and backward workers no longer oppose a halfpenny rate for tackling child poverty. There is no diatribe against 'monopolists of intelligence' and the 'very tall, thin man's' knowledge of parliamentary procedures is guillotined. The 'man with the red tie' no longer wants to soak 'Specimens of Liberal and Conservative upholders of the Capitalist System, 20 century' for 'a month or two in petrifying liquid', then hang them in a chamber of horrors. Harlow and Philpot threaten no violence. The renegade socialist's racist view of workers as 'wild beasts', 'on a level with Hottentots', goes unchallenged. Police harassment, and Owen's beating, are hushed up, but his social isolation is increased. His and Nora's open-minded position on Sunday schools, and the preparations for Frankie's visit, are spirited away. Mutual affection is minimised. Frankie does no chores, and shows no knowledge of socialist books, let alone a keenness to put them to work. Owen's domestic competence is sidelined. His ineligibility for the sick benefit club, and his response to advice about the unaffordable diet for his illness, disappear. Crucially, his link between 'Christian Duty' and capitalist property is broken.

Most of Noonan's sharpest attacks on employers' hypocrisies are blunted. Out go the passages on 'hands and brains' and 'Eat dirt, or eat nothing'. The fear caused by Rushton and Hunter's underhand practices disappears, as does Crass's vulnerability to replacement and the economic rivalries between workers. Most of summer goes, too, with the pressure to take on extra jobs and scamp them, and winter gets longer. Building-site eating arrangements and the worst working conditions are tidied away. Leaky drainpipes, 'saturated with fetid moisture and a stench as of a thousand putrifying corpses', are stopped up. The potential monopoly of air vanishes, as does the general speed-up as competition tightens. Above all, the repeated injunctions to 'Blame the system' are silenced.

Ball thought Pope was a Fabian socialist,[29] but Mike Smith-Rawnsley has found no evidence of her membership.[30] However, the 'revolutionary' Barrington vanishes altogether, and 'the Socialist group' at the Beano is reduced to Owen. 'The Great Oration' is cut by two-thirds, and there is no call to 'fill the House of Commons with Revolutionary Socialists'. Out go crucial links to 'The Great Money Trick', and to the role of education under capitalism. There is no description of how life could be in a socialist society, or of what would happen to the workshy. Owen's summer agitation, the Socialist Van's converts and its dogged persistence, never happen. The shootings at Belfast and Featherstone – even the character Sir Featherstone Blood – go unreported, as does the comment that such state-sponsored killings happened 'not once, but many times'. References to 'lazy' Labour MPs are impermissible. Finally, Noonan's optimistic conclusion is replaced by a scene from Chapter 34, where Owen, depressed by the misery around him, contemplates homicide, infanticide and suicide. So the 'imbecile system of managing our affairs' gets away with murder.

By 3 November Pope had met 'Miss Noonan' again, and was satisfied that

> her father was the character Owen in the book, that he followed the same trade – endured even greater privations – until his death three [sic] years ago. She said perhaps he had greater advantages than other workmen in the matter of education, but as he started his apprenticeship at 16 – and worked as a house-painter and decorator for various firms from that time till his death, without any outside support, I think his advantages must have been natural ones. In any case the book is the book of a working man pure and simple – there is nothing whatsoever scholarly about it – the work of a man who knows nothing really about the better classes – but a great deal about his own.[31]

Kathleen told Pope about Sir Samuel Croker, but 'I don't think she paid much attention to what I was saying – probably thought I was romancing'.

Unpleasant but fascinating

Pope's mangled version of The Ragged Trousered Philanthropists was probably completed by February 1914, and it was printed at the Mercat works, Edinburgh, for cheapness' sake. On 14 April Richards told Kathleen it was 'very important for the sale of the book that you should not see any writer from newspapers about it. It is not likely that they will find you, but if they did, please refuse point blank to see them.' Pope was 'most emphatic' about that, too. The book was published on 23 April, the day that Richards' successful divorce (on the grounds of his wife's adultery) appeared in The Times.[32] On 27 April he sent Kathleen 'a sheet that shows all that I am proposing to say about your father. But unless I am asked for further information I see no particular reasons in the circumstances for giving it.' He added: 'so far the reviews have been excellent in almost every case. The critics who have not liked the book must have been pur-blind or influenced in some way in their personal feelings.' 'Your cheque shall be sent to you next week.'

Richards' press release claimed that 'Robert Tressall was born in Ireland in 1871'. He told the Daily Chronicle that the author was a 'builder's labourer':

> He was often out of work, often starving, but he found time during some five years to write one of the most arresting and remarkable stories that has ever found their way into a publisher's office.
>
> 'The writer died some years ago,' Mr Richards continued, 'and he left the MS. containing some 500,000 words, to his daughter, a children's nurse. One day she showed it to her mistress, who, struck by the intense reality of the story, passed it on to Miss Jessie Pope ... She asked me to look at it. I confess that I delayed the reading — the length rather frightened me. But when at last I decided to tackle it I was amazed and delighted, and deeply sorry when I came to the end of the tale. It is full of the most intense pathos, yet rich in humour. But it is the work of a rebellious man — a man who rebelled against the rich, the capitalists, the Church.'

The manuscript had been 'reduced to the limitations of the ordinary 6s. novel.'

> But with the exception of the toning down of some of the language used by certain of the characters, not a line of it has been altered, and in this it differs widely from the volumes supposed to have been written in similar circumstances, which are so often faked. Even the title was Mr Tressal's [sic] invention.

It would have been hard to include more weasel words, half-truths and lies in so short a space. But the working-class author was dead, his child had been fobbed off, and Richards knew his market.

The Ragged Trousered Philanthropists was reviewed by over twenty national and provincial papers. The London Observer assumed it was autobiographical. The Saturday Review believed it to be 'a plain, unvarnished picture of the real labourer', and 'the actual record of hard experience'. The Daily Chronicle noted the 'Grim actuality' and felt workers' speech was 'reproduced with almost phonographic fidelity'. The book 'depicted the manners and customs of the wage-earning class with a frankness which might be called brutal, if the author was not one of themselves'; but the 'life of the skilled workman is not so black, certainly he is not so servile and dependent upon the good will of the employer and his foreman as the dead hand has painted'.

The Nation agreed: 'if the author was born into this mean environment, which we question, in spirit and in intellect he is entirely alien from the Mugsborough scheme of life'; while the Sunday Times deprecated 'the fallacy too often to be remarked in street-corner oratory that the workman's is the only really productive class in the state'. The Dundee Advertiser denied that 'employers are all conscious cheats', and that 'workmen who disagree with his hero are fools':

> None of them is a living being. The hero himself is not a man, but a lecture decorated with legs and other human attributes. Mr Tressall's sympathy with his fellows is a thing of the intellect; it arises from a creed, not from his anguished feelings.

So the paper damned the author's 'intellectual arrogance'.

However, the New Weekly experienced 'a painful scraping sense of fact'; The Christian World saw a 'challenge to Things as They Are'; and The Northern Whig found the book 'exaggerated, biased, in many ways untrue', but

> Its significance lies in the fact that it is an indictment by a class which undoubtedly believes it, and which is growing in power and in numbers, and who sooner or later, unless it is falsified, not merely by argument but by fact, will rise against what they believe misrule.

The Charity Organisation Review felt that 'this revolt against the wage system means a new phase in the collectivist doctrine'; and the Daily News and Leader found it 'impossible to read the book without sympathy with the most revolutionary ideas'.

Reviewers disagreed about the book's form. The Daily Sketch found it 'Formless and without a connected story', so it 'can hardly be called a novel. It is, rather, a series of character studies, conversations and incidents', though 'depicted with the minute exactitude Tolstoy employed'. In the *Edinburgh Review* Walter De La Mare praised 'a piece of pitiless satire that would hardly disgrace Flaubert'. Others were reminded of Swift, and one praised the author for having 'avoided altogether the pretentiousness and literary affectation that betrayed, for example, Mr H.G. WELLS' bath-chairman, MEEKS [sic]'. The *Review of Reviews* was 'doubtful whether any book, excepting perhaps *The Jungle*, can compare with this'. The *Scotsman* welcomed a 'human document' which 'rivals in interest Mr Patrick Mac-Gill's', but was 'more persistently and more ruthlessly realistic'.

One reviewer noted that some chapters 'have a suspicious resemblance to propagandist pamphlets'. The *Manchester City News* wondered 'whether or not a literary hoax has been perpetrated', while *The Times Literary Supplement* believed the 'tirades and dinner-hour lectures are unmistakably culled from newspapers or Socialist pamphlets'. The *Daily News and Leader* felt it was 'really a tract in favour of Socialism, and has the faults of a tract', since it 'misses the effect of reality, much as Dickens' "Hard Times" does, through overstatement'. Yet to the *Daily Telegraph* it was 'about as much fiction as is Defoe's "Journal of the Plague Year"'. It was 'terrible, but convincing; unbelievably sad, but suggestive', 'unpleasant, but fascinating'.

In the *Star* and *Birmingham Daily Gazette* James Douglas reminded readers that though this was 'a novel, and not a Blue-book', it was 'a real slice of life cut fresh from the loaf by a worker who had been through the mill', and was 'unmistakably based upon actual experience'. 'Slowly the workers are becoming articulate', and the navvy McGill and the painter 'Tressall' 'represent the new workman who is taking the place of the old workman', since they were 'not willing to put up with the hardships and privations and perpetual risks'. However,

> The painters who are described so realistically by Mr Tressall would doubt-less be rejected as gross caricatures by half the painters in this country ... He takes the employer at his worst, the foreman at his worst, and the journeyman at his worst. Trade unionism has raised the status of the painter far above these workers ... [W]e realise that Rushton & Co., Builders and Decorators, are not a Union house; and we see the need for trade unionism as an instrument for maintaining as well as raising wage-rates ... Nobody ought to lack food in a country which is teeming with superfluous wealth.

It was, nonetheless, 'an ugly slice of life'.

'Mr Tressall' was an enigma. The *Glasgow Evening News* assumed that com-pulsory education had made him 'arrestingly articulate. No such book could have been written thirty years ago.' *The Spectator* deprecated 'unbalanced discussions', but if 'the modern dislike of idealism is to be gratified, the story may be considered a masterpiece'. *The Nation* hailed the book's innovative tactics, but noted that whatever did not suit the socialist case was excluded:

> It is the portrait of British workmen of a generation back, foul-mouthed and beery, obfuscated and hide-bound, the product of generations of mean environments ... the author does not pretend to bring on the Mugsborough scene the higher type of Trade Unionists, the North-country artisans, but merely the rank and file of spiritless employees in a dreary town where there is chronic distress and unemployment every winter, and typical 'sweated industries'.

It was nothing less than 'A SOCIALIST NOVEL'.

Yet the reformist socialist *Daily Herald* and *Reynolds News* ignored the book, and Winifred Blatchford complained in the *Clarion* about its 'lack of genius' and 'lack of skill in storytelling and construction'. However, to Vanners

> now endeavouring to bring the British working man a few economic facts I recommend a day's reading of 'The Ragged Trousered Philanthropists'. It will prove invaluable, I am sure, and one or two chapters would be useful if read aloud from the platform of our new and handsome Van. Recommend particularly 'The Socialist Van', 'The Wise Men of the East', 'The Colony', and 'The Great Oration'.

The latter and 'The Oblong' would 'make splendid pamphlets'. Tom Johnson, writing in the Glasgow *Forward*, had thought the author was either Jack London or H.G. Wells. He felt this 'Book for the Foreman and the Boss' was a fitting successor to Blatchford's *Britain for the British*, and that its 'shocking realism' would leave 'My friend, the Capitalist' a 'changed man', if only the clergy would read out a chapter every Sunday.

The BSP's *Justice* felt that given 'the low level of culture in this country' it was 'not surprising that a genuine working-class literature is of tardy growth'.

> Of one thing we may be certain, however: when the new literature does arise, when the working men begin to write really great books, the motive will be found in Socialist criticism, and the inspiration in the Socialist ideal.

RTP was 'the fiery vengeance of a man whom Reality has put to the most exquisite torture', but whose 'realism has nothing cold-blooded about it'. There was a 'note of despondency', and 'the author's outlook might have been brighter had his lot been cast among a better organised section of the working class', yet his book came 'right out of the ranks of the workers themselves'.

But where was it going? The *Daily Chronicle* noted that the author 'fulminates even more strongly against his own class', but doubted that Mugsborough 'remained unaffected by the trade union movement'. The 'Socialistic preaching which pervades the book is vivid enough', though 'not altogether directed against the arch enemy, the capitalist and employer'. The *Observer* deprecated 'the pathetic Socialist programme that his author brings into every other chapter', while the *Athenaeum* commended his book 'to the sociologist and the politician alike'. The *Glasgow Evening News* believed it illustrated 'the lives of a large proportion of the men who paper and paint our houses at this season', and expected sales of ten thousand, while the *New Witness* hoped for 'tens of thousands'. The *Tatler* noted 'language at which the genteel will shudder', so RTP was 'not for un-imaginative people whose sensitive, silly heads are buried under the sand'. The *Saturday Review* called it 'a clarion call to working men to arouse themselves from their lethargy, take stock of their position, think, act'. Indeed, it was 'likely to do a great deal of harm if placed in the hands of un-educated or half-educated people'. Hastings newspapers seem to have ignored the book completely.

RTP's retail price of six shillings (30p) was equivalent to ten hours' wages for many skilled workers, but Richards' and Pope's main target market was probably the radical petty-bourgeoisie. The book was reprinted in May 1914, using thinner, cheaper paper, and became one of twenty nominations for the 'best novel of 1914' among readers of 'an intelligently edited periodical', though Conrad's *Chance* was the eventual winner. Richards noted that 'in its first three months it sold in England one thousand seven hundred and fifty-two copies' of two thousand put on the UK market, 'Then it died. In America it had the same fate.'[33]

Maynard Dominick, one of Richards' 'warmest friends', 'appeared on the scene'. He 'had a nose'. He 'read the subversive story, and, in spite of the fact that the conditions with which it dealt were English and had not even a superficial likeness to the conditions then obtaining in America, he arranged to publish it'.[34] In May 1914 Frederick A. Stokes of New York added a hyphen to the title and published *The Ragged-Trousered Philanthropists* under his own copyright, with 'All rights reserved', but with no printer's name. Upton Sinclair 'recognised its quality'.[35] Lucian Cary in *The Dial* thought the book too hard on working men – 'incapable of revolt he is

not'; and in The New Republic, Randolph Bourne stressed its international
relevance. That July an advertisement in the Socialist Party of America's
International Socialist Review quoted Robert Hunter's praise for 'the most remarkable human document that has appeared in my time', 'a masterpiece
of realism' ahead of Zola, Tolstoy, Gorky and London. It cost $1.25; but
in August ISR offered a copy and a year's subscription for $1.50, and it
was used in SPA training classes.[36] 'Richards sold fourteen hundred copies
to the Colonies apart from Canada', where Macmillan's sale 'amounted to
two hundred and fifty',[37] while William Tyrell in Toronto sold copies of
the US edition.

In June 1914 Kathleen had sailed from Bristol, and reached Paul
Meiklejon at Regina in Saskatchewan on 1 July. They married four days
later by special licence. On 4 August war was declared, 'everything closed
down', and Paul was 'Out of work'. By 1915 Kathleen was so hard up that
one trunk containing 'books, photographs, mss letters &c' from her father,
and 'probably, the copy of the "Evening Ananias" and other material', was
left at Winnipeg station when she 'could not afford to pay the storage
charges'. By then, RTP's overall sale of 3,400 copies was over eight times
higher than that of Joyce's Dubliners;[38] similar sales would have brought
him £87 (almost £4,000 at today's prices). In the UK Richards found that
the Great War 'killed every English novel of the season'.[39] That wasn't all
it killed, of course; but probably not many British Tommies thumbed this
expensive novel under shellfire in the Flanders trenches.

Alongside Marx and Paine

The Ragged Trousered Philanthropists did reach some working-class readers. Before
she sailed to Canada Kathleen Noonan gave one of her six complimentary
copies to the Cruttendens (which Edward later donated to Hastings Socialist
Library), and a May 1914 edition to Hugh Beney, her former landlord's
son at 241 London Road. Noonan's apprentice, Cradduck, heard Adams &
Jarrett workers 'talking about Tressell's book and tittering amongst themselves' soon after it was published;[40] though not every building worker
was enthusiastic about how the book represented 'us in Hastings'.[41]
However, a Bexhill man's borrowed copy 'laid the foundation of my
understanding of how the present system works and how terribly waste-
ful it is of peoples lives', and made him hope for the return of a Labour
government.

RTP got further afield than Sussex. A man from the SDP, ILP and Clarion Van tradition in Kent, 'could never stop talking about' it to his daughter. The 'literature Sec' at the Socialist Club in Pilgrim Street Arcade, Newcastle, got Charley Hall's father a copy, and from 1915 the ILPer saw himself as a Marxist.[42] Les Moss, then a young engineer in London, recalled how Wal Hannington would 'preach Marxism to us nearly through the night', so 'we hardly did any work'. Hannington brought him the *Communist Manifesto*, took him to BSP meetings and suggested he borrow RTP from the 'library'. Les read it, 'got much more interested and started to get the historical understanding of movements'. Later, he joined the Communists.[43]

Richard Coppock was a Manchester bricklayer, and Literature Secretary of the Openshaw Socialist Society, where he got hold of a copy of RTP. In 1916 he became divisional organizer of the Operative Bricklayers' Society, and by 1920 he was General Secretary of the National Federation of Building Trade Operatives. Jack Wills and George Hicks, both London bricklayers and 'keen industrial unionists', were 'among the first to be stirred by this book, and to make use of it to bring better and more militant trade union organisation into the life of the building workers'.[44] Hicks was an SPGBer for a time; but he was elected national organizer of the OBS in 1912, and then General Secretary in 1919, when he was also president of the NFBTO. In Scotland, building worker and guild socialist Jim Beveridge had a copy of RTP, and 'brought it alive' for Jennie Lee, the daughter of a Cowdenbeath miners' union activist and ILPer, who soon had his own copy in a glass cabinet in the parlour, alongside Marx and Paine.[45]

By 1916 the book was being used by socialist propagandists in London. One Sunday, teenager H.B. Thomas bought a copy at a meeting in Finsbury Park. He had read *Merrie England*, but this novel 'was 'both a revelation and an inspiration', and he joined the Herald League.[46] Another teenager heard of the book from the League. His father's East End barber shop was 'a sort of local political rendezvous', and RTP was an 'ideal book to enlighten the masses on their conditions, their cause and cure'. BSPer Abe Levy worked in a well-organised tailoring factory. He noticed that one apprentice read during the dinner break, rather than playing football, and 'very diffidently' offered him *Call of the Wild*, *The Iron Heel* and *The Jungle*. Hymie Fagan recalled:

> he touched very carefully on the lessons to be learned from them and the importance of trade unionism for the working man. He also spoke of Socialism, and slowly broke down all the prejudices which had been built up by school, the synagogue, the Mirror and the comics.

Then came *The Ragged Trousered Philanthropists*. As soon as he was sixteen Fagan joined the union. Later, he joined the Communists.[47]

As the war drew to an end an apprentice in a Sussex joiners' shop found that most of the 'elderly men' were in the Amalgamated Society of Carpenters, Cabinet Makers and Joiners, and 'one or two of these were Socialists'. 'Political arguments followed the lines' of *The Ragged Trousered Philanthropists*, and 'it was during one of these that the book was mentioned and later lent around among some of the men'. The apprentice joined the union. A conscientious objector loaned his copy to a friend, who was convinced it had been 'expurgated'; but he 'used repeatedly to quote large chunks from it', so his 9-year-old daughter 'knew quite a lot by heart before ever I read the book myself'. A Belfast apprentice ship's joiner was loaned a copy by a tradesman who had spent his war years in a torpedo factory in Greenock. For him and his mates 'it certainly was a turning point in our life'. Four years later he went to Cammell Laird in Birkenhead and became shop steward. A Shropshire activist in the Amalgamated Society of Engineers talked about 'what a tremendous book' it was, and understood that the original title was *The Ragged Arsed Philanthropists*. His son read his 'much thumbed, borrowed copy', and that led him on to *Capital*.

6

Pope's bloody mess-up of the work

Cutting politics while retaining the socialism

In 1915 Edward Arnold's representative was buttonholed by Mr Hardie of
the Reformers' Bookstall in Glasgow about RTP: 'Now there's a book of
which I could easily sell any number you like.' Harry Clifford told Grant
Richards, who, knowing that 'my Mr Dracott' would visit Glasgow, 'said
nothing and awaited events'. Hardie ordered 'a very large number'.[1] But
to retail at a shilling it had to be further 'condensed';[2] and Pope refused
a £5 fee, so the project stalled.[3] That January Richards had published *Jessie
Pope's War Poems*, and reprinted it twice by March. *More War Poems* followed.
One poem attacked food profiteers, but she told young men, 'Get to work
with a gun',[4] then worked with the war-blinded.[5] Wilfred Owen dedicated
his savage anti-war poem 'Dulce et Decorum Est', 'To Jessie Pope etc.' in
draft, but that became 'To a certain Poetess' in print.[6]

In 1917 Richards claimed he had not reissued *The Ragged Trousered Philanthropists* because 'paper was short and money for publishers scarce'; yet
knowing how 'money talks' he borrowed enough to buy paper for 50,000
copies of Bruce Bairnsfather's *Bullets and Billets*.[7] Frank Cooper recalled that
William Watson, president of the London Workers' Committee, told him
'on several occasions that he was personally responsible for the approach
to Jessie Pope' for the 're-compiling' of RTP;[8] but Watson was widely
suspected of being a Scotland Yard informer, and he may have lied. What
probably got Richards going was the October Russian Revolution, and the
release of the Clydeside political prisoners.

The 're-compiling' began late in 1917 or early 1918. Pope intended to 'cut out most of the *political* discussions', but 'retain much of the matter referring to Socialism'.[9] She kept 90,000 words, or just over one-third of the manuscript, so the thirty-six chapters of 1914 became twenty-five. The capitalist 'System' is made less systematic. Mugsborough politics, religious hypocrisy and monopoly are virtually eradicated. There is less of the 'usual reign of terror'. But Owen is more isolated, and still thinks about suicide at the end. This doubly mediated book was published in May 1918, claiming to be 'Reprinted' from the 1914 edition. Reportedly, Watson was outraged by Pope's cutting of 'the most important chapter of all, that on religion', and railed at her 'bloody mess-up of the work'.[10]

The shilling 1918 edition 'sold in scores of thousands at the various branches of the Reformers' Bookstall', and in Henderson's 'Bomb Shop' in London,[11] where one criterion ruled the choice of books:

> They must be rebel. Rebel a thousand years ago, rebel yesterday, rebel since lunch: not yet rebel at all, but likely to be rebel next week: rebel in politics, rebel in sex, rebel in religion – anything anyhow or anywhere rebel, anything smelling or tasting of rebel (even if a bit anachronistically) at once qualified for inclusion.[12]

As Victor Gollancz knew to his own cost, the Home Office kept an eye on the place. Yet Richards was always very keen to 'correct an impression' that the book was '"expurgated" for political reasons'.

> No such thing has occurred, but the first edition was 400 closely-printed pages and to reprint it at a low price was impossible. It was, therefore, condensed, but no political consideration was even thought of. 'The work was done reverently, the editor never losing sight for a moment of the spirit that animated the dead author'.[13]

Probably only he and Pope had read the entire manuscript, so he could lie with confidence. In any case, working-class access to socialist literature remained patchy. In a survey of the reading habits of six hundred adult manual workers in Sheffield, nobody mentioned Marx or Engels, let alone *The Ragged Trousered Philanthropists*.[14]

In October 1918 the 'abridged' edition was reprinted by W.H. Smith & Son on even thinner, cheaper paper, but still cost a shilling. (This time, the 1914 edition was not mentioned.) It could be had 'through the ordinary channels of the book trade, including the shops and stalls of Messrs W.H. Smith & Son', but also 'through the Socialist and Labour organisations of the country'. Richards named the Reformers' Bookstalls at Bradford,

Swansea, Glasgow and Paisley; the National Labour Press in Manchester and London EC; the BSP in Salford; Leicester ILP; the Scottish Co-operative Wholesale Society in Glasgow; the Builders' Workers' Union in Bermondsey; and Henderson's, Charing Cross Road, London WC.

Richards found that 'Ordinary bookshops sold it scarcely at all', but the *Herald* network 'assisted in its sale to the best of its ability', and a book which 'had hardly done more than pay the expenses of its production and its share of establishment charges, became suddenly a great success' in the UK, though in 'America there was no parallel revival'.[15] A journalist recalled that 'immediately following' the Great War,

> browsers in 'progressive bookshops', particularly in the north of England, came across a rather plebeian-looking book. Its price was a shilling, its pages just under 250, its paper was wartime worsted. But its title at once held the eye ... The book struck rather a new note, or rather an old note with a more urgent ring.

British troops were on their way home.

Len Green was in Portsmouth Hospital, and one of the orderlies said:

> 'When I come back from my leave I'll bring you a book back. It's called *The Ragged Trousered Philanthropist.*' Well, that didn't mean a thing to me. But he started to tell me about different parts of the book, and then when he said something about an Absconding Secretary of the Light Refreshment Fund ... that jogged my memory.

Before the orderly returned Len was sent home; but he mentioned the 'ragged trousered bloke' and his sister-in-law 'went and got a copy' of RTP from W.H. Smith's stall on Hastings station, as a Christmas present:

> The wife read it out to me, and we stopped up nearly all Christmas Eve, listening, and I knew ... all the characters that he meant them to be ... I knew Bob Tressall wrote that book ... He didn't mean that they should have their real names there to embarrass their families.

The model for 'Old Philpot' claimed he had the 'very table' on which Noonan wrote, but he 'never knew he'd written a book' until Len 'lent it to him'. Len's copy became 'a bit of a wreck' from regular use.[16]

A Bolshevik rising was likely

Early in 1918 the Bolshevik ambassador, Litvinov, had been given a friendly reception at the Labour Party conference; but the party leaders dissociated themselves from Bolshevik aims and methods, and proclaimed that 'the

Labour Party is not a class party but a National Party'.[17] Even so, their
new programme, *Labour and the New Social Order*, took account of the leftward
movement among the membership. It promised legislation on factories,
public health, housing, education, a national minimum wage, workers'
representation on company boards, a capital levy, nationalisation and
municipalisation. The Social Revolutionary Kerensky had been in favour of
allowing Kornilov's counter-revolutionary cavalry into Petrograd during
the revolution, first to declare martial law, then to smash the soviets and
their democratically elected Bolshevik majorities before his own comrades
removed him from office. Yet he was invited by the Labour leader to the
Labour Party conference, and took the opportunity to smear the Bolsheviks as the vanguard of German imperialism.

The British left was all over the place. At his third attempt ILPer George
Meek had been accepted by the Royal Sussex Regiment Pay Corps, but
was soon transferred to the Reserves. He thought Germans were 'a race of
human vermin which must be crushed and deprived of all power for
evil', but he got no chance 'to give some unspeakable Fritz' what was
'coming to him' at the front. By 1918 he hoped German civilians were
starving, since they were 'our brothers', 'just as much (and no more) as
are the inmates of Broadmoor ... Barbary pirates and Arab slave-traders'.
He also criticised 'ILP weaklings' and 'their Russian friends Lenin and
Trotsky', for having 'done the cause of Socialism more harm than can be
cured for ages to come'. Rather than be 'honoured' by the Kaiser, Meek
preferred to 'hang with such men as Robert Blatchford'.[18]

In October 1914 BSPer Ben Tillett had somersaulted to support the war,
then went round 'demanding munitions for our fighting men', and re-
peating government propaganda about alleged German atrocities.[19] In June
1916 he was in Hyndman's pro-war faction in the BSP which split to form
the National Socialist Party, while remaining within the Labour Party, and
by 1917 he was Labour MP for North Salford. Tom Kennedy fought in
Italy, and after he was demobilised he became NSP General Secretary.
Noonan's pal Alf Cobb got to the front line in France, but fell down a
railway embankment during a battle and injured his head. By December
1918 he was back in Hastings, suffering from epileptic fits. Yet he argued
successfully for the welcome home fund to be given to war widows and
their children, was elected onto the committee of the National Federation
of Discharged and Demobilised Soldiers and Sailors, and built a sizeable
electoral base for the BSP among the 1,600 Hastings unemployed, many

of whom were ex-servicemen.[20] Green recalled that Cobb 'cornered' a 'big Liberal', and won him 'over to the Labour Party'. The two souls of Mugsborough socialism were pulling in markedly different directions.

By October 1918 the Head of Special Branch was clear that 'We cannot hope to escape some sort of revolution', and he anticipated 'no passionate resistance from anybody'.[21] In November Field Marshall Sir Henry Wilson told the Cabinet: 'Our real danger now is not the Boches but Bolshevism',[22] and the armistice was signed next day. The so-called 'Great War' cost 800,000 British dead. Two million had been wounded, 180,000 gassed, and thousands more shell-shocked. Two million war widows, orphans and parents received grossly inadequate pensions or allowances. The economic cost was £8.7 billion, and the national debt had risen more than tenfold to over £7.4 billion.

In December 1918 the Labour Research Department *Monthly Circular* noted:

Nov. 1. Austrian Revolution.
" 6. German Naval Revolt.
" 7. Bavarian Republic.
" 9. German Revolution. Swiss General Strike.
" 10. Dutch Labour Disturbances.
" 13. Danish ditto. Spanish movement to Revolution.
" 14. Labour Party Leaves Coalition.
" 17. Hungarian Republic.
" 18. Portuguese General Strike.
" 23. London Labour Demonstration Refused Albert Hall.
Dec. 1. " " " in Albert Hall.

The Electrical Trades Union had threatened to cut off the lights for a victory ball unless the demonstration in favour of the Bolsheviks and the German Revolution went ahead. It did, and a 'Hands off Russia' Committee was funded by money Sylvia Pankhurst brought from Russia. The possibility of British workers getting all their own back was definitely on the cards.

At the hastily arranged 'Khaki Election' in December, and for the first time, all men over 21 were enfranchised, and about half of all women; yet under three-fifths of the new voters managed to exercise their right, and only a quarter of all soldiers, many of whom never received voting papers. In spite of that, Labour won 63 seats, compared to their previous 42, and their share of the vote trebled to 22 per cent. Even so, the Tories and their Liberal partners won comfortably. Many ILPers had a 'deep and ill-concealed contempt for ordinary people who were too "stupid" to recognise the abstract attraction of their socialism',[23] and their nickname for a conservative worker was 'ragged trousered philanthropist'.[24] Yet after the *Manchester Guardian* published the secret treaties released by the Bolsheviks, Field Marshall Sir Henry Wilson walked out of the Cabinet when it refused to contemplate that 'a Bolshevik rising was likely'.[25]

In January 1919 ten thousand troops went on strike and elected delegates at Folkestone. At Dover two thousand refused to sail to fight the Bolsheviks. At Osterley Park, soldiers commandeered army lorries, drove into London and marched down Whitehall in their uniforms, demanding their discharge. Up to eight thousand troops marched along Brighton seafront, and others demonstrated in Aldershot and Blackpool. Dominion troops took direct action. There were mutinies in the air force. At Milford Haven sailors ran up the red flag, and men at Rosyth refused to go to sea. Twenty thousand troops mutinied in France. Army and RAF top brass pretended that striking was not mutiny, and negotiated. After a show of force in Wales, Navy commanders followed suit. Trade unionists – including the South Wales Miners' Federation – showed solidarity, and the War Cabinet backed down. Demobilisation accelerated rapidly, and Churchill's anti-Bolshevik crusade was thwarted.[26]

Meanwhile, the Bolsheviks had announced that the Communist International would meet in March. The SLP committed itself to the dictatorship of the proletariat and to soviets, and tried to forge unity with the BSP and ILP. Economics linked to politics. A 'Hands Off Russia' conference was organised in London by the rank-and-file committee connected with the shop stewards' movement, and over five hundred delegates attended. Jack Murphy, chair of the Sheffield Workers' Committee, had now joined the SLP. He 'did not think that the revolution was on the door-step but I certainly thought it was somewhere down the street'.[27]

Ten thousand ex-soldiers were joining the job market every day when seventy thousand Glasgow engineering workers went on strike for a 40-hour week. BSPer Harry McShane recalled that when demonstrators got to Glasgow Green, police were 'lined up ready to attack us', but

> ex-servicemen pulled up the park railings, spikes and all, and the police ran for their lives. All over Glasgow, strikers went about cutting the trolley ropes and hundreds of immobilised trams blocked every route. Two policemen tried to intervene at the Saltmarket; the strikers stripped them and they had to run off naked.[28]

BSPer Willie Gallacher later admitted that a 'little more political understanding and a little less self-complacency would have been an advantage to the workers who were looking for leadership'. But they had 'no plan, no unity of purpose'.[29] First they were batoned, then they were jailed.

The key problem was the state. SLPer Tom Bell saw strikers marching through Glasgow, singing 'The Red Flag'; but next morning 12,000 troops

> occupied the city, including the post office and the electric power stations. Tanks were placed in the centre of the city and the market place in the East End. All the bridges over the canal and the river were occupied by soldiers, and for three days the town was practically under military control.[30]

The strike had just begun to spread into the Scottish coalfield, and delegates were sent to Belfast; but trade-union officials kept the struggle mainly within Glasgow. Gallacher later accepted

> we were strike leaders, nothing more; we had forgotten we were revolutionary leaders of the working class and while we cheered the flying of our flag, it had not for us the significant meaning it had for our enemies. They saw it as the symbol of an actual rising; we saw it as an incident in the prosecution of the strike.

'We were carrying on a strike when we ought to have been making a revolution.'[31]

Thanks to state pressure, the mismatch between mass organisations without socialism and small socialist groups without the masses was becoming increasingly clear. WSFer Harry Pollitt shared a platform with William Watson of the London Workers' Committee; but the state took confidence from the LWC's lack of mass support, raided its offices and charged Watson with sedition. Of course, only when Lenin wrote *The State and Revolution* (published in Russia in August 1917) did he fully grasp why Marx and Engels had argued for proletarian dictatorship after the bloody suppression of the Paris Commune. But it was 1919 before the BSP and SLP jointly published his book in English, and even then the BSPer and Scottish Workers' Committee organizer J.R. Campbell completely misread it as 'Lenin smashes Parliamentarianism'.[32] The Comintern met that March, but no British group was represented.

The ILP had lost ten thousand working-class members during the war; but after Labour's successes in the April 1919 local elections George Lansbury was enthused: 'The future is inevitably ours' and 'the next election will be our chance'.[33] This former SDFer, editor of the *Daily Herald* and founder of the Herald League, was being pulled by parliamentary reformism. Meanwhile, thousands of British soldiers had left their camps and returned home with their rifles and ammunition, and an interest in socialist ideas.

In May the *Daily Herald* published a War Office instruction requiring commanding officers to find out if troops would break strikes or parade for draft overseas, especially to Russia, and whether trade unionism had taken root. At Churchill's order, army officers were instructed to intercept the paper at railheads, so as to 'ensure that *no* copies are issued to the troops', but to do so with care: '*It is important that the collecting and burning of these papers involve as little publicity as possible.*' Yet the *Daily Herald* circulated 'underground' among troops in France, and published that War Office document in July.[34] In spite of all this, Ramsay MacDonald continued to argue that a parliamentary majority could 'proceed to effect the transition from Capitalism to Socialism'. He noted a station bookstall 'being used for the dissemination of leaflets on "Direct Action"', glanced at one, then 'laughed and wept at its rubbish'.[35] He completely failed to grasp the significance of the fact that the bookstall was in the middle of the Cairngorm mountains.

Caught on the ebb tide

By 1919 Bolshevik literature was reaching Britain. The BSP, SLP, WSF and South Wales Socialist Society met in London to discuss forming a united Communist Party, while the state went to great lengths to suppress Marxist ideas. Capitalists were happy to help. Shop stewards and 'literature sellers' were sacked wholesale from Vickers in Sheffield, though SLPers carried on propaganda in branches of the Plebs League.[36] This kind of Marxist 'study class' was a united front in which 'Socialists of every shade came together and worked harmoniously'.[37] The idea was taken up in factories. At a Slough engineering plant,

> Dinner-hour meetings and lectures on trade unionism and socialism became a daily feature and large quantities of socialist literature were sold. In several departments socialist book-clubs were organised in which groups of workers subscribed a shilling a week and drew lots to decide the week in which they would be entitled to receive and own a quantity of new books of their choice.[38]

The organizer was BSPer Wal Hannington. No doubt more copies of RTP found their place alongside Marx and Lenin.

In August 1919 the London and Liverpool police struck, demanding union recognition. Troops were called out, bayonets fixed, and tanks roamed the streets of both cities. There were reports of three warships anchored off Southend, and others were rushed to the Mersey from Scapa

Flow. It took mass sackings and the recruitment of unemployed ex-servicemen as scabs to smash both strikes. Meanwhile, the Triple Alliance of miners, transport and railway workers reappeared, led by ILP left-wingers like Robert Smillie, who recalled the prime minister's reasoning:

> 'I feel bound to tell you that in our opinion we are at your mercy. The Army is disaffected and cannot be relied upon. Trouble has occurred already in a number of camps. We have just emerged from a great war and the people are eager for the reward of their sacrifices, and we are in no position to satisfy them. In these circumstances, if you carry out your threat and strike, then you will defeat us.'
>
> 'But if you do so', went on Mr Lloyd George, 'have you weighed the consequences? The strike will be in defiance of the Government of this country and by its very success will precipitate a constitutional crisis of the first importance. For, if a force arises in the State which is stronger than the State itself, then it must be ready to take on the functions of the State, or withdraw and accept the authority of the State. Gentlemen', asked the Prime Minister quietly, 'have you considered, and if you have, are you ready?'

Smillie told Nye Bevan: 'From that moment on ... we were beaten and we knew we were.'[39] Both of them focused on the parliamentary road.

The British state was afraid of the rank and file. Scotland Yard's Director of Intelligence insisted that it 'must be remembered that in the event of rioting, for the first time in history, the rioters will be better trained than the troops'.[40] So while the government sent £100 million of 'London Gold' to support the counter-revolutionary generals in Russia, at home six million workers had their working hours reduced, without loss of earnings. Yet record numbers went on strike. Politically, there was some movement, too. The WSF had already applied for Comintern affiliation when, in October, the BSP followed suit. Unity negotiations dragged on; but in October and November there were two huge demonstrations in London against intervention in Russia. India was in revolt, and there was civil war in Ireland. Lenin was convinced that a pre-revolutionary situation existed in Britain.

In December, Gallacher and Campbell's pamphlet *Direct Action* was published by the Scottish Workers' Committee. It argued against the Bolshevik principle of the dictatorship of the proletariat, and for a national system of workplace committees linked to 'social committees' in working-class communities, whose 'ultimate function' would be to 'supersede the existing social organisation of capitalism' after a vaguely defined '*revolutionary struggle*'.[41] Revolutionary syndicalism seemed to work. That month railway workers won a strike, even with troops at stations, bridges and signal boxes. So as socialist organisations jockeyed for hegemony within the emergent Communist Party of Great Britain, many trade-union activists were more interested in the 35 million strike days that had been won that year.

Access to Bolshevik theory remained patchy. Harry Pollitt stored illegally printed copies of Lenin's *Appeal to the Toiling Masses* in his mattress, and 'each day took a supply to distribute amongst the workers in the docks and the shipyards' along the Thames. He knew it 'by heart', but 'had not yet had the opportunity of reading many of the basic works of Comrade Lenin'. However, SLPer Tom Bell advised him 'not only what to read of the Marxist classics then available for the first time, but how to read them'.[42] On the other hand, Socialist Prohibition Fellowship activist Bob Stewart said of the dictatorship of the proletariat: 'I don't know much about this and I don't think anyone else does here, but we know it is necessary.'[43] Sadly, such abject political dependence was all too common.

It was only during 1920 that Bolshevik and syndicalist ideas began fusing in practice. On 10 May London dockers and coal-heavers, led by Pollitt, stopped the *Jolly George* sailing for Poland with munitions for the anti-Bolshevik forces, and in June the WSF began calling itself the Communist Party. On 29 July parts of Lenin's *'Left-Wing' Communism: An Infantile Disorder* appeared in the BSP's *The Call*. The Communist Unity Conference took place on 30 July and 1 August; but the LWC and SWC, fearing it was 'going to be a glorified British Socialist Party', did not attend.[44] Neither did half the SLP, nor many members of the Herald Leagues. So the Communist Party of Great Britain began with just over five thousand members, half of them from London and Glasgow, and mostly from the BSP, ILP, WSF and SLP. They voted for the principle of the dictatorship of the proletariat, and the Comintern, yet they took into the CPGB much of the sectarianism that had bedevilled the British left since Noonan's day.

Meanwhile, the new TUC General Council, the Parliamentary Labour Party and the Labour Party had moved left. In order to put themselves at the head of working-class militancy they threatened a general strike against the government's warmongering in Ireland and its support for aggression against Russia, and set up three hundred and fifty Councils of Action. Field Marshall Sir Henry Wilson 'could not guarantee what would happen' if unprepared troops were sent into action against strikers.[45] Sir Robert Horne, the Minister of Labour and government 'strong man', 'never walked along Whitehall – sacred to the memory of Charles the Martyr – without paying very close attention to the lamp-posts'.[46]

Lenin was led to believe by ex-BSPers that the Councils of Action were soviets in all but name, but he argued that Communists should stand for parliament all the same. In September the CPGB voted in favour of seeking affiliation to the Labour Party, but only by 100 votes to 85. Tommy Jackson, former SPGB General Secretary, and one of the new party's foremost worker-intellectuals, told comrades he 'would happily take the Labour leaders by the hand as a preliminary to taking them by the throat'.[47] Such sectarianism was a godsend to Labour and trade-union leaders, who wanted nothing to do with revolutionaries. Unsurprisingly, the application was rejected; but the CPGB was unrepentant. *The Communist* announced: 'So be it. It is their funeral, not ours.'

Revolutionary syndicalism still appeared to work. Union membership reached over 6½ million in 1920, 2 million higher than in 1918, and more than 27 million strike days were recorded. Post-war wages rose in real terms by one-fifth, and a rail strike won a 48-hour week. But in September the state began planning for an emergency system of communications, the maintenance of essential services and the use of the army for strikebreaking. In December the CPGB leaders moved into their King Street headquarters, paid for with £24,000 from the hard-pressed Bolshevik government. Economic and political dependence fused.

Ex-SLPer Jack Murphy identified two key problems in the CPGB: the 'general political immaturity of the independent movement of the working class', and the fact that struggles 'grew spontaneously but were held back by sectarian ideas of the revolutionary leaders'.[48] In addition, Party members tended to be young, male and 'almost exclusively proletarian in character (too much so, in fact; with the added disadvantage of "anti-intellectualism").' Moreover, they 'had reached their appreciation of the social order more through their experience of working-class life and labour, than from theory.[49] The Party was 'so working-class that there was a real antipathy to what was termed "the intellectuals"' among many revolutionary syndicalists.[50] Turnover was considerable, and the original membership figure soon halved.

The strike wave continued in early 1921, but most struggles became defensive. Wages fell by one-fifth, and so did trade-union membership. In March an unemployed demonstration in Glasgow welcomed the Prince of Wales. A 'couple of thousand turned up and they were really wild, angry

men. Some of them were carrying hand-grenades they had brought back
with them from the front', and 'some even carried guns'.[51] In April the
coal owners locked out the miners and received state support. On the 4th
machine guns were posted at pitheads, and troops in working-class settle-
ments. On the 5th military leave was cancelled. On the 6th London parks
were commandeered for army camps; and on the 8th reservists were
called up. Then, on 15 April, 'Black Friday', the Triple Alliance leaders
called off a sympathetic strike. After that the Emergency Powers Act em-
powered non-unionised London police to club unemployed demonstrators with impunity. In the summer a severe economic downturn set in,
and unemployment rose to almost 10 per cent. The infant CPGB had been
caught on the ebb tide.

During 1922 the CPGB became economically and politically dependent
on Soviet Russia. Stalin became General Secretary of the Russian Communist Party in April; Lenin had his first stroke in May; and by August even
Trotsky was pessimistic about the likelihood of the revolution spreading
in the near future, though he and Lenin understood how vital that was.
Stalin and his allies built a network of supporters through the Comintern.
In Britain, a 'nucleus' was picked out, centring on ex-ILPer Palme Dutt,
with Salme Murrik acting as his political link to Moscow. Mikhail Borodin
('George Brown') reported to the Comintern on the CPGB, and noted its
failure to win union support, even though there had been 85 million
strike days in 1921, twice the previous record. By February 1922 Pollitt,
barely 31, was on the Comintern Executive.

The 'nucleus' quickly moved to 'Bolshevise' the CPGB. In February
1922 John Lewis, writing in *Plebs*, castigated the 'squabbling' 'intellectuals'. What was needed was training material aimed 'at helping those who
help the very ordinary and stupid worker'. Lewis wanted to 'banish everything but clear, positive and more or less assured results of study put in
so straightforward a form that *they are capable of being handed on* to the ordinary
man in a lecture'. In March, the night before the Party congress, Willie
Gallacher learned that some 'intellectuals', including members of the
Central Committee, had arranged to meet, so he went along and dispersed
them for acting like a faction. At the congress he proposed a Commission
on Organisation of three people chosen from outside the current leadership, and got his way. Dutt and Pollitt quickly marginalised Harry Inkpin.

Factions had been banned in the Russian CP 'for a brief period in 1921
by unanimous vote of the leadership, but only as an extreme measure

during an acute crisis'.[52] But in November 1922, ill as he was, Lenin exhorted non-Russian Communists to 'assimilate' the results of Russian experience, and not be 'content with hanging it in a corner like an icon and praying to it';[53] and in December he began opposing the growth of Stalin's power by writing a political 'Testament'. But then came his second stroke. Even so, by early 1923 Lenin was privately demanding Stalin's removal; but in March a third stroke took him out of politics altogether. By then the CPGB's *The Communist* had become the *Workers' Weekly*, edited by Dutt, and Gallacher's long-time ally, J.R. Campbell, was on the Central Committee. Throughout the Party the level of theoretical analysis and debate declined, while politically dependent super-activism flourished.

Books are weapons

The level of bigoted ignorance about Russia was enormous. Blatchford was barking that Bolsheviks were 'blood-thirsty savages'. (He ended up voting Tory).[54] ILPer George Meek saw no contradiction in being 'a class-conscious Socialist' and 'very much a race-conscious Englishman'; but he believed that the dispersal of the Constituent Assembly by the Bolsheviks represented 'tyranny' by 'a clique who have climbed into power by force and fraud on the backs of the working class'.[55] Meek evidently had no idea that the Bolsheviks had held the revolution back in July 1917, because they not won a majority in elections to the soviets, or that Social Revolutionaries keen on the Constituent Assembly had opposed it before the revolution, or that left-wing SRs had split away to join the Bolsheviks. During 1920 Meek condemned both war profiteers and miners who were 'never satisfied'; yet his own family depended on a small grant from the Royal Literary Fund, and Eastbourne notables supported his appeal to Lloyd George for a Civil List pension. When he died on 2 March 1921, no socialist organisation attended his funeral.[56]

Meanwhile, Hyndman slandered Lenin as a 'Communist Ivan the Terrible', and the Bolsheviks as 'Petrograd Butchers'.[57] Ben Tillett and Tom Kennedy voted against Communist affiliation to the Labour Party; and in 1921 Kennedy became Labour MP for Kirkaldy. The NSP sought to claim the heritage of the SDF by adopting the old name, but its politics bore almost no relation to those of the Marx-influenced organisation of which Noonan had been a member. However, in November 1920 Harry Pollitt had spoken on BSPer Alf Cobb's behalf during a Hastings Municipal election.[58] Cobb won easily, and created mayhem as long as his health allowed. When he died on 5 September 1921, his widow was adamant that the funeral procession should not start at the Town Hall steps, or include councillors; and the hundreds who followed Cobb's coffin yelled 'hypocrite' at the mayor and chief constable, all the way to his pauper's grave.[59]

What of Noonan's legacy? In September 1920 The Communist advertised copies of The Ragged Trousered Philanthropists at three shillings and sixpence – a hike of 350 per cent since 1918 – or fourpence more by post. On 24 November Grant Richards told Mrs Meiklejon in Canada that the 'cheaper' re-issue of the book 'has sold, and is still selling, well. When I am certain of your address I hope to be able to send you some additional payment'. Kathleen got £25, probably in 1921. That February W.H. Smith reprinted the 1918 version. It retailed at half a crown (2s 6d), or about two hours' pay for a labourer, and was on sale 'through the ordinary channels of the book trade', including W.H. Smith and the Socialist Labour Press, Glasgow, plus all the 'Socialist and Labour organisations of the country' mentioned in the 1918 edition. One of those, the 'Bomb Shop', now advertised itself in The Communist as 'Publishers and Booksellers to the Soviets of the World'. According to Gollancz, 'Henderson Senior, who officiated with two sons, looked exactly like Lenin; so much so indeed that a lot of people thought, after the November Revolution, that he was Lenin.'[60] And after all, Lenin insisted that books are weapons.

In January 1921 two middle-class intellectuals, Francis Meynell and Raymond Postgate, had left the Daily Herald, joined the CPGB and been put in charge of The Communist. Evidently Party chairman Arthur McManus 'didn't mind in the least' that Meynell was a Christian Socialist, 'knew no Communist dogma, had read no Marx or Engels, and had never heard of dialectical materialism'.[61] Most radicalised workers were in the same boat. In April Alice Pratt told Plebs readers that after she encountered Dietzgen's The Positive Outcome of Philosophy, she left 'feeling as though my brain had been stirred with a porridge spoon'. As she put it, the 'average man' needed something 'he can lap up with his Quaker oats – something he can read (and understand) as he runs'. A small book was 'more encouraging to beginners', written 'in language as simple as possible, consistent with the full text of the work'.

That July The Communist assumed that 'All who have read Robert Tressall's vivid story of working class life' would 'wish to possess a photograph of the author'. They happened to have some, postcard size, at threepence, or fourpence halfpenny by post, or a dozen for half a crown, post free. In September and November *The Communist* advertised RTP itself, and in January 1922 it noted bookshops where Communist publications could be bought. King Street, London, and West George Street, Glasgow, were Party offices. But the Herald League Bookshop in George Street, and the Reformers' Bookstall in Buchanan Street, Glasgow, were on Richards' list.

In June 1922 ex-ILPer Frank Horrabin did not mention RTP in 'A Short Syllabus on "Historical Materialism and Literature"' in *Plebs*; yet he encouaged young Communist Harry Wicks to read it.[62] The book was not on the 1923 Plebs syllabus, *What to Read: A Guide for Worker-Students*; but the son of a former president of both Cardiff Trades and Labour Council and Cardiff Labour ran a Saturday bookstall for the CPGB on the balcony of the city's Market Hall, and was 'at liberty to sell what I pleased in regards to progressive literature' to 'a number of advanced thinkers' from South Wales, including the miners' leader, A.J. Cook. The stock came from 'somewhere in London' – presumably the Workers' Bookshop. One item was RTP. The young Communist read it and realised he had had 'the same type of discussions with fellow workers who to my mind were extremely stupid'. The author 'obviously had advanced views for his time of life', and was 'very much portraying how things were', so the young man sold himself a copy.

The Ragged Trousered Philanthropists was finding readers in unlikely places. The Society Steward of a Methodist mission somehow bought ten copies for five shillings, and 'circulated them to friends and associates'. A teenager living in a Manchester slum thought she was 'very lumpen proletarian'; yet while she had read Morris, Barbusse, Marx, Engels, Lenin, MacGill and Sinclair, she found RTP 'seminal'. A Quaker and socialist couple who owned a factory in Edgbaston, Birmingham, run on a profit-sharing basis, gave a young working-class woman a copy. She assumed it was intended 'to interest my parents in Socialism', since she already 'believed in Socialism without knowing much about it' herself, having attended 'discussion groups' at the donors' home and 'learnt a lot from them and their friends'.

A Londoner found that the book made him 'a confirmed Socialist'. He put Robert Tressall on a par with Burns and Marx, and rested calm in the conviction that 'World Socialism' would 'come it will for all that'. But he gave no hint of what he might do to help. A 'pioneer Trade Unionist' joiner gave a copy to his son, an apprentice coach-builder, who knew that

Jokes were made of the Joiners Coat of Arms consisting of toasting a 'bloater' over the fire and a poor painter holding a slice of bread underneath the fish to catch the fat whilst being cooked. They would also joke about the painters 'skeleton kits' of tools they had brought on the job, which made me pity them more than ever. I can see now the small lad pushing the truck with the step ladders etc up the hill. The sacking of men at an hour's notice, or less.

The 'Great Money Trick' 'made' him a trade unionist, co-operator and a 'Socialist'. He joined the Labour Party, became a councillor then an alderman, and his son later became mayor of Reading.

In December 1922 J. Walsh, the NASOHSPD's executive member for Liverpool, focused on the 'enormous numbers of "rough" painters' working under rate. He argued that 'unless every man becomes a missionary for trade unionism, there is every prospect of the South of England retaining the unenviable reputation of being a drag on the forward movement'. He urged members to 'risk half-a-crown' on a book, which could 'be obtained from most booksellers', and 'once it is read can not be forgotten'. Walsh gave several quotations, stressing that the 'pitiless realism' included 'an occasional display of rather lurid language; yet it is so true to life that it never offends'. Moreover, 'if anything ever set up in print would appeal to the soul of a "skib", then the dreadful story recorded by Tressall should do the trick'. He was convinced that chapters like 'The Long Hill' had 'done more, to compel both *operatives* and employers to recognise their duty to the lads, than all the speech-making on the same subject'. Some members wanted 'to express appreciation of this wonderful book' and its author; but Walsh believed that

> to keep his memory green, and the most practical way of appreciating the service he has rendered, in exposing the seamy side of our trade in particular, is to devote our energies towards abolishing root and branch, the wretched conditions which he depicts.[63]

RTP was a union activist's tool-kit.

During 1922 Raymond Postgate had collaborated with Tommy Jackson on a book that defended the Bolshevik Revolution. But the writing was on the wall for non-'nuclear' intellectuals, so Postgate left the Party, as did Mark Starr, Ellen Wilkinson, Winifred Horrabin and Frank Horrabin. Postgate also left *The Communist*, and went back to the ailing *Daily Herald*, now owned by the TUC. His *The Builders' History*, commissioned by the NFBTO, appeared in 1923. It was meant 'to provide a further and much-needed weapon in the day-to-day struggle', and there was a cheap edition for Plebs and Labour College classes. Postgate thanked the retiring NFBTO president, George Hicks, for his 'advice and criticisms', assumed that RTP was 'absolutely essential' reading, and argued for 'a class-conscious Labour Party'.[64] Jackson, one of the very few leading Communists who remained active in the workers' education movement, described Postgate's appreciation as 'Very striking' in his *Plebs* review. At some point in the early 1920s a 'pirated' translation of RTP is said to have been published by the Russian All Union Council of Trade Unions.[65]

In 1924 a Hastings-born house-painter, who had been an apprentice in 1908 and knew Noonan, vouched that his book was a 'true description of life as it was in the building trade years ago in a small country town'. It remained relevant: 'men still fight like wolves to get a job that gives them a bare existence', resulting in 'no security, no peace of mind, no certainty of the future'. Trade unionism had grown stronger and 'younger operatives have had a better education and are beginning to think'; but little enough had changed on the job since Philpot's day:

> It is not exactly comfortable to stand on top of an eighty-rung ladder painting on a cold windy day. The hands and arms get frozen stiff, and every now and again an extra strong gust of wind almost blows one off ... Sometimes a weak spot in a ladder – there is a sudden crack – a snap and some poor unfortunate man is hurled 40 or 50 feet crashing to the ground.

There were still meal-time discussions on 'Evolution, Atheism, Socialism and other topics', yet Noonan's prediction had come true: 'the painting and decorating trade is almost debased to the level of an unskilled trade. Every true craftsman amongst the painters resents this.' But only a minority could find energy, after work, travel and bread and margarine, to be an active 'rebel', and be 'off to his union or a Socialist meeting to discuss how to alter his lot'.[66] Where would that minority go?

The very opposite of a class party

In November 1922 the Labour Party leadership let it be known that theirs was 'the very opposite of a Class Party',[67] yet the ILP 'Red Clydesiders' voted for MacDonald as leader. During 1923 George Lansbury rejected the CPGB affiliation, and at that November's general election Labour got over 4 million votes. Half of their 191 MPs called themselves socialists. The ILP won 46 seats, the SDF 4 and the Fabians 2, while Divisional Labour

Parties secured 35. Most Labour MPs were sponsored by trade unions, and Labour's manifesto contained no socialist pledges. Early in 1924 MacDonald's minority Labour Cabinet showed its true colours. Arthur Henderson reported on contingency plans for dealing with a threatened railway strike, and a Cabinet colleague, Jimmy Thomas of the National Union of Railwaymen, effectively undermined the dispute. MacDonald contemplated using troops against TGWU dockers, and a state of emergency was declared over a strike of London tram workers. The former pacifist presided over the construction of five cruisers, but he was not allowed to see his own security file, presumably because his government resumed diplomatic and economic relations with Russia.

Russia was changing. During 1923, and especially after the failure of the German revolution in November, Stalin and his allies stepped up their attack on Trotsky, who wanted the growing Party bureaucracy to be accountable to an informed membership. Trotsky's *The New Course* was effectively suppressed: old Bolsheviks were 'rooted up from positions of administrative importance, and shipped away to kick their heels in foreign embassies'; and almost 200,000 workers were allowed to become full Party members while a ban was imposed on any new 'intellectuals'. Lenin died in January 1924. His 'Testament' damned Stalin, Zinoviev and Kamenev on account of their serious political mistakes, but praised Trotsky, with reservations. Lenin wanted the Party Congress to hear his political 'will', yet only at his widow's insistence was it read to the Central Committee, and to a few delegates. Most of them discounted it, and it was kept from the membership at large. Tragically, Trotsky insisted that Max Eastman keep the 'Testament' an 'absolute secret'.[68]

Meanwhile, the CPGB was trying to build a revolutionary party in a non-revolutionary period, but failing to make much headway. Its five thousand members were 'practically all proletarians', young, male and white;[69] and Trotsky thought it a 'mere propagandist society', 'not a party, capable of directly leading the masses'.[70] However, Pollitt claimed that the CPGB was 'never so strong and influential in its history as it is now, and this despite the lack of finance, and the influences of doubting comrades'. In the April *Communist Review* Tommy Jackson argued that '"Organisation" has been made an end in itself', and asked: 'Is an ignorant membership necessary to the working of the plan of organisation?' Must they accept that the 'leading committee' understands, while their 'job is only to carry out all instructions at the double, and stand to attention until the next order comes'? He got responsibility for education and propaganda, but the 'nucleus' controlled the Central Committee.

During early 1924 CPGB membership climbed modestly. But on 25 July *Workers' Weekly* published an article by Pollitt calling on soldiers to 'Turn your weapons on your oppressors!' The Attorney General had the editor, J.R. Campbell, arrested, but MacDonald learned of the prosecution from newspapers, and the case was withdrawn. However, on 30 September MacDonald misled the Commons, then offered the government's resignation. On or about 10 October a document turned up in the Foreign Office. It was the work of two counter-revolutionary Russian émigrés; but thanks to the cooperation of top state officials, and of MI5 and MI6, the middle-man, Thurm, seems to have been paid £7,500 by Tory Party head quarters. On 25 October, four days before polling day, the *Daily Mail* published this 'Zinoviev letter', which called for pressure on Labour to make trade agreements with the USSR, and demanded Communist propaganda in the armed forces. The Labour Cabinet deferred judgement, yet their manifesto called for state ownership of the mines, railways and power stations, and a capital levy. They got 5½ million votes, but only 151 seats, while the Tories won 419. CPGB candidates won only 55,000 votes, and the Labour Party conference promptly barred Communists from dual membership.

In October 1924 Trotsky published *The Lessons of October* in Russia. He patiently explained how

> Lenin was ruthless in refuting the 'Old Bolsheviks' who 'more than once already have played so regrettable a role in the history of our Party by reiterating formulas senselessly *learned by rote* instead of *studying* the specific features of the new and living reality'.[71]

Stalin and his allies were able to impede the reprinting and distribution of this work so effectively that the public 'believed that the book had been suppressed'.[72] During 1925 Eastman's patience snapped. The Labour Publishing Company published *Since Lenin Died*. In it Eastman warned that the 'increasing rigidity' of what was coming to look like an 'aristocracy' in the Russian Communist Party was 'a fundamental danger to the revolution', not least because of the 'the irresponsibility, the childlike dependence' on the 'will and judgment' of Lenin which the new 'priesthood' sought to generalize.[73] That autumn Stalin and his allies insisted that Trotsky publicly deny the story about the 'Testament', because Eastman's book was 'objectively a tool of the counter-revolution'; and 'in order to prevent a renewal of the inner-party struggle', Trotsky 'denied what he knew to be true, and thus aided the campaign of falsification directed against himself'.[74] *Lessons of October* was published by the Labour Publishing Company later in 1925, but by then it was too late.

Towards the end of 1924 the CPGB leadership had chosen Stalin's side in the Russian power struggle, and the 'Bolshevising' process was 'begun in earnest'. After hearing Pollitt's report from the Comintern executive in December, Tom Bell wrote the first vicious anti-Trotsky article in the *Workers' Weekly*. In January 1925 two hundred London Communists voted against condemning Trotsky and the Left Opposition before reading their documents; but in February a TUC delegation to Moscow accepted the line against 'Trotskyism'. In April the Comintern adopted Stalin's anti-Marxist theory on the alleged stabilization of capitalism, and the TUC hosted an Anglo-Soviet Trade Union Conference. On 31 July the TUC General Council threatened an embargo on the movement of coal in support of the miners; and on 'Red Friday' the Tory government retreated. MacDonald damned them for encouraging Communists, while the Comintern criticised the CPGB for not disciplining members who held trade-union offices. Yet Dutt argued for greater powers to be given to the General Council, and Murphy denounced attempts to set up Councils of Action independently of that 'General Staff of the unions'.[75]

7

For circulation amongst the unconverted

Comrade Hicks

The one-time revolutionary syndicalist and SPGBer George Hicks was elected to the TUC General Council in 1921, and was courted by the CPGB from 1923. In 1924 ILPer John Wheatley needed support for his Housing Bill, and Communist Willie Gallacher took Hicks and Coppock to meet the minister, who convinced them to barter fifteen years of house-building and agreed wage rates for the 'dilution' of skilled work. Hicks supported *Lansbury's Labour Weekly*, which was begun in February 1925, and whose circulation soon reached over 170,000. But he also wrote for the Communist-controlled *Sunday Worker*, launched that March, which published articles on left-wing union leaders, 'uncritically extolling their virtues and fostering considerable illusions about their role in the TUC',[1] and had 'immediately halved' the circulation of Lansbury's paper.[2]

Hicks chaired the General Council's crucial Transport Sub-committee. In September 1924 he supported the CPGB at the TUC Conference, though Communists were barred from being delegates. Taking confidence from that decision, the Tories activated the first Labour government's strike-breaking plans and set up the Organisation for the Maintenance of Supplies. In October, after Labour's Jimmy Thomas stressed the need to 'Smash the Reds or they will smash us',[3] Pollitt and eleven other Communist leaders were imprisoned. The King Street offices were ransacked, and materials (including a mysterious object which turned out to be a lavatory ballcock) were removed. But an alternative Party leadership took over, and prosecutions under the 1797 Incitement to Mutiny Act gave wonderful publicity. Hicks addressed huge demonstrations outside the prison.

From January 1926 Hicks served on the TUC committee liaising with the Miners' Federation, and the CPGB believed he was part of an important group of General Council 'lefts', along with Albert Purcell and Alonzo Swales. In February Trotsky's *Where Is Britain Going?* was published in Britain, warning about the unprincipled and dangerous centrists, wobbling between reform and revolution, and stressing that the CPGB would be able to lead the working class 'only insofar as it enters into an implacable conflict with the conservative bureaucracy in the trade unions and the Labour Party'.[4] But while Trotsky's book was warmly welcomed by Dutt in that April's *Labour Monthly*, the CPGB did not criticise Hicks for supporting the TUC decision not to call a special conference to prepare for a general strike. They believed the state would back down. It did not; so a general strike was called for 3 May.

Workers responded magnificently, even in Hastings. But on 5 May police disabled the CPGB printing press. Two days later the General Council set about ending the struggle behind closed doors, and their advice to strikers was: 'Get into your garden ... Get into the country, the parks and the playgrounds. There is no more healthful occupation than walking.'[5] Ben Turner later claimed that he and other TUC leaders were 'Tricked, bamboozled, somewhere, somehow', by the Cabinet and the employers.[6] In reality, the 'Lefts' allowed the miners' leaders to be kept in the dark. On 12 May the number of strikers was increasing when the BBC announced that the strike was over. No arrangements were made for an organised return to work, and the miners were left to fight alone. Russian workers sent over £1 million, but Hicks denounced 'damned Russian money'.[7] Ironically, the Comintern had previously warned against relying on vacillating 'Lefts'.

In the *Sunday Worker* of 4 June Hicks claimed that the defeat of the General Strike was 'a great victory' which shattered the 'moral prestige' of the capitalist class. In July CPGB leaders called on members 'to behave as loyal trade unionists',[8] since TUC left-wingers had only lacked 'the necessary consistency and resolution'.[9] But by September Hannington, Gallacher and others publicly denounced their former allies: 'When the crisis came they ran away.'[10] Party membership climbed to twelve thousand, and the 'Elementary Course' insisted that new recruits, even 'the backward ones', had to 'think for themselves'. But the tutor was required to ensure that the class 'reaches the right conclusion', and to send 'a careful report on each member'.[11] Local 'leaders' were to be politically dependent on the 'nucleus', which was, in turn, increasingly dependent on the rising Stalinist bureaucracy in Russia.

After the miners' defeat in December 1926 recent recruits haemorrhaged out of the CPGB's ranks. Idris Cox believed that 'most of them had joined because they regarded the Communist party as the best fighter for their immediate demands', not because they understood and accepted Marxist theory.[12] So membership fell to what it had been two years before. Outside London, Glasgow and South Wales, the Party barely existed, and its strategy was in tatters. Yet in January 1927 the leadership invited Hicks to sign its 'Hands off China' appeal. By then it had dawned on him that whereas the General Strike had failed, Wheatley had delivered real reforms as a Labour minister, so Hicks and other TUC 'Lefts' wobbled right. In February they went along with the General Council's ban on co-operation with the Communist-led National Minority Movement in the trade unions, and they accepted the Labour Party executive's disaffiliation of branches that treated Communists as comrades.

A satire on all reformism

Even in its politically gutted form, The Ragged Trousered Philanthropists continued to help make socialists. A young man brought up by 'Socialist Parents with a great thirst for political Knowledge' bought copies 'through my Trades Union, the Furniture Trades Ass[ociation]', and 'loaned them out in their turn to different men'. He 'never had them returned'. A 'raw recruit' to the Labour Party read the book to find out 'what Socialism was about'. He already had 'a good idea of unemployment and poverty', and wanted to know 'who was responsible'. He learned 'that Land-Owners, Land-Lords and the Church were the Holy Trinity crucifying the masses', while 'it was the poor who were helping the poor'. Without Barrington, RTP did not succeed in 'pin-pointing the cause of the problem', but it 'gave me courage'. Yet in spite of MacDonald's government he was convinced Labour 'was a liberation party', and he did weekend 'outdoor propaganda' for twenty-five years.

The year 1924 had been particularly anxious for Grant Richards, but mainly because he 'took more out of the business than it could afford'.[13] The Ragged Trousered Philanthropists was reprinted in February 1925. That year a

George Hicks, 1927

German edition, *Die Menschenfreunde in Zerlumpten Hosen. Ein englischer Arbeiterroman,* translated by Kate Güssfeld, appeared from Neuer Deutscher Verlag in Berlin. Presumably Richards was paid a fee. Yet in February 1926 'the day came when a bill was not honoured' and he was bankrupt once again. Sir Joseph Dobbie (Director) and Maxwell Hicks (Receiver and Manager) reprinted RTP in October. In February 1927 the firm became the Richards Press, but Richards was left with 'so little control' that he resigned his chairmanship in July, though he remained a reader and editor.[14]

In June 1927 the Richards Press had published a 'Special Edition' of ten thousand copies of RTP, sponsored by the *Daily Herald.* The increasingly right-wing paper was losing £25,000 a year, and it was hoped that the book would be a circulation-raiser. It retailed at two shillings, and the Foreword was by none other than the General Secretary of the AUBTW, and 1927 President of the TUC, George Hicks. He argued that 'Tressall' was 'the Zola of the building trade operatives'. 'What he has described is true to life; we know that he lived it. We workers in the building industry know that he was one of us.' But 'to-day, when conditions are a little better and a little brighter', after 'hard struggles and ceaseless guerrilla warfare' by unions, 'the future is not so dark and hopeless as it was in the bad old times'. The novel was a 'Testament to the Cause of Socialism', and Hicks knew 'of no better book to give to the newcomer into our Movement, or for circulation amongst the unconverted'.[15]

The unconverted were legion. Union membership had halved since the General Strike, and strike days were at an all-time low. The Trades Disputes Act, known as the 'Blacklegs' Charter', made general and sympathetic strikes illegal, especially those aimed at the government. It also defined 'intimidation' so loosely that effective picketing was impossible, debarred Civil Service unions from affiliating to the TUC, and altered the trade-union political levy from contracting out to contracting in, thereby endangering Labour Party finances. In his September presidential address to the TUC Hicks asked workers to join bosses in a 'common endeavour to improve the efficiency of industry and to raise the workers' standard of life'.[16] Class struggle failed in 1926. Class collaboration was the way ahead.

RTP sold in scores of thousands. When one man 'first linked arms with Socialism' 'The Ragged' was '"required" reading, and he felt that the author was 'close by and a friend'. An apprentice whose parents were founder members of Worcester Labour Party, read it in the 'vicious aftermath' of the General Strike, when 'many employees took immediate advantage to tighten the screw on their workers'. Older workmates confirmed its accuracy. So he passed the book on, and felt it 'made many converts to Socialist thoughts'. An apprentice joiner in Caithness worked five ten-hour days plus Saturdays for ten shillings, and had to buy his own tools. His parents drummed into him that he was 'well off', but he knew he 'was a "Ragged Trousered Philanthropist"' when he acquired a copy 'by chance'. 'Robert Tressell became my solace' as 'a fellow traveller who understood ME!' RTP also 'provided much of the subject matter' in one young joiner's union branch, which became a talking shop once wages were slashed:

> The men tried to compensate by dropping slate clubs and TU subs. Membership fell off and things in the T.U. branches looked gloomy ... six of us attended the fortnightly meetings regularly 'to keep the branch open'. There was very little business to attend to and we just talked and told yarns mostly about the building trade.

A Wimbledon joiner was 'so impressed' after his wife paid three shillings and sixpence for a copy that he bought another and passed both of them round his woodworkers' union branch.

The politically eviscerated RTP could reinforce pessimism. A 9-year-old girl living in Norfolk read it 'because of' her father, a painter and decorator who was often unemployed. He got his workmates to read the book; but he believed 'the working class were their own enemies'. Yet it also provoked activity. Harry Weaver, then a building worker, recalled that its effect 'proved permanent', especially its 'simple but devastating exposure of the characteristic effects of capitalist exploitation and the clear statement of a Socialist alternative'. It had a 'capacity for gripping the reader and arousing a compelling desire to take an active part in fighting injustice'. He later became President of the AUEW. A Worthing woodworking machinist was loaned a copy by a workmate. He 'smiled at such a strange title', but read it, 'handed it to many of my friends', and went on to be a 'life-long Trade-Unionist' and a Daily Worker reader. A Midlothian man 'read "THE BOOK"', and it 'made me a fanatical supporter of my own class'. From the Labour Party he 'graduated' to the CP, and remained there for forty years. In Birtley, County Durham, Charley Hall read his Communist father's copy of the 1914 edition and drew Communist conclusions.[17]

By 1927 the Labour Party had lost hundreds of thousands of members, but centrist ILPers had no alternative strategy. So they wobbled between reform and revolution, while MacDonald and Henderson planned to take Labour policy back to before 1919. As for the CPGB, its latest training manual stressed that tutors needed to 'build up a synthetic picture of capitalism and the tasks of the workers in the pupils' minds'; but this misnamed 'thorough Leninist' document showed few signs of connecting with workers' agendas, above all in 'backward factory groups', and RTP was not on the extensive reading-list.[18]

In September 1927 Tommy Jackson welcomed the reprinting of the Daily Herald RTP in the Sunday Worker, even though he knew what Party hacks thought of its popularity:

From the 'expert' literary standpoint this is unaccountable. In form a novel the book is in fact a series of sketches of proletarian existence strung together by the merest thread of a plot. It has no exciting episodes, and its one and only sex episode is quite momentary and leads nowhere. It does not end, but breaks off hinting at horror. Its character-drawing is unaffectedly crude, and its hero is not beyond suspicion of sentimental priggishness. Quite half of its bulk is occupied with frank propaganda speeches presented as such – altogether a book which breaks every rule and ensures its own damnation from the first.

Yet it has gone through nine large editions, and will probably go on
selling indefinitely until the Revolution.
The reason for this is plain – the book is true.
The propaganda may be old-fashioned, but it is sound, and the general
background and atmosphere are such as every Worker can recognise and
sympathise with at sight.

'[R]eplace the term "Socialist" with that of "Communist" and the situation reappears in all its essentials.' Nine out of ten managers and foremen
in Britain were still called 'Misery'.

Jackson regretted the book's 'pessimistic contempt for the intelligence
of the ordinary unregenerate Worker and the intellectual superiority of
the Socialist hero'; yet he knew first-hand that

It was hardly possible then for anybody in the fighting line of the Socialist
Movement to escape the feeling of angry, embittered contempt for the
supine Workers who, apparently, simply would not see the plain facts before
them.
It must be confessed, too, that their Socialism was presented often in
such an aloof doctrinaire manner and so detached from the actual living
forms of class struggle that the proletarians could be forgiven for treating
them as 'half barmy' ...
Altogether, it is a book not only well worth reading, but – and I say it
in cold blood – well worth imitating.

'Half barmy' comrades who didn't understand workers' tastes, please note!
In only four months the first *Daily Herald* edition had sold ten thousand
copies, almost *one every seventeen minutes*. RTP helped to crystallise the choice
between reform and revolution.

During 1927 *Die Menschenfreunde* was published by Universum Bücherei
für Alle, Berlin. Its 'Foreword' noted that Robert 'Tressal' had experienced

neither the war nor the post-war period, nor therefore the school which,
by exposing and branding this system, could have led him on to the final
consequence, to the suggestion at least of clear revolutionary demands. But
what leaves a strong impression, a forceful lesson at the end of this workers'
book is that in the end all that remains for reformism is resignation, a
desolate nothingness. Meanwhile it has long since become a fact that in the
atmosphere of revolutionary struggle and action the proletarian has nothing
to lose but his chains, but a world to win.

The book 'acts through the weight of its facts as a shocking indictment of
the system of exploitation and exposes it in its last "human" refuge'.

The ideology of the working class in England, the classical country of
liberalism, is infected more than elsewhere by petty bourgeois and reformist

ideas. The tragic contradiction of this kind of liberal philosophy of the
'Ragged Trousered Philanthropists', force fed by the class enemy, by the
strangler himself, to the miserable existence of these unrestrictedly exploited people, stamps this story and makes it an especially unique publication in working class literature, and at the same time a shocking document
of proletarian life. A worker who has himself lived in the hell of immeas-
urable exploitation and deprivation of rights describes the cheerless life not
yet lit up by the idea of class struggle and revolutionary uprising and the
Philistine philosophy of these workers, their resignation often bordering on
simple-mindedness. The one worker, who puts forward the idea of class
struggle to his petty bourgeois workmates, is not understood by them and
is declared to be 'a bit mad'. While illuminating all these contradictions,
this little book becomes a satire on all reformism.[19]

The first real workers' play

The 1914 edition of The Ragged Trousered Philanthropists had made H.B. (Tom)
Thomas a socialist, and the October 1917 Revolution inspired him to join
the ILP, but by the mid-1920s he was a frequently unemployed stock-
broker's clerk, with an interst in drama. In 1924 ILPers and CPers founded
a Guild of Proletarian Art, and by April 1926 Thomas had become the
moving spirit of the People's Players, who were supported by Hackney
Trades Council. After the betrayal of the General Strike in May, Thomas
joined the CPGB. In that August's Labour Monthly, Dutt criticised the ILP-ish
London Labour Drama Association, arguing that the 'existing so-called
"advanced" plays are nearly all unusable from a working-class point of
view'. Consequently, workers had 'to develop their own plays from the
stories of the workers' struggle'. Moreover, during 1927 the Comintern
had ordered Communists to build a 'solar system' of organisations to act
as a 'bridge to the masses'.

Thomas liked The Ragged Trousered Philanthropists' 'tragic realism', and decided
to write a play which 'should be as unashamedly propagandist as the
novel, and should not depart from Tressell's words except as demanded
by dramatic effectiveness'.[20] Apparently, he aimed to produce it on the
West End stage, though this came to nothing.[21] However, in three weeks,
beginning in November 1927, the first scenes were 'put into rehearsal
while the others were being written'; and the play was staged at the
Ladies' Tailors' Hall, Great Garden Street, London E1, on 11 December,
with a cast of two electricians, two clerks, a book-keeper, a former able-
seaman, a tailor, a haberdashery salesman, two housewives, and two
cabinet-makers. Mark Chaney recalled that, instead of 'sitting back on our

haunches', 'we went out of our way to "sell" this first real workers' play'.[22]

They performed for CPGB branches, and though fifteen Labour branches had been disaffiliated for their Communist links, Chaney remembered 'various local Labour Parties finding halls and audiences'.

> I shall never forget the show we did at Braintree – we rolled up to the Town Hall in a coach provided by the Labour Town Council, who gave us a right royal welcome and incidentally a high tea, and then we all paraded the town with bell, book and candle, with leaflets and posters and the audience literally crammed the hall.

So 'instead of having to bear all expenses (or losses) we were actually being paid to perform and took a percentage of the profits'.[23]

In March 1928 they were invited to perform in Edmonton Town Hall;[24] but the use of the 'people's own language' presented political problems. Thomas recalled a meeting with the state censor:

> The Lord Chamberlain objected to the number of 'bloodys' in the text – 31. I pointed out that Shaw had broken the ice with a single and celebrated 'bloody' in *Pygmalion* and that I had already been guilty of misrepresenting the vocabulary of the building workers by leaving out all the numerous and then completely unprintable words with which their language was embellished. We finally compromised: 15 'bloodys' would be licensed, 16 or over, not. I agreed but left an all important question unanswered because unasked ... who would count the 'bloodys'?[25]

Chaney believed that 'the success we managed to maintain with those honest-to-God working-class audiences' was 'due, no doubt, to the fact that the humour was typical working-class', and 'the homeliness of the dialogue with the fifteen "bloodys" allowed us by the censor (which we expended in the first two scenes and sprinkled a few more for good measure) won their attention and support'.[26]

They also played workers' clubs, and 'had to compete with the usual club turns and the beer-swillers who sometimes left hurriedly before ten, to get their drinks'.[27] Mildmay Radical Club was the 'biggest and best working man's club in North London', but it had a rule about performances stopping at 9.45 p.m. before last orders. Yet when the bell went, to 'the consternation of the bar-tender', 'not a single soul got up to leave'. Altogether the Peoples' Players performed the play over a hundred times. Thomas felt it 'would be difficult to say who enjoyed it more, the audience or the players', since 'the audience participated in the triumph of Owen and his ideals'.[28]

Owen does not contemplate suicide at the end of Thomas's script, unlike the mediated novel. He argues that if bosses refuse to be pensioned off then workers *may* 'have to meet the owners' force by greater force':

> At all events, one thing is certain, that the degree of resistance of the owners will depend on the extent to which the workers are class-conscious and determined to succeed, and also upon the strength of their class organisations, the Trade Unions.

Harlow proposes that 'Socialism is the only remedy for unemployment and poverty' and, turning to the audience, asks for a vote. The script predicts that '*the curtain should quickly descend upon a great shout of "Ay" from the audience.*'[29] The appeal 'never failed to get the roaring cheers to decide the issue', and 'at curtain-fall the applause gave the actors time to scamper round to the exits to await the audience as salesmen of *The Workers' Weekly* and current pamphlets of the movement'.[30]

The company was in 'general demand by T.U. branches, especially of building workers'; and one print workers' branch 'honoured us by a special printing in gold leaf of a programme'. Chaney remembered that they did 'many shows for strikers',

> who were particularly impressed by the 'Join the Union' appeal at the end; and, at one historic show at the Hackney Manor Hall for the first Hunger Marchers who marched into the hall to the stirring music of a drum and fife band during the first scene of the play, we cheered with the rest of the audience and started the show over again for their benefit.

The play was 'direct and open propaganda', and was able to 'penetrate' Clubs and Institutes politically.[31]

During 1928 the Labour Publishing Company published *The Ragged-Trousered Philanthropists. A Play in Six Scenes. Adapted from the Novel of Robert Tressall* by 'Trudnik'. It had been 'licensed for public performance by the Lord Chamberlain, subject to certain alterations'. For amateurs the fee was 10 per cent of the gross takings, with a minimum of ten shillings and sixpence; though professional companies had to ask permission from The Richards Press Ltd. Costumes were available for hire, 'very inexpensively', and curtains could be supplied 'on special terms for schools and educational societies, or for charitable performances'.[32]

The published script sold very well indeed. In February 1929 it was performed at Stockport;[33] and that November *Workers' Life* reported that it was on at the Labour Hall, Peckham.[34] The Workers' Theatre Movement, which should have generalised that success, was 'almost moribund'.[35]

Anyway, not every socialist was an uncritical fan. Richard Fox argued that
The Ragged Trousered Philanthropists was 'part of industrial literature':

> It is a brilliant piece of self-expression by a building worker, clouded by the
> bitterness of ill-health and struggle so that in part it becomes a pamphlet-
> eering diatribe. But for all that its satirical and biting etchings of character
> have the ring of truth. Tressal [sic] leaves an impression of hopelessness and,
> looking back to the time when he was writing, this appears natural enough.
> To-day no one on the side of the working class doubts its coming victory.
> The only question is how and when that victory will come.[36]

In a similar spirit of messianic triumphalism, the CPGB made a disastrous
ultra-left turn into the political wilderness.

The final and absolute submission to Stalin

In May 1927 Jack Murphy, the British Comintern representative, was given
the 'honour' of moving Trotsky's expulsion. Murphy later reported that
'not in a single meeting was a voice raised in support of the Opposition'
at CPGB conferences.[37] Yet Party membership was below 6,500 and falling
fast, and the gap between it and the reformist left had widened. Talks
between Sir Alfred Mond and the new TUC President, Ben Turner, were
under way by January 1928. The Labour Party's manifesto, *Labour and the
Nation*, did not mention socialism; and MacDonald left the ILP. Yet when
miners' leader A.J. Cook and the ILPer Jimmie Maxton attacked TUC and
Labour class collaborationism, the CPGB denounced what they saw as an
attempt to divert workers from Communism.

In February 1928 the CPGB leaders confirmed their adherence to Stalin's
parody of 'Leninism', and the sectarian 'Third Period' was officially
launched in September. Their 'bridges to the masses' were blown up on
the right bank. The Labour Party barred Communists from being trade-
union delegates to its conferences, and members of the National Left-
Wing Movement from speaking on its platforms, while the TUC threatened
to withdraw recognition from Trades Councils that associated with the
National Minority Movement. Leading Communists found it 'necessary to
state quite frankly that there is no difference between the right-wing and
the so-called left-wing' in the General Council.[38]

During 1928–29 the CPGB lost over 2,000 members, and only 3,500
remained. Party member Harry McShane found that comrades in Vancouver
were 'already hero worshippers of Stalin':

> I didn't know much about Stalin, I had just heard his name, but they had
> Stalin on the brain. I couldn't understand it because I was still living in the
> communist tradition which saw Lenin as the leader but didn't have heroes
> in that way.

When Trotsky was deported from Russia, McShane was 'very angry about it; we had always placed Lenin and Trotsky together' as revolutionary leaders.[39] Yet he remained loyal when Stalin argued that Europe was entering a period of revolutionary upswing, and the 1929 CPGB programme came out 'in fundamental opposition' to Labour, 'the third capitalist party'.[40]

Class against Class meant abandoning Lenin's methods of analysis in the name of 'Leninism', and throwing away leading positions and close allies. In March 1929 A.J. Cook spoke on MacDonald's behalf at Seaham, against Pollitt, and was denounced for having 'joined the enemies of the revolutionary struggle' by his Communist friend and fellow miners' leader, Arthur Horner.[41] In the May general election Labour attracted over 8 million votes and took office. Of the 288 Labour MPs, two-thirds were ILPers. SDFer Tom Kennedy was made chief whip and a 'Right Honourable'. The CPGB got a grand total of fifty thousand votes.

In October 1929, as Marx generally predicted it would, the capitalist 'System' went into crisis. After the Wall Street crash, two-thirds of the CPGB leadership were replaced. The 'new forces' included graduates from the Lenin School in Moscow, though Pollitt and Dutt privately acknowledged that they were 'impossible fools and mechanical parrots and gramophones'.[42] By December Party membership was down to barely 2,500. The hitherto loyal (and Moscow-trained) Harry Wicks recalled that dissatisfaction was 'general throughout the party', and that among comrades he knew,

> the first significant break had come when he or she had rejected the non-
> sense that all people in the labour movement who did not directly support
> the party were 'Social Fascists'. The break came via practice, via an instinc-
> tive understanding that the vital need of the hour was united working class
> action, particularly in the face of the international growth of Fascism.[43]

The Party's London District Committee continued to disagree with the blanket condemnation of the left opposition; but Reg Groves watched 'critics and criticised alike scurrying to obey and conform to the latest commands, with leading Central Committee members twisting themselves into the most abject postures to placate the Comintern and retain their posts'. It was the 'final and absolute submission' to Stalin.[44]

RTP fan Tommy Jackson had published a hilarious article on 'Self Criticism' in the previous February's *Communist Review*, but he seems not to have known that likely losses on the proposed *Daily Worker* would be funded by the Comintern, so he objected to the closure of the successful *Sunday Worker* and his removal from the Central Committee enjoyed Comintern support. The cultural line shifted. Ness Edwards's *The Workers' Theatre* was published in 1930. He praised ILP work in Labour Colleges, and Plebs League and local Labour Parties for producing plays of 'a definite working class character', and wanted new plays put on in 'labour halls, club rooms, hired concert halls, and in the open air', which would act as '*an agitational force*', 'organising the working class', apart from 'slum defectives'. The chief targets should be unemployment, workshop incidents, workers' solidarity, 'the folly of conservative workmen' and 'political trickery'. Anything that showed 'the battle of life' and aimed at 'the destruction of capitalism, and the creation of a workers' republic', was fine. Yet RTP wasn't mentioned.[45]

Tom Thomas toed the line. From January 1930 his weekly column in the new *Daily Worker* argued for the development of an agitational, non-naturalistic theatre. In May he saw the German Workers' Theatre League in action, and in June a German 'contact' spoke at a Workers' Theatre Movement school. By July Thomas was proclaiming that the WTM 'rejects decisively the role of raising the cultural level of the workers through contact with great dramatic art which is the aim of the dramatic organisations of the Labour Party and the ILP'. What was needed was 'mass working class propaganda and agitation through the particular method of dramatic representation'.[46] So he dropped RTP from the repertoire, allegedly because it was too long and too complicated to stage. Instead he led a Red Troupe from London to Bristol and the Welsh coalfields with *Invergordon or the Sailors Strike*, *Speed-up*, *The Meerut Prisoners*, and a vicious sectarian attack on *Jimmy Maxton and the ILP*.[47] They also attacked Lansbury, even though he remained convinced that the 'complete abolition' of capitalism and the introduction of a 'system of co-operation' and 'international socialism' was the only future for humanity.[48]

As a young teenager, Manchester motor mechanic Jimmy Miller had found a Clarion Players' rehearsal 'very informal'. He was 'deeply disappointed and regarded the elderly producer with a good deal of disfavour' after 'what seemed to me to have been a complete shambles'. Miller remained a member of the group 'long enough to take part in a

production of *The Ragged-Trousered Philanthropist* [sic]. I don't think we ever
actually staged the full production though we did present odd scenes
from it at dances and socials.'[49] But once the line changed he formed his
own agitprop group, the 'Red Megaphones', with two weavers, a miner
and some unemployed youngsters.[50] Martin Bobker was YCL District Organizer, and Nellie Wallace was a Lenin School graduate. The Young Communist International sent a Russian, 'Kitty', to explain how Russian and
German comrades worked, and she put them in touch with the London
WTM and the German YCL.[51] (Ironically, Universum Bücherei für Alle in
Berlin reprinted *Menschenfreunde* in 1931.) During the 1931–32 Lancashire
textile workers' strikes the Red Megaphones' audiences totalled fifty
thousand, but while the YCL grew, the adult CPGB did not.[52]

In January 1932, Moscow allowed Pollitt to change the line, including
that on culture. The WTM had 'confused'

> the *negation* of bourgeois culture with the *destruction* of bourgeois culture. It
> did not seem to understand that the working class can make no contribution
> to art, science or any other field of human endeavour unless it takes over all
> that is best in previously-existing class culture.[53]

The 'average agit. prop. piece' had been a 'mass declamation for a small
group of players, dealing with a single political issue and ending in-
variably in a slogan reiterated with maximum decibel-output'.[54] At the
June WTM National Conference Pollitt argued against 'concentrating on
getting too much propaganda across of rather heavy character', and for
showing humorous aspects of working-class life.[55]

At this point Martin Lawrence was putting out translated Russian novels,
but it is not clear how many were read. However, *The Ragged Trousered Philanthropists* was 'required reading' in the National Unemployed Workers'
Movement, led by the Communist Wal Hannington. A student was given
a copy by his Labour College tutor. It was 'a must' in Faversham WEA
classes in 'Political Economy and International Affairs'; and a marine
engineering apprentice found it 'a shining light', especially "The Great
Money Trick'. In Liverpool James Larkin Jones wanted an explanation for
the poverty all around him.[56] Bill Bewley, 'a good old socialist and trade
union fighter' who had been active in the General Strike, got 'Jack' to read
the book.

> I couldn't life [sic] my eyes from its pages. It was so real in its exposure of
> much of the life around me and which I was beginning to experience in

my first job after leaving school. But the great significance of the book for
me was the simple, clear explanation of socialism.

From its pages I was encouraged to read more, to learn more; the
inspiration to become involved in the great cause of Labour was overwhelming!

It would not be true to say that the 'Ragged Trousered Philanthropist'
[sic] was my only introduction to socialist thinking but it provided a mighty
thrust in my emerging understanding about the need to change society.

I quickly acquired my own copy (since lost, like so many subsequent
copies to the 'borrower') and the book was a constant guide in workshop
discussions and Labour College classes.[57]

Unemployment was at 2½ million, and Jack wanted answers. Bill Barton,
'an old-style Marxist', persuaded him to become active in Liverpool Labour
College, so he took the evening and weekend classes for trade unionists.
In 1931 he was elected honorary secretary, and became a tutor. 'Classes
which I organised were as much practical as academic.' A 'collective method
of education suited us down to the ground'. Sometimes, 'we would read
a page from books like the *Ragged Trousered Philanthropists*' and discuss it. The
book 'was passed from hand to hand'; and it 'had a profound effect on
me as it did on tens of thousands of working people in my time'; but it
was 'the criticism of our class that affected me most'.[58] Jack joined the
Labour Party.

Others reacted differently. A boy from a 'deeply religious and politically Liberal' family in a 'typical West Wales mining village' found that the
General Strike changed his 'whole outlook'. He 'noticed the suffering of
the miners and their families', but also 'the ineptitude of the religious
and political leaders, including the labour leaders on local authority
bodies'. He 'felt quite strongly that something was very wrong', as he
'witnessed strong men being brought to tears by the insults', trying to
get 'a slip of paper to enable the family to eat the pittance of food'.

These men were not cowards but honest working men being trodden on by
this supposed man of God, a deacon at a local chapel.

I lost faith in religion, and politics, especially Liberalism. I became a
rebel without a cause and the family black sheep. The labour leaders disgusted
me as they only prayed on Sunday for the souls of these working people
who were every day struggling against the might of the capitalist classes.

Forced to leave grammar school and work at the colliery, he 'got into
arguments with religious and labour leaders on every possible occasion'.
His points were 'crude and not very effective', until a workmate convinced

him that 'reading and study of the subject' was required. 'The next day Will Evans brought me two books on loan; "The Ragged Trousered Philanthropists" by Robert Tressell, and "The Iron Heel" by Jack London.' They 'put before me in no uncertain manner the nature of this society', and 'the importance of an educated working class uniting to end for all time this class system based on exploitation and poverty of the people'. They opened 'the road to Marx, Lenin and all the great working class thinkers and leaders'. Later, he joined the CPGB.

The negation of everything the Labour Party stood for

In January 1931 the second Labour government committed suicide. Chancellor Snowden blamed the budgetary crisis not on the 'System' but on its victims, the long-term unemployed, and the first woman minister, Margaret Bondfield, helpfully suggested restrictions on women workers' rights. In July five rich men and two trade-union bureaucrats demanded expenditure cuts of £95 million. MacDonald bowed to the 'national interest', and the King flattered him into forming a 'national' government. But the pound was soon forced off the gold standard anyway, and the means test took thousands of Labour voters off benefits altogether. MacDonald was expelled from the party, and candidly acknowledged that the cuts 'represented the negation of everything the Labour Party stood for'.[59]

After the October general election the Tories strode back into office, with 'National Labour' support. The Labour Party got 2 million fewer votes and won 46 seats, and the ILP were reduced to 5. Union leaders tightened their grip on the Labour Party machine: Ben Tillett denounced Communists while accepting money from Tories; and Tom Kennedy was now a right-winger. In July 1932 the ILP wobbled left, disaffiliated from the Labour Party, and announced that its object was 'the complete overthrow of the economic, political and social organisation of the Capitalist State and its replacement by a Socialist Commonwealth'. It lost five thousand people, one-third third of its membership, within a year, then declined to a rump. The Labour left-winger Nye Bevan was still 'playing with the idea of a new Socialist Party', but his Communist pal Arthur Horner talked him out of it.[60]

The CPGB was not an option for the homeless left in 1931. Its total general election vote was under 75,000. Jennie Lee, no longer an ILP MP, visited Russia again, but noted the contradiction between starving people begging at the stations and the luxurious food available to her Cossack regiment hosts.[61] Leading CPGB cadres like John Cornford knew the Russian CP were 'quite deliberately responsible for a food shortage which c[oul]d be avoided if they slowed down the plan to export less grain', but, in spite of the man made famine in the Ukraine, 'They rightly won't.'[62] Jack Murphy remained critical of Trotsky even after he left for the Socialist League, which was formed by a few Labour lefts in October. Some 2,500 people joined the CPGB during 1932, but 2,000 left.

Up to this point Reg Groves, like 'most British communists had scant knowledge of communist oppositional groups abroad'. Then, 'one bright cold spring morning' he called at the 'Bomb Shop' in Charing Cross Road 'to buy some pamphlets and say hullo to old Henderson', and discovered that Jay Lovestone's US Labour Action and the Militant contained Trotsky's 'powerful indictment of Comintern policy'. Groves and his comrades were 'deeply shaken' by its analysis, and began 'secretly flirting' with the ILP; yet veteran Communist full-timer Tom Bell went to their Balham branch meetings and 'found nothing amiss'.[63]

However, when Hymie Fagan bought a copy of Trotsky's My Life for the Workers' Bookshop it mysteriously disappeared, though only Moscow-trained Bill Rust had a key. Soon after, Fagan saw the nasty side of Pollitt: 'It wasn't the Pollitt I knew.' He was 'accused of being a Trotskyist', then 'handed over to the secular arm of the Inquisition, in the shape of Frank Bright', who had completed the three-year course at the Lenin School. After refusing to kowtow – 'Bugger you mate, I'm not going to invent a confession' – Fagan narrowly escaped expulsion; but he was never trusted by the Stalinists again. Instead, Henry Parsons, 'who ran "Martin Lawrence"', had him checking Party bookshops,

> to see how they were being run, and to close them down if there was little hope of ever getting them to make a profit or at least pay their way. I found most of them semi-derelict, having become centres where unemployed members could spend the day, sitting in front of the fire, reading the books and pamphlets and making tea.

Three-fifths of Party members were unemployed; but if 'hardly a book or pamphlet was sold' Fagan loyally shut the shop.[64]

Then, in January 1933, Hitler was handed power. In March, while not admitting responsibility for the sectarian Third Period disaster, the Comintern permitted Communists to work with reformists. Unfortunately, the CPGB had recently ridiculed the ILP for suggesting a united front; and in

May Stalin further complicated matters by ratifying a pact of neutrality
and friendship with the Nazis. The new CPGB training manual understood that 'we are still largely isolated from the mass of the working
class', but blamed the members, and hoped 'new forces' from a 'united
front from below' would bypass them. It forgot the recent illusions in
TUC 'Lefts', and the German Communists' ultra-left lunacy, and falsely
accused the German Social Democrats of splitting the left and letting
Hitler in. But it quoted 'Comrade Stalin' approvingly when he insisted
that 'Social democracy is objectively the moderate wing of fascism.'[65]
Postgate believed that Labour Party delegates 'had had so large a bellyful
of Communist tactics that they would not, for however just a cause, associate with them'.[66] They got their socialist ideas elsewhere.

By now, in addition to the US, Canadian, Russian and three German
editions (one of which seems to have been of 15,000 copies), the 1918
'abridged' version of *The Ragged Trousered Philanthropists* had reputedly sold
100,000 copies in the UK. The two 1914 'complete' printings probably
amounted to 4–5,000. The first 1927 *Daily Herald* edition was of 10,000
copies, and the second printing was probably no smaller. Given the high
level of lending, the total UK readership of these 125,000 or so copies of
RTP could well have been half a million. Martin Secker claimed that Grant
Richards was 'never well off' after his second bankruptcy.[67] Yet he seems
to have supervised the republication of profitable back-list titles, and was
often seen in Monte Carlo. He wrote a guidebook to *The Coast of Pleasure*,
and remained addicted to the Café de Paris. In fact, he felt he 'might
myself be a Conservative, if I had the moral courage'.[68]

Richards Press reprinted *The Ragged Trousered Philanthropists* in August 1932.
It was described as the 1914 edition, which was a lie, though its price
remained at two shillings. However, George Hicks now acknowledged
that conditions were 'lamentable', and that 'industrial depression is having
disastrous effects on the Building Industry, as on all other industries'.

> The curse of unemployment is with us to an alarming and terrible extent.
> The continuous introduction of new machines and methods is, in addition,
> making employment for the 'Ragged Trousered Philanthropists' more pre-
> carious. Perhaps the future is not so dark and hopeless as it was in the bad
> old times, but it is gloomy enough in all conscience.

Hicks had been elected Labour MP for East Woolwich in a by-election in
April 1931, and held on to it in October; but he had no answers to a
'System' in deep crisis.

Grant Richards,
c. 1932

In 1933 De Arbeider Pers, of Amsterdam, published a Dutch translation of RTP, called *Menschenvrienden*. In the UK RTP fan Wal Hannington was forced off the CPGB's Central Committee. Twenty comrades were 'sent to Moscow' for training;[69] yet it was a non Communist who pointed to the

> fairly large number of working-class dramatic organisations in the country, associated with the Labour Party, Co-op., etc., as well as a number of semi-working class and petit-bourgeois groups, amateur dramatic associations and so forth. Even when these groups are middle-class in composition, they sometimes contain, or are capable of being captured by, radical thinking persons of semi-revolutionary or advanced views. Naturally, most of the plays they select are fairly realistic and straightforward. Yet many are waiting, even if unconsciously, for a new lead. Many would welcome plays expressing a definite anti-war, anti-fascist, socialist point of view.[70]

Others thought drama groups should be 'answering their own problems as they themselves saw them', and wanted 'a return to realism'.[71]

In January 1934 Left Theatre was formed, and Tom Thomas was on its committee:

> It became clear that in Germany the political warfare waged between socialists and communists had been tantamount to mutual suicide, and that in the rest of Europe survival would depend on an alliance of everybody threatened by Fascism. This wise attitude, when generally accepted, brought problems for the WTM. The whole of our work had been against the Labour Party and the ILP as well as against the National Government. MacDonald, Snowden, Jimmy Thomas and their ilk had been sitting ducks for our attacks even before they joined the National (Tory) Government. We had lampooned Jimmy Maxton and George Lansbury, and treated Labour and Tory as the same.[72]

The Rebel Players returned to 'earlier triumphs', and rehearsed The Ragged Trousered Philanthropists.[73] This 'convincing case for Socialism', put on by building workers in southeast London, 'certainly reinforced those beliefs' in one visitor from Bexhill.

Meanwhile, the novel continued its work. A teenager overheard two strangers in a railway carriage debating the merits of socialism and capitalism, and was 'so impressed with the argument for Socialism I felt "this is it – this is what the world needs"'. She went to her local library in East London, and the 'young lady' gave her '"Capital" by Marx, which was of course quite incomprehensible to me, and "The R.T.Ph."', which 'completely convinced me regarding Socialism'. She kept the novel and paid the two shillings fine. Another London teenager was allowed to read RTP, but only 'after a lot of thought' by her bricklayer father, because it was rather 'risqué'. She later became a union rep for a thousand civil servants. A young woman with an 'upper-class background & Grammar School education', while holidaying at Brixham, met a man who 'was pleased to talk to someone who wasn't a "True-blue Tory"'. He 'grew up in radical Cornwall, became a Socialist as a result of his wartime experiences, and worked in South Wales as a corporation blacksmith on de-mob', where he heard 'all the good Communist and Socialist speakers'. In Brixham the milkman would call round, 'sit the other side of the fire', and read RTP 'with tears running down his face'. When Labour supported non-intervention in Spain, she joined the CPGB, acknowledging that reading the novel had been 'the vital first step' in that direction.

A London carpenter and his workmates shared the book, which was 'more or less read to pieces as it did the rounds, and was minus its cover'. Communist building workers cottoned on. In October 1934 there was a successful nine-day strike at a site in Putney over the sacking of a shop steward. Frank Jackson, a carpenter-foreman, ran Noonan-like lunch-time discussions on subjects ranging from evolution to politics, and more than two hundred copies of RTP were sold. It inspired an attempt at workers' film-making, and a rank-and-file paper, *The New Builders' Leader*.[74] Charley Hall worked as a rep for the Workers' Bookshop. Every Communist 'local' (branch) was supposed to have a 'Literature secretary', who sold or raffled books; and even before the line changed, *The Ragged Trousered Philanthropists* was 'a steady seller'.[75]

8

A dream of Fred Ball

An organisation without a future

In 1934 William Campbell lived a privileged life in Russia, working as a clown. He was not a Communist, yet he knew there was 'hardly a single citizen of Leningrad, regardless of their attitude to the regime, who did not support Kirov', the city's Party boss. That December Kirov was assassinated, and some suspected that Stalin had removed a rival. William's stepfather, J.R. Campbell, arrived in Moscow as British Comintern representative in 1935, yet if he 'had been a petty official in a District Party Committee his name would have carried more weight'.[1] The CPGB was a sideshow. However, Palme Dutt was warned by Bukharin and Radek 'under the seal of absolute secrecy' never to enter the 'fatal path of conflict with the party', and this weighed on his mind 'like a nightmare'.[2]

In June 1935, at a Paris conference 'For the Defence of Culture', a Soviet delegate argued that Communists needed to 'overcome, in the shortest time possible, the survivals of sectarian traditions which have hindered them from finding a way of approach to the Social-Democratic workers'.[3] The Popular Front was officially launched at the Comintern's much-delayed Seventh World Congress in July–August. CPGB leaders loyally toed the Stalinist line. It seemed to work, since the 5,000 members of two years before became 11,000. Yet turnover was high among working-class recruits, who could not be retained without developing their theoretical understanding. Trotsky saw it as 'an organisation without importance, without influence, without authority, and without a future'.[4]

In 1937 the Left Book Club's publisher, Victor Gollancz, recalled Pollitt's opinion of the German Communist Willi Munzenberg: 'The booger! If I'd been soomoned to Moscow, and knew for certain that I'd be shot in the back of the neck the moment I landed, I shouldn't have hesitated for a second.'[5] Pollitt did not know that Stalin and Molotov were building a case against him, or that one day that year they signed over three thousand death warrants, then went to the cinema. Apart from the victims of the Moscow Trials, almost a million Russians and foreign Communists were killed, 2 million got prison sentences and 3 million were sent to the Gulag.[6] British Communist Rose Cohen was executed, and Pollitt was unable to prevent it. Yet the CPGB's new training course claimed Russian 'workers have power' and are '*happy*', so are 'working willingly for society (Stakhanov a forerunner of this)'.[7]

The Popular Front had cultural consequences. In February 1936 Martin Lawrence and Wishart & Co. amalgamated to form Lawrence & Wishart, which was placed at the Party's disposal. The policy of publishing tactfully edited novels under working-class writers' names was continued. However, Tom Thomas was 'very surprised when it was put to me' that as Workers' Theatre Movement organiser and the author of many lampoons on the Labour Party 'my continued leadership might be considered in some quarters a minor obstacle to the development of the Popular Front'.[8] So he resigned, and the New Theatre League, headed by the liberal Earl of Kinnoal, was aimed at everyone 'interested in progressive Theatre'.[9] London's Unity Theatre was founded, with the support of several CPGB intellectuals; while its opening night was not reported in the *Daily Worker*, there were soon hundreds of Left Theatre Groups all over the country.[10]

The Richard Press reprinted the 1914 'Complete Edition' of *The Ragged Trousered Philanthropists* in October 1935, which retailed at half a crown. It was claimed to be the '120th thousand', and noted that 'over 100,000 copies' of the 1918 abridged edition had been sold. During 1936 they published Tom Thomas's play script at half a crown, demanding 10 per cent of the certified gross takings, and a minimum of £2, almost four times the 1928 level. It had been revised. After Owen exposes capitalist exploitation with 'The Oblong' and 'The Great Money Trick', workers are neatly divided into sheep and goats. The narrative voice's pessimism is spoken by the renegade socialist, but Owen takes him on, especially about working-class 'Hottentots'. Nora speculates about a 'Workers' Commonwealth' built by 'Socialists in Germany, or France or even Russia', and Owen advocates abolishing 'the private ownership of the land, mines, railways, factories, and all other means of production', much as in the 1935 Party programme *For Soviet Britain*. 'Socialism is the only remedy for unemployment and poverty', the audience is told; but there is no mention of class warfare, revolution or proletarian dictatorship. Instead, the appeal is to 'get in the Union and stand up for ourselves as a beginning'; and the final stage direction continues to predict: '*the curtain should quickly descend on a great shout of "AYE" from the audience*'.[11] Hicks's 1927 Preface was quoted on the flyleaf, yet he was in a Labour Party deadset against Communist affiliation. So whose Socialism was being said 'AYE' to?

On 10 June 1936 the *Daily Worker* published a letter from a self-employed Hastings house-painter. J.H. Poynton had been a Hastings SDFer with the man he knew as 'Bob Newland', and he was aware of the editions his book had 'gone into and the languages into which it had been translated'. So he found it odd that such a 'masterly description of small builders' jobs of that day' was so little known that Upton Sinclair had thought it was 'getting about time we had another book from the able pen of Robert Tressall'. Fred Bower claimed that one night back in 1910, after he spoke at the Edge Hill Lamp, Liverpool,

> a short middle-aged, grey haired man of middle-class appearance accosted me. He spoke of how he had enjoyed the way I had delivered the goods. 'They'll come to our way of thinking yet', he said, by which I knew he was one of the elect. A few more words and we parted. Some ten minutes after this one of the comrades confided to me that the little grey man was the author of *The Ragged Trousered Philanthropists*.[12]

This was exceedingly unlikely, though Bower was clearly desperate to be associated with a book that had by 1936 become iconic in the British labour movement.

An underground book

Frederick Cyril Ball was born in Hastings Old Town on 1 March 1905.[13] He came from a long line of wheelwrights, ironsmiths, dressmakers and domestic servants. 'My great grandfather was at Crimea, I think. Other members of my family have fought at the siege of Ladysmith'; and Fred, too, was 'a great patriot'. His maternal grandfather, George Easton, was a building worker, and his mother, Grace, was a dressmaker. His paternal

grandfather had been one of Toby King's pupils; but from 1908 his own
father, Frederick, worked as a gardener at Telham Hill House, and this
involved the boy in 'pulling his forelock' when he passed his dad's
employer. In 1910 he went to Battle school; but by 1915 he worked part-
time as a garden- and coach-boy at Telham, while his father was away at
the front. Fred's mother voted Labour, but his father had 'always voted
Conservative' until he got back from the war, when he took the boy to
Cobb's meetings, and voted Labour. By the end of his life 'he'd have voted
Communist if there had been a candidate'.

In 1919, aged 14, Fred left school. He wanted to be a gardener, but was
apprenticed to Cousins the plumbers instead. However, his mother could
not keep him on five shillings a week; so in 1920, aged 15, he went to
work as a counterhand at Sainsbury's in London. Getting to the second
house at the pictures involved missing supper, and 'Seven o'clock closing
time (twice a week nine o'clock for knocking off) doesn't allow for night
school'; so he felt 'tied to a grocery business in which managership was
the only title to respect', and he 'wanted to spit this lot out'. He tried the
Esperanto Society, the Theosophical Society and the Spiritualist Church,
where he heard 'all kinds of half-baked notions'. There were middle-class
ladies 'reading my aura and things like that'. Probably in 1928, the poetry
of Burns and Clare 'had a profound effect' on him, and he wrote 'rather
naïve' sentimental and religious verse. Around 1933 he returned to
Hastings, went to WEA classes on Music and Literary Appreciation, and
found a friend, active in the Labour movement, who 'ridiculed all he
wrote'. T.S. Eliot's poetry cured him of 'literariness'; and for several months
he wrote 'nothing but comic doggerel'. He also met Jack Beeching.

Jack was born in St Leonards in 1922. His father had inherited land
and 'dabbled in business'; but the boy lived with his mother, a printer,
one of three trade unionists at her 'sweatshop' to join the General Strike
and lose their jobs. Around 1933 he went to grammar school, and wrote
poetry showing 'near contempt for economists, and those whom he held
responsible for the social and political catastrophes of the interwar years'.
He also got to know Ball. Sainsbury's 'paid rather high wages'; so it was
'fairly easy', after working there, 'to open your own little shop. This is
what Fred did.' But he 'was never cut out to be a small grocer; and he had
to sit there while his creditors decided whether or not to sell him up'.
Jack felt that the bankruptcy left Ball with 'a very bad anxiety neurosis'.
Ball's way of putting it was that poetry 'went into the ground a bit' as he

'began to get sidetracked' by politics. He had 'this political philosophical hotch-potch, a half baked mixture full up with this blinking passion to stick spears into society'.

In 1936 Ball became secretary of Hastings Left Book Club Poetry Group, and 'what I thought was a modern poet'. At Sainsbury's he worked along-side Peter Blackman, who had joined the YCL, even though 'rough lads with knuckle-duster rings' sometimes attacked their meetings on Hastings beach with stones. Ball saw them as 'fascists'. It all came together. The Spanish Revolution was under way. A vicar rebuked him for being 'too prejudiced in favour of the working class'. Ball had 'had a gutful of working for a multiple firm. The CP had a growing reputation, and Communism as an ideal seemed a more desirable system of social unity'. CPGB connections helped him publish poems in *Comment*, *Poetry and the People* and *Adelphi*. So he joined the Party, though he 'never desired a bloody revolution'.

Around this time 'some fellow, who was a house-painter' told Ball that *The Ragged Trousered Philanthropists* 'was one of the books that was most lent, and he'd been lent it, too'. 'This is a book you ought to read.' He did, and it was a revelation. It was the first English novel he had ever read 'in which men at work was the basic setting, and the working class the basic characters, and treated as real people, the kind of people I'd been brought up among, and not as "comic" relief'. His own family knew nothing of the book; and while 'some people knew it well ... others had never heard of it'. He could find no mention of its author in Hastings Library, yet the painter introduced him to two people who had known 'Tressell'; and at Christmas 1936 Ball gave a copy of the book as a present to 'Jim'. He found that it 'helped organise my ideas'. On 1 May 1937 Ball and his brothers, Robin and George, marched across London in a huge May Day demonstration. They were 'refreshed and assisted in keeping their vocal organs in good trim' by 'anti-Fascist chewing-gum and anti-fascist lemonade'; and they 'had sore throats for a fortnight'. They carried Noonan's SDP banner, 'retouched but not materially altered' by one brother for Hastings ILP. Yet Fred liked to think of *The Ragged Trousered Philanthropists* as 'a kind of underground book'.

Jack Beeching's grandfather – who may have been Ball's unnamed advisor – had been a painter before the Great War, and the book was his 'Bible'. In Jack's circle, 'The book was known, everybody read it, and they didn't make a critical assessment of it. As a picture of their own lives it was brilliantly, closely observed'. Some people had it as a 'consolation' for 'the failure of the General Strike, the retreat of the miners, the general feeling that the war and what caused it was not going to be put right'. But after hunger marches and Spain there was a 'left-wing revival', a 'mental stir-up', and 'many of the old militants, either ex-soldiers who'd been demobilised, or chaps who'd taken a militant stand', 'came over as a block as sympathisers of another sort of left'. During the Popular Front 'you couldn't win an argument with a Communist'. It 'seemed that every other social institution had fucked up, or was about to fuck up'. Other parties 'were hopelessly corrupt, stupid': 'we hadn't got twopence to bless ourselves with, but we had ... a confidence, partly of youth, and partly a feeling that history was right behind us'. RTP's 'despairing', 'slightly contemptuous' attitude was 'against the tone of the times'. The 'tone of the times was attack'.

Beeching was now secretary of Hastings LBC Poetry Group, and organ-ised recruitment. A procession of fifteen cars, with posters and streamers, drove to the seafront, and a collection was taken for Spanish Aid. Noonan's pal Bill Gower had joined the CPGB, and Jack went out with his daughter, who later died of tuberculosis. In 1938 the 16-year-old boy joined the Party. Looking back, 'Stalinism' seemed like 'a kind of extremely over-simplified Marxism-Leninism'.

> People at the time had a rather dim conception of Stalin's role, often distin guishing, for example, between the terror which was blamed on other individuals, such as Yagoda, and Stalin's responsibility for it. Some of his interventions in those years appeared to us politically impressive and he was surrounded with the prestige of the Seventh World Congress and the strategy of unity against fascism.

Ball wasn't in the Party at the time, and he and Beeching probably knew very little about Stalin's 'bloodsoaked tyranny'.[14]

In January 1938 the Daily Worker had dropped the hammer and sickle from its masthead. There was to be no more talk of the dictatorship of the proletariat. The build-up of production in preparation for war with Nazi Germany meant unemployed Communists were being pulled into indus-try, and could win leadership in trade unions. Inside the Party, workerism remained hegemonic. Bob Stewart warned congress delegates against 'un-scrupulous semi-intellectuals who pose as left-revolutionaries, who put their r's in barricades, instead of putting their arse on the barricades'.[15] He and others generalised uncritical loyalty to Stalin among recruits, and fostered 'socialist' nationalism. The influential journalist Claud Cockburn knew that 'a lot of English proletarian Communists' were bothered that the Comintern executive was 'composed of a pack of bloody foreigners'.[16] But the pull leftwards was strong. Bevan and Cripps's plan for a broad Labour movement had to be knocked on the head by Labour's executive with expulsions, and CPGB membership reached eighteen thousand by December.

Late in 1938 Fred Copeman, the former Invergordon mutineer on the CPGB Central Committee, was a British delegate to the Kremlin. He cheerfully supported any government which opposed the Nazis. CC member Bill Rust, who had been the British Political Commissar in Spain when Wally Tapsell went missing in mysterious circumstances, 'began to get fidgety', and reminded Copeman 'of a mobile jelly in the presence of some of these people. He dithered, as if he were begging alms from some great overlord. I felt they were all well aware of it and treated him accordingly.'[17] Comintern delegate J.R. Campbell later admitted that 'I knew a lot was wrong, but the Soviet Union was in danger of attack by Nazi Germany. Was I to break ranks?' He recalled speaking with someone who disappeared the next day, and was told: 'He was one of them.' So Campbell 'told Pollitt, but no one else, what he knew';[18] and by 1939 he was back in London at the *Daily Worker*.

In August 1939 most Communists were taken aback by the Hitler–Stalin pact, but not Freda Uttley. She had joined the Party after the General Strike, and married a Russian specialist in 1928. Her May 1930 article in *The Communist Review*, 'Economism Today', showed how the Third Period line contradicted Lenin's recently translated *Iskra* writings, which stressed the importance of intellectuals. Predictably, she was savaged by Moscow-trained hacks, and left for Russia, where she learned about the Ukraine famine, the privileges of Party members, and the secret police's camps. In 1936 her Jewish husband became one of their victims, and she escaped to the United States; but she did not lose her respect for Russian workers, or for Marx. Indeed, in 1940 she applied Marxist theory to Stalin's Russia and concluded: 'One can call the system state capitalism with the Bolshevik Party drawing the dividends', just like any other 'exploiting class'.[19]

During the later 1930s Fred Ball was often unemployed, with intervals as shop cleaner, window cleaner and firewood seller; though Beeching found him 'a very well read man, very learned in things like music', 'a thinker, in his own way', and 'heart and soul of the working class'. Fred's brothers became Communists, and they 'brought a lot of art students into the Party' to add to a local fisherman and 'people who were in the Left-Wing Movement'. But a 'couple of sociologists ... slowly took over, and their view of the working-class was as a sort of *deus ex machina*'. Fred saw them as 'a class enemy, who would use working-class people'. He had completed six chapters of a novel, *A Breath of Fresh Air*, but 'had to drop it then. I couldn't organise it'. However, in 1939 two of his short stories received 'very good notices', just before the Popular Front folded. That August the CPGB's knee-jerk loyalty to the Hitler–Stalin pact alienated Gollancz and split the Left Book Club leadership. The LBC Theatre Guild, which had reached 250 groups only eighteen months before, closed down in September, and in December the Club issued its first book critical of the Soviet Union. Ball and Beeching kept writing, and in 1940 they published *Personal and Partisan Poems*. Jack had intended going to university, but instead became a full-time sub-district organizer for the Party, 'hiding printing presses so that we'd be able to get a paper out', 'when the Germans came'.

Why you should be a socialist

During the Moscow trials Eddie Frow was a Communist cadre in Salford. He was active in the Left Book Club, and often visited Collet's in Manchester, but 'funnily enough, *The Ragged Trousered Philanthropists* escaped me'.[20] Yet a Salford teenager, whose father was 'a high class painter and decorator being paid a pittance for six months of every year', read his Labour College prize copy; and a Left Book Club member in Glamorgan noted that it 'was in much demand' from a library in a Liberal Working Men's Club. At Markham Welfare Association library RTP was the third most borrowed novel, behind Sinclair's *Oil!* and Gladkov's *Cement*, but ahead of Zola's *Germinal*.[21] A young council worker who 'had no time for politics' was lent a copy of 'the "Book"', and was struck by the similarity of his own position to the author's, though 'we were in many respects "better off"'. Teenager Robert Oakes was given an uncle's secondhand copy. He cut his 'political teeth' on RTP. It 'made me cry and made me bitter', and remained 'a friend and a guide' through life.

A man from Bootle, Liverpool, was one of eight children brought up by a lone mother. He found RTP 'truly represented the conditions and attitudes' he knew. He was 'well aware of Parish relief – visits to the pawnbroker, until there was nothing left to pawn, and the constant worry caused to my mother in wondering how to cope from day to day'; so the book confirmed his belief in the labour movement, and particularly in Bevan's statement that 'the Capitalist class will do anything for you, except get off from your back'. Another Bootle boy's grandfather had been in the Clarion Club, and cycled around Shropshire 'propagating the ideas of Socialism'. The boy's father, a Mersey tugboat engineer, 'continued my political education along the lines of Socialism'. Later, the young man found himself 'amongst some very progressive electricians', and became minute secretary of his union branch. The very small library he looked after soon included RTP. His working conditions were not much better, but when he tried to improve them he was sacked for being a 'rebel'.

Even German editions showed their influence. One refugee doctor's teenage daughter 'did not fully appreciate' the book at first, partly because 'my reaction to politics had previously been I wanted nothing to do with them'; but she read RTP after she joined the 'anti-fascist youth movement'. A refugee German building worker recommended a woman to read the 'haunting account of the exploitation of the poor'; it recalled her father's stories of building sites, and had 'the same effect upon my husband'. Leaders of Popular Front organisations cottoned on. George Elvin was joint General Secretary of the British Workers' Sports Association. In November 1937 he wrote an article for *Labour*, praising the recent production of Thomas's adaptation of RTP by the Reading Labour Dramatic Society as an 'excellent example of the use of the stage for propaganda purposes', and a key part of the Society's contribution to the local Trade Union Recruitment Week, after which the play was to be 'taken into the countryside'.

In 1938 Harry Pollitt noted 'a stirring far *outside* the usual circles of people who come to our meetings', yet the Party had not 'dug ourselves enough of a core of hard conscious students of Marxist theory'. Most members read very little except Party pamphlets and the *Daily Worker*. He knew that sales of fiction, especially 'proletarian fiction', were 'growing and can be used with great effect'; so every comrade 'should be also a literature seller'.[22] Stepney YCLers already ranked RTP among their '"literary" fare'. Local Communist Jack Dash read it the weekend before he began working on a building-site. He was 'all stirred up and ready to have a go', and by the end of the week the site was completely unionised.[23]

In Hertfordshire an old socialist carpenter loaned his copy of RTP to an apprentice, Eric Heffer, and it confirmed his own experiences:

'Misery' the foreman was very real. Good workers were often sacked because 'they were not fast enough'.

Carpenters were expected to hang doors, especially on speculative housing sites, at a fantastic pace. There was one story circulating amongst the men, that one joiner, told to hang sixteen doors a day, nailed them to picture rails, informed the foreman and walked off the job ...

Tressell's book had an enormous influence on me. It helped me to understand that Tories and Liberals were really different sides of the same capitalist coin. It explained simply but intelligently how capitalism worked, and why it was essential to get rid of it.[24]

Yet RTP was not the only accessible socialist literature available. John Strachey's The Theory and Practice of Socialism sold a quarter of a million copies. Hugh Dalton's Labour's Immediate Programme sold over 400,000. In two months during 1938 Strachey's Why You Should Be a Socialist sold a quarter of a million, helped by two Welwyn Garden City Communists who sold copies at three out of four houses in 'a systematic canvass of the whole town'.[25] Heffer read it, too, as well as Strachey's The Coming Struggle for Power and What Is To Be Done?

Heffer joined the LBC, but by 1939, aged 17, he was a LBC member and a Communist. He was sure 'Stalin was the greatest of men', the Soviet Union 'was a workers' state' and the CPGB 'was truly a workers' party'. He read Soviet Weekly, the History of the CPSU(B), Francis Cornford, A.L. Morton, Andrew Rothstein and T.A. Jackson. 'It was all important, it developed my education'. Yet 'propaganda about the Moscow Trials was accepted', and he was 'not exactly encouraged to read anti-Soviet, anti-CP socialist literature'.

We read Marx but not Bakunin, Lenin but not Kautsky, Engels but not Hegel. The anti-Marxists were referred to but not studied. Maxim Gorky was acceptable but others were not; although no index officially existed I did not read Ignazio Silone, George Orwell, Leon Trotsky, Andre Gide.[26]

But it was so impressive that Tom Thomas, the stage-adaptor of RTP, was in Heffer's branch.

Bourgeois literature with a slightly different slant

In 1937 Martin Secker bought the Richards Press, and in October 1938 he reprinted The Ragged Trousered Philanthropists. But in April 1939 the 'unrestricted' 25-year copyright lapsed, and Penguin negotiated to publish the 'abridged' 1918 edition, which fitted their policy of avoiding vulgar, 'dubious',

'sadistic' or 'salacious' books.[27] By October Penguin were 'putting in hand'
their paperback. In January 1940 Secker asked 'if the printers of your
edition remembered to save the text from which they set up', and noted
that Miss Pope had suggested that 'the Penguin people' print her foreword on the wrapper, since it was 'adequate introduction to the book'.[28]

In 1940 publishers were limited to two-fifths of their pre-war paper
usage, but Penguin's had been huge. Their sixpenny paperback RTP, mis-
described as 'Complete' and 'Unabridged', was published in April, in
what was probably a standard edition of 50,000 copies.[29] It appeared as
the Nazis overran Holland and Belgium, and Churchill became prime
minister in the wake of Dunkirk; and it was praised by *The Daily Telegraph*
and *The Times*. The printing sold out in one month – *a rate of over one copy every
minute*. It was reprinted in May, re-set to use fewer pages, and the sales-
rate slowed to one copy every seven minutes. The book fed into the
market formed by the LBC, whose July 1940 offering, *Guilty Men*, by
Michael Foot and others, lambasted the pre-war National Government,
and went on to sell 220,000 copies.

Penguin's RTP was small, light and cheap, and became a particular hit
in the armed forces. One soldier considered himself a socialist before he
read it, but was 'amazed how clear the theory of Socialism was put'. So,
even though the book 'gave the impression that whilst the system was all
wrong, nothing could really be done', he lent it to army comrades. An
army corporal was 'mooching about the Charing Cross Road bookshops'
when he spotted the book 'in a cheap hard-covered edition'. 'I had a few
shillings to spend and needed something to read.' He felt 'the bitter ending' was 'all too prophetic', yet the book taught him 'that in the last
resort my home comforts are due to the dirty jobs done by the working
classes'. Other members of the middle class had already learned that lesson.

George Orwell had been introduced to *The Ragged Trousered Philanthropists* by
a Leeds librarian in 1932.[30] In December 1940 he argued that before 1890
'very few genuine proletarians' could 'write with enough facility to produce a book or a story'; so he felt it 'was a big step forward when the
facts of working-class life were first got onto paper', and RTP was 'possibly
the first book that did this'. It 'has always seemed to me to be a wonderful book, although very clumsily written. It recorded things that were
every day experience but which had simply not been noticed before.' Yet
he was confident that the book was not 'the beginning of a new age in
literature'. Such 'heterogeneous literature belonging to a transition period'.

It was 'founded on the revolt against capitalism', but that was 'disappearing' in the wartime transition to a 'classless period'. He took Trotsky's perspective: 'I don't believe the proletariat can create an independent literature while they are not the dominant class. I believe that their literature is and must be bourgeois literature with a slightly different slant.'[31]

Penguin reprinted in January 1941. The paper quota was cut to one half of pre-war usage, and then to three-eighths. Some 20 million books had been destroyed by bombing raids, and in the summer a 'really prodigious demand for books set in'.[32] Sales of book tokens rose to over three-quarters of a million. Allen Lane of Penguin Books had recruited William Emrys Williams, former secretary of the British Institute of Adult Education and editor of the WEA's The Highway; and as wartime director of the Army Bureau of Current Affairs, between 1941 and 1945 Williams negotiated a deal between Pelican and the Forces Book Club. An RAF man in the Egyptian desert had read little after leaving school in Ireland four years before, but his unit of forty men had a 'very rudimentary lending library', run by the medical orderly, 'who had been a Bradford labourer before the war, and who, as far as I know, never read a book in his life'. 'Most of this small stock of books were paperbacks, supplied by the Red Cross', and 'the bulk of them were Penguin publications'. RTP was 'a much read book', and 'by the time I got to it was very limp, dog-eared and decrepit'. A young mother whose husband was overseas was loaned a copy by 'an "artisan" Socialist', who 'doubtless thought I ought to try and understand why!' She joined the Labour Party.

By 1940 CPGB membership had more than recovered, and the entry of the Soviet Union into the war in June 1941 seemed to change everything. The ban on the Daily Worker was lifted in September. Its enthusiasm for the war knew no bounds, and readership soon reached half a million. By 1942, after the Red Army's defence of Stalingrad, CPGB membership reached 56,000, or perhaps even 63,000, since members in the forces were supposed to drop their affiliation. However, some comrades believed the high membership figure was a 'pure fiddle': 'Eighty percent' were 'persons who paid a shilling a month to door-to-door collectors and never participated in Party branch meetings or any form of political activity'.[33] McShane believed that 'the whole character of the party changed'. 'For the first time we had a predominantly paper membership. Hundreds of people filled in membership forms during the huge Second Front meetings'; but 'only about a third of them ever turned up to branch meetings', and while members were 'educated', it was 'only along the current party line'.[34]

On the home front the Party line was to get involved in joint production committees (which had the full backing of Ernest Bevin's Ministry of Labour), to oppose all strikes (which became more frequent after 1942), to campaign against absenteeism and to argue against stopping work, even after fatal accidents in the pits. All that helped the war effort, and so Russia, but at the cost of making UK capitalism work more efficiently without an irreversible shift in power. In the forces it was different. Eric Heffer found a network of comrades in the RAF, and a ready audience for socialist ideas: 'I always carried some pamphlets on CP theory like Little Lenin Libraries, *Communist Manifestos*, and so on. I lent them out and got involved in discussions the whole time.'[35] John Sommerfield, an RAF fitter, took the line from Jack Lindsay's *England, My England* that 'Communism is English'. He was posted to a forward airfield in Burma, and 'there wasn't much to read. But I had a sort of little library that travelled with us, disguised as a box of 20-millimetre cannon shells.' Part of the ammunition was RTP. It 'was only a Penguin edition and, unfortunately, didn't last long, being handed around and read and re-read until it literally fell to pieces.'[36]

In January 1942 book-production standards were cut by the War Economy Agreement, yet Penguin's RTP was still selling one copy every fourteen minutes. It was reprinted in May, and published in Harmondsworth and New York. Opposite the title page was a note: 'FOR THE FORCES. Leave this book at a Post Office when you have read it, so that men and women in the services may enjoy it too.' Penguin understood that 'the most effective and persistent factor' in their sales was word of mouth.[37] A 'politically unaware' airman, staying with an uncle 'very active in national politics and the I.L.P', wrote that he had never experienced

> any of the deprivations, the sordid living conditions, the extreme poverty that many of my contemporaries had to face during the 20s and 30s. Frank challenged my rather smug middle-class arrogance and provided some insights as to the realities of capitalism. Before I left he gave me his copy of 'The Ragged Trousered Philanthropists' and that convinced me of the rights of the common man.

Frank Horrabin was still putting the book to work.

In Jamaica, Kathleen Noonan heard from an 'air force chap' that the book was 'one of the musts' in sociology classes. RTP was published in

Melbourne by Lothian (but with 'Penguin Books' on the cover) in October 1942. The South African paper Forward later took it for granted that 'Hundreds, perhaps thousands of South Africans have read' 'that classic of working-class life'.[38] But in the UK the novel had serious competition. From December the Beveridge Report sold over 600,000 copies. Nine-tenths of the population wanted its social security provisions adopted, and Labour got a National Health Service White Paper through Parliament. After victory in North Africa, and the German defeat at Stalingrad, every UK opinion poll showed a swing to Labour.

The book that won the '45 election for Labour

By September 1943 there were over four million men and women in the Britih forces. *The Ragged Trousered Philanthropists* circulated in the navy. In the army one man found that it 'influenced me greatly, because it related socialist thought to everyday life and work'; and what he saw in India 'reinforced the beliefs I had begun to form'. A Grenadier Guardsman took a copy into educational classes, where his friends, who were 'all young socialists', found it 'supremely clear'; but another squaddie claimed he was ordered not to read such 'subversive literature'! On the home front Percy Allott, city district secretary of the Shop Assistants' Union, contributed to Lawrence & Wishart's *Books against Barbarism*, and noted that RTP

> left an abiding impression upon my mind, a deeper conviction of the necessity for Socialist education and trade union organisation, and a stronger belief in the inherent truth of Marxism and the class struggle.
>
> I have been reading it again, and I find that for me it has lost none of its vital force, pathos and human appeal...
>
> Read this book; recommend it to all your friends, to all potential socialists and trade unionists; and to all who love literature which depicts life in all its stark reality – shot with pain – but also shot with promise.[39]

Who could deliver on such promises?

By March 1943 CPGB membership had gone down to 45,000, well below the mass base achieved by Communists in Italy and France; moreover, 85 per cent of them had been recruited since 1935. But in June Stalin abolished the Comintern, so the TUC was obliged to withdraw the 'Black Circulars', and wholesalers ended their ban on the *Daily Worker*. The CPGB rebranded itself as the Communist Party: the Central Committee became an Executive Committee; the Politburo was now the Political

Committee, and factory cells became 'groups'. Some 100,000 people left the Labour Party, and that figure 'almost certainly masked a greater decline'; yet 300,000 stayed in.[40]

By 1944 working-class people were open to socialist ideas. On average, they read for between three and five hours per week; and, as thoughts turned more and more to the post-war world, there was a surge in demand in bookshops and libraries. One chief librarian believed workers read RTP 'to understand the world better'.[41] Richards Press reprinted the 1914 edition of RTP as a hardback – 'the 125th thousand – in August 1943; and, as paper rationing eased slightly, they reprinted again in April, July and December 1944. The dustjacket showed a dispirited man leaning against a lamppost, and the book plugged this 'faithful picture of working men',

> driven by misery and want, ignorance and fear, into an anti-social attitude of hopeless despair. Their lives and thoughts, their work and leisure, their politics, their reactions to the message of a workmate who tries to help them understand the causes and cure of their poverty and squalor, are depicted with the stark realism possible only to one who has taken part in their struggle and has known at first hand their puny hopes and their ever-present fears.

Penguin also reprinted in 1944, on thinner paper, and with the pages kept together by staples. Their UK price remained sixpence, but a copy sold in Sydney, Australia, was over-stamped ninepence. After the landings in Normandy, both 'puny hopes and ever-present fears' and the war looked set to end, and in October 1944 the Labour Party announced that it would fight the first post-war election as an independent party.

By 1945 the LBC had put about 6 million books into circulation. But after Gollancz's experience of Stalinism, and even though, in his words, there had 'always been a certain detachment in my attitude to the Labour Party', he was 'almost painfully anxious' that Labour should be elected, since he could see 'little hope for humanity unless democratic socialism can be firmly established in this island, as a focus and model for the rest of the world'.[42] Labour's programme, Let Us Face the Future, was published in April. It did not propose to abolish the House of Lords, but hoped to be able to 'work towards' the nationalisation of land, and promised a National Health Service and the nationalisation of major industries. Yet its fundamental assumption was that post-war capitalism would bring 'full employment and the highest possible industrial efficiency', so that class struggle would diminish.

Could the Popular Front be revived? In February 1945, after Stalin,
Churchill and Roosevelt had agreed a carve-up of post-war spheres of
influence at Yalta, Dutt had argued for a post-war coalition, and insisted
that any Communist who predicted an independent Labour government
was being 'dangerously unrealistic'.[43] Thew idea of a coalition was well
received by delegates at the May Labour Party conference; but in the event
it was rejected. The war had helped create a larger working-class reading
public, and had definitely raised interest in socialist ideas, but not in
Stalinism. During May the formerly critical Richard Fox recalled in the
New Leader that RTP had 'made a deep impression'. Yet the Penguin edition
was unknown to one-time Workers' Bookshop rep, Charley Hall,[44] and CP
full-timer Ernie Trory hinted that the book was outdated.[45]

Towards the end of the war a young Liverpudlian found himself in an
Indian jungle. He read the Penguin edition of 'Tressell's great masterpiece', given to him 'by one of my company officers who had distinct
"left" inclinations', then loaned it 'to so many people (literally dozens of
them) that by the time that I brought it back to England it was in a very
sorry state indeed'. He had been a socialist since he was 16, but it 'certainly reinforced my views'. Another soldier recalled that it 'passed from
hand to hand' in the Parachute Regiment 'in semi-secrecy', since officers
'did not approve its searching expose of the system'; yet 'it was not even
safe to leave a copy down for even a moment' because it disappeared. It
'changed the views of many'. He was sure that 'at least 90 per cent of the
rankers voted Labour'.

At the July 1945 general election the CP slogan was 'Labour and a
progressive majority'. Party candidatures were cut to twenty-two, but
Labour opposed them all. Moreover, where the Party did not stand, Communists argued for a vote for Labour, even though this meant Bevin as
well as Bevan. The Daily Worker's eve-of-poll headline was 'Vote as Red as
you Can', but the CP vote was just over 100,000. Only Willie Gallacher
and Phil Piratin won seats, though about a dozen Communists were
returned as Labour MPs. Labour won almost 12 million votes and nearly
four hundred seats. What was on offer was not a choice between reform
and revolution, but between a small left-reformist party and a big one
that looked electable and pushed what sounded like socialist ideas.

The Communist Mervyn Jones found that 'what people mostly said in
explaining why they had voted Labour was that they were guarding against
a return to the unemployment and poverty of the thirties'. Let Us Face the

Future 'caught the mood', and 'the way to get things done was to be in the Labour Party'.[46] Heffer felt CP policy was 'to the right of some of Labour's policies and the views of many Labour Party members'.

> The 'Export or Die' policy was the official line of the CP. Workers going on strike were discouraged and often attacked. The government was defended when it seemed to us that the party should have exposed its policies, particularly as they affected the workers. But our main dispute with the leadership was theoretical and revolved around the attitudes that the party should adopt towards the state and revolution; Lenin's ideas were being abandoned.[47]

Former revolutionary syndicalist George Hicks was now Labour MP for East Woodford.

After the Labour landslide Nottingham teenager Alan Sillitoe was conscripted, and trained as an RAF wireless operator. Posted to Malaya in May 1947, he 'wanted something to read after fourteen hours taking down scarcely audible morse'. A signals corporal from Glasgow handed him a Penguin. It 'was obvious straight away that the writer, in not calling it "The Ragged-*Arsed* Philanthropists" had chosen its final and more proper sounding title knowing that otherwise it could not be published.'[48] Sillitoe 'ran through to the end without stopping', and

> from being a press-ganged participant in the Malayan Rubber War I was switched back to what I'd done – though not too unhappily – on leaving school: cleaning out suffocating flues of soot-blocked factory chimneys, scaling boilers from the inside in which candles flickered and went out every few minutes through lack of air. My first meeting with a 'proletarian novel' gave perspective to these things, showed me that the life I'd led was interesting enough to be written about.[49]

He recalled what his pal had said: 'You ought to read this. Among other things it is the book that won the '45 election for Labour.'[50]

9

King Street were lost

A shower of shits

The post-war history of *The Ragged Trousered Philanthropists* is bound up with that of the Communist Party. After being demobbed from the navy Jack Beeching worked at its King Street headquarters, but 'hated the place'. There were a few '*bloody* good blokes', 'there were bullies, and there were careerists' who had 'tumbled to the fact' that leading the working class 'didn't matter any more'. 'What you had to do was give the Russians a good report of what was going on – be their ears, so to speak – and give the English a good report of what was going on in Russia. If the Russians insisted on something being applied', then 'you jolly well did'. Hacks 'used to send the most lying reports about activity to the Soviet Union', and that 'made a clear, cultural and political line almost impossible'. However, 'King Street didn't speak with one voice', though it 'would liked to have believed that it did', so Russian control 'was never, I think, monolithic'. But the 'hard core of time-servers' were 'a shower of shits'.

Some people now like to believe that there was a 'cultural opposition' inside the post-war CP, which included Randall Swingler and Jack Lindsay; yet they rely on what ex-CPer Willie Thompson calls 'collective amnesia'.[1] During the Moscow trials *Left Review* refused to carry an advertisement for *The Case of Leon Trotsky*, a work which completely exonerated the former Red Army leader from Stalinist smears. Swingler told *New Statesman* readers: 'there is a line at which criticism ends and destructive attacks begin, and we regret that this line separates us both from Dr. Goebbels and from Leon Trotsky.' In *Tribune*, Lindsay argued that 'the cleavage between the men

145

who trusted the power of the masses, and the men who trusted only their own "cleverness" had to come'.[2] Stalin's assassin murdered Trotsky in 1940. In 1941, the CP line on the war was completely reversed, allowing Montagu Slater to become head of film scripts for the Ministry of Information. By 1945 he was chief drama critic at *Reynold's News*. Lindsay was on the London PEN Club Committee. Swingler wrote for literary journals, and owned Fore Pubs, which published *Our Time*, the successful wartime periodical. Their problem was that the CP was a 'very conservative organisation' with 'Stalinist reflexes',[3] which tended to be triggered by imaginative initiatives.

Early in 1945 the CP's Propaganda and Education Collective established a National Arts Advisory Collective. King Street apparatchiks Emile Burns, who edited *World News and Views* and had acted as Pollitt's deputy, and Robin Page-Arnot, who was a long-time associate of the 'nucleus' as well as being Dutt's deputy at *Labour Monthly*, invited Party writers to a meeting, and proposed forming a Party Writers' Group. A provisional committee of Slater, Lindsay and Edgell Rickword was appointed in April. Alick West, who had organised the Left Book Club Writers and Readers Group with John Lewis, was co-opted at the first meeting.[4] Beeching knew West was the literary figure whose brains Burns 'picked', though 'both of them were up the pole'.

The Party Writers' Group held its first meeting in June, at the Salisbury pub in St Martin's Lane. Page-Arnot was in the chair. At a subsequent meeting of the 'Salisbury Group' George Thomson and Edward Thompson had to defend Lindsay when he was 'unmasked' by Lewis as 'some kind of revisionist heretic'. Thompson recalled that Lindsay

> was high on alienation and reification … and had put Marx and Freud together in the bed of a single book. This book or another was (as I recall) 'withdrawn' as 'incorrect', and Lindsay was denounced at an enlarged 'aggregate' of the Writers' Group. I remember the immense shaggy head of the anthropologist V. Gordon Childe, just in front of me, shaking in fury at the general scene of dogmatism.[5]

In July came the Labour landslide. Culture moved up the Party agenda, Beeching believed, because 'King Street were lost'.

That autumn the USA dropped atomic bombs on Japan, and the Soviet Union called on all Communists to rally to its defence. At the British Party Congress in November there was 'only one slogan' – 'increase the sale of the *Daily Worker*'. Beeching recalled thinking:

they don't know what they're doing, don't know where they're going. The whole of the political movement was standing, not knowing which way to turn. What was one's attitude to the Labour Party? How would one criticise the things that the Labour Party were bringing in?

Pollitt was stuck in the Popular Front rut. He argued that there was 'a common interest between the working class and the progressive sections of the capitalist class', so conditions were 'objectively more favourable for the peaceful transition to Socialism than they have ever been'.[6] Delegates denounced his defence of blacklegging, but the CC blamed

> the sectarian outlook still prevailing in some sections of our party. To change this, it is essential that our members take a lively interest in all questions in which the people are interested, including social, art, music, literature, entertainment and sport.[7]

By March 1946 after the CP had lost three thousand members, the Comintern announced that each nation would 'effect its transition to Socialism' by 'its own road'.[8]

International events bore down on King Street. In March 1947 the 'Truman doctrine' committed the USA to oppose any revolution it saw as Communist-inspired. Moscow abandoned hope of peaceful coexistence. In April a CP National Cultural Committee was established, with Burns as Chair, and Sam Aaronovitch as Secretary. By May the NCC had identified 'a number of basic questions on which divergent view-points existed, which had better be thrashed out among ourselves'.[9] Maurice Cornforth, editor of Modern Quarterly, was involved. He was one of half a dozen Communists who formed a Cambridge cell in 1931. After acting as Secretary of the Cambridge City Branch, he bacame Party organizer in East Anglia. In 1939–40 he supported the Hitler–Stalin Pact on the grounds that the Soviet state 'can do no wrong, and is doing no wrong'.[10] To Beeching, he was 'a nice bloke, but they'd got him'. And Party writers

> soon discovered which way the cat was going to jump when Zhdanov in Petrograd (Leningrad) brought out his long, calculated diatribe against certain tendencies in biology, philosophy, and literature and so on. It was completely illiterate nonsense, but very clear and very calculated.

That spring's Modern Quarterly contained an article by Andrei Zhdanov, the Leningrad Party boss, who asked: 'if rubbish is tolerated in the education of the youth', was it not 'more serious guilt than the nonfulfilment of a production plan or the disruption of an industrial task?' Party writers were 'in the front line of the ideological struggle' and must 'educate the people and arm them ideologically'. Beeching knew 'this attack on the intellectual, cultivated, devoted left' was designed to show up 'their illusions about the way ahead, socially, and the role that communism would play'. The stubborn were quickly brought into line. Swingler's Fore Pubs was forced to sell *Theatre Today* and *Seven*, which subsidised *Our Time*, whose sales had halved. David Holbrook and Edward Thompson had been pressing for a more anti-American line, and when Swingler was attacked at a King Street meeting, they joined in.[11] Thompson recalled:

> Scolded in this way, these two immensely more wise, more deeply-political, and more cultured men ... sat passively, winced, and suffered without making a defence ... It was a shameful episode and I shared in the shame, for, however 'youthful' I was, I had allowed myself to be made use of as part of the team of uncultured yobboes and musclemen under the command of the elderly Burns.[12]

The Cold War was under way. In September *World News and Views* announced that the planet was split into the 'imperialist undemocratic camp' and the 'anti-imperialist democratic camp', so there was a need for a 'co-ordinated programme of action ... against American imperialism'. British and French Communists above all 'must take into their hands the banner of the defence of the national independence and sovereignty of their own countries', and gather around them all the democratic and patriotic forces of the people'. In October the Cominform propaganda offensive accelerated. Holbrook was put in control of *Our Time*, with an 'editorial commission' which included Slater and Beeching.[13]

In November *Our Time*'s editors contributed to the NCC discussion on 'Un-American activities', and their pessimism about 'the intelligentsia' became plain. They found

> defeatism, return to religion and/or obscurantism, and a general retreat from reality. Both because of the social pressure upon intellectuals to attack communism, and the profitability of such attacks, workers in all cultural fields are subject to continuous corruption whose end-product is a renunciation of *all* progressive ideas, *all* notions of the artist's social responsibility, and *all* belief in humanity.

Because of monopolistic mass media, the 'nation's mass culture tends to reflect a slick, dreary decadence'. So *Our Time*'s job was to 'help the development of a fuller national culture', not 'by appealing *directly* to ordinary cinema, "Daily Mirror", dog-race audiences', or to the 'Bloomsbury intelligentsia', but to the 'true intellectuals who are to be found in all sections of the community', especially 'intellectuals at the bench'. By December the NCC had limited the Writers' Group to professionals who were (or could be) members of PEN and the Society of Authors. Lindsay's name headed their list.

In January 1948 the NCC focused on the 'Penetration of US "Way of Life" into Britain' and planned a symposium on 'The British literary tradition'. They looked forward to 'improving the leadership of our work in the battle of ideas'.[14] A new policy document had recently been published under Pollitt's name. Looking Ahead assumed that Britain should 'survive as a great, independent nation', and not play a subordinate role as 'the slaves and cannon fodder' of the USA. So the 'people' had to be split from 'sections of the old reformist leadership', who, 'fearing and hating the mass movements of the people, turn to Wall Street, that democracy of millionaires and Negro lynchers', rather than 'engage in that hard class battle for the defeat of capitalism in their own country'. Labour had to 'declare an emergency situation', give ration books only to those willing to do 'useful work', stop emigration, strengthen Joint Production Committees, get workers in key industries to work one weekend in four, and purge 'compromisers with big business' and collaborators with Truman's foreign policy. Then the 'people' would be able to 'move towards Socialism without further revolution, without the dictatorship of the proletariat'. The 'people' included 'important sections of professional workers, technicians, artists, writers and thinkers', 'shopkeepers, working farmers and all who have a truly democratic and progressive outlook', plus 'doctors or teachers, scientists or architects, writers or singers, poets or painters, lawyers or small businessmen'.[15]

Communist Party members were disorientated. McShane believed that a 'whole bunch of middle-class people' took over the EC and 'drove the older members out'. Many 'saw no point now in working inside the Communist Party when the party was no longer distinguishable from the Labour movement. They might as well be in the trade union as officials, or inside the Labour Party'.[16] Looking Ahead was withdrawn, and John Gollan, then being groomed as Pollitt's successor, led the about-face. In February 1948 he argued in Communist Review that the pace of Labour's nationalisation 'could not be slower', that industry boards were 'the old gang thinly disguised, and that profit sanctified by the name of interest on State bonds still remains profit'. To achieve 'the inevitable victory of world Communism' in an age of 'new imperialism', comrades had to recognise that 'nothing fundamental has changed. It is still the Britain of profits and subsistence wages, of master and man, of privilege and lack of privilege, of class and class.'

At the March 1948 Party congress Burns argued that Communists had to 'defeat the imperialist propaganda, to expose its class character, whether it finds expression in open politics or in concealed forms in ethical, philosophical, historical or sociological ideas, or in the field of science, literature or art'.[17] Zhdanov had recently told a conference of Soviet music workers that 'Internationalism in art does not spring from the depletion and impoverishment of national art; on the contrary, internationalism grows where national culture flourishes.'[18] The April *Communist Review* reported an NCC conference attended by six hundred delegates, where Aaronovitch argued that the fight was on 'for a democratic people's culture that would inherit and extend the great achievements of our country'. In May *Our Time* celebrated not the centenary of revolutions in other parts of Europe but the comparatively modest British events of 1848. In June there was a serious rift between the Soviet Union and Yugoslavia. Burns closed 'The Soviet Discussions' in the autumn *Modern Quarterly*, insisting that 'cultural heritage is in its essence national'. Two months previously Zhdanov's early and unexpected death had been front-page news in the Cominform's English-language paper. Burns kept a copy in the NCC files, and *World News and View* stressed that comrades were 'strongly advised to study and re-study' Zhdanov's speeches.

The need to do away with capitalism

The Ragged Trousered Philanthropists remained politically active. Just after the end of the war Kathleen Lynne heard that it was being used as a textbook at the London School of Economics. A Durham miner had read the book 'many, many years' before, but his son, a mining engineer, knew it was always included in the books on sale at Labour College events, and at the Durham Miners' Gala. It reinforced 'our ideas and beliefs in Socialism'. A teenager found that, much more than her father's LBC collection, it 'caught my imagination and inspired a sense of the injustice of society which has endured'. After being 'one of a small band of working-class students' at Lady Margaret Hall, Oxford, she joined the Labour Party. Another teenager worked in an office with 'a very intelligent, very sensitive man some

twenty years older', who 'would question me upon my views about the
world'. She was 'very orthodox and very conventional', until he loaned
her RTP. She 'sat up far into the night absolutely absorbed'. It 'brought me
into contact with reality' and 'showed the blindness of the majority of
people to the true nature of the system in which they were exploited',
'converting me completely to the idea of Socialism' – the need 'to do
away with Capitalism'.

Brendan Behan's father was a Dublin painter, and 'the first book he'd
ever heard tell of was the painter's bible'. Both parents spoke of Irish
history and would 'come back by way of nineteen sixteen' to RTP. When
Brendan became a painter he found that 'on every job you'd hear painters
using the names out of it for nicknames, calling their own apprentice
"The Walking Colour Shop" and, of course, every walking foreman was
called Nimrod, even by painters who had never read the book.'[19] An Irish
worker recalled that when he first made contact with elements of the
British left, RTPs passed around 'with admonitions to be careful and return them when read as it was difficult to get other copies'. He and his
mates 'searched the bookstalls of the second-hand trade diligently, but
few people who had their own copies were making them available to the
second-hand trade'.

A Londoner, who had read the 'short version' of RTP before the war,
gave a copy to her plasterer husband. He found 'many, many jobs'

> had not changed very much and often conditions, toilet facilities, drying
> and eating arrangements (or lack of them) were too often just the same. He
> used the book constantly on various sites in and around London, and also
> in the film studios where he worked for many years. He was very active in
> the Union as a steward and official all his life.

During the war a London boy had helped repair bomb damage in his
school holidays, and had eaten sandwiches in 'filthy dust covered bug-
ridden rooms', where 'weak tea (rationing) drunk out of old jam jars was
common'. He read his father's copy of RTP in 1948, and it 'confirmed'
that conditions 'had changed so little'. He became very active in the
AUBTW, and a delegate to the Trades Council and the local Labour Party,
where there was a 'very low level of education', but he did his bit, using
the book. His father, a painter and decorator, had been a rail worker
during the General Strike, and was victimised. He normally 'voted Liberal
Tory or not at all', but RTP 'probably' made him vote Labour in 1950.

In September 1948 Thomas's adaptation of RTP was still being staged;[20]

but in May 1949 London Unity Theatre put on Bill Rowbotham's version, with an amateur cast and a professional producer. The actors' script was signed by the NFBTO's General Secretary, Sir Richard Coppock. It was a 'privilege', since the play '"Spotlights" those days with a compelling harshness which will make the audience appreciate the progress which the industry has achieved, and the great strength which the trade union movement has attained'. True, 'the system remains fundamentally the same; we still have an industry actuated by the profit motive'; but the play will 'spur us to fight for a building industry unfettered by Capitalism', and to 'achieve Robert Tressell's Socialism'.[21]

Rowbotham's script was largely a pastiche of Thomas's Popular Front version, but it was one of the few London Unity productions playing to full houses. *Picture Post* felt that Owen 'emerges as a bit of a bore', but acknowledged that nationalisation had 'disappointed those who expected a workers' millennium to arrive overnight with a change in control'. It hoped that 'the improvements in wages and conditions which his trade unions have obtained, our pension schemes and health service, and the end of the poor law, would possibly have won his approval of the way we're going'. There was no vote in favour of trade unionism at the end. The *Daily Worker* thought it would 'make recruits for our movement', but Len Green found the characters 'nothing like the men' he and Noonan had worked with.

The Grant Richards purchase action

Fred Ball claimed he was 'thrown out of the home guard' when he rejoined the CP, which was probably after 1941; but in 1942 he got interested in RTP again, and was 'amazed to discover that thirty years after the author's death no biography of him existed'. He wrote to the local paper, and to Grant Richards. Eventually, in March 1943 Richards offered to try to track down the manuscript, which he thought might fetch 'something like' £50. That was beyond Ball's means, and though 'someone suggested that the Communist Party Museum might be interested', it was 'beyond their pocket', too. However, in 1944 Ball interviewed Alice Meiklejon, Noonan's niece, and Edward and Phoebe Cruttenden.

Frank Swinnerton understood that 'before what was virtually his retirement from active publishing', Richards 'thought of his secretary', Pauline Hemmerde, who had served him with a lifetime's devotion':

Fred Ball, c. 1940

He could make no provision for her, could leave her no legacy, but there was the manuscript of The Ragged Trousered Philanthropists, to which she had first introduced him. He gave it to her. 'It may come in useful on a rainy day', he said.

It did. Evidently she sold it 'to a stranger across the marble-topped table of a London tea-shop' for £10,[22] 'just after the Second World War'. In November 1945 Robert Partridge of Harwell RAF Station offered Ball the manuscript for £315. In December Ball's literary agent, Andrew Kelt, claimed in the South African paper Forward that his client's 'information about Tressall in England' was 'almost complete'. Richards Press reprinted RTP in April 1946. After negotiations involving Richards and his agent, the manuscript price was cut to fifty guineas in August, then raised to £75.

Five years later Ball recalled that he bought the manuscript in a teashop near the Elephant and Castle Underground Station in London in September 1946, with sixty-three pound notes borrowed from 'a friend, Mr A. Kelt'. When Ball got it home 'a number of working-men – nobodies – were extremely interested and read it eagerly on my kitchen table'. It was 'agreed that seven people should subscribe ten guineas each and become joint owners of the MS. – the extra ten going towards incidental expenses and the balance towards the biography of the author'. So Kelt was repaid with 'no difficulty (as most of them were just out of the army and had fortunes varying from £20 to £30 each)'.[23]

Twenty-seven years after these events Ball wrote that Kelt arrived at the Elephant and Castle with the cash in his pocket and was actively involved in the 'momentous transaction'. Ball 'now had to raise the money for four shares to return to Mrs and Mrs Kelt who had decided to take two shares each themselves, and these I had no difficulty in raising from among the friends who had originally offered'. The four he named were Peter Blackman, George Jackson, Ernie Bevis and Gregory Gildersleeve.

> The six shares, we decided, should in fact be called seven, in event of resale at any time, the seventh being allocated to me in consideration of my efforts and expenses in obtaining the manuscript and for its safe custody as it was to be left in my charge.[24]

The 'shareholders' included a clerk, a window cleaner, a teacher, a Gas Board employee, and 'a couple' of unnamed 'personal friends'.

In the winter of 1946–47 Ball was out of work for three months and had begun writing his biography of 'Tressell'; but when he got a job with the South Eastern Gas Board, as a meter collector and clerk, the project stalled. P.J. Waters, then in his early thirties, worked with Ball for a time, and remembered Fred, his first wife, Elsie, Horace Chantler and Peter Blackman at 27 Edmund Road, Hastings, 'looking at the MS contents of a biscuit tin of the original story of the book'. Waters wrote up his notes as 'the Grant Richards purchase action'.

Richards Press reprinted RTP in March 1947. On 30 May Grant Richards could see 'no obstacle' to Ball's publication of the complete manuscript,

> if you can get hold of the Tressell heir, but your book, to be effective, would have to include the published parts, which are, of course, controlled by the Richards Press. This should not be very difficult. I have seen the Richards Press – the sooner we can have a look the better. Of course you could take the risk of no one turning up with claims as heir which would bear investigation – and I don't think there is a great risk.[25]

After failing to buy paper (which was still under wartime restrictions), Richards had a heart attack.[26] In August he travelled to Monte Carlo, where he died, aged 76, on 24 February 1948, leaving 'no fortune'.[27]

Jack Beeching knew about the manuscript 'quite early on'. Fred was 'very possessive of it'. He 'kept it under his bed, and wouldn't show anybody', since he 'was determined that it would also make his name'. He 'would exaggerate the amount of special knowledge he had of Tressell; and altogether it got mixed up with his private fantasies'. In June 1948 a 'letter' from 'Jack Salford ["Crass, the Foreman"], Edmonton' appeared in

Our Time. In July Lawrence & Wishart, Birch Books Ltd, Fore Publications Ltd and Central Books asked to see the RTP manuscript. One of Ball's brothers delivered it by hand as he 'wouldn't trust it to the post'. That same month Frank Jackson published an essay, 'Robert Noonan was not Defeatist', in the *New Builders Leader*. Then – 'the Party put me in there' – Beeching got Ball 'to consent to various things' concerning the manuscript. He 'didn't want to let it go. He didn't want people to know about it. If they didn't know about it, they couldn't do anything about it. If they did know it was there, they'd ask him to give a talk and pay him.' So Ball 'had to be rather heavily persuaded' to allow 'the existence of the book and the question of publishing it a public issue'. Ball later acknowledged there was 'a suspicion, that I have never been able completely to dispel, that I must have some personal advantage to gain through publication'.[28]

In October 1948 Beeching reproduced the manuscript's title page and last page, and quoted previously unpublished passages in *Our Time*. He argued that even the abridged RTP had 'probably made more socialists among the English working class than any other book. Working men who normally read no books have read it closely.' His own grandfather regarded it as 'holy writ', and as a child Jack had 'had one man or another pointed out to me as the original of a Tressell character'. But his main focus was on the rediscovered Barrington. 'Evidently it was Tressell's intention to show how the revolutionary Socialist movement is built on an alliance between the most honest and courageous intellectuals and the working-class movement.' Beeching noted that it was 'quite hard to find even a Penguin copy today', and suggested that 'a definitive edition' be published, together with 'a biography of its author'. Luckily, a TGWU delegate to Hastings Trades Council had spent five years writing just such a book.

That same month the Richards Press reprinted RTP. They noted that an 'abridged edition has been issued by Penguin Books Ltd', but emphasised their own copyright. George Bernard Shaw told Ball that he 'never knew of Robert Tressell and am not interested in him';[29] but Ball hoped the Associated Society of Woodworkers would buy the manuscript. However, Beeching persuaded him to offer the manuscript to Lawrence & Wishart. The book was useful ammunition in a larger CP debate. Beeching had already argued in print that the Popular Front had been 'a false dawn', since many intellectuals were joining 'the Anti-Popular Front'; so 'the survival of the English tradition' of the novel which he and others wanted to see was 'in the hands of the working class'.[30]

At King Street, as Beeching knew, 'everybody had their own theory about' RTP, however 'odd', but they were mostly 'very large palaces of theory with very little solidity about them'. To make matters worse, 'the Party as a whole, and it must be said in some ways the working-class movement as a whole, was philistine'. However, on the question of publishing RTP, while 'there may have been people who didn't see the point, people who saw the point but got the point wrong, wanted a different kind of book', 'there was no opposition', 'nothing of a political campaign' against it. Yet on 8 November Lawrence & Wishart told Ball that, given 'the number of editions on the market of the expurgated version and especially the number in the Penguin edition that must have been sold, the directors are of the opinion that the market has been flooded as far as the ordinary reader goes'. They suggested he 'might organise publication by subscription or by the raising of a national fund',[31] and turned the manuscript down.

The American threat to British culture

The 1945 Labour government had started with a lower level of national wealth than at any time since Napoleonic days, and debts of almost £11 billion. They then paid out over £2.5 billion (around £60 billion at today's values) for worn-out railways and pits. Even the Tory Harold Macmillan recognised that the National Coal Board represented not socialism but 'State capitalism'.[32] Labour instituted a national health service, but they also kowtowed to consultants. Moreover, they kept the same Civil Service advisers, and gave powerful positions on key government committees to bankers, industrialists and stockbrokers. The 1927 anti-trade-union laws were repealed, but the OMS provisions used to break the General Strike were put to work. Labour broke strikes with troops eighteen times (including two states of emergency), took strike leaders to court, and helped anti-Communist witch-hunting. They also marginalised most trade-union leaders, resisted equal pay for teachers and civil servants, cut council-house targets by one-third, and failed to raise the school-leaving age or increase the number of working-class students who went to university. In 1946 bread was rationed. In 1947 so were potatoes.

Urged on by the USA, six Labour ministers secretly decided to build a nuclear bomb at a cost of £100 million. The government maintained conscription, kept troops in Germany, and sent others to defend capitalist interests in tin and rubber in the Far East. In 1947–48 the cost of living rose by 9 per cent, but in 1948–9 wages were held below the level of inflation. By 1949 £350 million of 'hot' money had been exported by anxious capitalists, and one-tenth of national income went on 'defence'. NATO was formed that April. The pound was devalued in September. Labour's version of state capitalism without Stalin had stalled. In the February 1950 general election they received over 13 million votes, but their majority was cut to five. The Korean War began that June. Labour policy was now effectively determined by its military alliance with the USA.

In 1950 the CP's hundred candidates got just over 90,000 votes, but both MPs lost their seats, and only one other CP candidate saved his deposit. Membership began to slide. Nevertheless the NCC now had two subcommittees policing Party writers. In October Fore Pubs published the 'Key Poets' series, edited by Swingler and Lindsay, and the Party poets were invited to Marx House 'to meet a group of critics'. Beeching and others were put 'on a cockshy' as 'effete, literary intellectuals to an audience of hard liners', 'the philistine wing of King Street', with Burns 'playing Zhdanov'.[33] 'We were attacked as if we were a shower of shit.' The 'Pink Poets' were 'bourgeois', 'not Zhdanovite enough', 'not enough proletcult' and 'not enough devoted to the working class'. Yet 'they didn't know what the working class was, most of them'. As he looked along the table:

> There was Edgell Rickword, who won the MC in the trenches in the First World War. There was Randall Swingler, who won two Military Medals and been buried alive in Italy. I don't remember if Edward Thompson was there … he led the first tank up the Anzio beach-head. I'd been in the landing in the Royal Navy. There was John Sommerfield who, after fighting in Spain, had had his war in the jungle of Burma.

Then he looked at the critics. Later, he noted where they ended up. One became a *Daily Express* journalist. Another – presumably Lord Willis of Dock Green – 'wrote dialogue for a television series praising the police'. Another became 'a telly chat-show chap'. They 'justified their entry into the mass media in terms of 'are we getting close to the working class, are we putting the left-wing line through the mass media?' It was 'a very great justification for what would otherwise be your natural discomfort at receiving these high salaries and making these compromises, and certainly it doesn't give you a position of moral authority to attack serious poetry'. Beeching felt that the 'talented veterans' didn't "get a pasting" – *they did*'; but while a protesting letter from Lindsay appeared in the *Daily*

Worker in November, none of the 'Key Poets' was reviewed in Party publications.

Pollitt had praised Christopher Caudwell's work on cultural theory as recently as 1949, and it was used at the CP summer school in 1950. Yet in that winter's *Marxist Quarterly* Cornforth noted that Caudwell's writing was 'certainly not Marxism', since he 'followed bourgeois psychology by splitting man into two parts, natural and civilised'. So for him poetry had 'no connection with the real external world', but only with the 'inner world, the world of perception and the world of feeling', and these 'two worlds' 'fall apart in his hands', since 'they are nothing but the products of a metaphysical dualism', and very far from 'socialist realism'. Every Party 'intellectual' had 'at some stage to make a clean break', and 'to return to the Marxist classics and to read them again, again and again'. In October Tommy Jackson and Cornforth were 'visitors' at an NCC meeting; in November an NCC 'Discussion Statement' hammered *Marxist Quarterly* for its 'academic approach'; and in December the NCC and London District Committee organised a meeting on 'Art and Science in the Fight for Peace and National Independence', to be addressed by Comrade Pollitt.[34]

During 1950 Pollitt had pushed the Cominform line, yet the Russians now had the atomic bomb, and little use for small CPs like the British. King Street remained lost, so Pollitt had two discussions with Stalin, and in January 1951 a draft CP programme was issued 'for discussion'. Pollitt's Foreword assumed his audience were the 'great majority' of 'workers by hand or brain', who wanted 'to find the way forward to an independent, prosperous, Socialist Britain', avoiding war. The draft argued that in 1945 the 'people' had voted for 'great social changes which would weaken capitalism and open the way to Socialism', but while there had been working-class gains, 'no basic social change' had taken place. 'Nine-tenths of the wealth of the country is still owned by one-tenth of the population.' Labour's failure was 'not the failure of Socialism' but of the lack of a 'popular alliance' between industrial workers, farmers, professional people, scientists and technicians, housewives, teachers, shopkeepers and small businessmen, against 'the handful of big landlords, bankers and monopolists who exploit them'. Instead of 'capitalist nationalisation' there should be 'Socialist nationalisation' of the banks, big distributive monopolies, insurance companies and large land-owners' estates, and a state monopoly of foreign trade. There was no hint of revolution, or proletarian dictatorship, but if the right counterattacked a 'People's Government' would be able to 'rebuff' them if 'it restored command of the British Armed Forces to British commanders'. *The British Road to Socialism* called on 'all true patriots to defend British national interests'.[35]

In the spring 1951 issue of *Marxist Quarterly* George Thomson denounced Cornforth's 'mish-mash' of unhistorical methods, his ignoring counter-evidence, his selective quotations and his 'mechanical materialism'. 'To Caudwell, who died eleven years before the Soviet controversy on the arts, it was plain that there was a qualitative difference between bourgeois art and Socialist art.' But when Cornforth had published *Science versus Idealism*, nine years after Caudwell's death, 'there was no bourgeois science, only science'. However, Thomson agreed that 'one of the shortcomings in our writers and artists at the present time is their neglect of the theory of Socialist realism.' After this contribution Cornforth noted 'a regrettable oversight': 'it was not made clear in the last issue' that this was 'the second in the series'. In April the NCC organised a conference, which led to the June/July Special Issue of *Arena*. *The U.S.A. Threat to British Culture* was pushed hard, and later reissued as *The American Threat to British Culture*.

That summer Beeching argued in *Marxist Quarterly* that an adequately developed Marxist aesthetics was impossible 'until psychology is fully a science'. Courageously, Peter Cronin speculated that there might be 'an "idealist notion"' in 'Stalin's dictum that writers are "engineers of the human soul"'. But in the autumn Cornforth flatly told Party writers to 'rid our literary work and our literary criticism of the hangovers of idealism'. Edward Thompson was a 'bit potty about Caudwell', putting him alongside Marx, Engels and Stalin; but Beeching recalled no factional activity: 'I don't suppose anybody ever thought things out as clearly as that.'

Thompson recalled that Communist intellectuals were 'lacking in self-confidence when confronted by the intrusion of "the Party"'. The 'stream of "apostates"' was so full that all of us were apt to recoil, wilfully and unthinkingly, from the brink of any heresy for fear of toppling into the flood'. He liked to think there were a 'good many frustrated proto-revisionists in the Communist Party in those days', who resisted the 'di-dactic methods', 'wooden economism', and 'correct pabulum offered as "Marxism"' by the 'local Zhdanovs', 'designated the enemy as "King Street"' and denounced their 'Jungle Marxism'. Yet he acknowledged that this 'incipient heresy was unfocused, lacking in articulation', since no-body took responsibility for starting a public 'argument between dogmatic and creative Marxism' in this 'intellectual iron age'. So there was, indeed, 'a certain obliteration of the intellect'.[36]

Tressell of Mugsborough

In January 1949 Fred Ball was hopeful that Porcupine Press would publish the complete manuscript of RTP, but the project fell through. In May the National Society of Painters' solicitors, Ball, and a solicitor he was 'obliged to engage', had 'involved negotiations' with Richards Press. Ball offered 'to waive any claim we might have on the unpublished parts when it seemed at one time that the NSP intended to publish the whole', but they concluded that Richards Press had owned the complete copyright since 1913. Richards Press

> expressed their willingness to come to an arrangement with the NSP as to publication provided their ownership of copyright was recognised, but on 6 February 1950, nine months after the project was first mooted, the Society wrote that in view of the difficulties over the right to publish they had decided not to proceed any further.[37]

Richards Press's allegedly 'unexpurgated' RTP appeared in November.

The 1914 edition was still a valuable commodity because it was politically relevant. One woman used it as ammunition in an argument she was having with her next-door neighbour about nationalisation. A member of Dorking Labour Party recalled a 'group of us arranged for a group of amateur players to present "The Ragged Trousered Philanthropists" at a local school!' Probably they were the Unity Mobile Theatre Players, who, for at least five years from May 1949, took Frank Rhodes' adaptation to venues like Wortley Hall, Sheffield, the Derbyshire Miners' Holiday Camp, Skegness, and Gravesend in Kent, where Kenneth Price organised trade-union sponsorship.[38] A carpenter was working for a small builder in North London. At the ten o'clock whistle workers made their way to the 'canteen', a garage, where they 'sat on anything to hand from a cement bag to an upturned putty tin, and discussions took place precisely as described in "RT's"'. The foreman read out parts of the book, and it felt like 'day to day life':

> Our guv'nor crept round the back door; it was us who picked up the steps and pretended to be working; the language was everyday stuff to everyone but to see it in print ... and when 'Harry' read it out we roared with laughter at ourselves.

The book went its rounds. Social comment? we never knew it existed. When I got hold of it from 'Fred', he said 'read the first few chapters they are really funny – just like "Old Oddy" (our guvnor), and the apprentice pushing the cart up the hill and resting then being caught out, well it could have been before the war. Don't bother with the end chapters – they're not very funny'

They were working on a house used by a Russian trade delegation.

Ron Todd, the future General Secretary of the TGWU, was 'first inspired' by *The Ragged Trousered Philanthropists* as a commando during the Korean War. John Gorman, an East London teenager, read a secondhand copy, then *Capital*, and joined the CP.[39] A young railway booking clerk in London already felt that 'the only hope for a decent society was some form of Socialist government' when his brother brought a copy of RTP from work. It

explained so clearly the nature of capitalism – something which many of us had felt in parts but never been able to explain in such a complete manner. Yet at the same time it also painted a picture of a society which we were also aware of – one in which our very fellow workmen were often too selfish, stupid and ignorant.

He used it 'to explain such theories as surplus labour value', and it helped him understand more fully 'why I should be a socialist'. Yet in 1950 Tommy Jackson had made no mention of RTP in *Old Friends to Keep: Studies of English Novels and Novelists*, though he cheerfully referred to himself as 'a Stalinist, a Marxist, a Humanist and an ardent English Nationalist'.[40]

In October 1951 Lawrence & Wishart published Fred Ball's *Tressell of Mugsborough*. It cost twelve shillings and sixpence in a cheap binding, and eighteen shillings in hardback. Ball stressed he had 'received help solely from ordinary rank and file members of the Labour movement and from working-men', plus the London Council of Shop Stewards of the Associated Society of Woodworkers. His target audience was 'the rank and file worker', because most trade unionists 'knew rather less about the history of the British working class than about the history of old Joe Soap', so the Labour movement 'sees through one eye only and has no historical sense'. 'Fifty years of socialist agitation and propaganda haven't yet produced a mass body of educated and stable socialist opinion.' RTP was part of the answer. Socialists like 'Tressell' and Alf Cobb had 'believed in fundamental education', 'teaching the working-class socialist economics, not the re-hashed capitalist "economics" which passes in trade unions and Labour parties to-day'. Using large extracts from unpublished parts of the manuscript, Ball hoped to show the 'marvellous picture of us and our fathers and mothers as we toil in the shadows of that world to which it has pleased the devil to call us'. He hailed 'the world's first Socialist State', the USSR, and 'the great awakening of China and Asia'; and looked to a future with 'no race and colour bars'. But, sadly, Lawrence & Wishart let pass references to 'Niggers' and 'Fuzzi Wuzzis dressed like flunkeys'. Moreover, Ball damned socialist intellectuals for knowing 'far less about the working-class than do the Tories', and functioning as ruling-class 'agents in the Labour movement'. The 'Socialist Co-operative Commonwealth of the future' seemed a long way off.[41]

Reviewers focused on the novel as much as on the biography. *Reynold's News* believed there 'must be thousands of men and women in various parts of the world who first understood the theoretical basis of Socialism' from the 'Great Money Trick'. The *New Statesman* thought it 'tragic' that copyright problems 'prevent us from reading an unexpurgated edition' of the 'most authentic novel ever written about British workers'; and *Socialist Outlook* assumed the novel had a readership of 'millions'. The Hastings *Observer* noted 'Considerable trade union interest' in the book. A Bexhill man made Ball's acquaintance. He knew Bill Gower had a radio shop in Castle Hill Road in the 1920s, and he made a long tape of Len Green.

During 1951 Labour chancellor Hugh Gaitskell had increased taxes to pay for Britain's military involvements, but there was a balance-of-payments crisis. Meekly, the TUC acknowledged that employed workers' living standards would fall, as would those of the 2½ million people on the dole. Labour's reforms had left half the national wealth in the hands of 1 per cent of the population; and, in addition to legal overseas investments, £470 million (more than enough to deal with the crisis) was illegally sent abroad. At the October general election Labour recorded its highest ever vote of almost 14 million, but lost its majority of seats. A Labour researcher found that they 'dropped more votes from working-class men than from the whole of the middle-class'.[42] The CP's slogans were 'Save Peace – Save Britain' and 'End American Domination'; but its ten candidates got a total of only 21,000 votes and they all lost their deposits.

In January 1952 the CP's NCC required Communist professional writers to 'produce works related to the British working class struggle and based on the standpoint of Socialist realism'.[43] The April Congress told Party organisations to 'develop the cultural struggle as part of the political struggle', 'increase activity against the Americanisation of Britain's cultural life' and 'endeavour to make our national cultural heritage the pride and possession of the working-class'.[44] *The British Road to Socialism* went through on the nod, since Eric Heffer couldn't get a seconder to oppose it,[45] at a time when leading European Communists were being executed, and Pollitt, Campbell and Rust were 'frighteningly close to the terror',[46] Beeching noted King Street's 'feeble attempts' to 'wriggle free' from Moscow. They were 'not only financially dependent on the Russians to an extraordinary extent'; they were also 'ideologically dependent' and 'had no power of thought'. They were 'middle-men, explaining the Russians to the English, the English to the Russians, and of course they told more and more lies to both, confounding the issue generally'. Party membership was down to 35,000. For several months an average of one comrade an hour had left.

At a NCC conference of District Committee delegates Aaronovitch insisted that Party writers' work 'must be regarded as a weapon in the struggle'. In an NCC position paper, 'G[eorge] T[homson]' claimed that during the rise of a bourgeoisie, 'culture, national in form, is international in content; for it is based on humanism'; but in a period of decline it becomes 'cosmopolitan in form and fascist in content'. So the 'effect of American domination is, in Scotland and Wales, to intensify, and in England to reawaken, the national consciousness of the people'.[47] An *Arena* publication praised both William Morris and morris dancing as key elements of *Britain's Cultural Heritage*; and in the second issue of *Daylight*, Margot Heinemann noted that it was 'not passive suffering, but socialist-inspiration that has made a book like *The Ragged Trousered Philanthropists* a classic'.

Harold Smith worked in a Westminster library. He noted that while working-class readers sometimes got the title wrong – he felt they 'had been recommended to read it by a colleague', orally – they asked for RTP as much as for *The Iron Heel*. So it 'seemed ridiculous that what was considered to be a classic should not be available in its entirety'. In January 1952 he wrote to Richards Press, only to be told that 'the present text' was 'the best for general purposes', and that the 'largely increased costs of production' of the complete version would 'render the venture commercially impracticable'. Undeterred, Smith wrote to Ball and Slater.[48] In February the *Times Literary Supplement* reviewed *Tressell of Mugsborough*, and in March James MacGibbon asked to see the RTP manuscript. (Chapter 2 was published in the Russian popular magazine *Ogonyok* at around this time.) In April Slater wrote to the *TLS*, pressurising Richards Press. He was followed by J.W. Harper of the Amalgamated Society of Woodworkers, who suggested they might 'forgo' their rights, and MacGibbon, who wondered if profit-sharing might break the log jam.

Elements of the CP hierarchy then joined in. Walter Holmes noted in the *Daily Worker* that 'a small fortune has been made out of Tressell's book'. 'The great success of Unity Theatre's stage production, and the unflagging demand for the mobile unit's performances', provided 'promise of a good sale for a complete edition'. So if 'the publisher cannot afford a complete edition, should he not stand aside and let someone else try?' Richards Press suggested they might publish the censored sections separately. Could they see the manuscript? Ball declined; but he got union contacts to lobby Sir Richard Coppock OBE. By June the issue was on the agenda of the National Conference of the NFBTO, and that of the District Committee Annual Conference of the National Society of Painters. The National Union of Public Employees reportedly guaranteed a certain level of sales if MacGibbon & Kee would publish the manuscript; and it was thought that the electricians' union might buy it. *Electron* made RTP the first of its 'Books of the Month', and 'No. 1' in 'Your Labour Library'. 'Every member should read this book.' Yet Lawrence & Wishart continued to dither.

I O

Comrade Tressell

A sure-fire winner

During the early 1950s Fred Ball spoke at Labour movement meetings; but even he was taken aback when 'many scores of people from all over Britain, writers, students, teachers and workers, including a group of miners from the Scottish pits', took up his invitation to read the manuscript of *The Ragged Trousered Philanthropists* on his kitchen table. On 1 May 1953, at a Labour Party rally in Brighton, the local Trades Council wanted to 'put over a real trade Union message' to the new right-wing leader, Hugh Gaitskell, and they chose 'The Great Money Trick'. Following Ball's script, a planted 'Tory' intervened, and there was a heated argument in the audience, yet Gaitskell's anticlimactic answer to the question 'What can be done?' was 'Vote for us!'[1] In December Unity presented RTP at the White Rock Pavilion, sponsored by Hastings Trades Council, the NFBTO and other union branches. Len Green, having been disappointed first time, did not go.

Jack Beeching was now a director of Lawrence & Wishart. He had 'a very good political record', was acceptable to King Street, and could 'put projects in words that made them think they wanted to do it'. He was secretary of the Party Writers' Group, and working class — 'you could tell from my accent'. Lawrence & Wishart was 'one of our public faces where something could be got away with. The only trouble was it hadn't got any *brains*.' So Cornforth had been 'put in' to 'pull it round'. As for RTP, the firm 'hadn't made up their mind' about the manuscript: 'I don't think the

Party saw the point about the book. It wouldn't have helped if they had. They would have got it wrong.'

Some comrades thought it was 'a very good book' for all its 'weaknesses'. Yet it had 'a flavour of workers' power', which was 'not on'. It was 'especially not on after it became one of the tenets of POUM'. (POUM fought against Franco's fascists during the Spanish Revolution, but its members were influenced by Trotsky's ideas, and many were shot by Stalinists behind the lines.) RTP was also sometimes 'very contemptuous of the working class', so there was 'a very mixed feeling about it' among former syndicalists at King Street, who were 'philistines', and only 'involved in literary questions to the degree that they could make writers shut up and toe the line'. They 'used to tell teachers they were too articulate'. Fortunately, Cornforth 'had sufficient political experience to be able to talk sense to them occasionally, without making it sound like intrusive common sense'. Besides, the book was 'a useful thing to be able to throw in people's faces' if they jibbed at the Zhdanovite line. Then, in March 1953, when 5½ million Russians were in the Gulag, Stalin died.

During 1953 Communist academic Arnold Kettle noted that RTP and A Scots Quair were 'important and moving' novels. Moreover, they were 'the beginning of something new in our literature' and 'do not belong to the end of an epoch'.[2] Kettle sketched 'The Progressive Tradition in Bourgeois Literature' in an Arena publication, Essays on Socialist Realism and the British Cultural Tradition. Its Foreword acknowledged that, previously, 'We paid too little attention to what does influence the masses of the workers – the expression, through culture, deliberately fostered by British imperialism, of the outlook of social democracy.' Yet it was 'the masses of workers who must be united', and to 'reach them, to quicken all the forms of cultural activity which they already practise and we so often ignore, must be the constant and conscious aim of all our activity'. Then Aaronovitch laid down the line. In 'Capitalist Reaction against Socialist Realism' he quoted RTP on alienation; but in 'The Elements of Socialist Realism in Britain' his praise (and his mechanical materialism) knew no bounds. The 'real foundation of socialist realist literature in Britain' was 'laid by the housepainter Robert Tressall in his immortal novel':

> Much has been written of the sectarianism and doctrinaire weaknesses of Social Democratic Federation and similar bodies. But in the Ragged Trousered Philanthropists, though these weaknesses are also reflected, the Socialist movement showed its power and potentialities. Here we have the first true novel

of British working class life. Here for the first time the hero is a revolutionary Socialist.

Jack Lindsay filled in the organisational detail, stressing the political benefits of taking appropriate books to sell at trade-union meetings.[3]

Beeching knew that if Lawrence & Wishart published the RTP manuscript 'without paying a fee they'd have got in trouble', since Ball's title was 'very dubious'. So it was 'a dodgy business'. 'Had we got any right to the book? Did we own the copyright? What did we own? Did the man who sold it to us have something to sell? I think he was a shark.' Ball 'thought everybody was trying to do him down: not me, particularly, but me, yes, if it came to the push'. He also had 'grave misgivings' about Lawrence & Wishart, and he wanted a royalty:

> The question in Fred's mind was would I support him, or would I turn against him; and of course I would support him. But I was not going to support him in such a rabid way that I'd get other people's backs up, or we'd never get the book out.

Fortunately, Cornforth was 'able to win him over'. Beeching was 'sure Fred got his royalty, but I don't know'. 'I did nothing to stop it.' In December 1953 Lawrence & Wishart told Ball they had decided to 'proceed as quickly as possible with the full unexpurgated edition subject to your being willing to let us use the manuscript and to our reaching an agreement with the Richards Press',[4] who wanted 'compensation' for the remaining eleven years of copyright.[5] Their last printing appeared in February 1954, and retailed at seven shillings and sixpence. It was the twenty-third printing (but claimed to be the twentieth), and was advertised as the '138th thousand'.

Ball knew he had no copyright, but a fee would be appropriate for an editor. It was a big job. The manuscript came in two parcels, and in a damaged condition. Pope's pasted-over pages were read with a hand mirror, or

> separated by steaming-off with the kitchen kettle. The cut pages necessitated searching the MS many times in order to restore two parts of the same page … and sometimes this was only possible by matching the two edges left by her scissors.

The unattached chapter headings 'made it impossible to tell in many cases where chapters began and ended'; and 'almost all these title sheets were weeded out by Jessie Pope'. So Ball could 'only judge chapter length by

the subject matter indicated in Tressell's List of Contents'. He took the
Roman numerals for chapters to be 'certainly Tressell's own'.

> used red ink exclusively, not always, I fear, so neatly as I might, had I borne
> posterity constantly in mind, and where there are inconsistencies in the use
> of my pen this is because two other versions were prepared by me ...
> before it finally became possible to publish the MS as the author left it. For
> the sake of the record I should say that some of the red ink is in my wife's
> handwriting, who also laboriously strengthened the MS with the addition
> of sticky labels.[6]

However, while he acknowledged his wife's 'assistance throughout',[7] he
did not mention her name, or hint that Cornforth had helped edit the text.

The title page was redrawn, and Pope's Preface was omitted. The differently numbered and unfinished 'Mugsborough' chapter, which appeared
in Noonan's list of chapter headings, was annotated 'Deleted by Tressell',
and made into an Appendix. Subsequent chapters were renumbered accordingly. Ball accepted most of what appear to be Noonan's deletions
and emendations, including the rejection of the 'Internationale' chorus;
but he cut words and phrases, and made transpositions. He took over
summaries marked 'G[rant] R[ichards] Include', but made unacknowl-
edged additions, including that relating to Ruth's seduction. He silently
adopted Pope's additions to the 1914 edition, and amended previously
unpublished passages so as to conform to her style. Not all of his linking
passages were acknowledged. Some sentences in his hand, including the
first mention of Barrington, are annotated 'R.T.', without any supporting
evidence. Parts of pages are pasted together, not always for an obvious
reason. Ball's edited text did not go to the printers until December 1954.

Which socialist tradition did the book belong to? During 1954 James
Clunie ended his autobiography with verses dedicated to 'Robert Tressell',
the house painter and 'Literary Genius', who 'appeared as a symbol selected
by providence to speak through illness and hardship and craftsmanship.
Akin to the simplicity and sincerity of the fishermen at whose feet I was
nurtured.'[8] The one-time editor of the SLP's *The Socialist* was now a Labour
MP. In April 1955 Manchester Unity Theatre *Bulletin* wanted 'groups of
volunteers' to do 'a direct political job in the constituencies of Labour
Parties affiliated to us', after 750 people attended two performances of *The
Ragged Trousered Philanthropists*, staged with 'the very welcome assistance of
National Society of Painters who sold a third of the tickets'. 'Robert
Tressell's classic book, dramatised' was open for bookings by Co-operative

Guild Secretaries, and went 'touring the local circuit'. That August the Labour MP (and ex-CPer) Frank Allaun gave RTP a plug in The Paperworker. It was 'most inspiring to trade unionists in their struggle for a better life'.

In autumn 1955 Lawrence & Wishart's 'complete edition' was signalled by their distributor, Central Books, on 50,000 flyers, and many unions allowed branches to be circularised.[9] Books for Progress claimed that, had he lived, 'Tressell would have unquestionably become one of the foremost fighters in the ranks of the building workers.' A cheap edition would be available to those who could 'state trade union or other organization', and Ball was preparing a 'shortened version'.[10] Lawrence & Wishart's own announcement advertised five other novels by British writers.[11] On 1 October Harry Pollitt told readers of World News that he had 'read every edition of this novel that has been published'. Yet 'each time, while appreciating every word of it, I have felt something was missing'. In the 1910s, as a Gorton Tank apprentice in Manchester, he had known two socialists like Owen who

> were as sectarian as I believe he was; they despised their fellow workers, as he also gives me the impression of doing. They had no faith in them. They explained what they called 'the position' and what we now call 'the situation'. Yet they could not rally their fellow workers to their support.

Britain was 'in danger of becoming one huge Mugsborough because of what we tolerate', even though it had 'a Labour movement about which Owen could never have had any conception!' So Pollitt insisted: 'you simply must get this book by hook or by crook, and I particularly appeal to the "old 'uns" to ensure that the "young 'uns" read it'. Lawrence & Wishart were on to 'a sure-fire winner'.

A working-class classic

Lawrence & Wishart's 'Complete Text' of The Ragged Trousered Philanthropists was published in London on 6 October 1955. The 'De Luxe' 'Library edition' retailed at thirty shillings (about £24 at today's values), which was four times the price of the current Richards Press edition. Its dust jacket had a drawing of a gaunt, quizzical painter, and the publishers appeared to share his doubts, since it had a print run of only 1,500 copies. However, 3,500 copies of the 'Special Trade Union Edition' in 'limp cloth' sold at ten shillings and sixpence, since the NFBTO offered to 'ensure sales which

would offset the otherwise prohibitive cost'.[12] Curiously, Lawrence &
Wishart did not claim copyright.

The unsigned 'Publisher's Foreword' was written by Beeching and
Cornforth, but was apparently based on information supplied by Ball,
some of whose myths about Robert and Kathleen Noonan were uncritically
endorsed. They claimed the novel was the 'first account in English of the
lives and opinions of a group of working men, written with realism and
passion, not by an outside observer, but by "one of themselves"'. They
acknowledged that a 'few pages' had been 'entirely lost': some 1914 para-
phrases were included; 'necessary linking passages' had been 'supplied by
the present editor'; and 'Mugsborough' had been put in an Appendix.
Otherwise the text was 'printed exactly as the author wrote it'.[13] An
English-language edition was published for Russian students, with a
Russian Foreword.

Beeching believed 'there was not much marketing strategy'. But while
the descriptive aspects of the book were 'more and more irrelevant to
working-class life', it was 'different from the book people knew already'
in 'its tone and its attitude', and 'new things were happening in the
working-class movement'. The 'ruling classes were on the defensive': there
was 'a shift in the class feeling'; and RTP helped foster 'a certain, confident militancy' because 'its tone was more and more relevant … to the
aspirations of the politically conscious working class'. He felt ambivalent
about the Party's involvement: 'I don't know that the CP had *any* cultural
achievements', though 'individuals who were Communists' had. The novel
'sold itself'. Well, not quite.

Beeching's essay 'The Uncensoring of "The Ragged Trousered Philanthropists"' appeared in the October 1955 *Marxist Quarterly*. He attacked Pope's
'castrated and perverted' assimilation of the book to 'the right-wing Social
Democratic literary school – the literature of decaying liberalism with all
the radical backbone filleted'. Yet he acknowledged that the book was 'full
of contradictions', that it 'worries the pedants and is difficult to pigeon-
hole'. The second half of Pope's editions were 'episodic': their ends were
'dolefully pessimistic'; and Owen was a 'prig' who 'spends hours preaching at his workmates in the accents of the Almighty'. And yet,

> Go into any meeting room of the working-class movement in Britain and
> you will probably find at least one man present who could say, 'That book
> brought me to the movement. That book made me a convinced socialist.
> That book altered the whole course and direction of my life.'

Beeching acknowledged that many 'literary people outside the working-class movement' were 'perplexed to account for the phenomenal popularity' of the novel. But so were those 'of a theorising turn of mind inside the movement, who have formed a precise idea of what should (or should not) comprise the novel of "socialist realism"'. They argued 'that the socialist theories preached in the book are all "wrong", that they are mechanical, sectarian and crude; and we can do very much better ourselves now with very little effort; indeed, we have all the answers'. Such 'aesthetes and theorists' often lacked 'personal experience at first hand of wage-slavery such as the book describes', and so might be pulled by Pope's 'literary slumming', which was 'sometimes mistaken for socialist realism by the ignorant or malicious'. They should listen to workers.

As it happened, Beeching had been 'born within a stone's throw of the builder's yard' described in The Ragged Trousered Philanthropists, 'in the house of my late grandfather who worked for over forty years as a house-painter'. As a boy he 'had one man or another pointed out to me by him as originals of the characters', so the 'subject-matter of the book is in my bones'. Moreover, he could confirm that the book was acceptable to workers because of its truth-to-life. It was also 'a superb revenge for exploitation which threw a craftsman prematurely on the scrap heap after a lifetime's labour'. It demonstrated 'astounding fidelity to the moods of life under wage-slavery': it was 'the first to portray so unmistakably the main types of English working man', and its 'individual voices' raised 'arguments that may still be heard forty years afterwards on building jobs and in workmen's cafés'.

The book was also 'literature of permanent value, and 'firmly in the English radical-critical tradition'. Yet its 'most striking and instructive' aspects were 'its very departures from photographic fidelity to life', especially the omission of of the sea, 'a treacherous, noisy, seductive and dramatic element in our lives' and of 'the salt fields which charged no rent and gave shrimps, prawns, dabs and whitebait, not to mention excitement'. RTP's realism involved

> the abstraction of the inner truth of the subject-matter in its process of development; and the incarnation of this living truth in imagined characters. The 'imagined characters' in the book were in fact 'real characters' ... with the artistic irrelevancies stripped away. They did and said only those things which demonstrated the movement of society through the interrelation of their personalities. So they were more than living, larger than life, because they exemplified ... the truth that working people become fully human to

the degree that they develop a distinctive class consciousness and enter on the struggle for political power.

The book 'discards or suppresses all but those features of everyday life which bear directly or obliquely on the exploitation of the workers'. 'There may have been sponging in the Cricketers, but there was also decorous ceremonial drinking of friendly societies like the Oddfellows and Buffaloes. There was stark poverty, but there was also the co-operative renting of allotments.' So the novel was 'transitional', linking 'critical realism' not, as Zhdanovites believed, to a present, but to a future 'Socialist realism'.

Beeching argued that RTP was 'true to life' primarily 'because of the power of Tressell's imagination'. As a realistic writer he developed a

> vision of peculiar intensity, range and power, adequate to project in literature an imaginary world 'like' the real world yet different from it – a world on a bolder scale, more abstracted and selective in its sayings and doings; a world more generally significant because more generalised. A world of imagination above all capable of organising effectively the minds of men, and so transforming the world of reality itself.

Against heavy odds, Owen was 'gradually winning over his workmates', and so RTP demonstrates, as Marx had argued, that when workers struggle to change society they also change themselves. More than that, Barrington and Lenin both insisted that, unlike trade-union consciousness, 'socialist consciousness comes to the working class "from outside"'. Consequently, the book was highly relevant, because it focused on 'half-formed proletarians – broken to toil yet not turned to systematic rebellious struggle', so as to 'show the effect of socialist theory on men like these – to show how even the most "hopeless" will change when they discern that socialist ideas illuminate their own life experience and give them the hope they lack'. Under Labour some workers had 'acquired an unwarranted and grimly illusory sense of economic security', but under the Tories 'imperialism is more unstable than ever, and threatens every one of us with hunger and war'. The 'Complete Text' was an argument to be had with 'the vanguard of the working-class movement'. It was capable of making socialists in the here and now. Sadly, it had taken the 'vanguard' – King Street – 'a whole generation to catch up with and begin to seriously examine' a book which workers had cherished for generations.

On 6 October John Sommerfield offered 'The True Tressell Story at Last' in the *Daily Worker*. He stressed its 'blazing sincerity' and 'hatred for "the human enemies of humanity"', when, 'despite the National Health and television and trade union leaders with titles, we still have the rich and the poor, and the rich still rule'. Instead of 'extreme insecurities and horrors of poverty we're menaced by the insecurities and horrors of atomic war', and there were 'millions of philanthropists being duped to keep things the way they are', though 'the duping is more subtle and more high pressure'. RTP's 'final message is that the world hasn't got to be like this, it can be changed and life can be good if we fight to make it so'.[14] On 8 October in *World News* Bert Baker was struck by the author's 'bitter frustration with members of his own class, at their acceptance and even support of capitalism'. Yet RTP was still a 'working-class classic'.

Within a fortnight Cornforth had to do some explaining in *World News*:

The very heavy costs of paper, printing and binding made the production of this very long book extremely expensive. But we wanted to make it available as cheaply as possible to members of working-class organisations. The special edition which has been produced (on less expensive paper than the library edition, and bound in limp cloth) is being sold direct from publisher to reader at more or less cost price.

This could only be done by a method of direct sale; obviously, it ruled out any question of a seller's discount. For this reason the edition could not be on sale over the counter at any bookshop. It is not for sale to the general public, but is offered on special terms to members of working-class organisations only. You can obtain this edition by applying to the publisher, or to the publisher's central distributors, Central Books Ltd., 2 Parton Street, Red Lion Square, London W.C.1.

Arrangements have also been made for members of builders' trade unions to obtain it from the National Federation of Building Trades Operatives, and members of the Labour Party from the bookshop at Transport House or the Fabian Bookshop.

How do we explain Lawrence & Wishart's initial pessimism?

Catching the true voice of Tressell

Mervyn Jones had left the CP in 1951 over the prevailing 'submissiveness and self-deception'.[15] In *Tribune* in November 1955 he accepted that RTP was 'about the most detailed, fact-stored, utterly authentic account of working-class life and labour that we possess', but insisted that its author 'happened not to be an outstanding writer' and lacked 'knowledge of the form of the novel', there being only one. The

description of the book as a 'classic' is, in my opinion, great nonsense. What Tressall did was to set down what he heard and saw, with great honesty and in laborious imitation of the worst and most cliché-ridden prose of his age. And to set it *all* down.

True, it included 'long expositions of socialism', but they were 'so stilted',

and the character who makes them is such an insufferable prig that it's no wonder he converted nobody. But he was also a pessimist, and his scorn for his fellow-workers, who toiled blindly to enrich their enemies, is amply indicated by his title.

And the ending was 'phony, contrived, and unworthy'. So this edition was 'a hindrance rather than an aid to catching the true voice' of 'Tressall'.

Working-class *Tribune* readers didn't agree. Molly Mizen insisted: 'My husband is a plasterer and an ardent left-wing socialist, and ... I hear many stories from the site that sound like Tressall all over again.' Harold Smith predicted confidently 'how eagerly well-read men in overalls would dispute the view that Owen is "stilted", for have they not used, and been inspired by, his arguments in every workshop in Britain?' Donald Halls-worth, a Labour Party member, wondered if 'our' MPs had read the 'Ovation [sic]'. 'Do they know what socialism is, or have they forgotten?' 'We must confess we failed them once in 1945 when we had the power. Are we going to fail them again?'

Union officials joined in. In the November *Labour Monthly* Richard Coppock claimed to have 'read every edition of this book', and 'worked under the conditions as described'. 'The language used by the men, the back-biting, the cunningness, the betrayal, and the straightforward honest-to-God individuals are absolute demonstrations of the picture that is constantly being portrayed on the sites and the jobs.' So architects 'will get some understanding of the background of the life of the building trade operative and the tricks of the employers.' (Coppock hadn't been on the tools since 1916, and he didn't mention the knighthood.) In the December issue of *Labour Research* AUEW President, Harry Weaver, recalled his first reading of RTP: 'the effect on me was dramatic and proved permanent', and the new edition had lost none of the capacity for 'gripping the reader and arousing a compelling desire to take an active part in fighting injustice'. Another reviewer, Philip Hobsbaum, acknowledged that some 'conditions have altered very much for the better', yet

Nothing has basically altered: we are still the prey of Sweater and Hunter, but we call them by different names – rentiers, finance houses, pressure groups. The individual capitalist pointed out by Tressell has become a face-less board, an anonymous company.

So the 'bible of trade union organizers' still helped to 'convert workers to Socialism by the simple process of showing them the conditions under which they lived', and should rank alongside Blatchford's Merrie England.

Lawrence & Wishart's 'De Luxe' edition sold out in two months, and the 'trade union' edition in less than three, at an average rate of one copy every twenty minutes.[16] Reviews kept coming. In the Plebs of March 1956 A. Boyd accepted that the book was 'undoubtedly of interest to scholars and research-workers', but felt it 'possible in this age of speed, television and almost unlimited overtime that newcomers to the Labour Movement will prefer to read Tressell's classic in the shorter popular edition', which 'costs 11/–, 11/6 by post from the National Council of Labour Colleges'. (Evidently, Richards Press had jacked up their price by 30 per cent.) In May, Lilian Allaun, a former shop steward, recalled in The Paperworker how one passage took her back to when 'Dad, a plasterer, was drinking his last pint potful of tea.' 'Morning and night like a ritual, the dark, silent man, going and returning in the dark.' She was delighted that 'an ordinary edition' was to be published later that year. A newspaper correspondent noted that most workers still had a 'struggle to manage from pay-day to pay-day'; and he recognised how similar his workmates' arguments in defence of capitalism were to those used by Owen's: 'I think we can learn from the fact that the Owens of that time, when preaching socialism, did not tie it up closely enough with the need to fight for improved conditions under capitalism.'

As for the capitalist press, the Manchester Evening News hailed RTP as 'the only real working-class novel', though the Manchester Guardian thought it 'an achievement that nobody who is sane would wish to see repeated'. W.E. Brown in the Bolton Evening News claimed that the author's motive was 'a desire to propagate a very English kind of revolutionary socialism, that of William Morris and Robert Blatchford', so RTP 'ought particularly to be read by the innumerable grumblers at the welfare state', because 'this country has been belying the central thesis of the author that gradual reform was useless'. However, the Carlisle Journal argued that this 'brilliant book is worth a hundred political speeches, whether we agree with him or not'. 'If conditions like these were imposed on the working class half a century ago, it is a miracle that we avoided revolution.'

Late in 1955 Tyneside Unity Theatre had failed to stage an adaptation of RTP with a cast of eight, but Glasgow Unity were successful with 'The Great Money Trick'. Manchester Unity's October Bulletin noted its

Wythenshawe group had booked the Lesser Free Trade Hall for a performance of Rowbotham's adaptation, and it was a 'gamble that paid off'; but by November they were 'beginning to find that the mass organisations of the Labour Movement are no longer capable of sponsoring our shows and finding their own audience'. Merseyside Unity had also produced RTP, and the local NFBTO branches were asked for donations, actors and backstage workers. There were two 'full houses'. So Manchester Unity decided they 'must take our place alongside those who are fighting to restore the breath of life and militancy'. Early in 1956 their production of Rowbotham's RTP was sponsored by Stretford Divisional Labour Party.

We defended the indefensible

By 1955, as Jack Beeching recalled, Communist Party activity 'hardly got outside its own periphery'. Comrades in touch with workers, particularly writers, were finding it hard to make a living, but were 'feeding in signals from ordinary people, which didn't correspond with the dogmatic line'. King Street was 'shrinking back into a sort of masturbatory activity', and many members were demoralised. Only one-tenth of the *Daily Worker*'s circulation came from street and factory sales; and by early 1956 sales were half those before the Cold War. Malcolm MacEwen was on the editorial board. He and others saw themselves as 'democrats, humanists, socialists, engaged in the struggle for a humane, free, socialist democracy', and 'still looked to the Soviet Union as a model'. However, 'uncritical adulation of the USSR had become a source of increasing irritation', especially when the Yugoslav Party was expelled from the Cominform in 1948. Yet even after Tito was rehabilitated in 1955, MacEwen claimed that the Party as a whole 'had not the slightest inkling of the storm that was about to break'.

In February 1956 Nikita Khrushchev gave his 'secret speech' about Stalin's murderous practices. Harry Pollitt and assistant party secretary George Matthews were at a Moscow contraceptive factory at the time, and claimed they returned 'in total ignorance'. Dutt's whereabouts remain unclear, but the *Daily Worker* correspondent found out what was going on within hours, so Pollitt knew before he left Russia. However, most British Communists were kept in the dark until March, when the speech was leaked in Bonn. There was an attempt to keep the lid on: a proposal to describe the Hungarian leader Rajk's recent execution as 'judicial murder' was dismissed by a majority of the *Daily Worker* board.[17] Then the *New York Times* published a summary of Khrushchev's speech. In April Pollitt tried to blame Party 'intellectuals' for any mistakes, but in May he resigned on health grounds. Dutt sought to dismiss it all in *Labour Monthly*: 'That there should be spots on the sun would only startle an inveterate Mithraworshipper.' This outraged many members, so he retreated a little. In June the US State Department released the full text of Kkrushchev's speech. Days later the *Observer* did so in Britain, and the *Manchester Guardian* published a pamphlet version, *The Dethronement of Stalin.* Given the original CIA provenance, many Communists assumed the whole thing was 'yet another anti-Soviet lie'; but late in June came the shooting of the striking workers at Poznan. CP leaders were now 'almost as much at a loss as the rank and file'.[18] Peter Fryer, who had supported the original Hungarian trials, was sent to report on the 'rehabilitation' of Rajk and 473 others; yet *Daily Worker* editor Campbell was applauded by staff for admitting 'we defended the indefensible'.[19]

By July Manchester Unity's membership was down to twenty. Its one-sheet *Bulletin* noted 'discord', 'isolation', 'personalities' and

> distaste of the ethical behaviour of certain members, allegations of an overbearing attitude adopted by some committee members, attribution of base motives to fellow activists within the group and a virulent and unceasing criticism of … those who hold responsible positions

It appealed 'for a more comradely and cordial atmosphere as befits a left-wing theatre group, with the name of Unity', especially since Manchester City Labour Party had recently affiliated. However, London Unity went on the offensive with *World on Edge,* or *All Your Answers Questioned,* in which a man tore up his Party card and a woman slapped a Russian soldier's face. The cast and audience discussions 'went on half the night', and some 'roundly condemned both Khruschev and Gollan'.[20] Manchester Unity's Xmas *Bulletin* reviewed this 'important and unusual production', and invited members 'to submit suggestions for future plays' after RTP had caused 'an influx of new blood'.

Back in April Lawrence & Wishart had reached 'an agreement about copyright',[21] and reprinted their hardback at fifteen shillings. The Richards Press edition was now on sale at twelve shillings and sixpence; and in December they published 1,500 copies of Frank Swinnerton's *The Adventures of a Manuscript,* at three shillings and sixpence for twenty-eight pages.

Swinnerton claimed there were Czech and Polish editions of *The Ragged Trousered Philanthropists*.[22] Yet British Communist intellectuals remained timid about the book. Jack Lindsay argued that it was 'an important link between the classical novel and the novel of socialist realism', and 'any systematic inquiry into the precursors of the new literature would have to examine it at length'.[23] Late in 1956 Arnold Kettle hailed it in *The Marxist Quarterly* as one of 'only a handful of books written by working class writers about working class life from a working class point of view'. So those who wished to 'build up a working class literature' had to understand that 'only writers actually involved in working class life and struggle can bring into literature what is here needed – a working class sensibility, a particular way of seeing life and the scale of values implied in it'.

On 5 November British and French troops invaded Suez, and Warsaw Pact tanks entered Hungary. The *Daily Worker* attacked British imperialism but supported the Russian variety. However, Fryer found 'a mass uprising against tyranny and poverty that had become insupportable', given the brutality of the secret police. This genuine 'people's revolution' was being 'crushed by the army of the first Socialist State'. He also found that Rajk and others had been tortured and then blackmailed into 'confessions'; but the *Daily Worker* editors printed the official Russian line that Hungarian events were fomented by hooligan counter-revolutionaries. For Fryer it all brought back memories of how CP 'functionaries' put the paper 'under heavy fire' in 1949 over 'some very mild criticisms of certain inessential features of Hungarian life', and how a colleague, distressed by what he saw in Eastern Europe, was told by Pollitt: 'My advice to you is to keep your mouth shut.'

On 14 November the *Daily Worker* published a photograph of a lynched corpse of what it claimed was an ordinary Communist; but then another picture emerged with the same corpse wearing the uniform of a secret policeman. *Daily Worker* staff were not allowed to read Fryer's dispatches, so he decided to leave the paper though not the CP. However, London Party functionaries suspended him as soon as they discovered he was writing a book. The 'Stalinist hard core' were 'clearly prepared to destroy the Party as a political force rather than allow free discussion of their mistakes', but Fryer believed this was temporary, since 'honest Communists' would realise they had 'defended tyranny with all our heart and soul'.[24] This proved overoptimistic. John Gorman candidly admitted: 'we were all Stalinists in the sense that we believed that whatever he said was

indisputable. To quote Stalin gave the speaker unanswerable authority',
especially when reinforced by a 'bureaucratic centralism' which was a
complete parody of Bolshevik 'democratic centralism'.[25]

It was all 'a shocker' to Beeching, and 'a thing you daren't discuss at
Centre, except behind your hand with someone you knew very well'. He
was having a sandwich with Cornforth at Lawrence & Wishart one day:

> Maurice said, 'I've just heard the Dean of Canterbury … what a wicked old
> man he is. I'd never realised it before … he ran up the stairs, burst into my
> office, and said "Ahah, have you seen about the camps, the tortures, and
> death? I knew all the time".'

Denial was commonplace. Beeching knew a woman poet from 'right in
the heart of the Scottish proletariat', who insisted: 'We're protesting about
Suez, and we're trying to get rents down, and all the other things.' But
uncritical loyalty prevailed. Three-quarters of CP branches supported the
EC's position; under a fifth opposed; and the rest were undecided. At area
and district committee level support was 'much higher'.[26] Pollitt knew
British Communists had 'disappeared'; yet he claimed Stalin was 'a worthy
and indispensable leader both of the Soviet State and world Socialism',
and his portrait stayed on the wall at home.[27]

In January 1957 Beeching's 'Notes on Zhdanov' appeared in the Marxist
Quarterly. He argued that what united 'most of the honest writers of the
Left' was 'the defence of peace; loyalty to the overwhelming majority of
our nation, namely, the working class; and determination to end England's
parasite status internationally'. Yet 'Zhdanovism repels many who would
be our friends', 'Have not those of us who kept silent on the subject from
political loyalty been deliberately misleading ourselves and others?'

> Is literature an artificial cement that you slap on the cracks of a disintegrat-
> ing society; or flesh and bone of people's life experience, because it springs
> 'from the contradictions of material life, from the existing conflict between the
> social forces of production and the relations of production'.

Stalin's 'idealist response' was a distortion of Marx reinforced by an
'opinion-forming apparatus and techniques such as are at the disposal of
anyone at the head of a modern state'.

> It's maybe more hard, then, for the man at the top to discard whips and
> threats and hymns – particularly when they appear such superior and swift
> and proven methods, and so much that is life-and-death has to be done so
> quickly. 'Beat, and beat, and beat again', as Stalin is reported to have told his
> secret police.

Workers needed 'truthful and unfettered art', in England and in Russia. In his despair, Beeching had come to believe 'Art is the revolutionary activity'.

The Cold War hit RTP. On 1 March an anonymous review in the *Times Literary Supplement* suggested that in spite of 'long half-baked speeches on politics, anti-capitalism', *The Ragged Trousered Philanthropists* was 'the voice of the poor themselves' precisely because it illustrated

> the seeming backwardness of so many trade unionists to-day – the aversion against foreign workers, the clinging to restrictive practices, the suspicion of even good employers, the feeling of loyalty to each other that at times seems to override sense and reason.

In his response Ball meekly noted that this was 'the second occasion that the book has reached the portals of English literature, and one may hope that this time it may gain admittance', though the manuscript 'has not found a home in "the appropriate Trade Union" but is still under my bed in a cardboard box, uninsured at that, and the original soldiers' gratuities are still tied up with it'. Privately, however, Ball was sure that the book

> served as an example of how a masterpiece may be produced by a writer without the advantages of higher education, a masterpiece which may lack the polish and concise form of the professional product, but which transcends such work by its integrity, its exact observation, its faithful picture of the lives of those who ... 'worked on the building' in his day.

It had 'won a lasting place in the affections of the ordinary people because it is about us'.[28]

Yet a lot of 'us' continued to vote Tory. After all, the 1951–55 Tory government had retained the NHS, built more council houses than Labour, and abolished food rationing. In 1955 it was re-elected. Nye Bevan became Labour Party treasurer in 1956, with union support, but in 1957, as shadow Foreign Secretary, he supported the British bomb. Arthur Horner, CPer and member of the National Coal Board, was proud there had been no official strikes.[29] A Manchester miner told me that his CP branch was divided physically: 'workers' on one side of the room, 'intellectuals' on the other. There was no debate, and books were rarely present. Yet as Jim Higgins recalled, when Dutt and Pollitt toured branches, they got 'almost totally rejected and abused', because 'everybody knew they had been privy to at least some of the crimes'.[30]

Very few CPers knew that the Party remained in hock to Moscow, that Reuben Falber siphoned money from Progressive Tours without the staff's knowledge,[31] or that he 'picked up cash from a Soviet embassy contact

Jack Beeching

regularly' after 1957, sometimes more than £100,000 a year.[32] They knew that *Daily Worker* circulation had fallen to 57,000, and the new General Secretary, John Gollan, publicly announced that he expected membership losses of 30 per cent. At the April 1957 Special Party Congress factions were officially banned; but, as usual, the Stalinists organised factionally and managed to ensure that the minority report on inner-party democracy was ignored, while the majority report was carried by more than twenty to one. Andrew Rothstein (supported by Kettle), speaking for the EC, denounced 'backboneless and spineless intellectuals'; yet John McLoughlin, a shop steward at Briggs Motor Bodies, retorted: 'You are the enemy, you lying old swine.'[33]

CP 'intellectuals' Burns, Kettle, Aaronovitch, Cornforth, Lindsay and West all stayed. But Swingler went quietly, and so did Rickword, who carried on as manager of Collet's Hampstead bookshop and invested in a copy of Trotsky's *The Revolution Betrayed*. Brian Behan, a building worker, was the only EC member to leave, yet he insisted: 'The myth of a rock-like working class and the wobbly intellectuals should be thrown out once and for all. Many industrial comrades are worried about Hungary. Some very good ones have left.'[34] After a near-fatal car accident, Beeching left too. He later described himself as a 'communard', and his friends as 'bolshies rather than bolsheviks'.[35] Having 'flirted with the Communist Party for 20 years', Fred Ball left as well. Comrade Tressell was homeless once again.

11

The modern Lazarus

In the custody of the TUC

The Ragged Trousered Philanthropists survived the crisis of Stalinism. The Russian edition was reprinted in 1957, and in 1958 a German translation by Lore Krüger, *Die Menschenfreunde in zerlumpten Hosen*, appeared from Aufbau-Verlag in East Berlin, with a 'longish account of Robert's life and the finding and publishing of the full MS' by Günther Klotz.[1] Reportedly, the Stalinist authorities did not like its 'critical spirit'.[2] Lawrence & Wishart's edition was still getting reviews. In June 1958 the union journal *Red Tape* welcomed 'one of the best loved classics of the Labour movement', one which 'quite openly' 'intended to convert readers to socialism', but felt it 'probably no longer has the force of thirty years ago'. The contrary was the case.

One man made 'such a fuss' when his copy was not returned that, even though 'it looked an extremely boring book', his daughter read it and found it 'explained a great deal to me without any emotional distraction'. A bricklayer told a young labourer about it, and he found that older workmates had 'clear recollections of working conditions in the 1930s and even beyond', and knew earlier editions. A Merseyside ex-squaddie 'haunted bookshops for several years' until

> right before my eyes was 'IT'; a beautiful thick hard-back edition, priced 18/– (not cheap in those days). I had only 15/– with me, so I placed a deposit on the book, dived out of the shop, onto a bus home, and was back to collect my much sought after prize in one hour flat.

A Glasgow apprentice 'constantly heard painters talking' about RTP, and his father mentioned it when some incident sparked a memory. Then a copy 'leaped' into his 'range of vision' as he browsed in a bookshop. He 'identified' with Bert White. It 'blew the cobwebs away from my brain like a rush of fresh air'.

John Monks, a Manchester teenager, was 'encouraged to read Tressell's tale by others who had already been influenced by the story and its capacity to shape the way that readers view the world of wealth and its uneven distribution'. He went on to take a degree in economics at Nottingham University, but he continued to find that 'Tressell' was one of 'a few writers whose influence on your political philosophy goes deeper than your experience of current affairs or the analytical text books'.[3] At Parliament Hill School, North London, Sheila Gammon's English teacher put RTP on a list of 'books/authors that someone who considers themselves to be well read would have read', alongside Dickens and Lawrence.[4] A socialist 'Day Schoolteacher' recommended it to an apprentice, who passed it on to his mates, and to tradesmen. He noticed that it split readers into two categories: those interested only in 'cheap paperback' productions, and those who could 'enjoy discussions' about socialist ideas.

But to which political tradition did RTP now belong? In February 1959 former CPer Peter Fryer re-examined The British Road to Socialism. He found that the 'entire Marxist theory of the State, the proletarian revolution and the dictatorship of the proletariat' was 'twisted into an unrecognizable form'. To the CP,

> the workers are a social force, certainly, but a force to be manipulated from above. The party programme is not a programme for power, not a revolutionary programme, but a reformist programme. In essence it is no different from the Fabian conception of how socialism is to be achieved. Someone else, not the workers, will do the job.[5]

Party training was 'political pornography', not Marxism; yet what made Stalin's 'philosophical idealism' plausible to people was not 'gullibility' but 'hatred of capitalism and loyalty to the working class'.[6] Fryer edited the new Socialist Labour League's influential Newsletter; but after a coup by a group of 'orthodox Trotskyists' that September he resigned.[7]

Eric Heffer had been squeezed out of the CP in a particularly nasty way in the early 1950s, but by 1957 he was in the tiny Socialist Review Group, whose politics were influenced by Luxemburg, Lenin and Trotsky.[8] He argued that 'the power of the capitalist class must be completely broken', including the 'class state', and he denounced the 'class collaborationist policies' of the TUC General Council, which reminded him of post-war

CP policy – 'unity in words and conservatism in practice'.[9] In 1960 he became a Liverpool councillor. When the SRG became the International Socialists in 1962, he stayed with Labour, because it felt like 'a genuine workers' party'.[10] In 1963 he was adopted as a parliamentary candidate, and in 1964 he was elected MP.

Ball wanted to sell the manuscript but also wanted to keep it within the labour movement. His fellow shareholder Peter Blackman, secretary of the Sussex Federation of Trades Councils, wrote to Sir Richard Coppock of the NFBTO. In 1958 Ball took the manuscript to the union head office in Clapham, in a box marked 'Processed Peas'. Eventually, the Executive agreed to pay £130;[11] and the southern counties regional secretary, Kenneth Price, went to pick up the manuscript.[12] Ball had revised his draft 'history' to accompany it:

> To myself it has long been an inspiration that a house-painter, with no more advantages than the rest of us, should make such a contribution to the culture of the nation – about our part of that nation in which, for the first time, the lives of ordinary working-men, their wives & children, become the subject matter of literature – and a contribution which stands out precisely because the author remained true to 'his passion for justice & human brotherhood' & treated our lives seriously & not as a kind of comic relief in literature as lesser writers treat us.

Ball argued that the book was 'a mighty beginning to a literature of the common people' and had 'sprung from their great tradition of struggle for human rights'.[13] Lawrence & Wishart reprinted in 1959 at eighteen shillings. Ball was not present when Sir Richard Coppock presented the manuscript to TUC General Secretary Sir Vincent Tewson that January, though *Labour* was relieved that it was safely 'in the custody of the TUC'.

If you are mad, that makes two of us

In the early 1960s Stephen Lowe was a kid in Nottingham and an 'ardent communist for a period'. RTP was recommended to him by the manager of 'a flea-pit cinema and a miners' club':

> He claimed it was practically the only book he had ever read and had been given it by one of his mates in Malaya. He never seemed to me to be a socialist in any way, being just about the biggest con-man I ever met, but his heart somehow seemed to be in the right place. At any rate, I liked him, so I got the book from the Central Library and read it....
> The analysis of society was not what struck me because I already (obviously in a vaguer fashion) had come to those beliefs. It did not, in that

sense, convert me. It did something much more fundamental. It spoke to me directly, out of intense pain, saying 'You're not mad. You're not on your own. Or, if you are mad, well, that makes two of us.'

Both Stephen's grandfathers had been painters, but he wasn't getting on with his father, a former bricklayer and decorator who suffered from TB, Owen 'was the nearest to finding a father, a friend' that he 'had ever known'. He seemed 'a man alone who had not given in'. 'The bastards couldn't grind him down.'[14]

Jack Mitchell was introduced to RTP when he was a small boy, by his father, but it had 'no appeal' until his early teens. Later, he joined the CP, and in the May 1961 issue of *Marxism Today* he claimed that RTP was 'not only the first important working class novel in the history of English literature' but held an unequalled place 'in the consciousness of the vanguard of the British proletariat and progressive intelligentsia'. Artistically, 'Many of the established pre-conditions for socialist realism are apparently broken'; yet the book qualified 'as part of the first general breakthrough of the proletariat into the large-scale literary spheres' because of its 'proletarian sensibility'. Politically, it illustrated the 'central stumbling block facing the Labour movement' in Britain, the 'crippling gap' between 'the truly splendid working-class machine' and 'the low general level of clear political consciousness among the masses of the workers', which 'lags behind that of the French or Italian worker'. Owen was 'the old, uncompromising, dedicated English puritan hero, Mr Christian become a revolutionary socialist worker', and RTP told activists 'more of the truth about the tremendous difficulties facing them than any other novel'. It was 'the first strategic working-class novel in our history'.

Other comrades didn't necessarily agree. In the November *Marxism Today* David Craig acknowledged that The Ragged Trousered Philanthropists 'may, I think, be called the first work of socialist realism', and he accepted the new *Fundamentals of Marxism-Leninism* line on culture; but he was also a pupil of the Cambridge radical liberal academic F.R. Leavis., so he was concerned that the book was 'not subtle!' The working-class characters 'are valued for us in the crudest possible way': the bourgeoisie was 'taken over from the technique of the newspaper cartoonist'; and the 'lectures on socialism are bare and laborious'. Indeed, the book was 'full of defects compared to the matured socialist realism of Sholokov', and 'inferior' in 'profundity or consistent sharpness of detail' to Lu Hsun, the mature Gorky and Fedin. At best, RTP was a 'quite new type of work piecing itself together out of all manner of hitherto crude popular ingredients', and a 'unique effort to present the utter social truth, bared of all lies and illusions'. Craig taught classes for the National Union of Agriculture Workers in North Yorkshire, so he cyclostyled pages of RTP, and read bits aloud:

> Members latched onto him eagerly, saying things in discussion that amounted to 'He's really telling it like it is. Yes, that's what it's like. We know that stuff. We haven't come across it in books before. The bastards! (the foreman, etc.) Owen – aye, the thoughtful type. Couldn't he have given more of a lead?' The upshot was a feeling of quickening, of empowerment: members felt good that working conditions familiar to themselves and their fathers and mothers had been brought into the light of literature, and the minority of strongly militant members squared up eagerly to the question of 'what was to be done?' This usually meant 'putting a squib under that lot in White-hall/on the NEC, etc.'

But he felt only 'a minority' would have read the whole book.[15]

During 1961 Prelozila Dagmar Knittlove's translation of RTP, *Lidumilove v hadrech*, was published in Prague, with Ian Milner's account of the author's place in literature. It was dramatised for Czech television. Lawrence & Wishart's 1962 reprint cost twenty-one shillings; and, apart from an amended dust jacket and title page, it was identical to the edition published that same year by Monthly Review Press in New York, which retailed at $6. Yet Jack Mitchell was still dismayed by the lack of attention to the book by 'Marxist literary criticism' outside Russia and the Russian Sector of Germany. He accepted Aaronovitch's 1953 article, with its bizarre Zhdanovite line: RTP was 'at once international and deeply national'. Yet while he agreed with Beeching and Kettle that it was a link in the 'great epic realist tradition of the English novel', he did not explain why such a 'decisive step towards the founding of a working-class Socialist literature in Britain' was the 'only true national working-class epic in our language to date'.[16] Mitchell completed his Ph.D. on the book at Humboldt University in East Berlin in 1964.

In the early 1960s *The Ragged Trousered Philanthropists* continued to reach British workers. An apprentice joiner in Liverpool came to it after reading *Tressell of Mugsborough*, and reread it 'at least four times'. A young Irish painter found conditions in the novel 'immediately recognisable' at work; and it was a raffle prize at Wortley Hall, during the Fire Brigades Union's National School. A building-site labourer who became a Post Office worker in Northumberland found the book was well known by 'those of a thinking and socialistic bent'. A Belfast woman felt her socialism was 'something

of an external thing', until a friend suggested she read RTP. 'Sometimes it
angered me, sometimes it uplifted me, but from first to last it compelled
me irresistibly, reaffirming and substantiating what I believed'. It 'deeply
influenced' her decision to become involved in 'welfare work & then
Remedial Educ[ation] in one of Belfast's most deprived areas'. An apprentice painter with 'socialist sympathies' in Greenock had the novel recommended to him by a night-school teacher. He was having the same
arguments as Owen, and 'found the book a help in a practical sense'. It
'contributed to my understanding of Marxist ideas and action especially
within the trade union movement', because of its 'plain, simple, everyday
language that ordinary people can understand'.

The first great English novel about the class war

In 1958 the Author's Club voted Alan Sillitoe's *Saturday Night and Sunday
Morning* the most promising novel of the year. In 1959 Sillitoe argued that
'One of the reasons that the novel fails to acquire a bigger reading public
is that it tends to deal too much with middle-class life', while D.H. Lawrence and the 'proletarian novelists' of the 1930s were 'read mostly by a
middle-class audience'. In his view *The Ragged Trousered Philanthropists* out-
weighed Walter Greenwood's *Love on the Dole*, because of its 'bone-realism',
its 'Zolaesque greatness' and above all the way in which it raised the
question in readers' minds, whether it was about slum housing or the
hydrogen bomb: 'What can I do about it?'[17] In 1961 he gave the book a
walk-on part in *Key of the Door*.[18]

In 1963 Martin Secker sold the Richards Press; and in April 1964 *The
Ragged Trousered Philanthropists*' fifty-year copyright ran out. That December
Penguin's 'AG' enquired whether Dr John Burrow of Downing College,
Cambridge, had been asked for an introduction to a paperback edition.[19]
However, in February 1965 Panther, a subsidiary of Granada Publishing,
published their complete paperback edition at seven shillings and sixpence. They noted that 'Tressell's idiosyncratic grammar, spelling and punctuation (his way of conveying the spoken idiom of his characters), as well
as his somewhat inconsistent use of capital letters, have been restored';
and that this 'story of the most important struggle in history', that 'between the underprivileged and their oppressors', had 'sold hundreds of
thousands of copies'. No copyright was ascribed or asserted, though Lawrence & Wishart's written consent was required before this paperback

could be 'lent, re-sold, hired out or otherwise disposed of by way of trade in any form of binding or cover other than that in which it is published'.

Sillitoe's 'Introduction' was copyrighted. Having read *Tressell of Mugsborough* he accepted that, whatever the social origins of the novel's author, he had been 'grafted onto working-class life'. Moreover, the 'mass of personal detail keeps it a novel and not a tract', and the book is 'utterly unsentimental'. Speaking for and on behalf of working-class readers Sillitoe insisted that the book produced 'a bolstering of class feeling; pure rage; reinforcement for their own self-pity; a call to action; maybe a good and beneficial dose of all these things'. It was 'easy to read, like all journeys through hell'; but it was 'the first great English novel about the class war'.[20]

In his *Daily Worker* review, Arnold Kettle was unsure if the book was 'an interesting historical document, a record of things as they were' (like Engels's *The Condition of the Working-Class in England*), or 'more in the line of' Dickens, whose books 'can still delight and move us not so much by the facts they uncover as by the imaginative force of the world they create'. But he was quite clear that it was 'the first – one is almost tempted to say the only – successful attempt in English at what was later to be called "Socialist realism"'. Labour left-winger Michael Foot hailed it in the *Evening Standard* as 'the bible of trade union organizers and working-class agitators' and 'a document of the first importance in the history of the Labour movement'. But only its 'conception', and 'not, alas, the execution raises Robert Tressell to the level of the great mentor of Paine, Blatchford and Cobbett – Jonathan Swift'; so it was a 'misshapen masterpiece'. In the *New Statesman* V.S. Pritchett argued that this 'half-tract, half-novel' was 'one of those classics of underground life', but principally because it was 'rambling and repetitive and written out of the collective jawing of the people themselves'. He had more 'sympathy for the boss, the wretched little man, who won't allow two painters in a room together'.

In *New Society* John Torode christened it 'A Bible of Love and Hate'; while *Tribune* felt it 'broke a jagged hole in the smooth wall of middle-class values behind which a lot of books in England still get tidily composed'. 'The fear has gone, and the starvation workers are organised, the class war is blurred at the edges'; but for all its 'contempt for the stupidity of the working classes' it showed 'How to live on nothing, how to laugh with a bellyful of hate and dread, how to smash in the foreman's face and survive.' A newspaper correspondent urged people to carry it 'in a shoulder holster ready for the first oratorical oaf to speak of "the good old days", so that it can be rammed down his throat'. Another thought 'we still live in Mugsborough', so 'this book is still dynamite'. A third insisted: 'Every socialist, trade unionist, co-operator, communist, pacifist and humanist should buy a copy and lend it, lend it, lend it. It is a socialist nuclear weapon'. The guardian of actual nuclear weapons, Labour, were re-elected in March 1966 with a sizeable majority. That May, the Cabinet tried to bale out capitalism by imposing an incomes policy on the working class. The National Union of Seamen (including a militant John Prescott) resisted, and were branded a 'tightly knit group of politically-motivated men' – that is, Communists. Len Murray, one-time CPer but now TUC General Secretary, threatened to 'cripple' them.

Stuart Douglass had come across The Ragged Trousered Philanthropists at a London Unity Theatre production, and in March 1967 his own adaptation was being made into a television play for BBC2. Jack Duke, who 'had known men who'd worked with Tressall, and had passed copies of the book among his workmates', became technical adviser. Bert Baker plugged the project in the Morning Star, along with Tressell of Mugsborough, which was then out of print. He was confident that 'many readers already know Tressell's work and history', but for any who did not the Lawrence & Wishart hardback was available at twenty-five shillings. He neglected to mention that the Panther paperback cost only seven shillings and sixpence.

Douglass felt that Noonan was 'a true Marxist', but 'had to take liberties with the text, omitting some characters and incidents, even some of the more sacred scenes'. The producer, Michael Bakewell, told Ball, 'We've taken out a lot of the sex, but kept in all the socialism.' The adaptation was broadcast on 29 May, yet in spite of Hastings Trades Council's appeals, only on BBC2. Edward Fox starred as Barrington, the ever-present narrator, and stressed the gap between those 'helping to bring about a better state of affairs for the future' and those 'helping to perpetuate the present misery'. He argued for socialism, and suggested that acts of Parliament could abolish capitalism. In the final scene, Alderman Sweater is seen showing people round his house, bragging about the cheapness of the Moorish decorations, and announcing he would use the argument about 'the interests of masters and men being identical' at the next election. As in Noonan's book, no candidate would be representing working-class interests.

The *Observer* noted that, 'Far from aiming at realism', Douglass used 'an early film technique involving flickering captions in debased art nouveau lettering and balletic Chaplinesque characterisation', while his 'socialist heroes' were of 'a grotesque saintliness'. The *Sunday Telegraph* praised the 'triumph of abstraction', with 'little vignettes, each one separately framed', but found Owen a 'romantic idealist'. However, Robert Oakes felt that it 'does me good to go back to Robert Tressall [sic]'. 'It fills me with humility and makes me realise that I must go on even if I believe at times that man deserves what's coming to him.' He had been disillusioned with the Labour government, and 'with workers for supporting men like Enoch Powell, with nations for manufacturing horrific weapons and above all with our damn smug satisfaction'.

A mess of pottage

Fred Ball's novel *A Breath of Fresh Air* had been published in 1961. It came second to a book by Robert Graves in the Italia Prize, and was dramatised on radio. In June 1962 Sir Tom O'Brien, General Secretary of the National Association of Theatrical and Kine Employees and also Chairman of the Joint Advisory Council of the TUC, presided over the gift of a teak seat on the Hastings seafront. He claimed that many trade unionists present had read RTP 'as youngsters, with a great deal of delight, and rejoiced in the humour of the working class of that day'; but he 'regretted the modern working class had lost that sense of humour'. The mayor hoped the manuscript might be 'lodged in their own archives', or 'be loaned to them', and Sir Tom thought the latter might be arranged. Ball spoke, and was photographed standing behind Len Green, the 'last surviving character in Tressell's book'. The Trades Council placed a temporary plaque on 115 Milward Road. Two years later they installed a marble one. It was a modest beginning to 'Tressell' tourism.

In 1963 Ball began a book about his bizarre adolescent experience as a gardener, and *A Grotto for Miss Maynier* was published in 1965. He was living at 27A Elphinstone Road, and earning 'the greater part of his living as a bookie's clerk'; but he was working 'on a book about a man of his own age in the present day – although it is not an autobiography' – to be published in 1966, and produced on radio.[21] During 1966, aged 61, Ball retired to concentrate on his own writing, though his wife, Jacqueline, continued going out to work. Ball began collecting material for 'a history of working-class literature', focusing on Unity Theatre, *Poetry and the People*, *Our Time* and 'the amateur and more spontaneous activities sparked off by the movement'. He was still interested in RTP, but he didn't want 'to be tied to Tressell's apron strings'.

Ball believed that Kathleen Meiklejon (née Noonan) and her baby Joan, had been killed in a motor accident just after the First World War. In fact Kathleen had left Paul late in 1918. When he asked what the family should be told, she replied 'Oh tell them I'm dead.' So he 'invented the motor accident'. She used her stage name, Kathleen Lynne. Until 1921 Kathleen was a 'red hot socialist', but after a revelation she 'realised that if only we could convert the world to Christianity there would be no need for socialism', because 'we would have the true 'Brotherhood of Man'. *The Ragged Trousered Philanthropists* took a back seat, and it was not until 1956 or 1957, when Joan was working in a Christian Bookshop in England, that she 'discovered' the wartime Penguin paperback, though the Lawrence & Wishart edition eluded her. Kathleen wrote to Grant Richards, but her letter went unanswered by Secker. Joan returned to Canada in 1959, where she was accepted as a novice Anglican nun; but in 1962 she received a legacy. That September she and her mother decided to settle in England, and Joan was released from her vows to look after Kathleen.

Kathleen took a flat in Middlesex. She lived on her Canadian pension, although Joan paid her rent by running the Church Army Club, Canteen and Bookshop in the Forces Welfare Department at Lippstadt, Germany. In 1964 Joan married co-worker Reg Johnson. They worked in Algiers and Antwerp, before moving to Tudor House, Winchcombe, in Gloucestershire, where Kathleen now lived.[22] On 30 May 1967, the day after Douglass's RTP was broadcast, Reg wrote to *The Times*, pointing out the 'irony and pathos' of a situation in which 'Miss Noonan' had no television and could not see the programme, though she had sold the copyright for less than the cost of a set. *Times* reporter David Wilsworth came to Winchcombe, and his article appeared on 5 June. The woman who 'Sold rights to classic for £25' was quoted as saying 'I keep kicking myself for my own stupidity'. 'I don't want to be rich, but I would like to be able to buy some new curtains.' She had 'sold the book for a mess of pottage'.

A week later Maurice Cornforth of Lawrence & Wishart wrote to 'Miss Kathleen Lymme'. He stressed that she had 'no financial claims', since the book had 'been out of copyright since 1964', but enclosed a 'small cheque' for £25 as 'a token of good will, which we hope will at least help you

Reg Johnson

purchase the new curtains'. They expected to have to reprint RTP 'before long', and an 'inscribed copy' was in the post. He hoped she would give Fred Ball the information he needed. Ball's letter arrived from 53c Chiltern Drive, Hastings, next day. He asked Kathleen to grant an interview, and admitted that *Tressell of Mugsborough* was 'based mostly upon reminiscences of friends and workmates', and 'contains a number of misstatements'. He wanted to 'revise' it, and suggested 'we could make some arrangement'. Kathleen congratulated him on his 'recapture' of the manuscript, and asked to see 'Tressell of Mug', which she had not known about before. Ball sent his own copy on loan, only to be told that 'a great deal' was 'very far from the facts'. (Privately, Kathleen felt it contained 'quite a lot of propaganda'.) When Ball published 'More Light on Tressell' in the June issue of *Marxism Today* as an 'excerpt from a new book', it was carefully copyrighted.

Reg Johnson suspected that Ball's biography was 'a recent thought', and was anxious that Kathleen's unique knowledge should 'be used (exploited in its nicest sense) to her best advantage'. His solicitor saw

nothing in law to stop Mr Ball putting whatever slant he chooses on Joan's Grandfather's activities. The only thing you can do is ... try to correct the story. It does not sound as though you will be able to persuade Mr Ball to alter his 'slant' merely by offering him further factual information.

Ball met Kathleen on 29 June. She and the Johnsons felt he was 'expecting to receive on a platter all the information necessary for correcting the mistakes' in his first biography. However, none of the two-day conversation was recorded. Ball agreed that 'nothing was available for publication until otherwise agreed', and to consult the Society of Authors. In July, using headed notepaper, he told Kathleen that Hutchinson wanted the revised biography by Christmas, and promised to send the Society of Authors' response and his 'own opinions about an arrangement'.

Meanwhile, Rose Cruttenden told Kathleen that she had helped Ball with Tressell of Mugsborough, but had 'never seen him since', and that 'he had put in a lot of fiction'. She assumed he had taken a photograph of Kathleen, and 'some photographs of the Sunday meetings we used to hold on Hastings beach which showed the beautiful banner that your Dad painted'. Later, Rose responded to Ball's questionnaire, but 'he never acknowledged receiving it'. She signed off, 'still a Revolutionary, thoroughly disgusted with Wilson, Brown & Co'.

Ball had told Kathleen there had been plans for a Tressell Society before she came back from the dead. In fact the 'preliminary meeting' took place in mid-July It was a self-appointed body of nine people, and Ball was one of the acting secretaries. He argued: 'there is a great deal of feeling about Tressell in this country which has never been tapped or organised', so his committee planned to 'perpetuate the memory of Robert Tressell and his book; to promote and stimulate original creative work of all kinds; and to encourage participation in the arts as a means of understanding the society in which we live.' A permanent exhibition of 'Tressell-iana' was to be set up for the centenary of the author's birth, and 'an Honorary Historian' appointed to 'conduct research into Tressell and his times'. Ball was suffering from an ulcer, but was 'still negotiating with publisher'. His biography was commissioned by Lawrence & Wishart, but the Tressell Society was 'still in process of becoming' a year later.

In August 1967 Peter Blackman's name appeared on an article about 'The Robert Tressell Banner'. Ball's copy is marked 'Wrongly attributed', 'Written by F.C. Ball.'[23] He could not afford to travel, but he suggested that he and Kathleen swap photographs. He had approached the BBC about a biography of John Clare, and they suggested that he write his own. A play was commissioned by the Third Programme; he had a new

novel on the go, 'a sort of Everyman reflecting contemporary society';
and his 'standard biography' of Tressell was to be published in December.
He told Kathleen that 'a few socialist working men' wanted to buy her a
television set, but would 'have to seek National support'; and he enclosed
copies of 'letters on the subject of my responsibility' in relation to her
material, indicating that his own ideas were 'a little better'. The Society of
Authors stressed that Ball was 'under no legal obligation to give Kathleen
Tressell [sic] any part of the monies you make out of the book', but that
'there is some considerable moral obligation to do so'. They suggested a
10 per cent royalty 'on all the *net* income you make from the book during
her lifetime', with a reciprocal arrangement if she received 'substantial
sums' from press, radio or television interviews. On behalf of Lawrence
& Wishart, Cornforth argued that Kathleen should not be in the contract:
'if she is poor, you should bear in mind that you are too. And *you* are the
one who does the work, and must support wife and child.' But Ball might
care to 'pass on to her a bit of the earnings', up to £50, 'if her services
really are substantial'. Reg's solicitor thought a 10 per cent contractual
royalty was fair to Kathleen, with no upper limit if Ball got 10 per cent
of her net income.

On 4 September Ball sent Kathleen his own proposals for an arrangement, and four days later he arrived at Winchcombe, 'prepared to collect
material'. Reg recalls that conversations 'took place over a couple of days
with the tape running at different times during the day and well into the
night', and there was 'no chronological order' to the questions.[24] Kathleen
began reading her notes about her paternal grandfather, then Ball quickly
interrupted: 'Who told you, or how did you get the idea?' He was gen-
tly put in his place: 'Dad told me. Or maybe Dad and aunt Adelaide.'
Soon after, the recorder was switched off, and Ball became more circum-
spect. Kathleen made laconic comments about her father, 'the wicked
Irishman', but she refused to have words put in her mouth. She insisted
that Robert's supposed words, when handing her the manuscript, were
'rubbish'. The stories of its being tied up in a pink ribbon and kept
under her bed, and the alleged visit to the soup-kitchen, were dismissed
out of hand. Rose Cruttenden wasn't her childhood friend – that was her
elder sister, Edith. Kathleen's cousin Alice 'never liked me, anyway', and
possibly 'didn't like Dad'. Ogilvy's article was 'a fairy tale'. Ball became
notably less confident; but he desperately wanted her consent to the idea
that his oral sources – Gower especially – had 'quite a good picture' of

Robert's 'essential character', though 'wrong in some little particulars of fact, possibly'.

On 14 September Ball sent a receipt for three tapes and for copies of various documents and photographs. Reg recalls: 'No formal agreement was entered into.' 'There was an open-ended verbal agreement to "wait and see". Depending on the success, or otherwise, of the book a financial settlement would be negotiated.'[25] However, on 25 September Kathleen gave Ball 'first refusal on the right to publish the original material and photographs passed to you' and 'further letters, press reviews and other notes promised for your use'. The period of payment was to be extended to read 'and thereafter to Mrs Joan Irene Johnson, née Lynne daughter of the aforesaid, grand-daughter of Robert Tressall'; though Ball was to take his expenses into account before calculating the sum to be paid. Kathleen assumed the 'standard form of contract' would cover all other eventualities. That month the Balls moved to 4A Cotswold Close.

Ball did not contact Kathleen again until January 1968. He had 'hardly touched Tressell', had yet to transcribe the tapes, and put the onus on her to contact his agent about the 'Agreement', make notes, establish her ancestry and send him a list of all names mentioned by her father. In April he sought to reassure her about contractual issues, and asked for a copy of her father's last letter. He also enclosed 'a few' questions, though his questionnaire on 'South Africa' had twenty-four headings, and many sections required multiple answers. Yet in May he asserted that Tressell of Mugsborough 'is not only a true and faithful portrait in general, but is practically one hundred per cent true in particulars', and added that it was 'very unfortunate that you are able to add so little', since

> I didn't want to do this book, I want to do my own books, but a whole set of circumstances make me obliged to. I have been doing research ever since Tressell of Mugsborough was finished in 1950, without help and at my own expense, not counting time and I can assure you, only out of a sense of historical duty – there hasn't yet been any money in Tressell for me and I don't think I shall ever earn the time I spent, but I want to make as good a job as I can and forget all about it!

He nagged her again for a copy of Robert's last letter, which was 'the only personal document surviving of Tressell and will probably in time be regarded as a little historical treasure'. His questionnaire on 'England' had forty-six headings, and 'Going to Liverpool' had thirty-one. But he stressed that 'I shan't necessarily be putting everything you tell me into the book.'

By July Kathleen had sent Ball 'about 10,000 words'. He had a play accepted for broadcasting, a novel under way, and was 'overwhelmed with "work" on the Tressell book'. Jacqueline's job brought in £5 a week; but he could not get work, or qualify for dole, and would not 'beg from National Assistance'. In December Kathleen used the rent money to go to Hastings for the presentation of the television set, licence, aerial, cheque and TUC Centenary Badge. Of her two specially invited guests, Rose Cruttenden attended and Cornforth did not,[26] though the prospective Labour parliamentary candidate for Hastings was there. Kathleen's speech was recorded by David Haines, who also filmed her 'as a historical record'; and she signed copies of RTP in Hastings Library. A reporter noted: 'At least one British trade union presents a copy' of this 'Workers' Classic' to 'each new member'. Kathleen admitted to 'publicity shyness'. But 'Kate Tressell is another person altogether – she doesn't mind!' She was 'The Modern Lazarus'.

Stuart Douglass had told Kathleen that The Ragged Trousered Philanthropists 'has haunted me for most of my life', and in view of the 'paltry sum' she received from Richards, he promised 'to pursue your case as far as I can', though the BBC was under no legal obligation. Late in 1967 he had taped an interview with her for the Arts section of the CP's Labour Monthly, which he edited 'in an unpaid, honorary capacity'. An edited transcript appeared in June 1968. Kathleen noted the errors: 'it sounded as though someone had listened to the tape and then written the article later'. When Douglass's dramatisation was broadcast to mark the TUC's centenary, Kathleen had to visit friends to see it. In December Douglass's play script was staged, with his permission, by Wandsworth School in London. There was an illustrated booklet relying on Ball's biography, and the producers had access to Leonard Jones's research.[27] Tribune noted: 'The System is still as pernicious, and perhaps its days are still numbered, but its subtlety and resilience are disconcerting and the alternative is no longer so bright or clear as Tressell believed.' The Putney & Roehampton Herald did not comment on the fact that the unctuous Reverend John Starr was played by Roy Jenkins, namesake of the right-wing Labour minister.

Mere academics

During 1967 Kathleen had learned that Jack Mitchell's forthcoming book aimed to 'establish' RTP as 'one of the great works of English literature'.

Yet in July Brian Mayne of the University of British Columbia claimed that its popularity had 'waned steadily' since 1947 in both 'England' and North America.[28] This was nonsense. Richards Press had published the book four times between 1948 and 1954, while Lawrence & Wishart had issued five printings since 1955, and did so again in 1968 at twenty-five shillings. (Perhaps some canny librarians were having the Panther paperback rebound, since the hardback publisher's claims concluded: 'and without a similar condition including this condition being imposed on the subsequent purchaser'.) Since 1955 there had been a hardback printing for the US market, two in Russia, and others in Germany, Czechoslovakia and Bulgaria. In 1967 and 1968 Panther reprinted their paperback edition at seven shillings and sixpence, with a still from Douglass's television production on the cover. In January 1969 they graciously returned Kathleen's cheque and sent her three copies free of charge.

Kathleen's knowledge was becoming a commodity, but she was losing control over its use. In 1968 *Labour Monthly* sent her a cheque from Eric Bolton, who had used the transcript of the Douglass interview for his Lancaster University M.A. Bolton concluded that because of Noonan's middle-class 'background and experience', he may have 'believed in the justice of the cause' of socialism, 'but not in the ability of the working class to play its part'.[29] So he told Kathleen he was anxious that Mitchell seemed 'almost determined to make RTP a virtually flawless work because of his own political commitment'. He 'very much sympathised' with Mitchell's Communist politics, but felt his approach was 'dangerous and in the long run will work against the proper recognition' of the book. In 1969, Bolton worked as a builders' labourer to raise money to get to East Germany, and 'all the men I met had read "The Philanthropists" and were very interested to hear that I had met Robert Tressell's daughter'. By then, David Smith's Auckland University Ph.D. on RTP was under way. He and his wife had 'read and re-read' the book 'until the covers have fallen loose'. Yet when Kathleen queried some of Ball's conjectures, and mentioned the scholarly interest, he told her he was sure his biography would 'survive because I am not a mere academic'.

Raymond Williams had joined the Communist Party when he was a Cambridge undergraduate before the war. But he did not rejoin afterwards, because he and his friends 'knew we were to the left of the Labour Party' and the CP was 'irrelevant because of the intellectual errors it had made'. Besides, it 'had absolutely no implantation of any kind I could respect in any of the fields of work I was involved with'.[30] In 1946 Williams got a full-time staff tutor's job in English Literature, based in Sussex, and sometimes dropped in at the CP house in Hastings. He was finally alienated by the Stalinist suppression of the East Berlin building workers' uprising in 1953, and worked for the Labour Party in the 1955 general election. In 1961 he took up a fellowship at Jesus College, Cambridge (which, as he told students, 'came out of the blue', and 'seemed like a good idea at the time'). It is not clear whether Williams joined the Labour Party;[31] but Wilson's governments and the failure of the centrist *May Day Manifesto* network to go anywhere in 1968 may have helped him changed his mind about RTP. Late in 1969 Lawrence & Wishart published Jack Mitchell's *Robert Tressell and The Ragged Trousered Philanthropists* in hardback at forty-five shillings. Williams contributed a 'Foreword' which claimed that 'some failure of communication' in his Welsh, working-class youth meant he read the abridged RTP only during the war, and was 'incredibly late' in reading the complete edition. (He told his students that the title put him off.) However, he now understood that the novel was 'part of the altered popular culture of the British people after the Industrial Revolution'.[32]

Mitchell agreed with Kettle that *The Ragged Trousered Philanthropists* prefigured 'socialist realism' with its 'mature working-class sensibility' and 'proletarian humanism'. It had 'no plot in the traditional sense'; yet the prose was 'plain, sober, concrete – a clear glass, or rather lens, through which the reader views reality'. So the novel went beyond 'popular critical realism' in a way impossible before 'the general maturing of the working class in the age of imperialism'. In fact it was comparable to Gorky's *Lower Depths* and prefigured Brecht. Politically, the book represented 'part of the stripping for the fight which hall-marked this period of preparation before the Great Unrest', when, 'under a militant rank-and-file leadership, the modern British working class as a whole went over to its first full-scale offensive'. By 1914 'it was touch and go which would come first, world war or social revolution'. In 1915, 'the men and women of Clydeside picked up where the Great Unrest had left off, and it was here, in 1916, that Tressell's *Philanthropists* entered directly into the struggle.' It was nothing less than 'a 'revolutionary working-class novel'.

Any weaknesses were the price of innovation. The stereotyping of bosses was to show they were agents of 'a perfectly impersonal and universal law' of profit, 'working itself out through them as individuals'. The exclusion of a 'love story' helped head off any '"inner" or "outer" emigration'.

'Something of the sectarian S.D.F. schoolmaster remains in Owen', but the omission of union activity was unimportant, since the 'most efficient trade union machine in the whole capitalist world' could now be taken over by new engineers. RTP showed the 'gap between the organisational efficiency and the relatively low level of political consciousness', which was 'the main stumbling block' to a British revolution, and the book was 'indirectly, a criticism of the working class', but 'a merciless self-criticism was top priority. All comfortable self-delusion and imposed illusion had to be cauterised away'. Mitchell claimed that the 'militant working class'

> accepts Tressell's merciless criticism because it is true, because it was writ- ten by a man who was clearly one of themselves, because, by addressing a great novel to them, he implicitly accepts them as the people who will eventually change the state of affairs which he depicts.

Indeed, this 'tale of misery, unrelieved gloom and (except for the last paragraph) defeat' was 'most dangerous to the powers that be', since 'we learn why there has been no socialist revolution in Britain – yet'.[33]

In the New Statesman V.S. Pritchett noted that this 'Marxist polemic con- tains all the well-known cliches which stick out like ironmongery on the page'. Mitchell was a 'dogmatic critic', since the 'real drama lies in the conflict between socialist argument and the lazy-mindedness of people living from day to day'. After all, Noonan had not answered 'Social Revo- lution' to the question, 'What can they do?' In any case, 'Technology and the power of militant trade unionism, two wars, and a new industrial revolution, have left only small pockets of "philanthropists".' In 1970 Raymond Williams gave the novel half a page in The English Novel from Dickens to Lawrence. It 'offered a conscious political position', so its form had to be different. Its strength was 'the anonymous, collective, popular idiom through which a working world is strongly, closely, ironically seen'. Its 'final judgment' had 'a generous irony, from within the working class, and as such humane'. But it was 'one significantly isolated case'.[34]

Barbara Salter was a student of English at Manchester University. She saw herself as 'apolitical', but while her supervisor regarded it as 'a bit of a chore', she completed her M.A. on The Ragged Trousered Philanthropists in August 1971.[35] She felt it was 'nearly great', but could not stand 'close scrutiny':

> Stark reality and absurd fantasy, vivid comedy and laboured propaganda are brought together in this novel where neither plot interest nor character analysis predominate. There is much repetition, poor structuring, tired prose.

The arguments are rarely intellectually exciting, nor are they fully wedded
to the narrative. The end is contrived.

'The novel can no longer rely on the force of its arguments to disguise its
flaws: ultimately, it succeeds or fails as narrative art.'[36] It was definitely
succeeding commercially. In 1971 Lawrence & Wishart's sixth printing was
selling for £2, while Panther's fourth cost 50p.

By 1972 Salter was working as a schoolteacher. She noted the 'shortage
of literature which is other than middle class in outlook, and which is
suitable for young people'. RTP 'was much too long to ask the reluctant
4ths and 5ths to read', but extracts went down well. So she suggested
that Lawrence & Wishart should publish a shortened version for schools.
All Noonan needed was a good editor. The directors were 'entirely in
agreement' 'as to the general principles'. She should 'condense linking
passages and some of the phatic dialogue', and 'most (or all?) of the
comments/outbursts of anger/diatribes/spelling out of significance where
they occur in the flow of the narrative', thereby halving the book's length.
Cornforth was happy to spare 'poor modern kids' the 'SDF material', but
he wanted Ball consulted, though he 'would never be able to prepare
such a thing himself'. Salter was encouraged to get on with the editing.
In October Cornforth suggested chopping out most of the 'summer'
chapters, including lumps of the 'Beano' excursion and 'The Great Oration'.
But in March 1973 printers' estimates indicated that the new version would
be too dear, unless investment 'were made in a far bigger printing'. At the
height of a period of industrial struggle comparable only to 1926, it was
a risk Lawrence & Wishart were not prepared to take. They closed the
project down.[37]

12

One of the damned

The sob story effect

By 1969 Fred Ball's work had been translated into French, German and Norwegian, and broadcast in several European and Commonwealth countries. His autobiographical 'From Oblivion to Obscurity, or How to Make Your Fortune as a Grocer', was broadcast on BBC radio in January, and repeated in February, when he appeared on BBC2 television's *Late Night Line-up*. He told Kathleen he 'deeply regretted having been obliged to do' the revised biography, and had 'long since taken to cursing Robert Tressell who seduced me when I was young and foolish'. He hoped to finish it 'in weeks', and claimed he could have completed it 'a year ago with as much knowledge as I have now', yet still nagged for 'documents'. Kathleen suggested: 'It might have been better for you if I had remained "dead" for a longer period and you could have had your book finished earlier, then I could have put out a refutation of inaccuracies.' She noted her father's 'integrity, his burning zeal for justice, his infinite compassion, his hatred for cant and hypocrisy and, as I have realised lately, his humility, added to these his absolute regard for the truth.'

In May, Ball wondered if Kathleen minded being asked a 'few questions'. By June he was 'getting along now with the write-up'. But in July he was 'wading through 70 trays of material' and hoped to 'emerge sometime later this year', though 'it still won't be a definitive biography'. In September the book was 'well under way but not finalised yet'. Reg and Joan Johnson went to London 'doing research', and took legal advice. In January 1970 Ball reported that the biography was 'coming along now.

Only 70 boxes left.' As for the centenary of her father's birth that April, 'it doesn't seem as if we're doing anything but readings', and Ball 'had neither time nor money to help', though he was continuing to find 'Tresselliana'. When Kathleen challenged his speculations, he insisted: 'you and I will never agree on interpretation'.

In August 1970 David Haines 'discovered' Noonan's murals in St Andrew's church, Hastings, as it was being demolished. Ball told interviewers there had been thirty or forty 'Tressells', including 'murals and frescoes in restaurants, public houses, churches and private houses'. Yet Hastings had 'never been proud of Tressell. Nothing is made of him in the schools, and the education committee even turned down a recent offer by a London school to put on a dramatised version of "Philanthropists" for Hastings children.' In reality, Ball turned down several offers, including one of £600 in cash, to help preserve the church mural; and the curator of Hastings Museum gave £40. Evidently, relying on Ball, a reporter believed that Hastings was 'as unwilling to be reminded of [Noonan's] ideas in 1970 as it was in 1914'. The Labour Party's national youth officer and the TUC Education Department visited. It was reported that 'the original templates from which Tresswell [sic] worked were recently discovered in a builder's store and destroyed because it was not realised that they were of any value'. The secretary of Hastings and St Leonards Central Aid Council remained unimpressed with 'chunks of (let it be whispered) somewhat indifferent art', and a former St Andrew's vicar called it 'a drab, dark area'. A Mr Knights complained that the mural was vandalised four years before, yet 'not one of the champions of Tressell' 'appeared to help in the cleaning up operations'. Ball wrote on his cutting: 'Typical of hatred name of Tressell still evokes.'

Ball's 'A Pair of Tressells' appeared on *Late Night Line-up* later in September. Haines, stressing he was 'not a socialist', offered Kathleen a piece of the mural and a colour photograph of the panel. In October a copy of a Noonan family document unaccountably appeared in an article lauding Ball's and Haines' work. BBC television's *Late Night Line-up* wrote to 'Mrs Lin' to confirm she would be filmed with her daughter 'being taken around places associated with Robert Tressell in Hastings', starting from Ball's house; but when the crew went to Congress House to film the manuscript it was a long time before it was tracked down in the box marked 'processed peas'.[1] In November BBC Radio 4 broadcast Ball's *One of the Damned*.

In June 1971 Ball was still 'putting final touches to M.S.', having been required to cut over 30,000 words from his biography. He hoped Kathleen had seen herself singing on television – he understood the BBC 'would send you a telegram' – and asked more questions. In August he reported that there was a Bulgarian RTP, that he had a copy of 'the Jap version', and that the book was 'being translated into Swahili'. (Reportedly, a French translation was also being planned.[2]) Kathleen received Ball's typescript in September, except for the last chapter, which had yet 'to pass the publisher'. Ball acknowledged he had condensed her and Joan's stories, and lost 'a lot of my historical background', but he hoped the book would be published within a year. Kathleen patiently explained that Gower's tale of seeing boxes instead of furniture in their flat was mistaken, unless it was just after they had moved; that she never did her homework in the room where her father was writing; and he did not have 'asthma'; though these and other 'inaccuracies' did 'add to the "sob story" effect'.

Early in 1972 Ball's publishers indicated that they 'like the book but want cuts made', yet he was still asking Kathleen for information in June. As for acknowledgements, he 'would merely use the expression "members of Robert's family" as I don't want to disclose prematurely the surprise of Kathleen's reappearance. Hope this is OK.' In October Ball asked for the 1905 photograph of the St Andrew's mural. Weidenfeld & Nicolson, now Ball's publishers, asked for it three more times, noting 'Mr Ball has first copyright' on others. Reg Johnson pointed out that Ball had undertaken 'to negotiate an agreement with Mrs Lynne in return for her contribution towards providing material for the biography of her father', so permission would be delayed until the publishers could 'prevail upon Fred Ball to finalise the agreement.' Kathleen moved to Westbury-on Trym, near Bristol. Her letter against the Church profiting from the apartheid regime in South Africa appeared in the Church Times. But she did not hear from Ball for some time.

The appropriate standard

In the early 1970s Heath's Tory government brought The Ragged Trousered Philanthropists into focus for many readers. When Sam Webb was a child in North London during World War II his parents' politics were 'to the right of Margaret Thatcher', yet RTP was 'part of common speech'. One day, as a decorator was repairing bomb damage in their shop, Sam noticed that he broke rolls of wallpaper over his knee, then stuffed them up the chimney. Later in life, working as an architect on house conversions, Sam would put his hand up chimneys and 'fish out all manner of things from dead birds to broken rolls of lining or wall paper'. In 1968 he prepared evidence on behalf of Camden Borough Council for the public inquiry into the collapse of the Ronan Point tower-block; but the case failed against 'the full might of the Treasury solicitor, the massed ranks of QCs and the building industry. Oh and of course the government too.' In 1969–70, together with Paul Foot, a *Private Eye* journalist and an International Socialist, Webb 'stumbled upon the facts of what became known as the "Poulson affair"' (Poulson was the architect for Ronan Point). Yet Elwyn Jones, the Labour MP for Newnham South (where Ronan Point was situated), not only refused to meet Webb but threatened him with criminal libel. Senior Labour Party figures Andrew Cunningham and T. Dan Smith went to jail all the same. Webb thought it was time he read *The Ragged Trousered Philanthropists*. 'No bookshops stocked it. It wasn't in any public libraries including Camden's. Then one day in May 1971 I went into Central Books in Holborn, and there it was priced 15/–.' He 'couldn't put it down'. He still regards the book as 'my education' – an explanation of 'how the world worked'. When Webb had Ronan Point demolished, he found 1960s newspapers where concrete should have been. 'So it still goes on.'[3]

John Edmonds was born into a working-class family in South London. He first read RTP when he was 17, and 'enjoyed the stories', but 'found some difficulty with the structure', even though he had a scholarship to Oriel College, Oxford. Between 1968 and 1972 he worked for the General and Municipal Workers' Union in Hastings, where employment was 'heavily influenced by the master/servant relationship and the notion that workers in seaside towns should be very deferential towards their "betters"'. So 'money grabbing entrepreneurs would encourage their workers to forget about the dignity of their work and provide a shoddy service because bad work meant more profits'. Edmonds reread RTP's critique of the 'System'. It underscored his belief that workers 'have a right, not only to proper payment for their labour, but also to have their skills recognised and their talents developed'; whereas 'Capitalism tends to degrade not only the worker, but also the work.'[4] Yet he continued to believe that the way ahead for unions was to support the Labour Party.

The Communist Party was not an option, even though they had criti-cised the Russian invasion of Czechoslovakia in 1968. The CP tried to appear libertarian, yet there was serious concern about its inability to attract young workers in a period of rising industrial struggle, and about competition from the International Socialists.[5] Ian Birchall recalls that IS's founder, Tony Cliff, began referring to RTP in 1969, as Callaghan's Labour government began attacking public-sector workers. It was 'usually in connection with the problem of how to write in a way that was clear and accessible to workers', though he didn't use 'any of the jokes, illus-trations etc. I think it was the fact of RTP being a book that was widely read and appreciated by workers that impressed Cliff, rather than any particular aspect of its content', at a period when a Manchester building worker comrade was sending 'weekly reports of sales of 31 SW, 5 RTP'[6]

RTP helped focus political attitudes. A former exploited apprentice com-positor concluded that 'life was very tough for both employer and em-ployee in the first half of the 20th century.' Yet whenever he felt 'utterly dejected by the greedy, grasping society in which we now live, I think of men like Robert Tressell and his spirit gives me fresh hope for mankind.' Sadly, he had 'failed miserably' to 'live up to his high standards' himself, but retained 'a feeling of sympathy for the underprivileged', if not for 'so-called socialists who live like kings but merely set out to disrupt our free country'. A Glasgow boss thought an electrician had a chip on his shoulder when he criticised him 'living in opulence'. But after reading RTP the electrician's 'veins were a lot clearer'. It 'cleared the fog, and gave me direction of thought and a goal to strive for': 'it was not the employ-er's fault, it was mine, and those like me who thought the system could not be changed'. In 1971 a Mansfield miner was asked if he would like to borrow a copy of RTP. He was 'deeply moved and deeply impressed', 'had it advertised on our notice board in our Pit Head Baths', and sent off for a further copy, which circulated round the colliery during the successful strikes of 1972 and 1974 'until it wore out'.

On building sites the book still came with the bricks. A self-employed carpenter was shocked that an apprentice had not read the 'Building Industries Apprentices Bible', 'The Ragged Arsed Philanthropist', and the boy was surprised that a foreman 'was equally a victim of the system'. A Motherwell labourer was told about the book by his brother, and it helped make him 'determined to do something, by the way of finding out more about socialism and of the "system" (if that's the right word) in which we live and work'. He went to night school, organised a site into UCATT, became a shop steward and Trades Council delegate, then started a two-year WEA course. In 1972 one worker was asked to join the union the day he started work on site. 'As soon as I signed up the steward gave me a worn copy of Robert Tressell's book.' 'It was my first introduction to Socialist ideas.' In North Wales Ricky Tomlinson had not read the book, but he was one of the militants trying to unionise sites. In 1973, after he became a 'prisoner of the class war', RTP was recommended by his prison governor.[7] Jim Arnison wrote up the case of the 'Shrewsbury Three'. He felt the best way 'to measure the improvements brought about through trade unions before the government onslaught of 1973–1974, on health, safety and welfare' was to use RTP as the 'appropriate standard'.[8]

His own real hero

On 2 November 1973 Fred Ball launched *One of the Damned: The Life and Times of Robert Tressell, author of 'The Ragged Trousered Philanthropists'* at a lecture in Hastings Public Library. It was published by Weidenfeld & Nicolson on 15 November, but only in hardback, at a cost of £5, and was marketed as a literary detective story. The *Spectator* felt it was 'naïve' and full of 'unsifted' facts. The *Daily Telegraph* focused on RTP, and argued it was 'a processional banner for the Left Wing of the Labour Party'. In the *Evening Standard* Labour left-winger Michael Foot wrote about RTP's 'truly Swiftian impact', but swallowed the myths in *One of the Damned*. The *Times Literary Supplement* stressed that Kathleen's material was the 'coping-stone', though Ball was his own 'real hero'.

The Socialist Labour League's *Workers Press* was less enthusiastic about RTP. 'From its obscure and bitter origins it has become a much-prescribed text in the universities and an essential part of the eclectic intellectual baggage of every reformist and Stalinist traitor in the labour movement.' The book's 'popularity in these circles is due to its weak side'. It 'never transcends a one-sided, pessimistic view of the working class', so the 'possibility of change remains at the level of ... ideas', while workers are 'doomed to remain divided, easily hood-winked, unreceptive' to reformist socialism, and appear 'basically stupid'. Noonan was still not Lenin, but he had a much bigger UK audience.

During 1973 Ingrid van Rosenbert noted how RTP encouraged its readers to 'think critically', mainly by the use of what she called 'Panorama techmique' – a pre-Brechtian shock effect of harsh vignettes and acid commentary.[9] In the UK, both Belt and Braces and 7:84 Theatre Company staged The Reign of Terror and the Great Money Trick, including 'a short history of twentieth century Britain in the form of an impersonation of all the Prime Ministers from Lloyd George to the present incumbent', Edward Heath.[10] The Guardian believed it showed 'the way in which Socialism has become corrupted', and that it offered a 'cheerful, even Socialist message'. Harold Smith tried to convince Albert Finney's agent that his client should star in a film.[11] Panther reprinted during 1973, and raised the retail price by 20 per cent, to 60p.

Contrary to Kathleen's express wish, Ball had published her father's last letter.[12] He also pastiched her memories, and repeated hearsay about Noonan's alleged 'tuberculosis' and death in a 'workhouse'. Unsurprisingly, he didn't know how to reach 'a settlement'. She told his publishers that 'Poor Fred'

> identifies himself so much with my father, and idolises him so much that he excoriates himself and multiplies his (Robert's) hardships. He reminds me of some of the early Christians who concentrated on CHRIST'S sufferings and tortured their own bodies in order to identify with Him.

Eventually, in May 1974, Ball managed to 'come to an arrangement'. Yet Kathleen remained sceptical about 'facts' taken from men 'who had probably forgotten all about Bob Noonan until Fred began questioning them forty or fifty years after his death'. She was 'not for one minute suggesting that they deliberately made mistakes but Rob[er]t had become rather a figure of romance and I dare say, many, like Fred took the book to be entirely autobiographical'. Her father's socialism was not that of the Labour Party, or that of Russia's communism. 'Neither is the real thing.'

The RTP manuscript appeared in the TUC's Trade Union History exhibition. Yet when the Johnsons went to see it at Congress House the receptionist

> didn't appear to understand just who we were nor what it was we were wanting to see. She did find somebody who knew of Tressell and wanted to do his best to help us. After a long search the MS was discovered in a laundry basket. We were allowed sight of the MS which was then replaced in its cardboard box and returned to the hamper.[13]

Later in 1974 a canvasser in Brentford and Isleworth knocked 'on the door of one very old man', who 'fetched down an original 1914 edition of the book', and said 'Here read this.' It made the activist 'realise the need to struggle EVERY DAY not just every few years at elections'. A fortnight after Labour scraped back into office on the back of working-class struggle, Kathleen received a letter from Downing Street. Mrs Mary Wilson had

> carefully noted the points you made about public ownership and passed them to my husband's office, where it is pointed out that some of your views are covered in the Manifesto, October 1974 which says ... 'we will introduce new legislation to help forward our plans for a radical extension of industrial democracy'.

Could she 'send on behalf of my husband and myself, our best wishes to the daughter of a man who made a lasting impression on Socialist thought in Britain?'

Late in December Kathleen heard from Ball. She and the Johnsons understood that his 'earnings from sales were little if anything, so he was never pressed to make a settlement'.[14] Over a year after publication Ball sent The Royal Literary Fund's £30 cheque for the loan of Kathleen's photographs. Reg noted that it arrived 'at a very opportune moment – just in time to stop the bank manager putting in the bailiffs'. Meanwhile, the Labour government's bailiffs, the International Monetary Fund, ensured that enacting Noonan's Co-operative Commonwealth was completely out of the question.

At around this time Andy Strouthous was a student, and struggling on his grant, but part-time decorating was 'a serious hindrance to the student lifestyle' and he was not getting enough sleep. He saw RTP at Bookmarks in Finsbury Park, and

> Robert Tressell came to the rescue. On reading his book I discovered the tip of leaning my ladder against the door, and, while the gaffer was away, catching up with much needed sleep. If the gaffer made a surprise return visit the ladder would stop the door from opening, I would jump up and shout 'hang on a minute boss, just painting over the door'.[15]

Andy later became a Central Committee member of IS's successor, the Socialist Workers' Party. The revolutionary left had grown, but its numbers were small. The last time Ian Birchall recalls Tony Cliff mentioning RTP was to German comrades in 1975, when he 'was stressing the importance of propaganda aimed at workers rather than the left intellectual milieu'. For IS, 'after the "downturn" and the turn to the "higher level of politics"', the point was to keep revolutionary organisation together.[16] For some left-reformists, it was to pay homage to dead heroes.

A clique in substitution for the mass movement

In 1975 there was a Swedish translation of 'The Great Money Trick'.[17] Panther reprinted RTP, and did so again in 1976, at 95p, when Lawrence & Wishart's new reprint cost £3.50. Ball was complaining that One of the Damned was not produced 'for the market for which it was intended': it was 'too dear to buy so it's being read in public libraries'. Consequently, it 'hasn't quite sold the first print yet and I haven't even covered my expenses'. But BBC Radio 3 asked him for a programme, and he 'finished off with a quotation from Robert about his vision of a society where we would put into practice the teachings of Christ'.

In March 1976 Alan O'Toole published an article in the Liverpool Free Press, based almost entirely on One of the Damned. O'Toole, John Nettleton, Billy Kelly and Eric Pye set up the Robert Tressell Memorial Committee, and got in touch with Ball. In a March 1977 meeting in Walton Trades and Labour Club with Eric Heffer in the chair, the Committee invited Jack Jones, General Secretary of the TGWU, George Smith, General Secretary of UCATT, and Len Murray, General Secretary of the TUC, to the unveiling of a headstone for Noonan's grave. Weeks later Kathleen was also invited, but was too ill to accept. The Committee published a list of contributors to the £2,000 bill. It did not include the TUC or the Labour Party (except for two branches); but £300 came from UCATT, and there were donations from TGWU and other union branches, Trades Councils, Merseyside CPGB, the Morning Star, Liverpool and London Unity Theatre, the Yugoslav Embassy, and dozens of individuals from as far afield as Australia and Japan.

According to O'Toole, on 18 June 'over 1,000 people', 'walked through the windy streets of Walton, banners flying', from County Ward Labour Party Rooms.[18] Heffer recalled a 'large contingent of construction workers'.[19] Ian Aitken of the Guardian saw 'some 600 or 700', 'largely working-class' people. He also noted that the 'bible of the Left' was 'part of the folklore' of his own family, since 'my maternal grandfather (John Levack, a one-time President of the Scottish Painters' Society) read the book aloud by instalments at his local branch meeting'. Norman Willis stood in for Len Murray; Albert Williams and George Smith were there from UCATT; and Stan Orme represented the Labour Cabinet. The Irish Post saw nobody from the Irish government, but Jack Jones had an Irish mother, and he read a passage from Wolfe Tone. Joan Johnson unveiled the black granite stone; O'Toole read out the William Morris poem inscribed on it; and Nettleton made a speech, as did Jack Jones.

Jones came from the left, but his political trajectory is emblematic of
those who drew pessimistic conclusions from RTP. Forty years before he
had 'listened, with increasing sympathy' to Leo McGree, the Liverpool
Communist and 'chief spokesman for the unemployed'. Soon after, he
volunteered for a CP-led hunger march, which won the 'sympathy and
support' of other Labour Party members. By spring 1934, when Mosley's
Fascists were meeting in Liverpool, the Labour leadership 'felt we should
"ignore" the Blackshirts, but that didn't seem much of a policy'. Jones
'formed an anti-fascist group' at the Trades Council, led 'young Labour,
ILP and Communist members in trying to speak out at Fascist meetings
and was forcibly ejected'. In 1936 he volunteered to go to Spain, but was
felt to be more valuable at home. He volunteered again, and was made
political commissar of the Major Attlee Company. He also met Attlee, who
'strengthened my faith in the Labour Party at a time when circumstances
were inclining me to move further towards the left'.

Attlee's 1945–51 government convinced Jones that socialists could reform the 'System', and by 1956 he wanted 'to promote more efficiency by
the encouragement of high wages related to high productivity', even
though this meant finding 'a more humane approach to mass discharges
of workers'. He hoped Wilson's 1964 Labour government would guarantee that 'we would be well on our way to achieving our Socialist aims',
and was elected to the Labour Party Executive. Yet by 1967 Jones was 'as
concerned as anyone to prevent strikes'; and by 1968 he favoured the
integration of trade unionists into collective bargaining procedures. Even
so, he was elected TGWU General Secretary, partly on the strength of CP
votes, and in 1969 he fought Barbara Castle's anti-union In Place of Strife. Yet
in 1970 he supported Tony Benn's proposed mergers in the car industry,
to make firms more competitive.[20] Capitalism was here to stay.

Under the cover of Heath's Tory government, Jones edged right. In
1972 he argued against a national strike in support of the dockers, and
ordered TGWU members to obey the Tories' National Industrial Relations
Court. He was criticised, not by the CP leadership, but by TGWU dockers.[21]
Labour got back into office in 1974. It established the arbitration service
ACAS, and passed the Health, Safety and Welfare at Work Act; so, as Wilson's
government ran into trouble, Jones rallied to its support, moving to the
right of the left-reformist CP by opposing pay policy.[22] In 1976, wages
rose only one-quarter as fast as prices, and unemployment reached 1.6
million. Jim Callaghan took over as prime minister. Jones refused a Lord-

Joan Johnson

ship, but accepted the even more exclusive Companionship of Honour.[23] At Noonan's grave-side in 1977 the former centrist used *The Ragged Trousered Philanthropists* as left cover. It had 'provided a mighty thrust in my emerging understanding about the need to change society', but not by very much.

Eric Heffer, Labour MP for Liverpool Walton, was reported as arguing that 'Tressell' had 'more influence on the growth of grass-roots socialism than the writings of Karl Marx'. The Grunwick strikers were photographed for the *Morning Star* in front of Heffer and Willis, having their hands shaken by Jones. Reg Johnson recalls 'so much jockeying for status and influence by politicians and trade union officials, not only within trade unions but between unions, that they were tearing themselves apart'.

> Joan, in a totally unscripted speech, called upon the assembled gathering to stop arguing amongst themselves and to concentrate on the vision of the man whose name they were honouring, and to come together with a collective voice to make this vision a reality.[24]

After the ceremony, Joan 'signed so many books and leaflets' that she 'was quite surprised not to have writer's cramp next day!' She also visited the Central Library to see the 'Robert Tressell Book-case'. In the evening, Merseyside Unity Theatre performed 'The Great Money Trick' at Walton Trades and Labour Club, where UCATT's Hastings branch secretary, Jim Robinson, presented Liverpool Trades Council with a photograph of someone looking very like Robert Noonan, apparently addressing a Hastings 'right to work meeting'. Ironically, a modern Right to Work Campaign, led by Socialist Workers' Party members – the former IS – and frowned on by union bureaucrats and Labour MPs, was then on the road.

Using a contribution from Granada Books, David Cope and some local building worker comrades 'plastered' Liverpool town centre with small posters saying that The Ragged Trousered Philanthropists was available from Progressive Books, the CP bookshop:

> The CP building workers in Liverpool sold well over a thousand p[aper]b[ack] copies; they would come in, often on Thursday nights when CP branches collected their lit[erature] and we were open later, and would take them S[ale] O[r] R[eturn] and hardly ever brought any back. There was one comrade in particular … a lovely man, not the most articulate of comrades and often the worse for drink, who probably sold close to 500 from 1975 when the shop opened to 1986 when I left. UCATT would also often order a dozen hardbacks at a time for presentations.[25]

RTP remained many CP trade union activists' political primer and icon. But it was not, and never had been, a guide to changing the 'System'.

Later in 1977 the Grunwick struggle was allowed to go down to defeat; and the Labour government attacked the Fire Brigades' Union. By then the CP was on the slide, and the old guard grouped themselves around the Morning Star. Ken Weller, who left the Party twenty years before, felt that its new recruits, even in the London building trades, 'weren't really politicos in the normal sense', and hadn't been for some time. They 'were part of a trade union network which happened to be CP'.[26] There was growing concern in the Party about the SWP,[27] and then the 1978 CP programme proved to be a more reformist British Road to Socialism. This was the last straw for the Stalinists, who left to form the New Communist Party. Harry McShane had left in 1951, but he supported the current SWP-led Right to Work March, and firmly believed what was left of the CP was 'a clique in substitution for the mass movement'.[28]

Our mate Bob's spot on

In June 1977 Kathleen Noonan Lynne appeared on The World this Week-end. She learned that Mr Dooley was 'doing a sculpture to honour Tressell's influence', using elements of the Last Supper and the 'Great Money Trick', and that Billy Kelly was painting her father's portrait. In July Joan wrote to the Guardian, noting that it was 'a matter of great regret' that she and her mother 'know so few of grandfather's admirers personally'.

May I please, therefore, invite your readers to write to me telling how they
came to know of 'The Ragged Trousered Philanthropists' in the first place,
what it has meant to them in their lives, and what opinions and beliefs they
have formed about the author himself.

Her letter didn't appear, so she wrote to the Morning Star, which published
it on 28 July, and to the Observer, which did so on 7 August. Joan could
not find a copy because printers had taken industrial action. But she was
probably unprepared for the avalanche that followed.

One woman recalled that her father was a 'great rebel' who admired
RTP enormously. A second had read her father's copy, and later gave it to
her children: 'anyone who shows interest is allowed to borrow it. I
consider this book the greatest argument I can muster, not being very
bright, when people who have never gone hungry ... start talking about
the trades unions as the lazier classes.' Another valued the book's 'insights
into what poverty and ignorance can do to friendships, to marriage, and
to all human relationships'. Her husband had 'loved its humour', and she
decided to 'have another read of it myself. I could do with cheering up.'
She thought the 'complete version' gave 'a much better development of
the political arguments', but she wondered 'when we lend the book to
people who read the Sun and the Mirror if the sheer length isn't a bit
daunting. Much as I prefer the full version I think the earlier one was
easier to spread around.' Yet a Worthing woman found it 'had been
borrowed continuously in three-week periods for several years' from her
local library.

A London man was one of the 'Socialistically oriented' amateurs who
performed Tom Thomas's play 'on a number of occasions' in the 1920s.
Thomas himself wrote from Welwyn Garden City, having been 'turning
over in my mind whether it might be possible somehow to arrange for
a performance of the play' on its fiftieth anniversary. Another Londoner
had found RTP so 'inspiring' that he wrote a book, and a Chelmsford
woman's children's books were 'not entirely uninfluenced' by it. The
former owner of Noonan's victim Arthur Du Cros's 'millionaire home' in
Coventry 'introduced the book to every tradesman who has ever come my
way in the course of repairs and decorations'. A small businessman in
Surrey had been shocked when a candidate for a rep's post presented a
list of terms and conditions far better than those in the factory, where
'good tradesmen who had worked for me for ten or more years were
deducted ¼ hour if 3 minutes late'. But then he thought of RTP, and his

own experience on the tools, and decided 'to correct these anomalies by raising rather than lowering standards'.

After 'a very "nice" middle class, extremely Tory upbringing', a woman student at Manchester University read RTP and had been 'a socialist ever since'. Another woman bought a copy for an evening class on 'Politics and the Novel', reread it, and was fired up again. A London teacher-training college principal loaned his 'flimsy first edition' to 'a young colleague' – 'a somewhat brash modern sociologist with a string of degrees in economics', who 'was disappointed that it had not come his way whilst at Cambridge'. Ruskin College students told their tutor that the book was 'in many respects' an 'accurate description of contemporary conditions in the industry':

> Throat cutting by low quotations, for 'lump' prices, lack of craftsman-ship, lack of proper apprentice training are all there and we pay a price for them. The brick work in our 10 year old semi is worse than stuff I was sacked for doing.

He felt 'only a cooperative or nationally owned industry will solve the problem'. A West German Ph.D. student found the book 'roused his interest' in the field, and when a painter spotted it in his London flat, he and most of his mates declared, 'that is a fine book!' A teacher's father had 'stories about unscrupulous foremen indicating two coats when the contractor stipulated three'. A mine safety engineer got a copy on a part-time course. Another student took his teacher's advice and RTP 'played a large part' in his becoming a socialist and active trade-union member. The book fed back from education into the labour movement.

Building-trade workers treasured RTP. A retired woodworking machinist believed that it 'identifies the working-class reader with himself'. A brick-layer credited the book with improvements in building-site conditions. A joiner was 'endeavouring to establish a Robert Noonan playground in this immediate neighbourhood using Job Creation Scheme money: 'He would have liked that, especially so when it will give employment to a number of men and boys now "out of collar".' Another joiner ensured copies were available for sale at his union branch meetings. A painter felt the book should be 'compulsory reading in schools', and be 'made into a major film financed in part by the TUC'. Someone else could not under-stand why the book was not 'a Film Classic'. Another noted that the TUC had recently loaned Noonan's manuscript for an exhibition at the Museum of Labour History in London. The icon should be on permanent display.

An apprentice bricklayer was recommended RTP by a labourer (who was later 'dismissed for having a chest condition which kept him from work in the cold weather'), and went on to become an FBU activist. The Mansfield miner had replaced the copy 'in circulation' round the colliery. A retired miner reread it because 'it has everything, humour, tragedy, phylosophy': 'it makes me laugh, cry, feel sad, and also very bitter'. Another man had found 'there has always been someone who has read the book' on nearly every job, and he heard it 'being discussed and recommended' in the Scott–Lithgow shipyard, small painting contracting firms and local council maintenance depots. Hunter, Crass and Slyme 'still exist in factories, offices and building sites', so he gave copies to workmates. A man who read it fifty years before found that it 'constantly gave me thought', since 'conditions' were 'not much better regards work, than they are today'.

RTP sometimes reinforced pessimism. A Londoner had worked with 'ready-made slaves'. 'Deprived of any meaningful education, trained only to create wealth for a privileged minority, they were and remain easy prey to any charlatan and smooth-talking apologist for the social-system which keeps them spiritually enslaved.' A retired Twickenham woman regretted that the Irish male nurses who had 'fought for reform in the hospitals, especially the mental hospitals' were no longer coming over, whereas she felt the Asians were 'not fighters, they are too gentle'. (Evidently she had taken no notice of the Asian women at Grunwick.) A Londoner in Hastings felt he had 'stepped back in time', since contracts of employment, overtime rates and unions 'seemed virtually unheard of'. He sympathised with Noonan, 'living in a town of blind people trying to convince them that there was such a thing as sight'; yet the book gave him 'something to lean on when having trouble trying to explain or get across some point in the many arguments I seem to find myself in with workmates who ... seem to thrive on being exploited'. A Canadian had been to Hastings: 'All the time I was thinking: Robert Noonan walked along this street – Robert Noonan entered that pub – Robert Noonan painted that big, old house.' 'Tressell' tourism was under way.

Many working-class activists focused on 'The Great Money Trick' because it was 'a simple explanation of Marx's theory of surplus value and explains the exploitation of labour by privately owned capital'. A former marine engineering apprentice stressed that 'The division of the bread has remained with me' after half a century. A builder's daughter believed it 'says everything about the plight of the worker cruelly exploited by the

Capitalist system'. Another woman won a political debate with her neighbour using the book's arguments. Three building trade-union activists had
been on the 'Blacklist' for 'quite a long time', and felt the book 'really
started us on the road to socialism'. For Des Warren of the Shrewsbury
Three and his supporters 'our mate' 'Bob' was 'spot on'.

RTP was part of the movement. A woman 'sunk from a very "upper"
layer of society' was recommended the novel by an 'old comrade in the
Edinburgh Trades Council'. A Sussex man heard of it from 'a comrade in
my local Labour Party', a former building worker, who had been put on
to it by Keir Hardie's nephew. He would 'relate how he had met many of
the characters from the book whilst working on the buildings and how
he had worked under at least half a dozen "Nimrods" in his time'. A
Droitwich man noted: 'for the many people who cannot read a serious
political work this book is a must.' A Watford man declaimed: 'The plun-
derers are still with us. The Nimrods, time serving. Wall to wall carpeting
does not change the economic structure of society.'

RTP was a socialist yardstick. For the chair of a Scottish Labour Party
social club it had been 'the political turning point of my life', and it
remained his 'Ten Commandments' on 'true Socialism'. A former Labour
conference delegate wondered what 'Tressell' would 'feel about the progress
we have made in taming capitalism!' One woman felt Noonan 'would be
disheartened by the development of the Labour Party and certain aspects
of the trade union movement'; and a man believed Labour had 'been
responsible for many reforms which, in themselves, are good but the
society envisaged by Labour Party members is, I think, a long way from
what Robert Tressell meant by socialism'.

RTP retained its therapeutic qualities, especially for Labour Party members. One turned to its ending when he felt 'downhearted'. Another had
spent thirty-four years propagandising, only to have to ask: 'please may
we eat, and how much'. It seemed like 'a wasted life', because the Labour
Party 'was not socialist nor did it intend to alter the system'. A Faversham
man wondered if 'the Dennis Healeys of our day ever take down what
must have been a well thumbed volume in their Oxford days. The shallow-
ness of men!' A veteran thought Bevan's socialism still needed to be got
across. A Gateshead mining engineer felt Noonan 'would have made a
good Labour MP', but 'in the best sense, not like some of the wishy-
washy men who have represented the people of late and who have been
anything but a credit to the Labour movement'.

Many of the disillusioned looked leftwards. One activist was bitter about Labour: 'even when they had a big majority' they refuse to 'make the effort to change the system to Socialism', while 'certain sections of industry that had a socialist basis are eroded to the point that the money-lenders gather the benefits instead of the people'. He was 'watching the USSR and their progress under their socialist system'. A man with 'a fairly affluent lifestyle' voted Labour, but no longer found 'the simple purity of Tressell's vision as convincing as I did', after 'the socialist waters had been muddied by Russian Communism'. Yet faith in 'actually-existing socialism' was alive and well among *Morning Star* readers. One 'granny' had worked for two years in Hanoi in 'the English language section of the publishing house, and was euphoric about the North Vietnamese people's 'prevailing state of contentment', for all the irregular electricity and the poverty: 'Socialism is beautiful, and tho' it's had a struggle here – it *works*!' Other veterans were less confident. A one-time member of the Labour League of Youth from Llanelli believed that RTP was 'truer now than it ever was, but I have no cure for our ills', except that young people needed its teaching about 'Virtue, a love of work & Imagination'. 'Our present leaders are fiddling in a circus and the tent is burning. Where have we been led?' – 'hope deferred makes the heart sick'. Other veterans plugged away. One found that a receptionist had not read RTP. He told her that 'her education was not complete', and that 'she would find it much more interesting than the goggle box'. He hoped she would buy a copy and pass it on to 'anyone else on the staff who have not read it'; and he gave her a copy of the *Morning Star* containing Joan's letter.

Faith in the political effectiveness of RTP was widespread. A retired miner had recently presented a copy to young Appalachian miners, and another to his son, a painter and decorator working for Dyfed County Council. He believed trade unions should give 'each young member on his introduction to his trade union a free copy'. The Secretary General of the Council of Post Office Unions 'long since wore out my first copy' and 'had to buy a second', which was 'recently read by my 16 year old daughter'. Another 'ardent socialist', aged 71, borrowed the book from the local library. He got half-way through, then someone else requested it; but he would give his sons copies for Christmas. One man's daughters – both 'ardent socialists' – had read the book. He hoped 'our grand-children will read it, and sometime in the near future I hope they and all mankind will benefit by getting a System where *planning for people and not for profit* will be the priority'.

Youngsters warmed to the book. One noted 'that crucial combination of manual and mental labour which will be a feature of future communist society'. Another, from Portsea, who had been told about the book by a 'middle-aged vagrant who had been ruined by alcoholism', read it and got 'involved in the Labour Party and the labour movement generally', but was experiencing 'disenchantment with socialism'. He blamed his 'disappointment and frustration' on the 'the inert conservatism of "respectable" working people'; yet the book gave him 'the chastened hope' that 'the labour movement could be saved from that selfish indifference to people which permeates the capitalist system', but 'only by genuine involvement with, and concern for, the lot of men and women in field, office, factory'. After ten months on the dole, socialism (with a dash of Kropotkin) still seemed possible. A building site labourer had once thought 'a Labour Party in power was socialism but after the invigorating experience of reading that book I learnt sadly that that wasn't the case'. He 'would like to see a socialist society and not the clap-trap mouthed by party politicians'.

In August 1977 *The Ragged Trousered Philanthropists* featured in a *New Statesman* quiz, and Kathleen appeared on 'Woman's Hour'. By September Joan had to produce a standard letter to acknowledge all her correspondence, though Len Murray at the TUC never responded to her inquiry about a 'living memorial' for 'Tressell'. However, Hastings Borough Council approved the naming of a Robert Tressell Avenue. A local Young Socialist hoped to commemorate his hero with the support of Labour Party branches. The Johnsons wanted 'something that would help people in some way rather than an inanimate plaque or monument', and suggested he might 'tap' Sussex trade unions. Months later, Hastings Trades Council sponsored a scholarship for an apprentice to attend a Ruskin College summer school.

Fred Ball was now living at 2 Fearon Road, a 'modest house', 'the first he has ever owned'; but complained he was suffering from 'blood pressure brought on over the years by tension, anxiety and such'. His biography of Noonan 'didn't do him much good': in fact, it 'made him a bit of a marked man'.[29] In November, BBC Radio 3 broadcast his dramatised documentary, 'A Search for the Identity of Robert Tressell', and *The Ragged Trousered Philanthropists* was BBC Radio 4's 'Book at Bedtime'. One listener was anxious that 'a certain class of reader, usually elderly', rather likes wallowing in misery that he can feel was of past time. But that's his loss, because a strangulated cry of agony like Tressell's is for all time, like Christ's supposed, 'My God, why has thou forsaken me'. It is the core of bitterness at the book's centre that gives it the aseptic quality that will forever keep it alive, certainly as long as 'class' survives (and that looks like forever at this dark moment).

He worried, would 'today's battle-cry' become 'tomorrow's lullaby'?

13

The end of history?

The ardour of immature revolutionism

In the late 1970s UK intellectuals continued to patronise *The Ragged Trousered Philanthropists* and its readers. Robert Barltrop observed that 'the most remarkable of all books about working-class life' had been 'immensely popular amongst working men'. Yet its author 'was not a writer; he did not know how to select, to do away with the superfluous and make his material work to its best effect'.[1] Alan Swingewood believed that the book conformed to the post-1933 'Frankfurt School' model of 'a society of total management and manipulation, a system in which the contradictions are assimilated and negated by an overpowering, monolithic and fairly rigid capitalist ideology'. So RTP 'represents a conservative affirmation of the subordinate role played by the working class through a culture which is no more than the sum of habit, customs, superstition, ignorance and the compelling exigencies of everyday life'.[2]

Neither critic explained why Panther went on to reprint their paperback in 1977, and twice in 1978 (at £1.50, three times the 1971 price); or why Lawrence & Wishart reprinted their hardback in 1978 (at £3.95, twice the 1971 price), and Monthly Review Press issued a paperback edition in New York, let alone why on 3 February 1979 seven Japanese men and women founded 'a dwarfish organisation named JAPAN SOCIETY FOR ROBERT TRESSELL' at the home of T. Hironaka, RTP's Japanese translator. Hironaka's book 'did not sell as well as we expected', 'solely because the publishers are not financially strong enough to develop necessary publicity activities'. However, his translation of Mitchell's book was serialised in his high school's teachers' magazine, and Ball's *One of the Damned* was translated.

In the UK most Noonan-related activity took place outside Hastings. Merseyside Unity Theatre performed 'The Great Money Trick' for shop stewards on a WEA course, and also for Young Christian workers.[3] Liverpool City Library planned an exhibition. In November 1978 Joan Johnson was invited to speak at Northern College, near Barnsley. The principal claimed RTP was 'one of the books we encourage students to read here and it has always been a basic book in the courses with which I have been associated at Sheffield University Extramural Department'. In fact Joan's letter had been drawn to his attention by a student, who told her that 'Most of the students at this college have read it', as had most people where he was shop steward. He knew an East Berlin schoolteacher who had to take an examination on it. 'When I am trying to convert I always loan or recommend the book.' He was 'out to change the system'.

In East Berlin Mary Ashraf was puzzled by RTP:

> As a political educator (in spite of the primitive economics and undialectical presentation of capitalist relations) and as a trade-union recruiter (in spite of the union having so little positive role in the book beyond passing reference to the defensive function of the Operative Painters' Society) it had a great record.

Yet why did Owen's exasperation at workers' 'stupidity and individualism (at times bordering on contempt), awaken not repulsion but a strong sense of kinship and mutual interest'? RTP was a 'virtually plotless masterpiece of panorama, the life cycle of the workingman and the revolving scenes of labour's year', and 'through and through a parable – not symbolic but drawing universal example out of the actual and particular. It is all sermonising, not a line wasted, not one neutral paragraph', while its 'loose structure' allowed it 'to be read discontinuously as a series of episodes'.[4] Yet Ashraf failed to notice that its politics could be read discontinuously, too.

In the UK, young adults' attitudes to RTP were not always positive. It was recommended to Janet Cole by a former Lowestoft bus driver, who was now a fellow philosophy student at Warwick University. Janet had been brought up in 'a Quaker, socialist household and was already broadly aware of, and in sympathy with, the views expressed'; so the book didn't convert her, but it 'must have made an impression'. However, her copy was last seen 'in the baggage room of my hall of residence, being abandoned in a cardboard box with many other books too numerous to accompany me onwards in my life'.[5] Paul Brook was 'radicalising rapidly'. Comrades in the Labour Party, CP and SWP talked about RTP's political usefulness, yet it 'didn't sound very inspirational' or even 'particularly attractive as a novel', compared to Strumpet City. He read part of the first page, only to find it 'miserable'. He much preferred George Dangerfield's Strange Death of Liberal England, which led him on to The Communist Manifesto, and then, via Kapp's Eleanor Marx and Huberman's Man's Worldy Goods, to McCann's War and an Irish Town. Eventually, Paul joined the SWP.

Many socialist students simply had not encountered The Ragged Trousered Philanthropists. Jeremy Hawthorn read it 'after completing a degree in English literature'.[6] Bernard Sharratt felt his own delayed encounter was due to 'the arrogance of youth', when New Left Review displaced any involvement in politics with theoretical 'praxis' and impenetrable jargon. 'It wasn't in fact until after I'd seen a dramatic adaptation of the novel, by the Joint Stock Theatre Company that I finally opened the book'.[7] Left-wing lecturers were not impressed. David Craig and Michael Egan felt it was written 'in styles often painfully pieced together from the shop-talk, demagogy, and pamphlet literature which bulked large in the language-culture of working men'. Moreover, 'even realists like Tressell' and Upton Sinclair tended 'to soar into a peroration as they close', and 'swept beyond the facts to an unlikely vision of a revolutionary future somewhere beyond the skyline' with 'the ardour of immature revolutionism'.[8]

Stephen Lowe read English at Birmingham University, but 'Tressell was never mentioned'.[9] In 1977–78 he was resident playwright at Dartington College of Arts when Joint Stock Theatre Company asked him to write a stage adaptation of RTP. This time the book 'attacked' him. He considered himself 'at best as a woolly socialist', but he asked fundamental questions: 'What is poverty? What is the direction we should take now? What is missing in the thinking of the left?' Joint Stock's Bill Gaskill, who had been a member of the Committee of 100 in 'Ban the Bomb' days, asked him if he 'really believed in a revolution'. Lowe 'waffled wildly' since his politics were largely 'spiritual', but he acknowledged: 'One can move up or fall down. Hopping on the spot is not a choice'.

At first the cast treated the 'Brigands' as individuals, 'with real differences and disagreements', until Lowe insisted that 'while their grotesqueries might take different forms, the main factor was their over-riding solidarity'. Gradually, they focused on 'the central question, "What has changed, if anything?'' Gaskill had them painting in the mornings and rehearsing in the afternoons. He insisted that Owen 'accepts his position with mere resignation'; so they needed to 'illustrate a man not being allowed to do good satisfactory work because of the capitalist system' and 'show the nature of his action or passivity when he is faced with a crisis'. This led to discussions about current political options. One of them hoped social-ism might come via the Labour Party, though they were 'not altogether convinced'. Then the sponsors, mainly 'councillors, money men, business men' and governors of Dartington, popped in for a wine-and-cheese party, and the cast had to wait on them. The Arts Council demanded fifteen weeks' touring per year. After that the company concentrated on the 'ceiling of consciousness'.[10] To rub it in they had a two-month lay-off while Lowe went back to his job in Scarborough to write the play script.[11]

It was the hardest job he had ever done.[12] He made the building-site language realistic. At a time when the Anti-Nazi League was confronting the National Front on the streets, he represented Crass and Sawkins as racists. Owen's TB was made explicit, and Barrington was left out; but Harlow becomes a trade unionist, then a socialist, and delivers part of the 'Great Oration'. Towards the end he announces: 'We're 'aving that public meeting, now, top o' the hill. 'Cos if we get enough support, London say they may put up a Labour man. There's still time.' Owen demurs: 'It's a dead end.'

> If we go into their game, if we enter the House of Parliament on the back of the Unions, they'll just buy us off. We've got to hold out for the works, not go for the crumbs. Even if we force Capitalism to eliminate poverty completely, the cancer will still be in the air. Dog will still eat dog. We've got to tear it out by the roots, and build a new world.

Harlow persists: 'Are you coming with us or what?' '*Owen raises the banner, on which is written Workers Unite.*' '*They hold the tableau as the light builds to full. Blackout.*'[13]

Starting in Plymouth in September 1978, Joint Stock played to packed houses. The *Sunday Times* noted of the Riverside Theatre performance in London that 'nothing much happens', yet 'the economic theory now sounds like a speech by Michael Foot updated to about 1907'. *The Times* thought the play 'no substitute' for the novel. One *Guardian* reviewer damned it with faint praise, while another pronounced it 'One of the highlights' of the year. The *New Statesman* asked, 'have the realities of economic power altered so vastly since 1906?' But *Time Out* spotted that the ending

departs entirely (but convincingly) from Tressell to debate the nature of
opposition to capitalism and the problem of whether trade unionist and
Labour Party social democracy is really the way to defeat capitalism. Joint
Stock leaves this question open.

An extra performance soon sold out, and the play script was published.

Contact Theatre put on Bob Tomson's adaptation of RTP at Manchester
University Theatre. The local *Evening News* patronised this 'sincere but too
earnestly over-committed' 'bit of a bore'; while the *Daily Express* thought
the arguments 'too simplistic', though appropriate to 'the grubby obverse
side of the golden Edwardian era'. Yet the *Morning Star* found it 'good to
hear the message of Socialism put once more in such clear, simple terms,
and to see the theatre filled with young people'. One performance was
completely booked by UCATT, whose officials 'still present dignitaries and
visitors with copies' of the novel. UCATT also provided the banners,
while other props came from the CP's Progress Books. Ironically, the only
real activism came from Equity members who collected for colleagues in
Theatremobile, recently sacked by the Mid-Pennine Arts Association for
alleged 'left-wing bias'.

Lawrence & Wishart approached Ball about publishing a paperback
edition of his biography. In April 1979 *One of the Damned* was broadcast
again on BBC Radio 3. But in May came a general election. Labour's 27
per cent of the poll was their lowest since 1918. Yet there was no sizeable
socialist alternative. The CP was in disarray, and the SWP was the 'smallest
mass party in the world'.[14] So the Tories benefited from working-class
votes. That September Lawrence & Wishart published a paperback edition
of *One of the Damned*, retailing at £3.25. It was launched in Hastings Library,
which was full to overflowing. One of the audience noticed that the 1962
'Tressell' seat had gone missing. Updating the biography, or making cor-
rections, had been considered 'too expensive', and Kathleen noted the
persistent errors. Adelaide never intended to travel to Johannesburg. The
deed to the plot of land in South Africa was stolen from Paul's lodgings.
Her father always drank tea, to which he was addicted, never coffee.
Gower was an electrician, and an employee of the local theatre, not an
apprentice painter. The *Morning Star* pushed Ball's book, but the *Yorkshire
Miner* recommended that RTP, the 'immortal treasure', be read first.

Marx simplified into the working men's understanding

From 1979 Thatcher's Tory government extended Labour's monetarism and developed its attacks on organised workers. They began with a full-scale assault on right-wing-led unions like the steelworkers and on the less well organised in the public sector, but backed off from the miners. Ball got 'a lot of public speaking jobs' at shop stewards' and Labour meetings, and at union conferences. Panther reprinted RTP in 1979 and again in 1980, when Lawrence & Wishart reprinted *One of the Damned*, including a 'Special UCATT edition', 'Not for sale to the public'. There was uncritical praise for the biography and the novel in *Tribune*. Gordon Gostelow gave a talk on 'Robert Tressell and F.C. Ball and the preservation of *The Ragged Trousered Philanthropists*' in Hastings. The London *Observer* marked the anniversary of Noonan's death.

At this point the recently appointed WEA tutor–organizer responsible for Hastings, David Alfred, had 'only a faint recollection' of seeing the television adaptation of RTP, but at Vernon Hull's suggestion he got the book out of the library, read it, and 'started thinking of ways in which it might be used'.[15] Ball declined giving a WEA 'day-lecture', but Haines agreed. He told Kathleen: 'Fred gave a wrong picture of Tressell', since, 'he was looking for himself' in his hero. Noonan 'wasn't really a political man at all. He was a deeply religious man who simply couldn't believe in religion.' On 3 May 1980 seventy people turned up to hear 'The Strange Case of Robert Tressell'. Haines 'expected a bit of trouble from communists'; but even Ball disagreed only about 'the workhouse and the cause of death', though he 'insisted that Hastings would have burnt the manuscript if he had sold it to the local museum – which, of course, is rubbish'. When Haines suggested a Tressell Society – the previous attempt had foundered because 'with Fred in the chair I'm afraid we got nowhere!' – eighteen people volunteered. South East Arts made a generous grant; and, after discussions with Raphael Samuel of Ruskin College, Oxford, the Robert Tressell Workshop was established in October.

There were signs of a growing interest in RTP in London. In September 1980 a day-long event at Goldsmiths College marked the sixtieth anniversary of Greenwich, Lewisham and Southwark CP branches. Robin Page-Arnot spoke, as did veterans of the Workers' Theatre Movement, the National Unemployed Workers' Movement and the National Minority Movement. Unity Theatre performed Laurence Davies's adaptation of RTP, for the first time in many years. Kathleen heard from a London Labour councillor that a carpenter friend who was originally from the West Indies had found the book 'illuminating and absorbing' when he 'first became interested in his youth in the TU and socialist movement'. He was now a Labour councillor, too.

In January 1981 the *Guardian*, then the *Morning Star*, reported that Irene Wright, a 32-year-old former gardener with Lewisham Borough Council, had discovered that pieces of Noonan's St Andrew's mural had been lying in Hastings Museum Library cellar for ten years. She had read *The Ragged Trousered Philanthropists* in 1972: it was 'the first book to put into words things I had felt over the years. It made me realise I was a socialist', and she began a coampaign to restore the mural. By November sponsors included Eric Heffer, who claimed he had read the book eight times, and Jack Jones. In December the Robert Tressell Mural Panel Appeal Committee launched an appeal for £1,500, using a poster and circular that noted that 'unless the money is raised publicly it will continue to deteriorate in its damp boxes in the Museum works'. Apparently, the cellar roof was 'held up by an old trolleybus stand'.[16]

The Committee wrote to trade unions and trades councils. Only two letters of support came from Hastings; yet sponsors now included Barbara Castle, Alan Sillitoe and Neil Kinnock. The *Observer* reported that Noonan died of tuberculosis in a 'warehouse', and was 'thrown into a pauper's grave', 'discovered in 1977'. Haines understood the interviewee was a Ball 'disciple', and was 'very sorry to say that this Mural Fund looks as if it's run by very left-wing people' who 'seized upon the legend for political purposes'. He was also worried about the Robert Tressell Workshop. David Alfred was co-opted onto the Mural Committee. When asked why Noonan had been ignored in Hastings, he was clear: 'Because he's a red hot socialist, that's why. He makes Tony Benn look like a right-winger.' Alfred wanted to see a 'Tressell museum', and to 'bring big name speakers down annually'.

The first Robert Tressell Memorial Lecture was planned to commemorate the seventieth anniversary of Noonan's death. It was given by John Nettleton, a veteran of the National Union of Seamen's Reform Movement and secretary of Liverpool's Robert Tressell Memorial Committee, who was about to be made redundant from the Courtauld factory where he was TGWU convenor. On 28 March 150 people heard him claim that RTP was 'universally read' by painters on Merseyside; though he came

across it as a seaman, after reading *Tressell of Mugsborough*. He noted that the
Liverpool joiners' union official, Leo McGree, regarded it as his 'bible';
but he did not mention that McGree was a Stalin loyalist. Nettleton understood that 'The Great Money Trick' was 'done at branch meetings' and 'in
what they call the "hut" at building sites whenever they're rained off'

> I know lads who have got that off by heart. And every new apprentice who
> ever comes on the building site on the Liverpool Cathedral, that's his first
> lesson. And he learns that before he learns about the trade; ... and that's the
> way it should be.

'It's a common saying in Liverpool socialist circles that for every person
brought into the movement by Marx, there's ten brought into the Movement by Robert Tressell.' 'I've been a shop steward for twenty years. If I
were to go on the shop floor and read *Das Kapital*, I wouldn't be a shop
steward for long.' Yet 'The Great Money Trick is *Das Kapital*', but 'simplified
into the working men's understanding'.[17]

Alan O'Toole read extracts from the novel; Ball signed copies of *One of
the Damned*; and Irene Wright announced that nearly £1,000 had been
raised for the Mural Appeal. By May the Committee's target had been
achieved, and they hoped to see the restoration completed by the following Easter. Eventually, the Appeal topped £2,200. Manchester UCATT sent
£100, the TGWU gave £100, and other unions chipped in. 'Much of the
rest came in small cheques of £1, £2 and £5', but *Socialist Worker*'s contribution was not given wide publicity.[18] That autumn Nettleton's talk and
Alfred's 'Report Back' appeared in *History Workshop Journal*, edited by Raphael
Samuel.

In December 1981 Nigel Townsend's stage adaptation of RTP was performed by the Cockpit Theatre Company at the Inner London Education
Authority's Cockpit Theatre, and then at Theatre Space in Central London.
The cast were mostly unemployed people in their early twenties, though
some had been drama students. They had 'devised' the scenes in six weeks,
then Townsend wrote the play script. 'Tressell', 'Kathleen' and 'Grant
Richards' were chorus and commentators, and the play included elements
of *One of the Damned*. The *Morning Star* preferred 'the famous Unity Theatre
version', but felt that 'The Great Money Trick' was 'as effective as ever',
and was glad the young audience went out humming Edward Carpenter's
socialist hymn, 'England Arise'. *News Line*, the daily paper of the tiny Workers'
Revolutionary Party (the rebranded Socialist Labour League), regretted
that the adaptation 'shifted a bit too much towards the elements of back-

wardness in the workers' ideas and Owen's despair', and left out Noonan's 'vision of the glorious fabric of the Co-operative Commonwealth, rising from the ashes of the capitalist system'. The Hastings *Observer* published a faintly supportive review, but too late for readers to catch the final performance. The *Times Educational Supplement* noted that only one of the eighteen cast had got a job after the show ended. But during 1981 Panther reprinted the novel twice, and jacked the price up by 30 per cent to £1.95.

There were signs of life in Hastings. In March 1982 the South Eastern District WEA, the 'Robert Tressell Workshop' and the Trades Council showed a film about Noonan's life, made by Mr R.C. Milsted. Nigel Townsend was asked to talk at the Unemployed and Claimants Advice Centre: 'Please bring a coat in case it is cold and there is not enough heating.' Meanwhile, Irene Wright's committee was trying to get the owners of Noonan's mural, the Museum Committee, to agree about where it should be displayed.[19] In Liverpool, John Nettleton was out of a job, but he was active at the Walton Unemployed Centre and in the TGWU 6612 Unemployed Members Branch. In April, billed as 'Secretary of the Robert Tressell Memorial Committee', and giver of 'the Robert Tressell Memorial Lecture at Hastings', Nettleton spoke on 'Robert Tressell: His Life and Times' for the WEA Northern District, supported by the Newcastle Trade Union Studies Information Unit and Newcastle Trades Council.

Nettleton was a supporter of left-winger Tony Benn, who lost the deputy leadership of the Labour Party to Denis Healey in September 1981. According to opinion polls, Benn's popularity among Labour voters was half that of his rival, and he appealed to only one-fifth of the electorate; so he promised not to stand again. Healey, however, did not appeal to socialists. By December Labour's support had halved in one year. Some former Labour left-wingers moved right. In April 1982 long-time pacifist Michael Foot supported Thatcher's Falklands task force, with Benn's guarded agreement. Labour Party membership fell by a quarter. The Executive was dominated by the centre-right, even before several key right-wingers broke away to form the Social Democratic Party.

Neil Kinnock inherited much of Benn's electoral support inside the Labour Party, especially from lay and full-time trade-union officials, and in May the chief opposition spokesman on education opened the Hastings General and Municipal Workers' Union and Constituency Labour Party offices in Wellington Square as 'Robert Tressell House'. His press release claimed he had read *The Ragged Trousered Philanthropists* 'many, many times', since it was 'a normal part of reading in the kind of working-class family I came from'. It functioned as an 'armoury of ideas', against 'ignorance, superstition'

> and gullibility of people who think that injustice, dishonesty, conflict and fear are the unchanged and unchangeable natural order that has to be accepted and obeyed as 'bad luck' or even respected and supported in the name of order or respectability, or enterprise or national greatness.

Yet today, 'mortgagors vote for the mortgagees, the borrowers for the lenders, the sacked for the sackers, the mice for the cats', believing 'we can have better hospitals, homes and schools by spending less on them', and 'they can keep jobs whilst all around are losing theirs'. The 'descendants of The Ragged Trousered Philanthropists live on' in the Tory-voting working class.

However, Kinnock's main target was a 'minority' of socialists inside the Labour Party who 'cannot see the people for the slogans',

> so self righteous that it refuses to deal with realities, so busy chanting that it never stops to listen to anything or anyone that does not patronise its simplicity. That minority appears to believe that a small, organised vanguard equipped with the right ten-point plan can use the anticipated despair of depressed masses to win power. That is foolish. It always has been.

Kinnock used RTP as left cover. The one-time adult education tutor and fervent supporter of CND invoked Nye Bevan, that late convert to atom bomb 'deterrence', and misquoted Engels in an attempt to damn Lenin. 'Tressell', apparently, 'would have been disgusted' with members of Militant, who were 'weakening the Labour movement by dividing it ideologically' and 'making idealism look like madness'. A press photograph showed Kinnock holding One of the Damned, and posing next to its author. A wholly uncritical report appeared in the Morning Star.

Very good, according to legend

Not all socialist academics were pulled right after three years of Thatcher's savagery. Raymond Williams now understood that The Ragged Trousered Philanthropists was 'founded, from the beginning, on a view of class relations' as seen from the uncomfortable position of 'a participating and exposed observer, seeking transformation rather than reconciliation'.[20] In his May 1982 Robert Tressell Memorial Lecture, 'Writing about Working People: The Case of "The Ragged Trousered Philanthropists"', Williams argued that 'there was a basic lack of fit between the shape of working-class lives and the inherited forms of the novel'. Moreover, RTP was not about 'archetypal working-class communities', which, 'so to say, deliver class consciousness'. Its author was 'in certain respects very conscious of his difference'. So perhaps this was why his book 'has always appealed especially to relatively isolated militants and questioning men [sic]'.[21]

In September Kathleen Noonan Lynne learned of a posthumous award to her father by the Irish Post, she told a reporter that he 'envisaged The World Wide Brotherhood of Man irrespective of race', so it was 'funny' that

> so many people claim to be communist or socialist when they do not really know what they are claiming to be! Russia is certainly not truly Communist nor the labour party socialist: Socialism is 'All for One and One for All'. Now it seems to be all 'me, me, me'.

She was sure her father would not join a union today, 'without upsetting the apple cart'. That month Ball unveiled Noonan's mural panel at Hastings Museum, and Eric Heffer called 'Tressell' 'the greatest Socialist writer Britain has ever produced' – he 'should be honoured every year on a par with the Tolpuddle Martyrs'. Ex-CPer John Gorman 'suggested Tressell would have been an ally of the health workers', then defending themselves against an increasingly confident and vicious Tory government. Red Hot News, 'Bulletin of Mugsborough Communist Party', focused on Ball's account of the mural discovery.[22] Ball found it 'somewhat surprising that the audience was from many differing political views and walks of life'. The Guardian noted that 'Hundreds of Labour Party enthusiasts' were present, and claimed that the restoration cash had been raised 'thanks largely to the generosity of its readers'. Gordon Gostelow, 'Royal Shakespearian Actor' read extracts from RTP. This was followed by a 'Beano'. Hastings Library put on a small display. Joan Johnson told a reporter that her grandfather would have had no use for the Labour Party or the CP: 'They don't live up to socialism in the way that Grandad taught.' 'He would have had a fit at Stalinism and tower blocks.'

The struggle over symbolic possession of Noonan's book, and the interpretation of its politics, continued. It had its lighter side. In Sue Townsend's The Secret Diary of Adrian Mole aged 13¾ the hero notes:

> Pandora's mother said I could call her Tania. Surely that is a Russian name? Her father said I could call him Ivan. He gave me a book to read; it is called The Ragged Trousered Philanthropists. I haven't looked through it yet but I'm quite interested in stamp collecting...[23]

In December 1982 *The Robert Tressell Papers* was published. It had support from Hastings WEA, six nearby WEA branches, South East Arts and the southern regions of the GMWU and UCATT, and could be obtained 'for £2.00 incl. p&p from: Robert Tressell Workshop, c/o Robert Tressell House'.[24] Alfred wrote a review of *One of the Damned* in the CP's *History Today*.

Meanwhile the Arts Council had commissioned Spectre Productions to make a film about Noonan and his book. *Give Us This Day* relied heavily on *One of the Damned*. The National Theatre programme noted that it began with Noonan's arrival in 'the picturesque resort of Hastings', and went on

> to reveal the gradual disillusionment he felt with the conditions of his own life and the lives of those around him. It shows the various ways he struggled against these conditions, and how the writing of the book came out of that struggle and was part of it.

There was an 'SDF Man'; but the contrast between Noonan's political activity and the lack of it in RTP was largely ignored. The film got its first public showing in North London in November, and was available for hire at £19. North Islington Labour Party used it as a fundraiser. In January 1983 it was screened on Channel 4. David Haines wondered if Kathleen 'roared with laughter' at her father as a 'sort of tubercular Robin Hood'. In fact she 'dropped off and missed the beginning', and was 'quite asleep before the end', but while Frank Grimes was 'too gentle' in the role of her father, the rest was 'very good "according to legend"'.

By March 1983 *The Robert Tressell Papers* had sold 800 copies. That year's Robert Tressell Memorial Lecture, 'Robert Tressell and the Trade Unions in the 1980s', was given by Norman Willis, deputy General Secretary of the TUC. He acknowledged that RTP made socialists; but he was keen to split 'democratic Socialism' from 'the day-to-day protection and work of trade unionism'.[25] Workers should join unions and Labour, but leave things to the full-time officials. In June Greenwich Young People's Theatre Powerplay Workshop, supported by the Inner London Education Authority, the Arts Council, the Borough of Greenwich and the Great London Arts Association, staged an adaptation of RTP. There was a benefit for a youth exchange with young actors from Yugoslavia, to which Kathleen sent £5, though she was too ill to attend. Bizarrely, Act 1 began with Noonan's death, complete with priest; and 'Tressell' became the authorial voice. In spite of 'The Great Money Trick', the overall stress was on changing attitudes *before* acting to change the world. The play ended with Owen hinting at the slaughter of the Great War, while the rest of the cast sang

'England Arise'. One reviewer was grateful that the 'plight of the working man in 1911' was not 'used as a platform for the ravings of today's left-wing extremists'.

In June 1983, Kinnock's Labour Party got 3 million votes fewer than in 1979. Its candidates attracted the lowest average vote of all time, and its number of MPs was the lowest since 1935. Stephen Lowe had been concerned about Labour for some time, but he remained interested in 'those rare moments when societies, or bits of them, have a chance to change direction'. He hoped that by seeing such moments represented 'we might be wiser next time'; but he wanted to know 'if we put our faith behind it again, what demands do we make so we are not betrayed again?' He returned to RTP. He saw it as 'a force for revolutionary change, not just a critique of the system as it stood', but also 'a critique of what's holding back the working classes from consciousness'.

On 13 July Lowe's revised adaptation was staged at the Half Moon Theatre, London, subsidised by the Arts Council, Greater London Council and the London Borough of Tower Hamlets. The marketing material for this 'underground classic' focused on 'work, the lack of it and the manipulation of both workers and management alike by the Capitalist system'. Lowe's programme notes (written in June) were openly political:

> Last night, Labour was defeated at the polls in an election dominated by a suicidal nostalgia to return to the so-called stability of Victorian life (which Tressell exposes), and a media intent on creating an alternative party that would fudge the fundamental challenges we are all facing. And already, there is the first sound of voices arguing that Labour's failure was attempting to re-unite with the socialist vision that Tressell would have understood, and that it should have remained 'moderate', only nominally committed to socialist principles. Those on the Left are faced with the question of whether to return to such 'dreams', 'utopian fancies', and to re-unite again, as under Wilson and Callaghan.

He wanted to hold on to RTP's 'vision' of 'the essential nature of socialism', yet cling on to reformism and not follow Noonan in advocating the revolutionary smashing of the capitalist 'System'. Harlow and the very reluctant Owen 'hold the tableau as the lights build to full'. 'Blackout', once again.[26]

The *Evening Standard* thought that suggesting 'Tressell's vision' was 'more akin to the hard left of the Labour Party rather than to the mushy politics of Wilson and Callaghan' was 'dreadful'. If he had witnessed

> the blinkered economics of union bosses, the unfairness of the closed shop, the affluence of the working class in capitalist societies and the tyranny and

mass murder in Socialist ones, he might have been less keen on unfurling the Red Flag than such Left-wing reactionaries as Mr Lowe.

City Limits complained that the play had 'nowhere near' the 'crude subtlety' and 'fear and loathing' of a novel 'even more relevant in these days of the Blessed Margaret', and that it effectively supported a 'pragmatic Labour Party consciousness', while the Guardian got little sense of 'a commitment to change'. The Spectator complained about a lack of 'historical or political perspective' – 'Even Ian Mikardo left at the interval on press night.' Tribune felt that 'this brilliant expose of paternalism and forced labour is unfortunately bitterly appropriate', and the Morning Star hailed 'a political winner'. Cannily, the Irish Post discerned an emergent Noonan 'industry'.

In November 1983 Fred Ball was at the GMB's Woodstock College, arguing that RTP represented a 'British brand of socialism'. He got a positive response. Give Us This Day had won the Grierson award. Panther reprinted at £2.50 (a 28 per cent hike); Lawrence & Wishart reprinted too. By now Kathleen had read Methuen's revised play script and wrote witheringly to Lowe, who was 'deeply, deeply disturbed' by her critique. He 'did insist on attending the last week of rehearsal', and had asked that 'a large number of swear words' be cut. However, he was able to reassure her about take-up for the novel, since 'large numbers were sold at the box office'. However, RTP fan Sean O'Donoghue, a UCATT shop steward in West London, recalled that his 'bible' did not find its way onto building sites he knew, though he met 'all the characters' in the book, and some of the subcontractors were 'animals'.[27]

A spiritual elect?

In March 1984 retired TGWU General Secretary Jack Jones gave 'Robert Tressell's Message for Today' as that year's Robert Tressell Memorial Lecture. On 6 April an article based on the talk appeared in Tribune. RTP 'provides a clear cut case for Socialism, as valid now as when it was written', so

> Neil Kinnock, Tony Benn, Roy Hattersley, Len Murray and the rest who claim leadership in the Labour movement, and not least those who write in support of the movement, should read this book again and again, and try to emulate the clarity of its expression, the sincerity of its spirit.

Jones acknowledged that in the 1930s it was RTP's 'criticism, in a way, of our own class that affected me most', and that 'much of it is still true today'. 'Ignorance and divisions still stand in the way of a rapid advance to the socialism of Bob Noonan's dreams':

> How far have we advanced in the elimination of ignorance since Noonan's day? I ask the question knowing from my own experience of the inertia and lack of comprehension which prevails among many people. It's an alarming condition, almost as frightening in its way as a nuclear threat.
> If our schools, colleges and universities were turning out a nation of reasoning, critically-minded but public spirited citizens, well-informed on economic and political subjects and able to recognise and control their prejudices, our life would be a lot simpler. Political parties, for example, would be able to put a reasoned case before the electorate and expect to win on its merits.
> It is a reflection on all of us, on our education system and on the Labour movement, that a large part of the British population remains half-educated with a narrow and self-centred outlook.

'The danger is that a new wave of Goebbels-type methods is beginning to spread in our country', where the 'clever, scheming, wealthy class is able to play off one section of the population against the other'. How could gullible workers ever evade brain-washing and achieve the Co-operative Commonwealth?

Jones suggested that RTP needed updating: 'What was missing was the message of fighting together. The workers needed to be organised and united and shaken out of their apathy', and any socialist who

> fails to organise in trade unionism fails in the purpose. Equally, the working man or woman who is content merely to be a trade unionist and fight on the industrial front, to build a union no matter how financially strong – is fighting with one hand tied behind his back.

Like Noonan, Jones separated economics from politics: 'we must build a stronger Labour Party combined with strong unions so that we can fight with two hands'. His October talk to Preston WEA, published as 'The Ragged Trousered Philanthropists and Its Relevance Today', was even less optimistic, but by then the TGWU had allowed some of its lorry drivers to cross miners' picket lines for months.

The NUM leadership had shown dangerous bureaucratic weaknesses from the start of the Great Strike. Arthur Scargill, a life-long fan of RTP, remained true to his Stalinist roots. He refused to go over the heads of his regional officials to ask for rank-and-file support for picketing out Nottinghamshire scabs, but he accepted CPer Mick McGahey's divisive argument for keeping Ravenscraig steel plant open. Crucially, in June 1984 the NUM failed to close the Orgreave coking plant.[28] Of course, Scargill's mistakes were compounded by timidity and opportunism within the Labour Party, of which he was a member. Neil Kinnock, the MP for a Welsh mining constituency, visited an NUM picket line for the first and only time in January 1985, after nine months of bitter struggle. Sadly, Kinnock's sworn enemies, the Militant Liverpool councillors, failed to open a second front against the Tories by defying rate-capping, and *Militant* denounced Tony Benn and the Campaign Group for disrupting the House of Commons with demands for a debate on the state's attack on the miners' strike and on mining communities.

For left reformists the loss of the Great Strike was a huge ideological defeat. Reactions varied. Eric Heffer walked off the platform at the Labour Party conference when Kinnock launched his assault on Militant, but Heffer believed Labour's transformation into 'the SDP Mark II really got under way' when former 'soft-left' colleagues ditched him.[29] In reality it was not the supposed class struggle in Parliament that was decisive. Rank-and-file socialists and trade unionists had helped feed miners and their families – upwards of half a million people – for a whole year. Artists helped ideologically. In May and June 1984 Glasgow novelist Archie Hind's bleak and uncompromising Scottish adaptation of RTP was taken on tour with 7:84 Scotland, subsidised by the Scottish Arts Council, and they played to huge working-class audiences. Capitalist publishing profited. Panther reprinted RTP twice in 1984, the second time at £2.95 (a rise of 18 per cent), and again in 1985. Lawrence & Wishart also reprinted.

One of the sourest reactions to the Great Strike was that of Raphael Samuel, founder of Ruskin History Workshop and *History Workshop Journal*. He was born in London in 1935. His mother was a CP activist, but his father left home and lived at the Liberal Club. After his parents divorced 'Raph' was sent to boarding school; and in the later 1940s he became a YCLer. Palme Dutt was 'our foremost theologian'. The boy 'read no forbidden books', and 'entertained no dissident thoughts'. He 'attempted to "clarify" an aunt and uncle who were "confused about Yugoslavia", and had come to doubt the Moscow Trials', and he 'turned amateur agronomist to defend the theories of Academician Lysenko'.[30] In 1953, aged 18, Samuel wore black and wept the day Stalin died. He left the CP in 1956, but didn't go far away, and was troubled by the serious rows inside the Party in the 1970s.

In 1980 Samuel still felt that RTP, that 'magnificent testament', was 'surely the central text for an understanding of the political psychology of socialism' of 1880–1914, and 'arguably the most important single contribution of British Marxism to the making of the labour movement'. Yet by 1985 he had become disoriented by 'the question mark which – ever since the Social Democratic secession of 1981–82 – has seemed to hang over the very existence of a labour "movement"'.[31] That March he gave the Robert Tressell Memorial Lecture. He argued that The Ragged Trousered Philanthropists was 'one of the great texts of our literature'; but it was 'very much like a Pilgrim's Progress of our time, in which the lonely seeker after salvation finds himself beset by weakness and temptation on all sides', while its socialism had 'so many affinities' to the Salvation Army. What irked Samuel most was the book's optimism, which tallied with his own former experience, especially the 'idea that you were being carried as if you were on history's back and that you were realising a historical mission'. But Marxism was now only 'a mystical vision'.[32] Any whippersnappers who thought otherwise were, as Samuel had once been, members of a self-deluding, utopian and messianic 'Spiritual Elect'.

Soon after, Samuel attacked what was left of the Communist Party in articles in New Left Review. He argued that the Morning Star's 'real affinity' was 'not with the Hard Left of the Labour Party but with the Centre-Left' of the trade-union movement. 'Its ideal-typical leader is the newly elected secretary of the TGWU, Ron Todd.' Its 'real heartland' was

> in the trade union offices, among full-time functionaries – organizers keeping faith, by their own lights, with their members, yet differently positioned in life and, as recent experience suggests, sometimes tragically distanced from the real flow of rank-and-file sentiment ... and the star billing which it gives to articles by General Secretaries suggest that it is in danger of becoming a house journal for the TUC.

Yet he saw no alternative. 'On the ultra-Left – the dissidence of Dissent – a dozen "vanguard" parties and as many tendencies and groups, compete for the honour of leading a non-existent revolutionary working class.' He found it 'difficult to take the idea of non-Party Marxism seriously'.[33] 'Marxism' had belonged to the Party, and as that went, so did hope.

14

Tressell, Marxism and hope

Against the new conformists

In 1985 Fred Ball was 80, and had joined no party for thirty years. 'I don't think Communism stands any chance in any country that seems to make some effort to help all the population.' The Communist Party 'has never known where it's going or where it has been. Many of its opponents know more about Marxism than it does'. There was 'still a radical section' in the labour movement, 'wanting to develop the social side of socialism', but Ball saw himself as an 'evolutionary socialist', if that: 'I'm nothing more really than an old-fashioned English Liberal-radical – not really political at all.'

The Ragged Trousered Philanthropists remained relevant. During 1985 Alan O'Toole and John Nettleton gave six free lectures at the Merseyside Unemployed Centre. Keva Coombes, who had been present at Noonan's graveside in 1977, was now chairman of Merseyside County Council. In October he opened the Robert Tressell Museum of Local History in No. 2 Lodge at Walton Park Cemetery, praising the way RTP 'puts forward the human values of socialism'. The Museum's secretary, curator and 'history consultant' was O'Toole, and Nettleton was chair of the trustees. They received a grant of £6,500 from Merseyside County Council, but the project was run by volunteers, plus a few people on one-year Manpower Services Commission contracts. The Museum 'attracted many visitors', yet it closed in a matter of months. Comrade Noonan was not to be a New Labour priority.

The writer Edward Upward had left the CP in the 1950s, but in October 1985 he characterised RTP in the *Times Literary Supplement* as 'the most underestimated English novel of the twentieth century', 'one of the great classics of English Literature' and, indeed, 'of world literature'. Tony Benn agreed. In his May 1986 Robert Tressell Memorial Lecture, 'Tressell the Teacher', Benn hailed the 'socialist classic', but sought to recruit Noonan to 'revolutionary Christianity'. He was clear about the political role of the police at Orgreave, during the Great Strike, and more recently at Wapping, where he had seen baton charges against peaceful pickets. He also acknowledged that change in favour of the working class has 'always come from below', since Parliament 'has always been the last place to get the message', yet he dismissed the idea that any organisation except Labour 'can ever be the instrument of the British working class'. A speaker who criticised Labour's record from the left was dismissed in an uncomradely manner, but Benn was not completely confident. He read both the *Morning Star* and *Socialist Worker*: 'who am I to know which view is going to be the one that turns out to be right in the long run?'[1] In the short run Labour won only 31 per cent of the poll in the 1986 general election, while Panther reprinted *The Ragged Trousered Philanthropists*.

In academia, the pull of pessimistic bourgeois feminism grew stronger. In April 1987 Eileen Yeo became the first woman to give a Robert Tressell Memorial Lecture. In 'Women and Socialism in Robert Tressell's World' the Sussex University history lecturer spoke on behalf of all women, about all men. She felt Mugsborough was largely 'a man's world' seen through a 'masculine eye', and spoke confidently about 'men's sense of self and especially their idea of their own masculinity'. But are we to frown on Owen for coping with TB, getting soaked going to tell Jack Linden about a job, organising a whip-round for Mrs Newman, standing up for Bert, and supporting Nora when she was unwell? And why is Ruth 'defenceless' for living independently of Will? Half the women in Noonan's day had three children, and a quarter had more than five, though no Mugsborough woman has more than two. Yet Yeo insisted that 'we get the idea that Tressell would prefer to keep his women protected at home'.[2]

Revealingly, Yeo's model of a strong working-class woman was Hannah Mitchell, who joined Manchester ILP in 1908, and was supported as Poor Law Guardian, Manchester city councillor, JP and member of the Public Assistance Relief Committee by her male comrades. Yet Mitchell was outside the Labour Party by 1930, and had left the ILP by 1935, in order to devote herself to exercising power, largely over working-class women and men, on the magistrate's bench. Abstractly, Yeo acknowledged that socialists fight for the emancipation of the whole human race, yet concretely she assumed that it had to be won for them, from above, by the middle class. She also ignored the fact that Labour leaders have consistently put the interests of the 'nation' – that is, those of the ruling class and its middle-class hangers-on – before those of working class men, women and children. She took it for granted that there was no alternative, and ignored a question about the possibility of a non-Stalinist Marxism.[3]

During 1987 *Filantropy v rvanykh*, by 'Robert Tressel', was published in Russia. Jack Mitchell continued to praise the book as a 'socialist national-ist classic'. It had an 'ability to present the "habits and customs" of the working class as something contradictory, containing creative potential in an estranged form', in spite of 'satire on the delusions of workers, the lonely, often thankless fight of the isolated socialist' and 'the actual de-scending spiral of social misery under maturing capitalism'.[4] That May, Metro Theatre staged Lowe's adaptation at Newport Pagnell, directed by Steven Daldry and sponsored by Milton Keynes Trades Council. Metro also played at Cheltenham Fringe Theatre, handy for the victimised trade un-ionists at GCHQ. In June they were at Hastings, where the Robert Tressell Workshops Ltd were opened in a former railway building. Supported by the local co-operative development officer, and Hastings Voluntary Serv-ices, the project was based on a £10,000 grant, a £30,000 interest-free loan, plus £36,000 for five years running costs from (or via) the borough council. The aim was to provide workshop accommodation, secretarial services, advice and training for first-time businesses and co-ops run by ten unemployed people aged 16 to 25. Rents would undercut market rates, and the management's target was fifty units. During 1987 Panther reprinted *The Ragged Trousered Philanthropists* at £3.95, a hike of £1 in two years.

Kathleen Noonan Lynne died in Bristol on 12 March 1988. Fred Ball wrote an obituary, but died himself on 14 April. Ball had recently supported Newark and District Trades Union Council, who were planning an event focusing on RTP. It was also supported by local trade-union branches and committees, Liverpool, Hastings and Dublin Trades Councils, the East Mid-lands TUC, the president of the Nottinghamshire NUM, the General Secretary of the National Union of Public Employees, the joint General Secretary of the Manufacturing, Science and Finance Union, and Norman

Willis, now General Secretary of the TUC. Labour MPs were keen to have
their say in the programme. Joe Ashton recalled reading RTP, aged 16,
'during my dinner hour and tea breaks while working on a lathe. It had
a deep and long-lasting influence on me and was a far better education
than any seminar at Ruskin or any speech I have ever heard in Parliament.'
Neil Kinnock saw it as 'a warning of what life could become again if our
generation doesn't argue and organise for democratic socialism'. David
Blunkett believed it should be part of the Tories' national curriculum.
Ball's posthumous piece stressed that the political situation 'could and
must be changed'. Stephen Lowe, whose adaptation of the novel was the
main attraction, felt that his 1979 version had foreseen 'the dangers of a
rapid growth of unemployment, and the threatened attacks on trade unionism', while Noonan's novel 'shows us the reality for the workers of so
called Victorian philanthropy and Free Enterprise', and 'outlines the central choices of direction for the left'. It 'does not give us easy answers,
but it certainly clarifies the questions'.[5]

Another academic, Bernard Sharratt, Reader in English and Cultural
Studies at the University of Kent, gave the 1988 Robert Tressell Memorial
Lecture. In 'Tressell and the Truths of Fiction' he argued that the book
didn't tell you to be a socialist, but offered 'exercises in understanding,
which readers can try out for themselves, within and beyond the text
itself'. It was a kind of socialist propaganda kit, at the heart of which was
'The Great Money Trick'.[6] RTP continued to be staged. John Lowe's adaptation, then on tour, promised 'squabbles, thoughts and dreams and tales of
their families and sweethearts', as 'Robert Owen', played by Eric Richard
'takes on the bosses and unites the men' in 'A Show With Songs, Passion
and Laughter'. The Guardian missed the 'pained, put-upon soberness of the
troop of decorators' of an earlier production. But the Daily Telegraph noted:
'What a cast! Neil Kinnock, Michael Foot and the Tonys Benn and Banks
all adorn the programme'; and observed that the play particularly appealed to 'excitable youngsters in the front stalls'.

That November The Robert Tressell Lectures 1981–1988 was published by the
WEA at £3.90. (It advertised a new edition of The Robert Tressell Papers.) John
Nettleton made a point of stressing that Jack Jones was 'a personal friend'.
Jones, now president of the TGWU Retired Members Associations, argued
that 'Robert Tressell's message for today' was about 'the ignorance, the
divisions, the subservience' of the working class. There was 'something
wrong yet with our society: a mentality, in a sense, born out of centuries

of slavery and serfdom'. As for the idea that a reasoned socialist case could convince a British working-class electorate: 'That's like saying if pigs could only fly.'[7] However, Tony Benn continued to ask extremely pertinent questions:

> Why, more than seventy years after the book was written, has so little advance been achieved by working people in Britain in their relationship to the structure of power in society, despite the existence of the biggest and strongest democratic socialist labour movement in the world which is officially committed to socialism and to the transformation of society? Was it that Tressell's ideas were tried and failed? Was it that they were not tried? Or were there other factors to it?

His answer signalled a leftward shift:

> Because Labourism, operating a narrow electoralism within the unchanged structure of the bourgeois state under capitalism, and the Labour Party, which wasn't explicitly socialist, worked on very different principles than the ones that Tressell set out.

The 'basis of social change must be do it yourself'. In struggle, people 'get an education for which there is no substitute'.[8] Any classical Marxist could agree.

In 1989 Eric Heffer was too ill to give his Robert Tressell Memorial Lecture, 'Tressell's Impact on Working-Class Socialist Politics'. But after the impact of the fall of the Berlin Wall, many academics were pulled by that peculiar form of sophisticated despair known as 'post-modernism'.[9] In 1988 Wim Neetens had described RTP as 'revolutionary'.[10] Yet by 1991 he felt it offered 'a glimpse of what literature *tout court* could be'.

> Both the novel's form and its career stand witness to the possibility of a democratic modernism which hopefully negates the dictates of the literary market place by being intelligent and experimental without being academic or obscure, popular without being trivial, oppositional without being marginal, instructive without being patronising or dull.[11]

On the other hand, Raymond Williams had worked in his local miners' support group during 1984–85, and, like Benn, had shifted leftwards. Yet when he died in 1988 he was still 'one of the very few – shamefully few – literary critics to have taken Tressell as seriously as he deserves'.[12] In 1988 Panther reprinted RTP, and in 1989 they did so twice, now at £4.50, while Lawrence & Wishart's hardback reprint cost £8.99. Williams's posthumous volume *The Politics of Modernism* also appeared in 1989. Its subtitle was *Against the New Conformists*.

What we are fighting for

By 1990 a tiny fragment of Fred Ball's archive had been acquired by Hastings Museum. Late that year it was put on exhibition. Joan Johnson loaned some Noonan family material, and the TUC sent part of the RTP manuscript. A performance of the Popular Productions one-man show, *Tressell*, was sponsored by the National and Local Government Officers Association. One journalist thought the audience seemed 'largely middle class', and managed to find three working-class women with glowing memories of the town in Noonan's day. The TUC's John Monks wrote a piece for *Public Service*; the Irish Congress of Trade Unions gave support; and Lawrence & Wishart advertised RTP and *One of the Damned*. Hastings Museum and Trades Council provided a 'Reception and Buffet', with Ron Todd, General Secretary of the TGWU, as guest speaker. Todd invited Joan Johnson to be photographed with him for the union journal, signing copies of her grandfather's book. *Tressell* went on to have eighty performances in the UK and Eire. Panther reprinted '"one of the most popular books" that the Labour Party sells'.[13]

During 1991 the paperback RTP appeared under the Paladin imprint, retailing at £5.99. Paladin was a subsidiary of HarperCollins, owned by Rupert Murdoch, yet the blurb stressed the novel's focus on 'the most important struggle in history, the struggle between the underprivileged and their oppressors'. Lawrence & Wishart's and Panther's previous printings were noted, but some of the author's stylistic practices had been 'restored', so the text was 'almost in its original form', and copyright applied only to Sillitoe's 1965 Introduction. Meanwhile, Lowe's adaptation of RTP was revived by Birmingham Rep, sponsored by the Arts Council and the GMB and directed by Steven Daldry. The production brought in full houses as far away as Birmingham Alabama.[14] Methuen republished the play script, which was introduced by Labour's Mark Fisher, shadow minister for arts and media. He stressed that one of the first acts of the Tory government had been to undermine health and safety laws. 'Philpot dies again, three times every week', and his employer is fined £400, while the battle against privatisation of public services was 'far from won'. Yet RTP reminds us 'what we are fighting for'.[15]

At this point Hastings Labour Party was 'desperately short of money to fight the Tories', and 'unable to raise enough funding locally to rent new premises – however small'. So it started a 'Robert Tressell Appeal Fund' by commissioning a local artist to design a bone-china mug bearing a picture of Noonan. Their publicity credited him with having written 'one of the opinion forming books which created a climate for the early Labour Party and the trade-union movement to flourish and become effective'; but no mention was made of the SDF, or Owen's anti-capitalism, or Barrington's perspective of sending revolutionaries to Parliament. A Brighton history teachers' cooperative called itself 'Tressell Publications'. 'Tressell' was becoming a useful marketing tool.

There was now a Robert Tressell Memorial Committee in Dublin, consisting of members of the National Union of Journalists, the plumber's union, UCATT and the Irish National Housepainters and Decorators Union. In May 1991 Joan Johnson unveiled a plaque at Noonan's birthplace, 37 Wexford Street, in the presence of the president of the Dublin Council of Trade Unions and the General Secretary of the Irish Congress of Trade Unions. Nobody came to represent Hastings, and the Irish Labour Party was not invited; but John Nettleton was able to bring across an exhibition about the life and work of the author. (Tours of Liverpool's Irish connections now took in Noonan's grave.) In July Joan was asked to approve the naming of a Tressell Ward at Hastings' Conquest Hospital, for people with breathing difficulties. At least that use of his name was appropriate.

In 1992 Labour was defeated in the fourth successive general election. Methuen reprinted Lowe's play script. In 1993 Brighton Labour Party member Trevor Hopper arranged a 'One Day School', sponsored by the WEA, and a 'Robert Tressell Walk' around Hastings. That November, visitors to Central and Ore branch libraries were entertained by extracts read from RTP by the Labour chair of the county council's libraries and records committee. Paladin's sixth reprint in three years now retailed at £6.99, before HarperCollins issued it as a Flamingo Modern Classic.

In 1994 Hastings WEA decided to revive the Robert Tressell Memorial Lectures. Dr John Lovell of the University of Kent spoke on 'The Ragged Trousered Philanthropists and Trade Unionism in the Edwardian Era'. He ascribed Noonan's marginalisation of unions and the Labour Party to his 'dedicated socialist' perspective, and he agreed that, had he lived, the author would have felt 'more at home' in the Communist Party. So it was particularly paradoxical that RTP had become a 'Bible' of Labour Party leaders.[16] That June Tony Benn spoke to a 'packed audience' at Hastings Library in support of the Robert Tressell Foundation, 'brainchild' of Labour councillor Terry Randall. They hoped to commission a 'bronze bust' costing up to £10,000 to commemorate the 125th anniversary of Noonan's birth, and to establish a 'Foundation Literary Fund' to 'promote the writing and publishing of books about the life of working people in modern Britain'. Randall was acting chair of a steering group of people from unnamed 'groups and organisations', and money was subscribed; but the Foundation failed to materialize. Meanwhile, the Robert Tressell Workshops went into administration. Trevor Hopper deplored the 'demise of such a valuable project', but added some 'good news for Tressell fans': 'Southern Labour Heritage' would commemorate Noonan's anniversary with a guide to 'Tressell's Hastings'. However, in spite of the Johnsons' best efforts, the anniversary was allowed to pass without an appropriate public celebration.

In May 1995 the Robert Tressell Memorial Lecture, 'Robert Tressell and "New Labour"', was delivered by yet another academic, Professor Ben Pimlott of Birkbeck College, University of London. He was anxious about a possible 'break with the past', given that Labour had been built on working-class union organisation in heavy industries, and not on any coherent socialist theory or analysis. He was convinced that the party's late 1970s problems were the result of union leaders' 'refusal to move with the times'; but its 'long-term survival' was now 'in the balance', since the class-based loyalty of its 'uneducated' voters could no longer be taken for granted. Pimlott was 'in many ways a supporter of New Labour', and he hoped that, once elected, the Blairites might become 'more radical'. But anyone who shared Tressell's socialist aspirations was 'likely to be disappointed'.[17]

RTP was in danger of being absorbed into the heritage industry. That October there was a month-long programme of 'Roots, Radicals and Writing in Sussex', organised by the marketing department of Sussex Arts. Tony Benn spoke on 'Tressell – South Coast Socialism'; and In Toto Theatre Company presented *Mugsborough* at the Stables Theatre, Hastings, sponsored by South-East Arts. Largely ignoring RTP, this 'black physical comedy celebrating the coming centenary of the class war' followed the group's policy of 'presenting complex ideas in their purist, most absurdist form'. In November Trevor Hopper argued in *Tribune* that it was 'the system itself, not individuals, that needs changing', but he took the opportunity to add that his *Robert Tressell's Hastings* was available for £4. It was 'amended and reprinted' in December.

During 1996 academics, Labour politicians and entrepreneurs large and small all claimed 'Tressell' as their own. In May Maire McQueeney organised a tour of 'Robert Tressell's Mugsborough', in collaboration with the WEA, to coincide with a Robert Tressell Memorial Lecture on 'Robert Tressell and the Literature of Commitment'. Speaking on behalf of 'the common reader' and all artists, Terry Eagleton, the Warton Professor of English Literature at the University of Oxford, focused on the book's 'impure realism', rather than on the political commitment to change the 'System' which inspired its socialist author.[18] The booksellers Dillons found that *The Ragged Trousered Philanthropists* was Labour MPs' favourite book. Fred Ball's widow, Jacqueline, was invited by East Sussex County Council's Head of Library Services to unveil an enamel panel commemorating Noonan at Hastings Library. This she did in October; but the dates were wrong, and it had to be re-enamelled.

Dr Gary Day of De Montfort University, Leicester, had been paid £250 by HarperCollins for a new introduction to their Flamingo *RTP*, which was still selling 'a steady eight thousand copies a year'.[19] Day argued that Noonan's philanthropists 'cannot see the truth – because there is none to see'. The truth was that 'there is no single truth', though it was true that the book had 'its roots in the Marxist analysis of society'. However, Marx was out of date: 'the idea that capitalism is not going to be violently overthrown has now been accepted.' For Day, Marxism's 'main tenet' was that 'the economic base of society entirely determines what Marx called the superstructure, that is its social, political and cultural forms'. (As it happens, this idea is not in Marx's writings; but it was often at work in the mechanical materialism which hegemonised the Communist Party.) Day also argued that 'utopia never goes out of fashion'.[20]

In January 1997, 25,000 voters in a Waterstone's 'books of the century' survey put *RTP* in sixty-second place. On 1 May New Labour benefited from a landslide vote against the Tories. Two days later Gary Day gave his Robert Tressell Memorial Lecture, 'Class, Culture and Literary Criticism: The Case of *The Ragged Trousered Philanthropists*'. He was concerned that the Labour election poster, 'Young Offenders Will Be Punished', could 'easily have come from the Tories'. He was outraged that Labour Home Secretary Jack Straw, and his Tory predecessor Michael Howard, both 'rushed to condemn the strike by Essex fire-fighters' against cuts in services. Mimicking Kinnock's anti-Militant rhetoric, Day was scathing about 'the Labour, *yes* Labour, MP' Frank Field's claim that welfare recipients were 'the enemy within'. RTP remained Day's political yardstick: the 'real cause of poverty is the division of society into two classes'; and the rich were getting richer while the poor got poorer. Yet New Labour praised capitalism. Day asked, 'Are you listening Tony Blair?' But he seemed to sense that the answer was no.[21] What were Blairites fighting for? The Murdoch empire's 1997 reprint retailed at £7.99.

All we've got to look forward to, the past?

In September 1997 the Johnsons learned that something called the Robert Tressell Centre had a website under construction. Early in 1998 the new New Labour MP for Hastings invited Trevor Hopper to speak to the local Fabians; and in February Hopper led a day school on 'Robert Tressell and *The Ragged Trousered Philanthropists*' for the University of Sussex. In July he informed the Johnsons that he and 'several others' had met the previous week. The Labour Party were 'allowing us free use of a room at their HQ in Bohemia for a year', and the Labour MP was 'to provide some stationery' with 'a logo of Tressell'. The 'long term aim will be to hold a Tressell festival and to raise funds for a permanent exhibition and home for Tressell's work' plus a 'research and resource centre', where 'we can house what remains of Tresselliana'. He assured them: 'No one will make any money', and 'the centre should be non-political'.

By September 1998 the Robert Tressell Centre website was up and running, courtesy of Labour-controlled Hastings Borough Council. The anonymous home pages argued that RTP's message was that 'working people had to change the capitalist system, of which they were the direct victims', and claimed that the book was 'partly responsible for the original outline of the Welfare state'.[22] However, there was considerable unease about the withering away of reformist gains, the drop in union membership, the collapse of the Communist Party and the arrival of New Labour.

By October Hopper's booklet had sold three hundred copies, and he led a guided walk of 'Robert Tressell's Mugsborough', to fit in with the Robert Tressell Memorial Lecture. 'The Well Trousered Philanthropists: The Future of Utopias', was given by Professor Fred Inglis of Sheffield University, a Fabian of thirty years' standing. He praised the 'benefits' of Sainsbury's, Tesco, John Lewis and Marks & Spencer: 'This is how a virtuous and benignant state in utopia ought to look', since, apparently, 'we all wear M&S underclothes'. He acknowledged that 'free markets are unjust, that capitalism is cruel, and that these things must be opposed and may be overcome'; yet he had no suggestions as to how this might be achieved. Evidently Stalinism and fascism were twins; and Stalinism was to be laid at Lenin's door, and maybe that of Marx. Anyway, the collapse of Russian 'Socialism' meant that the 'power of capital is invulnerable at the moment for any projectible future', while the 'appeal of the Marxist Left to revolution' is somehow both 'inaudible and inane'. Citing the grandfather of postmodernism, Theodor Adorno, Inglis argued that the world cannot be understood as a whole. In common with every other authoritarian liberal he assumed there were no grand narratives except his: 'Utopia will now wear motley.' Sadly, he was not coherently opposed from the floor.[23] This Robert Tressell Memorial Lecture proved to be the last.

By February 1999 the Robert Tressell Centre website was linked to 'Maire McQueeney's Novel Outings'. In May, as 'part of a Council initiative to increase awareness of the town's heritage', the Centre organised a 'Robert Tressell Event', sponsored by the GMB, two other unions, a few Trades Councils and Hastings Borough Council. The Labour mayor of Hastings opened the proceedings. Brighton Labour supporter Dr Hopper conducted a guided trip, and the New Labour MP unveiled a memorial plaque to Robert Noonan at 241 London Road, en route. The principal of Ruskin College, Oxford (Labour) spoke, and a Labour councillor presided over an 'evening of diverse entertainment'. Next day the Labour leader of Hastings Borough Council opened a panel discussion, which included Dr Hopper (Labour) and a Labour MP. A former East Sussex Labour county councillor spoke on 'Robert Tressell, Libraries and Socialism'; and there was an evening drink at The First Inn Last Out, hosted by the landlord, another Labour councillor. On the third day, Dr Clive Griggs, a contributor to Tribune, spoke about George Meek, and Dr Gary Day (Labour) gave a talk. The Labour Cabinet had signed a copy of RTP, and the raffle draw was presided over by the New Labour MP. Subsequently Dr Hopper's booklet was doubled in size, and supported by the GMB.

From January 2000 the Centre began producing a quarterly newsletter. Late in May there was a second 'Robert Tressell Event'. The marketing department of Hastings Borough Council helped with publicity, and Hastings Museum was opened on a Sunday to show the mural fragment and the even more fragmentary 'Fred Ball Archive'. The principal sponsors were the Hastings Branch and Southern Region of the GMB, who also loaned their minibus. The principal speaker was the GMB General Secretary,

John Edmonds. He denounced 'narrow profiteering', and claimed Noonan
would have wished to see capitalist entrepreneurs give 'good value for
money'. Unlike Inglis, he also condemned Marks & Spencer for sacking
European workers so as 'to increase profits by paying poverty wages to
workers in S.E. Asia', and for refusing to pay 'a penny of compensation',
help redundant workers find other work, or support re-training. M&S
'should listen to the wise words of Robert Tressell'.[24] Yet why should
they? After all, Noonan had insisted that the fundamental problem was
not any single capitalist firm but the entire capitalist 'System' and those
who made their peace with it. During 2000 the architect Sam Webb was
busy investigating 'suspect system built tower blocks' in Birmingham,
which had gas supplied in spite of health & safety regulations.[25]

By now Joan Johnson was seriously ill. Such was the respect for her
and her grandfather that John Monks, General Secretary of the TUC, wrote
a kindly letter. She died on 8 October 2000. The obituary in the Hastings
Observer was written by Derek Norcross, a Liberal Democrat. Her death was
mentioned on the Robert Tressell Centre website below the result of the
raffle for a signed copy of RTP. RTC now advertised 'Tressell' badges, a CD
of 'A Brass Band Musical', In the Red (said to be based on the novel),
another of *Songs of Irish Labour*, including 'A tribute to Robert Tressell', and
extracts from RTP for £1. Meanwhile, there was serious talk of raising
£750,000 to make the novel into a film. Lawrence & Wishart were having
difficulty in finding the capital to reprint the hardback edition, and there
was 'a curious legal matter about the paperback rights'.[26] Then Project
Gutenberg put the entire book on the Web, and this seems to have formed
the basis of a machine-read (and completely unlistenable) CD talking
book.

Some Centre website visitors were interested in a reprint of Ball's *One
of the Damned*, though Reg Johnson, representing the estate of Fred Ball and
the family of Robert Noonan, had to complain about the failure to secure
authority for this advertisement.[27] Many visitors stressed that the socialist
appeal of RTP was alive and well in Australia, Belgium, Eire, France,
Germany, Korea and the USA; yet visitors kept coming back to the New
Labour government, and noted that, by Noonan's socialist yardstick, it
had failed comprehensively. Gary Day acknowledged that the society
Noonan described 'sank from view for a short time in Britain from 1945
to 1979', but 'the return to free market economics and the relentless
pursuit of money' make the book 'even more relevant to our under-

standing of the world'. Another visitor believed 'Tressell' would be hor-rified at the betrayal of socialist policies by their local New Labour MP, and felt strongly that somebody should make sure the Cabinet reread RTP to remind them why they joined the Labour Party in the first place.

In 2001 the GMB completely underwrote the third Robert Tressell Event. Extracts from a stage adaptation of The Ragged Trousered Philanthropists, done by Trevor Hopper and Vincent Mahon, showed Philpot with a beer bottle in his pocket before he falls off the ladder. That was their invention, and it revealed a sadly typical New Labour attitude to working-class people. The Labour leader of Hastings Council and the GMB regional secretary acted out the parts of turn-of-the-century SDF members on Hastings beach. They demanded to be heavily heckled, and were, but they failed to con-vince a sceptical audience that New Labour had a political strategy for arriving at a Co-operative Commonwealth, and even tried to dismiss Blair's support for Bush's new imperialism on the grounds that the PM had had 'a bad day'. A reporter thought it was a real political meeting, and, in a way, it was. Many ex-CPers and Labour left-wingers felt, if not yet home-less, then on the edge of eviction. The bookstall, with copies of RTP, was provided by Hastings SWP.

In April 2002 a new German translation of Menschenfreunde by Else Tonke was launched at the Frankfurt Book Fair. In May, Lawrence & Wishart borrowed money to reprint a thousand copies of the hardback.[28] The Flamingo edition was the best-selling book at that year's Unifi conference. HarperCollins are coy about sales, but given the 'steady eight thousand copies a year' they were selling in 1996–97, the forty-three printings from 1965 to 2002 (including those of Panther) could well have averaged 10,000 copies apiece. Penguin kept no records of print runs in the 1940s, but their six printings probably totalled 300,000 copies. At today's paper-back price of £9.99 these combined sales would be worth £7.3 million. As for hardbacks, Lawrence & Wishart's computerised records – the only ones now accessible – show sales of 6,700 from 1987 to 1998.[29] Given they reprinted in 1989, it is likely that their first twelve printings were each of 5,000 copies (as the 1955 edition certainly was), though their 2002 reprint was of only one thousand copies. At today's hardback price of £16.99, 61,000 copies would bring in £1 million. The Richards Press claimed sales of 138,000. Calculated at their last retail price of 12s 6d (52.5p), that represents the equivalent of over £1.2 million today, which tallies with Beeching's 'fairly educated guess' that they made £60,000 profit by 1955.[30] Even without the twenty overseas printings (one of which was probably of 15,000 copies), that represents a grand total of £9.5 million at today's values. The real figure could be much higher.

Kathleen Noonan received £25 and six free copies from Richards in 1914, and another £25 in the early 1920s. She received £25 and a hardback from Lawrence & Wishart in 1967, and three paperbacks from Panther in 1969. Had she got the 10 per cent royalty which James Joyce received from Grant Richards, by the time Richards' copyright ran out she would have received the equivalent of at least £500,000 at today's values, and twice that sum if she had benefited from the profits made by Lawrence & Wishart, Panther, Paladin and Flamingo. Unsurprisingly, Reg Johnson feels the same now as he did in 1967: 'Kathleen was a victim of the system Robert wrote about and the family have paid the price ever since.'[31]

Shaking the optimism of the bourgeois world

Today, John Monks feels that The Ragged Trousered Philanthropists is 'a complete one off, a towering peak rising out of a desert'; but he continues to find it subjectively important:

> It is one man's solitary cry against injustice, but it is a solitary cry which has strengthened the resolve of many, myself included, to do what we can to change the world for the better and to root out the modern equivalents of the inequality against which he rages so eloquently.[32]

John Edmonds is proud that 'we now have a Robert Tressell Festival each year',[33] and though it failed to take place in 2002 he knows better than most that with Private Finance Initiatives, Public–Private Partnerships and attacks on firefighters it is hard for anyone who claims to be a socialist to support New Labour on its pro-capitalist road. A socialist novel finished in 1910 remains politically influential in the twenty-first century because, as Rita McLoughlin, a GMB shop steward in Manchester, argues, it 'relates to working class lives, any time and any place'. This is why her millworker father read it to her when she was a child, and why it continues to inspire trade union and socialist activists today. Ironically, Marxist intellectuals have generally ignored or patronised the book, but not all of them.

Friedrich Engels was not a professional literary critic, and his taste in novels has recently been very properly criticised.[34] Nevertheless he made several useful theoretical points when he argued that

the novel of socialist tendency wholly fulfils its mission if, by providing a
faithful account of actual conditions, it destroys the prevailing conventional
illusions on the subject, shakes the optimism of the bourgeois world, and
inexorably calls in question the permanent validity of things as they are,
even though it may not proffer a solution or, indeed, in certain circumstances, appear to take sides.

To do this, socialist novels should be 'realistic', and give a 'truthful repro-
duction of typical characters under typical circumstances' by 'conscien-
tiously describing the real mutual relations' in capitalist society.[35] Tressell's
novel does all of that, and more.

In 1989 Ian Birchall argued (as had Raymond Williams) that Noonan's
descriptions of workers being exploited at the point of production could
not fit into the form of 'classic realism'. Moreover, RTP was unable to
cope with all of working-class history, so that is why Owen, like Kafka's
K., was a man virtually without a past. Neither could it deal with the
future, because 'moving into the realms of speculative Utopia' would, by
definition, involve moving away from the real. Consequently, whereas the
traditional realist novel tends to have characters, a plot and some form of
narrative closure, Noonan's realism breaks with those conventions. However, RTP also has a dialectical character, and (potentially) politically clari-
fying effects, because it underlines the lack of fit between bourgeois
ideology and workers' experience of capitalist social relations. So it is a
one-off, but Birchall agrees with Jack Beeching (and so disagrees with
Jack Mitchell) that it should be seen not as Stalinist 'Socialist Realism', but
as a foundation text of 'proletarian modernism'.[36]

Birchall's ideas are interesting, but they do not account for all of the
book's peculiarities. Beeching pointed out that Mugsborough is isolated,
even from the sea; David Craig noted that the bourgeois figures are stereo-
types; and Eileen Yeo stressed that women are necessarily sidelined by the
book's focus on men's work. Added to that, most of the planet is ignored,
working-class history is virtually abolished, and the trade-union, socialist
and suffragette traditions are marginalised or left unrecorded. Realistically, Mugsborough workers are split into the hopeless, the intermittently
hopeful and an ambivalent majority, yet Mugsborough time repeats itself,
and bourgeois power seems all-pervasive and unalterable.

As we have seen, RTP's narrative voice offers to articulate the inner
thoughts of Mugsborough workers, and sometimes functions as a pessimistic inner dialogue between Owen's socialist ambitions and his varying
levels of confidence. Early on, we are told, he sits listening to a 'pitiable

farrago with feelings of contempt and wonder', and asks: 'Were they all hopelessly stupid? Had their intelligence never developed beyond the childhood stage? Or was he himself mad?' (25). In the middle of the book he focuses on the 'great barriers and ramparts of invincible igno-rance, apathy and self-contempt' (396). Realistically, Owen and Barrington go through ideological struggles with workmates. In the process they demonstrate how bourgeois ideas are knitted together inside workers' heads, and, on bad days, inside socialist activists' heads, too. Owen tries to separate key arguments and nail them down, but very often either he is interrupted – and he is always being interrupted – or his big ideas slither back into a hopeless muddle. But for all that, the narrative voice ends by proclaiming 'The Golden Light that will be diffused throughout all the happy world from the rays of the risen sun of Socialism' (630). So how do we get from pessimism to optimism?

In the 1920s the Russian literary theorist Valentin Vološinov argued that some forms of written 'inner speech' – especially what he called 'quasi-direct discourse', that ambiguous mixture of narrative and reported speech – are literary devices for representing *class struggle in the head*.[37] In RTP, that includes the reader's head, too. But the narrative voice leaves open whether we should identify with the vacillations of Owen's 'inner speech', his reported utterances and Mugsborough workers' differing reactions, or with his activity. It also mimics the hopes, thoughts, anxieties, frustra-tions and, yes, fantasies, like the exploding Rev. Belcher, which pass through socialist activists' heads, especially during a hard argument, and above all during political downturns. What could be more *realistic* than that? So RTP is a dialogue with us, its readers, about faith in the working class as an agency of socialist transformation and, therefore, about the possibility of hope.

Of course, *The Ragged Trousered Philanthropists* is not a magic wand. TUC-sponsored shop stewards' courses continue to act out 'The Great Money Trick'.[38] But what fully socialist strategy has the TUC ever advocated? Irish political prisoners in the Maze were impressed with Noonan's book. But what irreversible movement towards socialism has revolutionary national-ism ever achieved? In the early 1980s the South African Allied Workers' Union and Federation of South African Trade Unions used RTP as part of union educationals.[39] But does the Soweto housing problem show any signs of being solved? And as for New Labour, like Lenin's corpse under Stalinism, Noonan's socialism has been politically embalmed. Meanwhile, the capitalist 'System' which Noonan wanted smashed still exists world-wide, and is wreaking its customary bloody havoc as I write, and, no doubt, as you read.

Many socialists have learned from the past, and do not wish to repeat others' mistakes, but that involves breaking through what Stephen Lowe called a 'ceiling of consciousness', as I discovered when my own politically optimistic view of RTP was tested at the SWP's 'Marxism Ninety Eight'. All but two or three of the hundred or so people who turned up early that Sunday morning had read the book, and I confidently expected to be taken to task for daring to criticise a working-class icon. Yet the discussion was very comradely. One speaker had been tested by a next-door neighbour, to check he was clear that the cesspit above 'The Cave' was capitalism, and that Bert's rest on the way uphill symbolised a pause workers had to take in the struggle for socialism. Another found the book a brilliant way of 'lifting a veil' from the 'System', and therefore a useful 'stepping-stone' for workmates on their way to Lenin's *State and Revolution*. One by one, speakers reluctantly agreed about the downside of RTP. It made them angry, or allowed their anger to surface, but they had serious qualms about it how it let the employers off the hook, while it 'never hesitated to stick it to the workers'.

The most telling story came from a militant who used to work in a Merseyside textile factory. Around 1980 he had been 'agitating' at a union meeting. Afterwards the convenor gave him a copy of RTP, saying, 'Here you are, that'll sort you out'; 'any questions on the book, please come to me, I am the foremost authority'. The book made the young activist so angry that by 1981 he had become union chairman. But then the management threatened to close the factory:

> We had to take a stand. And I can remember chairing a meeting of two thousand people, very angry, wanting to tear the heads off the employers … We were waiting for the convenor to come along and address this meeting. He was the guy who was going along, telling us, 'This is the way forward. Read this book'.

At this point the chair was handed two pieces of paper. One said: 'Sorry, the convenor can't make the meeting tonight, since he is doing a talk on *The Ragged Trousered Philanthropists* in Manchester'. Previously, the convenor had been telling the threatened, angry workers to put complete reliance in Tony Benn's campaign for the deputy leadership of the Labour Party. To the militant chairman it felt like being told: 'Just put your cross on a piece of paper. Leave it to us. There's nothing you can do.' So he had to choose, whether to read part of The Ragged Trousered Philanthropists, or the other paper, 'which related to the struggle, and which moved the struggle forward' – which said 'Yes, we need to fight, but we don't want to go along the road where people like [the convenor] are going to leave and sell you out'. He read out the paper from the comrades in the SWP.[40]

Over twenty years later, and for the first time in British history, we have three large pro-capitalist parliamentary parties. As I write, Labour Cabinet ministers who recently gave themselves a 40 per cent rise are still trying to smear firefighters, who risk their lives, for a similar increase to their much lower wages. That veteran seafaring militant of 1966, deputy Prime Minster John ('Two Jags') Prescott, gets four times as much as firefighters, but, as activists in the Fire Brigades Union point out, he and Blair have no qualms about spending billions of pounds on helping President Bush kill innocent civilians in Iraq. At home, for all Mark Fisher's rhetoric, the Health and Safety Executive failed to investigate over 3,500 construction site 'accidents' in 2000–01, and the overall number of inspections has fallen by 43 per cent since New Labour came to office. As for David Blunkett's 1988 proposal to put The Ragged Trousered Philanthropists on the National Curriculum, that was quietly forgotten when he became Minister of Education.

Getting all our own back

Ricky Tomlinson seems to have drawn his own conclusions. He gave The Ragged Trousered Philanthropists a hearty plug on ITV's Stars and Their Lives, and he repeatedly recommends the 'best ever book' in newspaper interviews. He also supported both the Socialist Alliance and the Socialist Labour Party in the 2001 general election. The Hansard Society's research shows that turnout was down to 59 per cent, the lowest figure since 1918, when a hundred candidates stood unopposed. The younger you were, the less likely you were to vote. The main reason for abstention (as Noonan understood) was that the main parties were pro-capitalist. This is why the author of The Ragged Trousered Philanthropists did not join Ramsay MacDonald's Labour Party, but the 'Marxist' SDF. His model for Philpot, Dan Pankhurst, reportedly joined its successor, the SDP.[41] Neither Owen nor Barrington was politically sectarian, and they were close to the cutting edge of British socialism by 1910 standards. In 'The Great Money Trick' Barrington engaged with

Marxism. Jack Beeching recalled that in the 1920s the boy who some think was partly the model for young 'Bert' signed up with the CPGB.

However, as we have seen, the CP, the ILP and the various Labour Lefts ran into the sand because they opted for a strategy of trying to deliver socialist reforms from above, within the constraints of the capitalist 'System', rather than struggling to win irreversible democratic control from below. This fundamental choice is built into RTP. Is socialism something which can be legislated into existence; or is it the case, as Marx insisted, that 'the emancipation of the working classes must be conquered by the working classes themselves'?[42] The key argument, R.H. Tawney noted in the 1930s, is about the state: 'Onions can be eaten leaf by leaf, but you cannot skin a live tiger paw by paw; vivisection is its trade, and it does the skinning first.'[43] Those of us who experienced the attentions of the British state during the Great Strike of the British miners, or of the Italian state in Genoa more recently, understand that we are not dealing with an onion. True, Barrington's perspective of sending revolutionaries to parliament has not really been tried in Britain, except for a few individual exceptions, but it was tested in Chile in the early 1970s, and tens of thousands of workers paid with their lives to warn us against putting all our faith in that strategy.

As ever, we have to decide whether, in the words of the current Flamingo blurb, Noonan is to be marginalised as 'a journeyman-prophet with a vision of a just society', and his writing excavated as 'a complete and living archaeology of the speech of a particular human group', or whether his socialist ideas need to be put to work to 'rouse his fellow men from their political quietism', and women too. Clearly, we must not repeat the SDF's determinism, abstentionism and sectarian mistakes. Neither must we, like so many Communists, give unthinking loyalty to leaders wholly unequipped to do any genuinely Marxist analysis. Moreover, it is no use laughing, crying and feeling smug and superior, like Owen. Fighting the class struggle in our heads, and blaming other workers on building sites, in call centres or in schools, simply makes no difference. The 'System' remains unchallenged, and the 'Idlers' continue to win. What we need is a clear strategy for getting *all* of our own back.

The choice between the two souls of socialism — reform and revolution — is a key reason for RTP's continued appeal. However much they pay lip service to him and his book, that is what separates the unprincipled opportunism of the Ramsay MacDonalds, Ramsay McKinnocks and especially the Ramsay McBlairs (if that is not too unfair on MacDonald) from Noonan's socialism. Of course, it would be nice if there were short cuts to the Co-operative Commonwealth; and in periods of defeat and quiescence reformist ideas can be persuasive. On a bad day, the working class can seem 'congenitally stupid, corrupt, apathetic and generally hopeless', and, however reluctantly, demoralised socialists can be pulled by the idea that 'change must come from "superior" people'.[44] Realistically, that corrosive, elitist and authoritarian Fabian, New Labour (and ex-Stalinist) despair sometimes appears in Noonan's book, and it seemed to fit Britain in 1914 and 1927, Germany in 1925–31, and Britain again in 1985. But it is vital to recall that as RTP was being finished the Great Unrest was getting under way, that the effects of the betrayal of the General Strike did not last for ever, that the Nazis were beaten in World War II and in the later 1970s in Britain, and that they will be beaten again. The miners' Great Strike prevented Thatcher transferring £8 billion to the 'Idlers', and the massive rejection of the poll tax helped to finish her off.

Today, for the first time in years, socialists have the opportunity to work with hundreds of thousands of other anti-capitalists who have demonstrated at Seattle, Prague, Nice, Genoa, Brussels, Rome, Barcelona, Seville, London and Florence, and will continue to do so elsewhere.[45] Whether Noonan's anti-capitalist politics lead to the Co-operative Commonwealth depends on where we put our talents and our energies. It will need optimism, willpower and socialist ideas, but first it will require a ruthless critique of the pessimistic aspects of Noonanism, and a form of organisation quite different to the sectarian Social-Democratic Federation, the Parliamentary Labour Party,[46] the Communist Party,[47] or the Stalinist Comintern.[48]

Should we send revolutionaries to parliament? Yes, of course. But they should treat it like the 'dunghill' Lenin knew it to be. Should we not honour Robert Noonan? Absolutely. But it is high time we stopped uncritical ancestor-worship. Have we modern-day Owens and Barringtons suffered? Of course we have. But we must stop being proud of strings of glorious (and supposedly inevitable) defeats, and forget silly squabbles and self-defeating sectarianism. What we have to do is to put the optimistic elements of Noonan's socialist perspective into practice, building on the last century's experience and avoiding all the known dead ends. As Ian Birchall argued in 1989, the real resolution to The Ragged Trousered Philanthropists can take place only outside the novel.[49] And as Noonan was beginning to understand in 1910, the Co-operative Commonwealth can come about only by changing the capitalist 'System' irreversibly.

Notes

Introduction

1. Ian Birchall, personal communication.
2. WEA 1982: 21.
3. Reg Johnson and Jacqueline Slocombe, personal communication.

Chapter 1

1. Ball 1973: 7.
2. Ward n.d. Unreferenced Ward quotations derive from this letter.
3. Irish Chief Secretary's Office Registered Papers, National Archives, Dublin, courtesy of Jim Herlihy.
4. Ball 1967: 180, 182.
5. Ball 1967: 180 82.
6. Ball 1973: 5.
7. Callan 1997: 121.
8. Ball 1973: 5, 6.
9. NASA Cape Town, CSC 2/1/1/336 no.30, courtesy of Jonathan Hyslop.
10. NASA Cape Town, CSC 2/1/1/336 no.30, and NASA Pretoria, Thomas Lindenbaum's Death Notice, 30 November 1937, courtesy of Jonathan Hyslop.
11. Ball 1973: 13.
12. Anon 1960; Ball 1973: 16.
13. Ogilvy 1945; Ball 1973: 16, 17.
14. NASA Pretoria, WLD 5/45 617/1904

and WLD Illiquid Case 14/1905, courtesy of Jonathan Hyslop.
15. Hyslop 2001: 75, 77.
16. Ogilvy 1945; Ball 1973: 16.
17. McCracken 1999: 23, 25–8, 36, 37.
18. Anon 1960.
19. Ball 1951: 24.
20. McCracken 1999: 19.
21. Donal McCracken, personal communication.
22. Jonathan Hyslop, personal communication.
23. Ball 1951: 27, 34.
24. Pakenham 1988: 116.
25. Ball 1951: 34.
26. Douglass 1968: 262.
27. Reference courtesy of Reg Johnson.
28. Walsh 1922: 9.
29. Ball 1973: 30.
30. Douglass 1968: 261.
31. Ball 1951: 39.
32. Walsh 1922: 9.
33. Carlyle 1932: 151, 152.
34. WEA 1982: 56.
35. Ball 1973: 32–3, 71, 114.
36. Walsh 1922: 9.
37. Ball 1973: 37, 39.
38. Ball 1973: 64–6.
39. Postgate 1923: 390.
40. Tressall 1927: Foreword.
41. University of Warwick Modern Records Centre, NASOHSPD 2/1/1.

42. NASA Pretoria, WLD Illiquid Case 14/ 1905, courtesy of Jonathan Hyslop
43. Mitchell and Pritchard 1913: 14.
44. Ball 1973: 63.
45. Anon 1988: 21; Ball 1973: 54.
46. Ball 1951: 48.
47. Ball 1951: 42, 44, 51; Ball 1973: 62.
48. Ball 1973: 68, 100.
49. Ball 1951: 19.
50. Walsh 1922: 9.
51. Ball 1973: 81.

Chapter 2

1. Hyndman 1911: 192, 205.
2. Marx 1986: 113.
3. Marx and Engels, MECW 47: 245.
4. Thompson 1988: 366, 379, 410.
5. MECW 48: 246, 252.
6. See Charlton 1999.
7. Thorne 1989: 63, 76.
8. Thompson 1951: 109, 134.
9. Blatchford 1908: 127–8, 243–6.
10. Engels and Lafargue n.d.: 339.
11. Dutt 1963: 122–3.
12. Lansbury 1931: 77, 79.
13. Thompson 1951: 130.
14. Meek 1910: 1, 3, 21–2, 34, 62, 112–13, 139, 161, 169, 172–3, 178, 180, 196, 228, 256–60.
15. Matthews 1991: 33.
16. Meek 1910: 260.
17. Ball 1973: 82–3.
18. Thomson 1951: 150–51, 155–7.
19. Thompson 1951: 150–62.
20. Ball 1973: 84–5.
21. Blatchford 1902: 43, 75–6, 98, 100, 171–2.
22. Tsuzuki 1961: 128.
23. Jackson 1953: 67–8.
24. Challinor 1977: 9.
25. Challinor 1977: 15.
26. Milton 1973: 20.
27. Budgen 1970: 83–5.
28. Macintyre 1980: 207.
29. Challinor 1977: 12, 14.
30. Macintyre 1980: 18.
31. Woodhouse and Pearce 1975: 23.
32. Tsuzuki 1961: 154.
33. Rose 2001: 42, 131, 305.
34. Blatchford 1914: 252, 269.

35. Campbell 1981: 16.
36. Jackson 1953: 54–6.
37. Hopper 1995: 4, 10–11, 16; Hopper 1999: 9–11
38. Ball 1973: 84–5.
39. Hopper 1999: 12, 36.
40. Matthews 1991: 18–19.
41. NDL membership card, Hastings Museum.
42. Meek 1910: 261.
43. Coxall and Griggs 1996: 114, 116.
44. Meek 1910: 261–2.
45. Matthews 1991: 20.
46. Coxall and Griggs 1996: 117.
47. Meek 1910: 261–3.
48. Coxall and Griggs 1996: 121.
49. Matthews 1991: 1–4, 18–20, 26.
50. Ball 1973: 85.
51. Connole 1961: 12.
52. Ball 1951: 68.
53. Matthews 1991: 22.

Chapter 3

1. Hopper 1999: 13.
2. Ball 1973: 85.
3. Coxall and Griggs 1996: 122.
4. Matthews 1991: 28–9.
5. Milton 1973: 31, 34.
6. Matthews 1991: 5, 8.
7. Matthews 1991: 22–4.
8. Hopper 1999: 32–3.
9. Matthews 1991: 29, 38.
10. Ball 1973: 90–92, 112; Ball 1951: 63.
11. Matthews 1991: 31–2.
12. Meek 1910: 263–5, 267.
13. Coxall and Griggs 1996: 145, 171.
14. Thompson 1910: 16, 19, 22.
15. Coxall and Griggs 1996: 130, 148–9.
16. Matthews 1991: 34–6.
17. Ball 1951: 52–4, 71–2.
18. Coxall and Griggs 1996: 159.
19. Meek 1910: 280.
20. Coxall and Griggs 1996: 123, 433–4.
21. Challinor 1977: 51.
22. Quelch 1912: 13, 15.
23. Matthews 1991: 13.
24. Hopper 1999: 39.
25. Hopper 1999: 38.
26. Matthews 1991: 15, 33.
27. Matthews 1991: 35–6, 38–40.

28. Ball 1973: 88–9, 115.
29. Ball 1951: 40–41.
30. Ball 1973: 101, 111.
31. Gower 1926.
32. Ball 1951: 69.
33. Ball 1951: 78.
34. Ball 1973: 113.
35. Poynton 1936.
36. Ball 1951: 39, 43, 174.
37. Ball 1973: 187.
38. Poynton 1936.
39. Blatchford 1908: 140.
40. Tsuzuki 1961: 205.
41. Matthews 1991: 42–3.
42. Ball 1951: 78; Ball 1973: 72–3.
43. Hopper 1999: 17.
44. Matthews 1991: 41, 45–9.
45. Ball 1973: 111.
46. Matthews 1991: 15–16.
47. Hastings CP 1982: 7.
48. Matthews 1991: 51–3, 56; Ball 1951: 71.
49. Smith 1978: 8, 28, 29, 34.
50. Douglass 1968: 263.
51. F.L. 1926: 99.
52. Matthews 1991: 58–61, 65.
53. Hopper 1999: 40.
54. Matthews 1991: 76–82.
55. Ball 1973: 110, 141.
56. Poynton 1936.
57. Blackman 1967.
58. Ball 1951: 82; Ball 1973: 141, 150–52.
59. Coxall 1992: 23, 27.
60. Ball 1973: 143.
61. Coxall 1992: 27; Coxall and Griggs 1996: 205, 248.
62. Ball 1973: 143.
63. Poynton 1936.
64. Ball 1973: 147.
65. Walsh 1922: 10.
66. Poynton 1936.
67. Matthews 1991: 12–13.
68. Ball 1973: 30.
69. Gower 1926.
70. Mitchell 1969: 13.
71. Ball 1973: 229–30.
72. Ball 1973: 157.
73. Bower 1936: 193.
74. Alfred 1988: 15.
75. Gower 1926.
76. F.L. 1926: 99.
77. Ball 1973: 160–1, 253–4.
78. Gower 1926.
79. Bower 1936: 193.

Chapter 4

1. Page numbers refer to the Lawrence & Wishart edition of RTP.
2. I owe this point to Reg Johnson.
3. Klaus 1982: 72.
4. Salter 1971: 10.
5. Ball 1973: 100.
6. Matthews 1991: 24.
7. Salter 1971: 14.
8. Hobsbawm and Rudé 1970: 106, 109, 215.
9. See O'Brien 1995.
10. See Charlton 1999.
11. Matthews 1991: 4.
12. Eagleton and Pierce 1979: 82.
13. Alfred 1988: 84.
14. Gauldie 1974: 100.
15. Ball 1951: 166–9.
16. Matthews 1991: 81.
17. Mann 1967: 93.
18. See Siegel 1989.
19. Hopper 1999: 42.
20. Matthews 1991: Preface, 86.
21. Matthews 1991: 11.
22. Hopper 1999: 34.
23. Ball 1951: 159–60.
24. Matthews 1991: 11.
25. Poynton 1936.
26. Poynton 1936.
27. Wicks 1992: 5.
28. Ball 1951: 85.
29. Anon 1960.
30. Ball 1973: 16.
31. Ball 1973: 50; Ogilvy 1945.
32. Matthews 1991: 12–13.
33. Cf Klaus and Knight 2000: 71–83.
34. Ball 1973: 121, 122.
35. Blatchford 1931: xiii, 222, 225.
36. Thompson 1951: 229.
37. Bolton 1968: 104.
38. Bellamy and Saville 1987: 200.
39. WEA 1982: 39.
40. Bolton 1968: 122.
41. Hyndman 1911: 397.
42. Bellamy n.d.: 39, 45, 184, 208.

43. Thompson 1910: 62, 81, 98.
44. Hopper 1999: 35.
45. Thompson 1910: 96.
46. Alfred 1988: 27.
47. Gower 1926.
48. Bolton 1968: 157.
49. Thompson 1910: 107–9.

Chapter 5

1. Meacham 1977: 206.
2. Tsuzuki 1991: 150
3. McShane 1978: 38.
4. Milton 1973: 64.
5. Connole 1961: 68.
6. McShane 1978: 47.
7. Meek 1910: 280–1, 290–91.
8. Matthews 1991: 89, 91, 102, 108.
9. Anon 1912.
10. Coxall and Griggs 1996: 301, 306–9.
11. Coxall and Griggs 1996: 313, 315.
12. Matthews 1991: 89, 91, 102, 108, 123.
13. Ron Clarke, personal communication.
14. Wicks 1992: 41.
15. Tressall 1914: Preface.
16. Swinnerton 1956: 7.
17. Richards 1960: 66, 81, 104, 108; Richards 1932: 132.
18. Richards 1960: 52.
19. Richards 1960: 222–3.
20. ALA.
21. Swinnerton 1956: 8.
22. Scholes 1963: 154.
23. Swinnerton 1956: 8.
24. Swinnerton 1937: 78.
25. Richards 1960: xiv.
26. Tressall 1914: Preface.
27. Ball 1957: 5.
28. Swinnerton 1956: 8, 17–18.
29. Ball 1973: 167.
30. Mike Smith-Rawnsley, personal communication.
31. Swinnerton 1956: 10–11.
32. Reference courtesy of Mike Smith-Rawnsley.
33. Richards 1960: 223.
34. Richards 1960: 109–10, 223.
35. Swinnerton 1956: 18.
36. Young 1985: 288.
37. Richards 1960: 223.
38. Scholes 1963: 158.

39. Swinnerton 1956: 19.
40. Ball 1973: 187.
41. Alan Burgess, personal communication.
42. Charley Hall, personal communication.
43. Moss 1979: 21, 22.
44. Craik 1964: 99.
45. Lee 1981: 28–9; Hollis 1997: 9.
46. Samuel 1985: 78–9.
47. Fagan n.d.: 45–6.

Chapter 6

1. Richards 1960: 223.
2. Postgate 1923: 391.
3. Ball 1973: 179–80.
4. Pope 1915: 11.
5. Bebbington 1972: 87.
6. Day Lewis 1971: 55.
7. Richards 1960: 220, 221.
8. Ball 1973: 181.
9. Ball 1973: 180.
10. Ball 1973: 181.
11. Richards 1960: 223.
12. Gollancz 1953: 297.
13. Postgate 1923: 391.
14. Rose 2001: 190–5.
15. Richards 1960: 223.
16. Ball 1973: xiii.
17. Murphy 1972: 170.
18. Coxall and Griggs 1996: 214, 216–17, 317, 320, 323, 326, 334.
19. Tillett 1931: 267; Schneer 1982: 187.
20. Matthews 1991: 123–6.
21. Kendall 1969: 168.
22. Milton 1973: 180.
23. Haynes 1984: 104.
24. Macintyre 1980: 205.
25. Kendall 1969: 189.
26. See Rosenberg 1987.
27. Murphy 1942: 83.
28. McShane 1978: 107.
29. Gallacher 1940: 226.
30. Bell 1937: 46.
31. Gallacher 1940: 220, 221.
32. Macfarlane 1980: 195.
33. Bush 1984: 98.
34. Lansbury 1925: 73–4, 122–3.
35. Morgan 1987: 77, 85.
36. Darlington 1998: 51, 54.

37. Jackson n.d.: 135.
38. Hannington 1967: 66–7.
39. Bevan 1952: 20–21.
40. Davies 1992: 101.
41. Gallacher and Campbell 1972: 27, 30.
42. Pollitt 1940: 112, 123, 124–5.
43. Stewart 1967: 89.
44. Bell 1941: 187.
45. Kendall 1969: 193.
46. Smillie 1924: 278.
47. Thompson 1992: 39.
48. Murphy 1972: 166.
49. Dewar 1976: 35.
50. Stewart 1967: 102.
51. McShane 1978: 128.
52. Trotsky 1974: 3: 123.
53. Lenin 1980: 431.
54. Thompson 1951: 227, 232.
55. Coxall and Griggs 1996: 327, 363.
56. Coxall and Griggs 1996: 400, 456–8.
57. Tsuzuki 1961: 239, 240.
58. Ball 1951: 66.
59. Matthews 1991: 131–5, 139.
60. Gollancz 1953: 296.
61. Meynell 1971: 127.
62. Wicks 1992: 37.
63. Walsh 1922: 4, 5, 8, 10.
64. Postgate 1923: xiv, xvii, xx, 450.
65. Ball 1973: 257.
66. F.L. 1926: 94–5, 99, 102, 105–7.
67. Macintyre 1980: 175.
68. Eastman 1925: 26, 82–3, 92, 98.
69. Thorpe 2000: 786.
70. Trotsky 1974: 1: 18, 179.
71. Trotsky 1987: 23.
72. Eastman 1925: 123.
73. Eastman 1925: 100, 106.
74. Cliff 1991: 95–6.
75. Darlington 1998: 117.

Chapter 7

1. Woodhouse and Pearce 1975: 93.
2. Lansbury 1931: 196.
3. Klugmann 1976: 65.
4. Trotsky 1974: 2: 119.
5. Horrabin 1927: 40–41.
6. Turner 1930: 314.
7. Woodhouse and Pearce 1975: 144.
8. Woodhouse and Pearce 1975: 151.
9. Klugmann 1976: 322.
10. Hallas and Harman 1986: 17.
11. CPGB 1926: 6, 7, 14.
12. Cox n.d.: 24.
13. Richards 1960: xvii.
14. Richards 1960: xvi; Brockman 1991: 278.
15. Tressall 1927: Foreword.
16. Cliff and Gluckstein 1986: 283.
17. Charley Hall, personal communication.
18. CPGB 1927: [2], 102.
19. Translation courtesy of Mary Phillips.
20. Samuel et al. 1985: 83.
21. Mitchell 1969: 1.
22. Kemp-Ashraf and Mitchell 1966: 155.
23. Kemp-Ashraf and Mitchell 1966: 155.
24. Ball 1973: 215.
25. Samuel et al. 1985: 82–4.
26. Kemp-Ashraf and Mitchell 1966: 155–6.
27. Kemp-Ashraf and Mitchell 1966: 155.
28. Samuel et al. 1985: 83, 84.
29. Thomas 1928: 61, 63.
30. Salford 1948: 242.
31. Kemp-Ashraf and Mitchell 1966: 155–6.
32. Thomas 1928: [2].
33. Ball 1973: 215.
34. Reference courtesy of Dave Cope.
35. Samuel et al. 1985: 87.
36. Fox 1928: 85.
37. Darlington 1998: 157–8.
38. Hinton and Hyman 1975: 47.
39. McShane 1978: 160–1, 246.
40. CPGB 1929: 5, 8.
41. Davies 1987: 165.
42. Morgan 1994: 72.
43. Wicks 1992: 139.
44. Groves 1974: 7, 22.
45. Edwards 1930: 2, 67, 68, 70, 72, 75.
46. Bradby 1980: 219.
47. Worley 2000: 79.
48. Lansbury 1931: 8, 13.
49. Goorney and MacColl 1986: xix.
50. Bradby 1980: 219.
51. Frow 1993: 67–8.
52. Gloversmith 1980: 254.
53. Jones 1974: 272.
54. Jones 1974: 272.
55. Bradby 1980: 221.

56. Jones 1986: 22
57. RTMC 1977.
58. Jones 1986: 24, 48–9; Jones 1984: 3.
59. Morgan 1987: 194.
60. Horner 1960: 63.
61. Lee 1981: 103–9.
62. Sloan 1978: 55.
63. Groves 1974: 45–7, 52.
64. Fagan n.d.: 83–6, 91.
65. CPGB 1933: 5, 22, 34, 39, 42, 73, 80.
66. Postgate 1934: 182.
67. Richards 1960: 228.
68. Richards 1932: 37.
69. Samuel et al. 1985: 93.
70. Jones 1974: 274.
71. Tuckett n.d.: 5.
72. Samuel 1986: 77.
73. Jones 1974: 278.
74. Clark 1979: 262–5.
75. Charley Hall, personal communication.

Chapter 8

1. Campbell 1981: 118, 132, 140–67.
2. Callaghan 1993: 280.
3. Wood 1959: 39.
4. Trotsky 1974: 3: 29.
5. Gollancz 1968: 42.
6. Haynes 2002: 120–22.
7. CPGB 1937: 6, 8.
8. Samuel 1986: 77.
9. Gloversmith 1980: 251.
10. Jones 1974: 271.
11. Thomas 1936: 26, 72–3, 85, 89.
12. Bower 1936: 193.
13. Unreferenced material about Ball comes from his published work, plus Blackman 1967, Hastings CP 1982, WEA 1982, Alfred 1988 and cuttings in Hastings Museum and RTFP.
14. Thompson 1992: 15.
15. Thorpe 2000: 786.
16. Cockburn 1959: 49.
17. Copeman 1948: 166, 167.
18. Beckett 1995: 130, 143.
19. Uttley 1940: 218–19. Cf Cliff 1996.
20. Samuel 1987: 81.
21. Rose 2001: 252.
22. CPGB 1938: 3, 9–10, 12, 14.

23. Dash 1969: 36.
24. Anon 1977.
25. CPGB 1938: 25.
26. Heffer 1991: 16–17, 22.
27. Williams 1956: 22, 55.
28. ALA.
29. Williams 1956: 31, 58; Donald Muir, personal communication.; Russell Edwards, personal communication.
30. Crick 1982: 221.
31. Orwell 1984: 54–8, 60; see Trotsky 1991.
32. Brophy 1942: 31.
33. Higgins 1965: 158.
34. McShane 1978: 235, 236.
35. Heffer 1991: 26.
36. Sommerfield 1955.
37. Williams 1956: 44.
38. Ogilvy 1945.
39. Anon 1943: 18–19.
40. Rose 2001: 231, 233–4.
41. Pimlott 1986: 186.
42. Gollancz 1952: 146.
43. Callaghan 1993: 212.
44. Charley Hall, personal communication.
45. Trory 1945: 18.
46. Jones 1987: 79.
47. Heffer 1991: 33.
48. Sillitoe 1975: 145.
49. Sillitoe 1959.
50. Tressell 1965: 7.

Chapter 9

1. Thompson 1992: 62.
2. Woodhouse and Pearce 1975: 235, 239.
3. Thompson 1992: 109, 215.
4. NCC 1/1; Croft 1994: 6–7.
5. Thompson 1979: xxvi.
6. Morgan 1994: 142.
7. Croft 1994: 3–4.
8. Callaghan 1993: 239.
9. NCC 1/1.
10. Callaghan 1993: 185.
11. Croft 1998: 152; Croft 1995: 30.
12. Thompson 1979: xxvi.
13. Hobday 1989: 242–3.
14. NCC 1/1.
15. Pollitt 1947: 6, 10, 24, 67, 72, 75,

83, 85, 90, 100.
16. McShane 1978: 240–41.
17. Branson 1997: 172.
18. Zhdanov 1950: 62.
19. Behan 1990: 293.
20. Ball 1973: 215.
21. Rowbotham n.d.: Foreword.
22. Swinnerton 1956: 20, 21.
23. Ball 1951: 102–4.
24. Ball 1973: 191–3.
25. Ball 1973: 194–5.
26. Brockman 1991: 279.
27. Richards 1960: 228.
28. Ball 1973: 201.
29. Ball 1973: 186.
30. Fox 1948: 12–13, 16.
31. Ball 1973: 195–6.
32. Fyrth 1993: 66.
33. Croft 1998: 159.
34. NCC1/1.
35. CP 1951: 3–6, 10, 13, 14, 17, 18.
36. Thompson 1979: xxvi, xxvii; Thompson 1977: 234, 270, 273.
37. Ball 1973: 196–7.
38. Kenneth Price, personal communication.
39. Gorman 1995: 198, 211.
40. Jackson 1950: 10.
41. Ball 1951: 7, 8, 15, 72–4, 84, 196, 210, 215, 217–18.
42. Fyrth 1993: 264.
43. NCC 3/6.
44. Margolies and Joannou 1995: 198.
45. McShane 1978: 251.
46. Beckett 1995: 125.
47. NCC 3/6.
48. Harold Smith, personal communication.

Chapter 10

1. Ball 1973: 198, 215–16.
2. Kettle 1969: 61.
3. Anon 1953: [3], 45, 49, 66.
4. Ball 1973: 202.
5. WEA 1982: 21.
6. Ball 1957: 5–8.
7. Ball 1958: 8.
8. Clunie 1954: 94, 95.
9. Ball 1973: 202–3.
10. Copy courtesy of Dave Cope.

11. Dave Cope, personal communication.
12. Ball 1957: 4.
13. Tressell 1955: 5–6.
14. Sommerfield 1955.
15. Jones 1987: 119.
16. Ball 1973: 203.
17. Miliband and Saville 1976: 24–6.
18. Miliband and Saville 1976: 45.
19. Beckett 1995: 131.
20. Miliband and Saville 1976: 85.
21. Ball 1973: 217.
22. Swinnerton 1956: 27.
23. Lindsay 1956: 233.
24. Fryer 1956: 7, 9–10, 20, 26–7, 33, 79, 80, 87, 91, 93, 96.
25. Gorman 1995: 250, 254.
26. Miliband and Saville 1976: 48.
27. Cohen 1997: 111, 113.
28. Ball 1957: 8–9.
29. Horner 1960: 192.
30. Higgins 1997: 9.
31. Cohen 1997: 92.
32. Beckett 1995: 2.
33. Wood 1959: 213.
34. Birchall 1974: 94.
35. Beeching 1993: 6–7.

Chapter 11

1. Ball 1973: 205.
2. www.gruene detmold.de zeitung.
3. John Monks, personal communication.
4. Sheila Gammon, personal communication.
5. Fryer 1959: 121.
6. Fryer 1959: 121, 125–6.
7. Widgery 1976: 61–2.
8. Widgery 1976: 34.
9. Higgins 1965: 86–9, 135.
10. Heffer 1991: 70.
11. Ball 1973: 226.
12. Kenneth Price, personal communication.
13. Ball 1958: 9–10.
14. Lowe 1979: 3.
15. David Craig, personal communication.
16. Mitchell 1962: 33, 34.
17. Sillitoe 1959.
18. Sillitoe 1965: 233, 238.

19. ALA.
20. Tressell 1965: 7–10.
21. Fred Ball's CV, Hastings Museum.
22. Reg Johnson, personal communication.
23. Cutting, Hastings Museum.
24. Reg Johnson, personal communication.
25. Reg Johnson, personal communication.
26. Reg Johnson, personal communication.
27. Booklet, Hastings Library.
28. Mayne 1967: 73.
29. Bolton 1968: 158.
30. Williams 1979: 65–6, 92.
31. Woodhams 2001: 100.
32. Mitchell 1969: ix, x.
33. Mitchell 1969: 2, 28–9, 46, 53–4, 64, 73, 85–6, 112, 118, 121–2, 194.
34. Williams 1974: 126.
35. Barbara Phillips (née Salter), personal communication.
36. Salter 1971: 17, 71.
37. Correspondence courtesy of Barbara Phillips.

Chapter 12

1. Ball 1983.
2. Ball 1973: 205.
3. Sam Webb, personal communication.
4. John Edmonds, personal communication.
5. Reid 1969: 31–4.
6. Ian Birchall, personal communication.
7. Sam Webb, personal communication.
8. Arnison 1974: 15.
9. Rosenberg 1973. Translation courtesy of Gila Breitenbach.
10. MacLennan 1990: 207.
11. Harold Smith, personal communication.
12. Reg Johnson, personal communication.
13. Reg Johnson, personal communication.
14. Reg Johnson, personal communication.
15. Andy Strouthous, personal communication.

16. Ian Birchall, personal communication.
17. Adolfsson 1975.
18. Anon 1988: 27.
19. Heffer 1991: 111.
20. Jones 1986: 37, 40, 42, 59, 67, 133, 146, 152, 158, 167, 185, 200, 202, 217.
21. Darlington and Lyddon 2001: 176.
22. Jones 1984: 284–5.
23. Jones 1986: 286, 333.
24. Reg Johnson, personal communication.
25. Dave Cope, personal communication.
26. Samuel 1987: 87.
27. CPGB 1977: 17–18.
28. McShane 1978: 253.
29. Sam Webb, personal communication.

Chapter 13

1. Barltrop 1978: 189.
2. Swingewood 1977: 55, 58.
3. Dawson 1988: 41.
4. Ashraf 1979: 85, 169
5. Janet Cole, personal communication.
6. Hawthorn 1984: viii.
7. Alfred 1988: 93, 95–6.
8. Craig and Egan 1979: 146, 162, 167.
9. Lowe 1979: 4.
10. Lowe 1979: 4–7, 24–5, 27, 30–31, 42.
11. Walter 1999: 71.
12. Stephen Lowe, personal communication.
13. Lowe 1978: 42, 43.
14. See Birchall 1981.
15. Alfred 1981: 194.
16. Dennis Nolan, personal communication.
17. Nettleton 1981: 164, 170, 171.
18. Ian Birchall, personal communication.
19. Flyer and letters, Hastings Library.
20. Jefferson and Martin 1982: 64, 65.
21. Alfred 1988: 20, 25, 26, 31.
22. Copy courtesy of Dave Cope.
23. Townsend 1983: 86.
24. Flier, courtesy of Sam Webb.
25. Alfred 1988: 39.
26. Lowe 1983: 5, 48.

27. Sean O'Donoghue, personal communication.
28. Callinicos and Simons 1985: 47–119.
29. Heffer 1991: 216.
30. Samuel 1985: 49; Samuel 1986: 70.
31. Samuel 1980: 48–9; Samuel 1985: 17.
32. Alfred 1988: 55–7, 64, 67–9.
33. Samuel 1985: 7, 23, 33.

Chapter 14

1. Tape courtesy of Ann and Neil Bates.
2. Alfred 1988: 79, 80, 82, 84, 85.
3. Tape courtesy of Neil and Ann Bates.
4. Klaus 1987: 59, 65, 70.
5. Anon 1988: 5, 7, 8, 34.
6. Alfred 1988: 109.
7. Alfred 1988: 11–12, 45–7, 50.
8. Alfred 1988: 71, 74, 75, 77.
9. See Callinicos 1989.
10. Neetens 1988: 88.
11. Neetens 1991: 154.
12. Alfred 1988: ix.
13. Croft 1990: 7.
14. Stephen Lowe, personal communication.
15. Lowe 1991.
16. Notes courtesy of John Lovell. WEA tape courtesy of David Alfred.
17. WEA tape courtesy of David Alfred.
18. WEA tape courtesy of David Alfred.
19. Gary Day, personal communication.
20. Day 1997.
21. Notes courtesy of Gary Day.
22. See www.1066.tressell.

23. Notes courtesy of Fred Inglis. WEA tape courtesy of David Alfred. See Harker 2000.
24. Notes courtesy of John Edmonds.
25. Sam Webb, personal communication.
26. Dave Cope, personal communication.
27. Reg Johnson, personal communication.
28. Dave Cope, personal communication.
29. Dave Cope, personal communication.
30. Mike Harker, personal communication.
31. Reg Johnson, personal communication.
32. John Monks, personal communication.
33. John Edmonds, personal communication.
34. Birchall 2002: 124–6.
35. MECW 47: 357; MECW 48: 167.
36. Birchall 1994: 54, 55, 58, 61.
37. Volosinov 1973: 140–59.
38. Geoff Brown, personal communication.
39. Hyslop 2001: 82–3.
40. Harker 1998.
41. Ball 1973: 141.
42. Anon 1962: 288.
43. Pimlott 1986: 41.
44. Draper 1996: 36.
45. See Bircham and Charlton 2001.
46. See Cliff and Gluckstein 1996.
47. See Eaden and Renton 2002.
48. See Hallas 1985.
49. Birchall 1994: 55.

Bibliography

Adolfsson, Eva (1975), 'Robert Tressell – Englands "okande" proletarforfattare', and 'Stora pengatricket', *Varaforfattare*, 2 (Stockholm: Kulturfront Forlag), 312–32.

Alfred, David (1981), 'The Robert Tressell Workshop, Hastings', *History Workshop Journal* 12: 12–14.

Alfred, David, ed. (1988), *The Robert Tressell Lectures 1981–88* (Rochester: WEA).

Anon (1912), *The Miners' Next Step* (Tonypandy: South Wales Miners' Unofficial Reform Committee).

Anon (1943), *Books Against Barbarism* (London: Lawrence & Wishart).

Anon (1953), *Essays on Socialist Realism and the British Cultural Tradition* (London: Arena).

Anon (n.d.), *The Paint House* (Johannesburg: Herbert Evans).

Anon (1962), *Documents of the First International*, 1 (London: Lawrence & Wishart).

Anon (1977), *Robert Tressell* (Liverpool: Robert Tressell Memorial Committee).

Anon (1988), '*The Ragged Trousered Philanthropists*. Souvenir programme' (Newark: Newark Trades Council).

Arnison, Jim (1974), *The Shrewsbury Three* (London: Lawrence & Wishart).

Ashraf, P. (1979), *Introduction to Working Class Literature in Britain*, 2 (Potsdam: Humboldt-universität).

Ball, Fred (1951), *Tressell of Mugsborough* (London: Lawrence & Wishart).

Ball, Fred (1957), 'Authors Original Manuscript. The Ragged Trousered Philanthropists', Hastings Museum.

Ball, Fred (1958), '*The Ragged Trousered Philanthropists*, by Robert Tressell. A Short History of the Original Manuscript' (London: TUCC).

Ball, Fred (1967), 'More light on Tressell', *Marxism Today* 11: 177–82.

Ball, Fred (1973), *One of the Damned* (London: Weidenfeld & Nicolson).

Ball, Fred (1983), 'Robert Tressell'. Tape, TUCC.

Barltrop, Robert (1978), *Jack London* (London: Pluto).

Bebbington, W. (1972), 'Jessie Pope and Wilfred Owen', *Ariel* 3(4): 82–93.

Beckett, Francis (1995), *The Enemy Within* (London: John Murray).

Beeching, Jack (1948), 'The Ragged Trousered Philanthropists', *Our Time* 7: 196–9.

Beeching, Jack (1955), 'The Uncensoring of The Ragged Trousered Philanthropists', Marxist Quarterly 2: 217–29.

Beeching, Jack (1993), A Memoir of Thomas McGrath (East Grand Forks, MN: Spirit Horse Press).

Behan, Brendan (1990), Borstal Boy (London: Arena).

Bell, Tom (1937), The British Communist Party (London: Lawrence & Wishart).

Bell, Tom (1941), Pioneering Days (London: Lawrence & Wishart).

Bellamy, Edward (n.d.), Looking Backward (London: Routledge).

Bellamy, Joyce, and John Saville, eds (1987), Dictionary of Labour Biography 8 (London: Macmillan).

Bevan, Aneurin (1952), In Place of Fear (London: Heinemann).

Birchall, Ian (1974), Workers against the Monolith (London: Pluto).

Birchall, Ian (1981), The Smallest Mass Party in the World (London: SWP).

Birchall, Ian (1994), 'Proletarian Modernism? Form and Content in The Ragged Trousered Philanthropists', Notebooks (Middlesex University) 1: 48–69.

Birchall, Ian (2002), 'Zola for the 21st Century', International Socialism, Second Series, 98 (Autumn 2002): 105–28.

Bircham, Emma, and John Charlton, eds, (2001), Anti-Capitalism (London: Bookmarks).

Blackman, Peter (1967), 'The Robert Tressell Banner (Where Is It Now?)', The Journal, Birmingham Trades Council, August 1967.

Blatchford, Robert (1902), Britain for the British (London: Clarion).

Blatchford, Robert ['Nunquam'] (1908), Merrie England (London: Clarion).

Blatchford, Robert (1914), Not Guilty (London: Clarion).

Blatchford, Robert (1931), My Eighty Years (London: Cassell).

Bolton, Eric (1968), 'The Ragged Trousered Philanthropists in its time', unpublished MA dissertation, University of Lancaster.

Bower, Fred (1936), Rolling Stonemason (London: Jonathan Cape).

Bradby, David, et al., eds (1980), Performance and Politics in Popular Drama (Cambridge: Cambridge University Press).

Branson, Noreen (1997), History of the Communist Party of Great Britain 1941–1951 (London: Lawrence & Wishart).

Brockman, William (1991), 'Grant Richards', Dictionary of Literary Biography, 12 (Detroit: Gale): 272–9.

Brophy, John (1942), Britain Needs Books (London: National Book Council).

Budgen, Frank (1970), Myselves When Young (London: Oxford University Press).

Bush, Julia (1984), Behind the Lines (London: Merlin).

Callaghan, John (1993), Rajani Palme Dutt (London: Lawrence & Wishart).

Callan, Charles (1997), 'Robert Tressell and His Fellow Philanthropists Reconsidered', Saothor 22: 113–22.

Callinicos, Alex (1989), Against Postmodernism (Cambridge: Polity).

Callinicos, Alex, and Mike Simons (1985), The Great Strike (London: Socialist Worker).

Campbell, William (1981), Villi the Clown (London: Faber).

Carlyle, Thomas (1932), Reminiscences (London: Dent).

Challinor, Raymond (1977), The Origins of British Bolshevism (Beckenham: Croom Helm).

Charlton, John (1999), It Just Went Like Tinder (London: Redwords).

Clark, Jon, et al., eds (1979), Culture and Crisis in Britain in the Thirties (London: Lawrence & Wishart).

Cliff, Tony (1991), Trotsky: Fighting the Rising Stalinist Bureaucracy (London: Bookmarks).

Cliff, Tony (1996), *State Capitalism in Russia* (London: Bookmarks).
Cliff, Tony, and Donny Gluckstein (1986), *Marxism and Trade Union Struggle* (London: Bookmarks).
Cliff, Tony, and Donny Gluckstein (1996), *The Labour Party* (London: Bookmarks).
Clunie, James (1954), *Labour is My Faith* (Dunfermline: A. Romanes).
Cockburn, Claud (1959), *Crossing the Line* (London: Readers Union).
Cohen, Phil, ed. (1997), *Children of the Revolution* (London: Lawrence & Wishart).
Connole, Nellie (1961), *Leaven of Life* (London: Lawrence & Wishart).
Copeman, Fred (1948), *Reason in Revolt* (London: Blandford).
Cox, Idris (n.d.), 'Personal and Political Recollections'. NMLH, CP/IND/MISC/ 213.
Coxall, Bill (1992), 'Bridging the experience gap in the early 1900s: H.G. Wells and George Meek', *Literature & History* 3(2): 19–38.
Coxall, Bill, and Clive Griggs (1996), *George Meek* (London: New Millennium).
Communist Party (1951), *The British Road to Socialism* (London: CP) [January, Draft].
Communist Party of Great Britain (n.d. [1926]), *Elementary Course of Communist Party Training* (London: CPGB).
CPGB (1927), *Communist Party Training* (London: CPGB).
CPGB (1929), *Class against Class* (London: CPGB).
CPGB (1933), *Communist Political Education* (London: CPGB).
CPGB (1937), *Four Lesson Course* (London: CPGB).
CPGB (n.d. [1938]), *Books & Pamphlets. How To Sell Them* (London: CPGB).
CPGB (1977), *Trotskyist Organisations in Britain* (London: CPGB).
Craig, David, and Michael Egan (1979), *Extreme Situations* (London: Macmillan).
Craik, William (n.d.), *Central Labour College* (London: Lawrence & Wishart).
Crick, Bernard (1982), *George Orwell* (Harmondsworth: Penguin).
Croft, Andy (1990), *Red Letter Days* (London: Lawrence & Wishart).
Croft, Andy (1994), 'Writers, the Communist Party and the Battle of Ideas, 1945–1950', *Socialist History* 5: 2–25.
Croft, Andy (1995), 'Walthamstow, Little Gidding and Middlesbrough', *Socialist History* 8: 22–48.
Croft, Andy, ed. (1998), *A Weapon in the Struggle* (London: Pluto).
Darlington, Ralph (1998), *The Political Trajectory of J.T. Murphy* (Liverpool: Liverpool University Press).
Darlington, Ralph, and Dave Lyddon (2001), *Glorious Summer* (London: Bookmarks).
Dash, Jack (1960), *Good Morning, Brothers!* (London: Lawrence & Wishart).
Davies, Andrew (1992), *To Build a New Jerusalem* (Michael Joseph).
Davies, Paul (1987), *A.J. Cook* (Manchester: Manchester University Press).
Dawson, Jerry (1988), *Left Theatre* (Liverpool: Merseyside Writers).
Day, Gary (1997), Introduction to Tressell 1997.
Day Lewis, Cecil, ed. (1971), *The Collected Poems of Wilfred Owen* (London: Chatto & Windus).
Dewar, Hugo (1976), *Communist Politics in Britain* (London: Pluto).
Douglass, Stuart, ed. (1968), 'Talking to Kathleen Tressell', *Labour Monthly Arts Section* (June): 261–5.
Draper, Hal (1996), *The Two Souls of Socialism* (London: Bookmarks).
Dutt, Rajani (1963), *Problems of Contemporary History* (London: Lawrence & Wishart).
Eaden, James, and David Renton (2002), *The Communist Party of Great Britain since 1920* (Basingstoke: Palgrave).

Eagleton, M., and D. Pierce (1979), *Attitudes to Class in the English Novel* (London: Thames & Hudson).

Eastman, Max (1925), *Since Lenin Died* (London: Labour Publishing Company).

Edwards, Ness (1930), *The Workers' Theatre* (Cardiff: Cymric Federation).

Engels, Frederick, and Paul and Laura Lafargue (n.d.), *Correspondence*, 3 (Moscow: Foreign Languages Publishing House).

Fagan, Hymie (n.d.), *An Autobiography*. Brunel University Library, Working Class Autobiographical Archive (2–261).

Fox, Ralph (1948), *The Novel and the People* (London: Cobbett).

Fox, Richard (1928), *The Triumphant Machine* (London: Hogarth).

Frow, Edmund and Ruth (1993), 'The Workers' Theatre Movement in Manchester and Salford, 1931–1940', *North West Labour History* 17: 66–74.

Fryer, Peter (1956), *Hungarian Tragedy* (London: Dennis Dobson).

Fryer, Peter (1959), *The Battle for Socialism* (London: Socialist Labour League).

Fyrth, Jim, ed. (1993), *Labour's High Noon* (London: Lawrence & Wishart).

Gallacher, William (1940), *Revolt on the Clyde* (London: Lawrence & Wishart).

Gallacher, William, and John R. Campbell (1972), *Direct Action* (London: Pluto).

Gauldie, Enid (1974), *Cruel Habitations* (London: Allen & Unwin).

Gloversmith, Frank, ed. (1982), *Class, Culture and Social Change* (Brighton: Harvester).

Gollancz, Victor (1952), *My Dear Timothy* (London: Gollancz).

Gollancz, Victor (1953), *More for Timothy* (London: Gollancz).

Gollancz, Victor (1968), *Reminiscences of Affection* (London: Gollancz).

Goorney, Howard, and Ewan MacColl, eds (1986), *Agit-prop to Theatre Workshop* (Manchester: Manchester University Press).

Gorman, John (1995), *Knocking down Ginger* (London: Caliban).

Gower, William (1926), 'The Real Robert Tressall', *Daily Herald*, 11 July.

Groves, Reg (1974), *The Balham Group* (London: Pluto).

Hallas, Duncan (1985), *The Comintern* (London: Bookmarks).

Hallas, Duncan, and Chris Harman (1986), *Days of Hope* (London: SWP).

Hannington, Wal (1967), *Never on Our Knees* (London: Lawrence & Wishart).

Harker, Dave (1998), 'The Ragged Trousered Philanthropists: A Critique' (London: SW Recordings).

Harker, Dave (2000), 'Adorno and Marxism' (London: SW Recordings).

Harman, Chris (1988), *The Fire Last Time* (London: Bookmarks).

Hastings CP (1982), *Red Hot News* 2, September.

Hawthorn, Jeremy, ed. (1984), *The British Working-Class Novel in the Twentieth Century* (London: Edward Arnold).

Haynes, Mike (1984), 'The British Working Class in Revolt: 1910–1914', *International Socialism*, Second Series 22: 87–116.

Haynes, Mike (2002), *Russia: Class and Power 1917–2000* (London: Bookmarks).

Heffer, Eric (1991), *Never a Yes Man* (London: Verso).

Higgins, Jim, et al. (1965), *A Socialist Review* (London: IS).

Higgins, Jim (1997), *More Years for the Locust* (London: IS Group).

Hinton, James, and Richard Hyman (1975), *Trade Unions and Revolution* (London: Pluto).

Hobday, Charles (1989), *Edgell Rickword* (Manchester: Carcanet).

Hobsbawm, Eric, and George Rudé (1970), *Captain Swing* (London: Readers' Union).

Hollis, Patricia (1997), *Jenny Lee* (Oxford: Oxford University Press).

Hopper, Trevor (n.d. [1995]), *Robert Tressell's Hastings* (Brighton: Hopper).

Hopper, Trevor (n.d. [1999]), *Robert Tressell's Hastings* (Brighton: Hopper).

Horner, Arthur (1960), *Incorrigible Rebel* (London: MacGibbon & Kee).

Horrabin, Frank (1927), *A Workers' History of the Great Strike* (London: Plebs).

Hyndman, Henry (1911), *The Record of an Adventurous Life* (New York: Macmillan).

Hyslop, Jonathan (2001), 'A Ragged Trousered Philanthropist and the Empire', *History Workshop Journal* 51: 65–85.

Jackson, Thomas (1950), *Old Friends to Keep* (London: Lawrence & Wishart).

Jackson, Thomas (n.d.), 'Interim Report', Part II. NMLH, CP/IND/MISC/11/1.

Jackson, Thomas (1953), *Solo Trumpet* (London: Lawrence & Wishart).

Jefferson, Douglas, and Graham Martin, eds (1982), *The Uses of Fiction* (Milton Keynes: Open University Press).

Jones, Jack (1984), 'The Spirit of Robert Tressell', *Tribune*, 6 April, 6–7.

Jones, Jack (1986), *Union Man* (London: Collins).

Jones, Leonard (1974), 'The Workers' Theatre in the Thirties', *Marxism Today* 18(9): 271–80.

Jones, Mervyn (1987), *Chances* (London: Verso).

Kemp-Ashraf, P., and Jack Mitchell, eds (1966), *Essays in Honour of William Gallacher* (Berlin: Humboldt-universität).

Kendall, Walter (1969), *The Revolutionary Movement in Britain 1900–1921* (London: Weidenfeld & Nicolson).

Kettle, Arnold (1969), *An Introduction to the English Novel*, 2 (London: Hutchinson).

Klaus, Gustav, ed., (1982), *The Socialist Novel in Britain* (Brighton: Harvester).

Klaus, Gustav, ed. (1987), *The Rise of Socialist Fiction* (Brighton: Harvester).

Klaus, Gustav, and Stephen Knight, eds (2000), *British Industrial Fictions* (Cardiff: University of Wales Press).

Klugmann, James (1976), *History of the Communist Party of Great Britain, 1925–1926* (London: Lawrence & Wishart).

L., F. (1926), 'Painter', in Margaret A. Pollock, ed., *Working Days* (London: Jonathan Cape), 93–114.

Lansbury, George (n.d.), *The Miracle of Fleet Street* (London: Victoria House).

Lansbury, George (1931), *My Life* (London: Constable).

Lee, Jennie (1981), *My Life with Nye* (Harmondsworth: Penguin).

Lenin, Vladimir (1980), *Collected Works*, 33 (London: Lawrence & Wishart).

Lindsay, Jack (1956), *After the Thirties* (London: Lawrence & Wishart).

Lowe, Stephen (1978), *The Ragged Trousered Philanthropists* (London: Margaret Ramsay).

Lowe, Stephen (1979), *Joint Stock and The Ragged Trousered Philanthropists* (Totnes: Dartington College of Arts).

Lowe, Stephen (1983), *The Ragged Trousered Philanthropists* (London: Methuen).

Lowe, Stephen (1991), *The Ragged Trousered Philanthropists* (London: Methuen).

McCracken, Donal (1999), *Macbride's Brigade* (Dublin: Four Courts).

Macintyre, Stuart (1980), *A Proletarian Science* (Cambridge: Cambridge University Press).

MacLennan, Elizabeth (1990), *The Moon Belongs to Everyone* (London: Methuen).

McShane, Harry (1978), *No Mean Fighter* (London: Pluto).

Mann, Tom (1967), *Memoirs* (London: MacGibbon & Kee).

Margolies, David, and Maroula Joannou, eds (1995), *Heart of a Heartless World* (London: Pluto).

Marx, Karl (1986), *Capital Volume 1* (Harmondsworth: Penguin).

Marx, Karl, & Frederick Engels (1975–), *Collected Works* (London: Lawrence & Wishart).

Matthews, Mike (1991), *Alf Cobb* (Hastings: Matthews).

Mayne, Brian (1967), 'The *Ragged Trousered Philanthropists*', *Twentieth Century Literature* 13(2): 73–83.

Meacham, Standish (1977), *A Life Apart* (London: Thames & Hudson).

Meek, George (1910), *George Meek* (London: Constable).

Meynell, Francis (1971), *My Lives* (New York: Random House).

Miliband, Ralph, and John Saville, eds (1976), *Socialist Register 1976* (London: Merlin).

Milton, Nan (1973), *John Maclean* (London: Pluto).

Mitchell, John (1962), 'The *Ragged Trousered Philanthropists*', *Zeitschrift furAnglistik und Americanistik* 10(1): 33–55.

Mitchell, Jack (1969), *Robert Tressell and 'The Ragged Trousered Philanthropists'* (London: Lawrence & Wishart).

Mitchell, J., and J. Pritchard (1913), *The Parish of St Andrew, Hastings* (London: Sherlock).

Morgan, Austen (1987), *J. Ramsay MacDonald* (Manchester: Manchester University Press).

Morgan, Kevin (1994), *Harry Pollitt* (Manchester: Manchester University Press).

Morris, William (1993), *News from Nowhere* (London: Penguin).

Moss, Les (1979), *Live and Learn* (Brighton: Queenspark).

Murphy, Jack (1942), *New Horizons* (London: John Lane).

Murphy, Jack (1972), *Preparing for Power* (London: Pluto).

Neetens, Wim (1988), 'Politics, Poetics and the Popular Text', *Literature and History* 14(1): 81–9.

Neetens, Wim (1991), *Writing and Democracy* (Brighton: Harvester).

Nettleton, John (1981), 'Robert Tressell and the Liverpool Connection', *History Workshop Journal* 12: 163–71.

O'Brien, Mark (1995), *Perish the Privileged Orders* (London: Redwords).

Ogilvy, Stewart (1945), 'Story of Tressall's Life on Rand', *Forward* (South Africa), 14 December.

Orwell, George (1984), *The Collected Essays, Journalism and Letters*, Volume 2 (Harmondsworth: Penguin).

Pakenham, Thomas (1988), *The Boer War* (London: Abacus).

Pimlott, Ben (1986), *Labour and the Left in the 1930s* (London: Allen & Unwin).

Pollitt, Harry (1940), *Serving My Time* (London: Lawrence & Wishart).

Pollitt, Harry (1947), *Looking Ahead* (London: Communist Party).

Pope, Jessie (1915), *Jessie Pope's War Poems* (London: Richards).

Postgate, Raymond (1923), *The Builders' History* (London: NFBTO).

Postgate, Raymond (1934), *How to Make a Revolution* (New York: Vanguard).

Poynton, J. (1936), 'Building Worker Whose One Book Still Lives', *Daily Worker*, 10 June: 7.

Quelch, Harry (1912), *Economics of Labour* (London: Twentieth Century Press).

Reid, Betty (1969), *Ultra-Leftism in Britain* (London: CP).

Richards, Grant (1932), *Memories of a Misspent Youth* (London: Heinemann).

Richards, Grant (1960), *Author Hunting* (London: Unicorn).

Rose, Jonathan (2001), *The Intellectual Life of the British Working Classes* (New Haven, CT: Yale University Press).

Rosenberg, Chanie (1987), *1919* (London: Bookmarks).

Rowbotham, Bill (n.d.), *The Ragged Trousered Philanthropists* (London: Unity Theatre).

Salter, Barbara (1971), 'A Study of *The Ragged Trousered Philanthropists* by Robert Tressell', unpublished MA dissertation, University of Manchester.

Samuel, Raphael (1980), 'British Marxist Historians', New Left Review 120: 21–96.
Samuel, Raphael (1985), 'The Lost World of British Communism', New Left Review 154: 5–53.
Samuel, Raphael (1986), 'Staying Power', New Left Review 156: 63–113.
Samuel, Raphael (1987), 'Class Politics', New Left Review 165: 52–91.
Samuel, Raphael, et al. (1985), Theatres of the Left 1880–1935 (London: Routledge & Kegan Paul).
Schneer, Jonathan (1982), Ben Tillett (Beckenham: Croom Helm).
Scholes, Robert (1963), 'Grant Richards to James Joyce', Studies in Bibliography 16: 139–60.
Siegel, Paul (1989), The Meek and the Militant (London: Zed Books).
Sillitoe, Alan (1959), 'Proletarian Novelists', Books and Bookmen (August), 13.
Sillitoe, Alan (1963), Key to the Door (London: Pan).
Sillitoe, Alan (1975), Mountains and Caverns (London: W.H. Allen).
Sloan, Pat (1978), John Cornford (Dunfermline: Borderline).
Smillie, Robert (1924), My Life for Labour (London: Mills & Boon).
Smith, David (1978), Socialist Propaganda in the Twentieth-century British Novel (London: Macmillan).
Stewart, Bob (1967), Breaking the Fetters (London: Lawrence & Wishart).
Swingewood, Alan (1977), The Myth of Mass Culture (London: Macmillan).
Swinnerton, Frank (1937), Swinnerton (London: Hutchinson).
Swinnerton, Frank (1956), The Adventures of a Manuscript (London: Richards).
Thomas, Tom ['Trudnik'] (1928), The Ragged-Trousered Philanthropists (London: Labour Publishing Company).
Thomas, Tom (1936), The Ragged Trousered Philanthropists (London: Richards).
Thompson, Edward (1977), 'Caudwell', Socialist Register 1977 (London: Merlin): 228–76.
Thompson, Edward (1979), 'Edgell Rickword', PN Review 6(1) Supplement: xxvi–xxviii.
Thompson, Edward (1988), William Morris (Stanford, CA: Stanford University Press).
Thompson, Laurence (1951), Robert Blatchford (London: Gollancz).
Thompson, Wilfred (1910), Victor Grayson (Sheffield: J.H. Bennett).
Thompson, Willie (1992), The Good Old Cause (London: Pluto).
Thorne, Will (1989), My Life's Battles (London: Lawrence & Wishart).
Thorpe, Andrew (2000), 'The Membership of the Communist Party of Great Britain, 1920–1945', Historical Journal 43: 777–800.
Tillett, Ben (1931), Memories and Reflections (London: John Long).
Townsend, Sue (1983), The Secret Diary of Adrian Mole aged 13¾ (London: Methuen).
Tressall, Robert (1914), The Ragged Trousered Philanthropists (London: Richards Press).
Tressall, Robert (1927), The Ragged Trousered Philanthropists (London: Richards Press).
Tressell, Robert (1965), The Ragged Trousered Philanthropists (London: Panther).
Tressell, Robert (1997), The Ragged Trousered Philanthropists (London: Flamingo).
Trory, Ernie (1945), Mainly About Books (Brighton: Acorn).
Trotsky, Leon (1974), Trotsky's Writings on Britain, 3 Volumes (London: New Park).
Trotsky, Leon (1987), The Lessons of October (London: Bookmarks).
Trotsky, Leon (1991), Literature and Revolution (London: Redwords).
Tsuzuki, Chushichi (1961), H.M. Hyndman and British Socialism (Oxford: Oxford University Press).
Tsuzuki, Chushichi (1991), Tom Mann, 1856–1941 (Oxford: Clarendon Press).

Tuckett, Angela (n.d.), The People's Theatre in Bristol 1930–45 (London: Our History).

Turner, Ben (1930), About Myself (London: Humphrey Toulin).

Uttley, Freda (1940), The Dream we Lost (New York: John Day).

von Rosenbert, Ingrid (1973), 'Robert Tressels Arbeiterroman', alternative 90: 148–60

Vološinov, Valentin (1973), Marxism and the Philosophy of Language (New York: Seminar Press).

Walsh, J. (1922), 'Editorial Remarks', NSP Monthly Journal 2(4): 3–10.

Walter, Harriet (1999), Other People's Shoes (Viking).

Ward, William (n.d.) Letter to Hubert Williams. Hastings Museum.

WEA (1982), The Robert Tressell Papers (Rochester: Robert Tressell Workshop).

Wicks, Harry (1992), Keeping My Head (London: Socialist Platform).

Widgery, David (1976), The Left in Britain 1956–1968 (Harmondsworth: Penguin).

Williams, Raymond (1974), The English Novel from Dickens to Lawrence (London: Paladin).

Williams, Raymond (1979), Politics and Letters (London: New Left Books).

Williams, William (1956), The Penguin Story (Harmondsworth: Penguin).

Wood, Neal (1959), Communism and the British Intellectuals (New York: Columbia University Press).

Woodhams, Stephen (2001), History in the Making (London: Merlin).

Woodhouse, Michael, and Brian Pearce (1975), Communism in Britain (London: New Park).

Worley, Matthew (2000), 'For a Proletarian Culture', Socialist History 18: 70–91.

Young, James (1985), 'Militancy, English Socialism and The Ragged Trousered Philanthropists', Journal of Contemporary History 20(2): 283–303.

Zhdanov, Andrei (1950), On Literature, Music and Philosophy (London: Lawrence & Wishart).

Index